*New Age and Neopagan Religions in America*

*The Columbia Contemporary American Religion Series*

**Columbia Contemporary American Religion Series**

The spiritual landscape of contemporary America is as varied and complex as that of any country in the world. The books in this new series, written by leading scholars for students and general readers alike, fall into two categories: Some titles are portraits of the country's major religious groups. They describe and explain particular religious practices and rituals, beliefs, and major challenges facing a given community today. Others explore current themes and topics in American religion that cut across denominational lines. The texts are supplemented with carefully selected photographs and artwork, and annotated bibliographies.

———

*Roman Catholicism in America*
CHESTER GILLIS

*Islam in America*
JANE I. SMITH

*Buddhism in America*
RICHARD HUGHES SEAGER

*Protestantism in America*
RANDALL BALMER AND LAUREN F. WINNER

*Judaism in America*
MARC LEE RAPHAEL

*The Quakers in America*
THOMAS D. HAMM

# NEW AGE AND NEOPAGAN RELIGIONS

## in America

Sarah M. Pike

COLUMBIA UNIVERSITY PRESS

NEW YORK

COLUMBIA UNIVERSITY PRESS
*Publishers Since 1893*
New York    Chichester, West Sussex

Library of Congress Cataloging-in-Publication Data

Pike, Sarah M., 1959–
    New Age and neopagan religions in America / Sarah Pike.
        p.    cm. — (Columbia contemporary American religion series)
    Includes bibliographical references and index.
        ISBN 0–231–12402–3
        1. New Age movement—United States.  2. Neopaganism—United
States.  3. United States—Religion—1960–  I. Title.  II. Series.

    BP605.N48P55    2004
    299'.93—dc22                                          2003061844

Printed in the United States of America
c 10 9 8 7 6 5 4 3 2 1

# CONTENTS

# INTRODUCTION

When I was a freshman in college in 1977, I became a vegetarian and frequented the local food cooperative and vegetarian restaurant in Durham, North Carolina. I met students who meditated, practiced yoga, and volunteered at the J. B. Rhine psychic research center and community members who were in occult study groups. Although not a full participant in any of these practices, I was endlessly curious about alternative spiritual and healing techniques. My friends' and student colleagues' activities and interests were part of a small but vibrant subculture. When I entered Duke University my declared major was zoology, but I soon ended up in the Department of Religion, where I discovered theories and histories that helped me situate and understand the alternative spiritual paths I saw around me. Twenty-five years later, vegetarian Gardenburgers® are available in supermarket chains and yoga classes are offered at every neighborhood health club. Activities that were suspiciously esoteric to most Americans when I was an undergraduate are now often accepted as part of popular culture even when they are dismissed as trendy or "flaky."

Since those college years I have been an observer of and occasional participant in the many activities that can be grouped under the umbrella of New Age culture. When I began attending Neopagan festivals for my dissertation research, many of the practices I encountered were familiar from my earlier contact with New Agers. I immediately saw the significant overlap between the two movements and started to investigate the differences that set them apart, at least in their own eyes. I also became aware during my graduate work that the communities and subcultures I had been learning about were part of a larger field of study.

The study of new religious movements was shaped into a field during roughly the same years that I was discovering and later researching New Age and Neopagan religions. Early studies, such as British sociologist Bryan Wilson's *Religious Sects* (1970), were written by sociologists who were interested in issues of institutionalization, the "routinization of charisma," and the opposition of cults and sects to society. These works took seriously what many people thought were bizarre cults that developed outside the confines of mainstream Protestant and Catholic religiosity. Also in the 1970s and 1980s, religious studies scholars ventured into this field, and they were looking at different issues than the sociologists. Historian of religions Robert Ellwood's *Alternative Altars: Unconventional and Eastern Spirituality in America* (1979) traced the historical impetus behind the supposedly "new" religions and located them within an alternative stream of American religiosity. Ellwood's later work on spirituality in the 1950s and 1960s placed alternative religious choices alongside other cultural phenomena of those eras. Over the following decade, comparative and historical studies of new religious movements were published, such as R. Laurence Moore's *Religious Outsiders and the Making of Americans* (1986) and Mary Farrell Bednarowski's *New Religions and the Theological Imagination in America* (1989). Catherine Albanese's *Nature Religion in America* (1990) placed the New Age movement and Neopaganism within a history of nature religion and Timothy Miller's *The 6os Communes: Hippies and Beyond* (1999), a study of religious communes during the 1960s and 1970s, described the communal movements in a historical context that included discussion of the New Age movement. None of these works provided in-depth accounts of the historical origins and religious lives of Neopagans and New Agers, though they touched on some aspects.

Public tragedies involving new religious movements, such as the group suicide of the People's Temple in Jonestown, Guyana (1978), the Branch Davidian tragedy in Waco, Texas (1993), and the Heaven's Gate suicides (1997) that attracted mainstream media attention spurred research into new religions as well as determined opposition to them. Scholars of new religions were called on to comment about and analyze these religious communities and to critically appraise their relationship to the broader culture and were consulted by law enforcement, the news media, and politicians given the task of investigating these events. Waco in particular generated a wealth of scholarship about the relationship between new religious movements and their cultural context, including James Tabor and Eugene Gallagher's *Why Waco? Cults and the Battle for Religious Freedom in America* (1995) and Catherine Wessinger's *How the Millennium Comes Violently: From Jonestown to Heaven's*

*Gate* (2000). These studies called attention to the need for better understanding of the historical origins of new religions, the meaningful lives participants create within them, and the points of conflict (and convergence) between new religious movements and the broader society.

The flourishing of new religious movements in the 1970s and 1980s and the increasing criticism of them by the media, family members of participants, conservative Christians, and the anticult movement increased the need for scholarship in this area. Deprogrammer Ted Patrick's *Let Our Children Go!* (1976) represented the most extreme view, but many other books based on questionable scholarship argued that power-crazy "cult" leaders used aggressive mind control techniques to draw in and keep converts. The worst cases of criminal misconduct within new religions were used to scapegoat all of them. Generalizations about "cults" were painted with broad strokes; many of the charges leveled against them also characterized the communal structures of early Christianity or the insular world of the Amish or Hasidic Jews. Anticult forces tended to rely on sensationalized news stories and the need of ex-cult members to distance themselves from their former communities, and were often driven by a conservative Christian agenda. In response, studies of specific new religious movements such as *The Making of a Moonie* (1984), Eileen Barker's careful statistical analysis of the Unification Church, advanced an understanding of the religious worlds of the so-called "cults" that set themselves apart from the rest of society.

Many of the studies of new religions have been polemical, apologetic, or inaccessible to the general reader. The field has often been polarized between scholars who are critical of new religions and those who are more sympathetic with them, in part because of the extreme separation from society advocated by some of these movements and their experience of persecution by law enforcement and other religious communities.

The New Age and Neopagan movements are not typical new religions because they lack one charismatic leader and are not physically separated from the world. They are fluid networks of individuals, organizations, books, and Web sites. They have been difficult to study, however, because they do not have founding texts or leaders but rather are highly decentralized, antiauthoritarian, and personalized, even though some small communities within the broader religious movements may focus around charismatic leaders and create authoritarian structures.

Studies of Neopaganism and the New Age movement by scholars of American religions and new religious movements were nearly nonexistent until the mid-1990s, even during the 1980s as they emerged and became important features on the North America and British religious landscapes. *Drawing Down the Moon: Witches, Druids, Goddess-Worshippers and Other Pagans in America Today* (1979), an excellent journalistic account of the diverse forms of American Neopaganism by National Public Radio reporter Margot Adler, was thorough, but too long and detailed to be used effectively as an introduction to Neopagan religion. Anthropologist T. M. Luhrman's *Persuasions of the Witch's Craft* (1989) was the first ethnographic study of Neopaganism, but focused on magical groups in London, England.

The New Age movement attracted more attention, but mostly from British scholars who did not situate it in the context of American cultural and religious history. J. Gordon Melton at the Institute for the Study of American Religion was one of the few people to systematically document what was happening in the United States in several articles and then in *The New Age Encyclopedia* (1990) and *The New Age Almanac* (1991), which have been important resources for scholars and general readers, but did not go into New Agers' everyday rituals and belief systems. Then in the mid-1990s several studies were published within a period of a few years: Wouter Hanegraaff's *New Age Religion and Western Culture: Esotericism in the Mirror of Secular Thought* (1995), Michael York's *The Emerging Network: A Sociology of the New Age and Neo-Pagan Movements* (1995), Graham Harvey's *Listening People, Speaking Earth: Contemporary Paganism* (1997), Paul Heelas's *The New Age Movement* (1996), and Jon Bloch's *New Spirituality, Self and Belonging: How New Agers and Neo-Pagans Talk About Themselves* (1998). These books, by scholars who, with the exception of Bloch, were all based in England or Europe, offered scholarly overviews but tended to focus on the development of these movements in Britain, engage in scholarly theoretical debates, or discuss theology with little attention to religious practice. Few of these works, regardless of their contributions to scholarly conversations, offered general readers an entry into the religious worlds of New Agers and Neopagans.

By the last years of the twentieth century and the opening of the twenty-first, more ethnographic and focused work was being done. For instance, Michael Brown published *The Channeling Zone: American Spirituality in an Anxious Age* in 1997, the first ethnographic study to focus on a specific New Age practice—channeling. Steven Sutcliffe's *Children of the New Age: A History of Spiritual Practice* (2003) described the emergence of the British New Age community Findhorn from the teachings of important figures like Alice Bailey and Sheena Govan and provided short ethnographic portraits of British New Age communities. Helen Berger's *A Community of Witches: Contemporary Neo-Paganism and Witchcraft in the United States* (1999) drew on quantitative and qualitative data to create a profile of Neopagan religion, as did *Voices from the Pagan Census* (2003), a book she coauthored. The most thorough and scholarly historical study of Neopaganism's roots was Ronald Hutton's *The Triumph of the Moon: A History of Modern Pagan Witchcraft* (1999), though it too was largely focused on Neopaganism in Britain. I published my ethnography of American Neopagan festivals, *Earthly Bodies, Magical Selves: Contemporary Pagans and the Search for Community* (2001), and witnessed first hand the growing numbers of undergraduate and graduate students at American Academy of Religion meetings who wanted to study or were already writing about the Neopagan community.

These examples suggest that over the last few decades attention to New Age and Neopagan religions has been steadily increasing, but the work that is available leaves many gaps in our knowledge about these religious cultures, and no books provide accessible overviews of the subject. Because much of the research has been done either by British scholars whose work is skewed toward their specific cultural and historical contexts, it is encyclopedic and useful for reference but does not provide a full sense of the religious lives and concerns of Neopagans and New Agers worldwide.

When I have taught courses on new religious movements I have not been able to find engaging books on New Age and Neopagan cultures that introduce readers to the main concerns and daily lives of participants. In this book, then, I have tried to offer a readable account of how these cultures emerged during particular moments in American religious history and developed particular kinds of religious expression. In order to provide a general picture of how these movements have carved out a place for themselves on the American religious landscape I have consulted academic sources, memoirs, contemporary commentaries, practitioners and participants in the movements, newspaper articles, Internet Web sites, and listservs.

My most challenging task has been to clarify in a straightforward way the distinctions between Neopagan and New Age communities as well as the many concerns they share. For this purpose I have situated both movements within a particular story of American religious history and developments in American life after the 1960s, especially the increasing personalization of religion and the sexual liberation, feminist, and environmental movements. Because they attract widespread popular attention, I have also been concerned with describing how New Age and Neopagan movements successfully promoted themselves through publishing and on the Internet. The popularization of their ideas has been an important development.

The first two chapters of the book introduce readers to the religious worlds of Neopagans and New Agers. Chapter 1 provides an account of a festival workshop, describes Neopagan aesthetics, and discusses some deities and ritual practices. Chapter 2 is an overview of New Age and Neopagan religions in which I sketch their commonalities and differences and introduce the themes to be examined in more depth in later chapters.

Chapters 3 and 4 describe the historical emergence of New Age and Neopagan movements. Chapter 3 outlines their various historical antecedents. Although I briefly describe these early roots, the chapter is largely concerned with "the spiritual hothouse" of the nineteenth century that nourished movements built on older beliefs, but included religious innovations that were to be important for New Age and Neopagan attitudes toward life, death, and the supernatural. Chapter 4 discusses the growth of identifiable New Age and Neopagan groups out of the 1960s counterculture. During the 1960s the New Age movement's dual emphasis on self-transformation and planetary healing was evident in the writings of important leaders, gurus, and modern-day prophets like Timothy Leary and Ram Dass, as well as in the beliefs and practices of the people they inspired. This chapter also introduces key figures, institutes, retreats, and centers around which New Age and Neopagan concerns coalesced and then became identifiable as movements.

The last three chapters look at central concerns that these religions share. Chapter 5 takes up the variety of healing practices that are at the heart of much Neopagan and New Age spiritual life. I look at how standard narratives of healing and spiritual autobiographies bring order and meaning to experiences, and the ways in which these stories are shared and circulated. Healing and other rituals require certain tools, such as tarot and medicine cards, astrological charts, how-to books, crystals, incense, herbs, and other objects, and I explain how these might be used. Chapter 6 explores the important impact of the feminist and gay liberation movements on gender roles and sexuality within Neopagan and New Age communities and the ways these religions have also shaped discourse about gender in the broader culture. One of the most obvious ways in which Neopagans and New Agers have shifted their understanding of gender roles is in the public recognition of female leaders and religious specialists. This chapter explores a range of examples of how men and women play with gender roles within these movements and create new rites of passages. Chapter 7 examines the notion of a "new" or "Aquarian" age that these religions have envisioned and promoted more or less from their beginnings. I also explore some of the controversies concerning New Age and Neopagan practices and offer some thoughts on future developments on the Internet and in actual communities.

My approach to the study of new religious movements has been shaped by the assumption that a sympathetic but critical approach is most useful. My view is not that of an insider, but I hope that participants in New Age and Neopagan communities will recognize themselves in these pages, even if they disagree with the labels I have given them or feel uncomfortable with my decision to discuss them side by side. I am sensitive that scholarly work on new religions takes place in a charged cultural arena in which religious persecution and legal struggles are a reality in the lives of participants. My hope is that this work may help to dispel negative stereotypes that have been perpetuated by the media, anticult groups, and religious competitors, and that it will introduce readers to the historical emergence and lived religions of Neopaganism and the New Age movement.

I am indebted to the many New Agers and Neopagans who spoke with me, responded to my e-mails, and welcomed me to their rituals and festivals. Thanks especially to Sharon Knight for agreeing to let me write about her Pantheacon ritual, described in chapter 1, and for responding so generously to my questions. M. Macha Nightmare and the many Neopagans and scholars on the Nature Religions Scholars network e-mail list moderated by Chas Clifton have provided valuable insights into the lives of Neopagans and fascinating accounts of and information about rituals, beliefs, activist events, legal struggles, media coverage, and debates. Many other people have also helped me to understand the lives of contemporary New Agers and Neopagans, and I can only thank some of them here. Sabina Magliocco, Jone Salomonsen, and Adrian Ivakhiv offered new points of view and clarified my thinking about Neopagan and New Age communities through our conversations and their research. Jason Beduhn toured me through Sedona and sent me New Age materials. Lucy Pike, M.D. shared with me her observations on alternative healing methods and their relationship to mainstream medical practice.

I am much indebted to the friendly and helpful folks at Columbia University Press, especially James Warren, Plaegian Alexander, and Leslie Kriesel; and to photo researcher Elyse Rieder. Working with all of them has been a pleasure.

I also thank California State University, Chico, the College of Humanities and Fine Arts, and the Department of Religious Studies for their support and a semester-long sabbatical that allowed me to write up the results of my research for this book. My colleagues have been supportive and interested throughout the research and writing, and I especially want to thank Micki

Lennon for her close reading of many of these chapters and her insightful editing suggestions. The mistakes and oversights in this book are all mine, of course.

Laird Easton, Robert O'Guin, and Dianna Winslow (who also generously read and made helpful suggestions on chapter 5) took care of me and celebrated my successes, and I thank them for their friendship and intellectual companionship while this book was under way. Above all, my children, Dasa, Jonah, and Clara, deserve special thanks for allowing me to hole up in my office writing when they would have preferred my attention elsewhere.

*New Age and Neopagan Religions in America*

*Part One*

# CHAPTER ONE

# Ancient Mysteries in Contemporary America

San Jose, "Silicon Valley" central, is the heart of the late twentieth-century technological revolution and home to a large community of Neopagans and New Agers, many of whom have converged on a local hotel. The expansive lobby and atrium area of the Doubletree Hotel features a restaurant and bar, luxurious lounge chairs, elegantly dressed doormen—and dozens of people walking around in velvet cloaks, leather corsets, and other costumes. As I passed through on my way to a late-morning ritual, a traditional English longsword dance had taken over the lobby. Fiddle and guitar players kept time to the kilted dancers, and passersby gathered to watch them go through their steps. This was the yearly Bay area New Age and Neopagan convention called Pantheacon, and the scene was not out of the ordinary for a hotel that also hosts science fiction and Star Trek conventions. Down the hall from the lobby were information tables with flyers advertising henna hand painting, soul journeys, a shamanic healing arts center, Earth activist training, a fire drum circle, and *The Hieroglyph* newsletter for Egyptian revivalists. The hallway opened onto the "Vendor's Room," a convention ballroom full of merchants selling Neopagan music CDs, gauze gowns, hooded cloaks, billowy silk blouses, leather bags, decorative knives and swords, crystals and colorful stones, herbal lotions and essential oils, incense and dried sage, chain mail jewelry, jewelry with Celtic designs, statues of Pan and voluptuous goddess figurines, tarot cards, and books about Mayan culture, Renaissance magic, astrology, ancient Greece, Welsh mythology, African Yoruba religion, Witchcraft, and more. Massages and aura readings were offered at some booths and a "Peace Altar" was set up in another, which invited participants to leave an offering or prayer for peace in "these interesting times." The hotel hallway was also filled with bulletin boards listing events that would take place over the three-day weekend. Hundreds of different rituals, workshops, and performances were listed, including "Intro to Shamanism," "Self-Hypnosis That Works," "The Quest Tarot," "Ancient Slavic Paganism," "Trance Middle Eastern Dance Workshop," "Druid Healing Ritual," "Hercules and the Hydra," "Liturgy for Athena," "Lord of the Rings—Chainmail 201," "Psychic Techniques," "Gaia Tribe in Concert," and "Being a Witch at Work," to name just a few.

Late Saturday morning a ritual called "The Jewel Without Price: Exploring the Grail Myth Through Tools of the Feri Tradition" was scheduled in one of the windowless convention rooms.[1] Participants who arrived for the ritual had read the following description in the convention program: "Musically accompanied workshop/ritual using Iron and Pearl pentacles to touch the mystery of the Grail, whose secret elixir of magick [with a K to distinguish it from stage magic] and inspiration has been sought by humanity throughout existence." The pentacle or pentagram is a symbol in the shape of a five-pointed star, with each point symbolizing one of the elements of earth, fire, air, water, and spirit. The ritual was to be presented by Sharon Knight, who, according to her informational flyer, was "a Feri initiate" who "has practiced magick for 20+ years. She is co-founder of the band Pandemonaeon and teaches music and magick in the Bay Area."

The description piqued the interested of many conventiongoers, and twice as many people as Knight had expected showed up in the conference room. Chairs were pushed to the back of the room and the lights were dimmed. More than fifty people stood or sat in a circle along the walls. Some were dressed in jeans and T-shirts and others wore ceremonial robes. There were no prerequisites or required attire. The entire convention and this ritual were open to anyone who paid the registration fee of $60 for four days. Knight wore a sapphire blue Renaissance-style gown, sleeves dripping with blue lace, a striking contrast to her long red hair, which she wore loose. Another priestess with blond braids wore a burgundy silk and velvet gown, fitted around the bodice and flowing through the skirt. The rich colors of their clothes and the period style were a welcome contrast to the nondescript hotel carpet and blank walls and helped to set the mood, as did a man softly playing acoustic guitar in the corner of the room.

In the center of the room was a large bronze grail, or cup, with tarot cards arranged face down in a circle on the floor around it. We stayed seated against the walls as Knight described each stage of the ritual, telling us exactly what to expect, how the steps of the ritual were to unfold, what chants we would be singing, and what she hoped to accomplish. As she talked, she realized that her original ritual plan would have to be adjusted to accommodate the large number of people who had chosen to attend that day. Instead of having everyone walk the shape of the pentacle, following the priestesses, they decided it would be more effective for us to stay where we were and to follow their movements with our eyes, imagining we were walking with them instead of actually moving around the room. Their original plan would have resulted in a confused melee of people with no idea what to do next.

When she was ready to begin, Knight asked us to stand, unless we were more comfortable sitting (no part of the ritual was mandatory, but most people followed directions), and she led us through a visualization to help us enter ritual space. She encouraged us to feel anchored to the earth, rooted in the bedrock beneath the earth's surface, releasing every distraction that might prevent us from being fully mentally and physically present for the ritual.

> Feel deep in your belly a glowing red fire. Let a strand of this red flame drop from your belly down into the earth, through all the layers of the earth, until you come to the very molten core of the earth. Let the fire of your core meld with the fire of the earth's core. As you exhale, let all your tensions and scattered energy pour down this red strand into the earth. As you inhale, draw up love and strength from the earth. Continue the cycle, pouring out your distractions into the earth and drawing up strength from the earth, until you feel focused. Then send your love down to the earth as you exhale and draw up love from the earth as you inhale. Chant, "Hail Earth, Mother of all."[2]

Worries, memories, concerns, and time fell away as we followed her instructions to visualize the "red core of energy" connecting us to the earth. Next we "cast a circle" in our minds by visualizing a sphere encompassing the ritual space, with the mundane reality of the hotel left outside. She instructed us, "Draw this red flame up through your entire body until it flows out your crown and up into the Heavens. Envision a sphere opening up about a foot above your head where an electric blue light flows into your body." Then the first chant began, Knight's strong and beautiful voice leading us and participants joining in as they learned the words. It was the "Vault of Heaven," an invocation of a deity (asking a spirit or deity to be present in a ritual) called the Star Goddess: "You who open the vault of Heaven, out of the blackness comes spinning of stars."[3] At the end of the chant she asked us to

Allow the essence of stars to pour through you, filling your body with the wash of spirit, flooding you and pouring all the way through to the center of the earth. Draw up the flame of the earth through your body and up out your crown, offering your earthly potency to the Goddess of Heaven. And let her starry wisdom rain down through you again until she grounds herself in the very core of the earth. And draw up the earth through your body until it fountains out your crown as an offering to the Star Goddess.

Then she told us to say to ourselves, "I contain the earth and the heavens within my center, the circumference of all." At that point the lights dimmed and the guitarist began playing again. Knight announced the purpose of the ritual and set us on our path: "What is the jewel without price? That for which we yearn in our deepest heart of hearts? That which drives us along the path of magick though we face misunderstanding, loneliness, and desolation? For what one kiss would you be willing to give all? . . . Come, let us walk the endless knot, and disentangle ourselves from limitation." The ritual focused on clearing psychological obstacles such as fear that kept us from knowing and acting to realize our full potential.

The "red wand priestess"—the blond woman in the burgundy dress—silently walked to each point of the pentacle while Knight followed behind her and led us through a visualization/meditation for each point; we followed their words and movements with our eyes and minds. The light of the wand, she said, "symbolizes the fire of earth we invoked that burns through our bodies and the blood that pulses through our bodies." The red wand priestess walked to the first point of the pentacle and began by raising her wand and pointing away from the center of the space. This first point was "Spirit and Sex," represented by a violet jewel and violet light running through our bodies. Knight asked us to think of all the ways that sex is empowering and positive, conjuring up our images of sexual power and shining violet light on them: "Feel your connection to the earth. Feel yourself opening to the Vault of Heaven. Notice the pillar of energy this creates, and allow this pillar to become flooded with a violet jewel tone. Here we invoke the powers of sex. Conjure within yourself all the images of your sexuality. How do you celebrate the deliciousness of sex? What joys does it bring you? In what ways do you feel strong in your sexual self?" We meditated on these questions, and then she asked us to notice any cloudy places in the violet jewel, places where we might be uncomfortable sexually, where our power might be blocked, where the violet does not shine, and to look into these places. "Where are your fears regarding sex lodged in your body?" she asked. "Trust your body-wisdom, and accept whatever feelings, images, or insights are given. Now clench even deeper into these fears. Accentuate the feelings of restriction they cause in your body, so that you really feel them. Take a deep breath . . . and release all the tension into the earth. . . . Shake it out, breathe it out," she instructed. A couple of people fell to the floor, some stomped, and others let their breath out with a rush. Knight rang a bell to signal the release and told us, "Flood yourself again with the pure jewel tone of violet, and stand in this clarity for a moment." We imagined the violet light permeating our bodies, shining through unimpeded, spreading through us as we held the images of sexual power in our minds.

The priestesses went through a similar routine for each point of the pentacle as we followed with our eyes and imaginations. Each time, Knight had us imagine a jewel-tone light shining through us, specifically associated with the element of that point (air—topaz, earth—emerald green, fire—ruby red, water—sapphire blue, spirit—violet). And each time we had to look for where the color was cloudy and our power blocked, mentally go into that cloudiness, see what was causing it, and clear it away by breathing out, then imagine the colored light filling us up again. Topaz and golden light were for the power of self-identity; red ruby, fire and pride for personal power, for our accomplishments and who we are; emerald for earth and power—where we see ourselves really manifesting our will on the concrete level, changing the world around us; blue sapphire was for water and passion flowing through us, passion for life more than sexual passion. "What are you most moved by in life?" Knight asked us. "What rouses your deepest emotions?"

When the priestesses walked toward each point, all of us turned in that direction and imagined walking toward it in our own way. Some lifted their hands up as if to hail the spirits of that direction, while others simply focused their eyes and minds there. Some ritual participants remained seated while others swayed back and forth as they stood and watched the priestesses.

After leading us through the visualization exercises for each element/color, the priestesses returned to the sex/spirit point where they had started. Here they repeated the same ritual in an abbreviated way, asking us to feel the Iron Pentacle (red fire coming up from the core of the earth where iron resides that represents the iron of our life's blood) as the red light of iron moved through our bodies.

At the head, they said, "We invoke Spirit and Sex," and asked us to visualize red flame tracing from our head to our right foot.

At the right foot—"We invoke Fire and Pride"—we were to visualize
red flame from our right foot to our left hand.

At the left hand—"We invoke Air and Self"—we were to visualize red
flame from our left hand to our right hand.

At the right hand—"We invoke Earth and Power"—we were to visualize red flame from our right hand to our left foot.

At the left foot—"We invoke Water and Passion"—we were to visualize
red flame from our left foot back to our head.

Then we were told to repeat the process while tracing a red pentagram
over our body, and to speed up, saying only, "Sex, Pride, Self, Power,
Passion" at the respective points.

Then there was stillness and the music began again. Knight led us in an invocation of the Celtic goddess Brigid, whom she called the "Keeper of the
Cauldron of Inspiration in Celtic lore." Knight circled around the grail,
swinging a silver branch of bells and singing a song to Brigid:

*Oh light in times of darkness, Lady come down to us*
*Mother Serpent, Mystic Rose, Lady come into us*
*Eerie One of the Ivory tower, Lady come through us*
*Fountain of Crystal, Mouth of Music, Lady come out of us*
*Oh Lady of the Cauldron, warmed by the breath of the sacred Nine*
*Oh Lady of the Cauldron, warmed by the breath of the sacred Nine.*[4]

We all joined in, repeating the song many times to let the energy from our
singing fill the room. The guitarist in the corner kept playing as the song
slowly died down and Knight invited us to come up and look into the grail,
"to scry"—a process of seeking visions and insight by looking in a mirror or
water into other realities. She also instructed us to choose one of the tarot
cards that were arranged face down on the floor around the chalice, turn it
over to see which character it was, then put it back and concentrate on what
it signified. People spontaneously left the outer circle and gathered around
the grail a few at a time. When they had finished and returned to the circle,
others took their place. Some people sat by the grail and meditated on what
they saw there or on their card for a few minutes before returning to the
circle.

We went through a similar process with the Pearl Pentacle, visualizing
pearly white light flowing through our bodies and turning into color at each
point. We did this several times quickly, filling the room with our energy.
Knight explained what we were doing this way:

As the Iron Pentacle is the work and wisdom of our human selves, so the Pearl Pentacle is the work and wisdom of our Divine Selves, our transpersonal magick, the quickening that comes from gaining awareness of the True Will. Pearlescent energy drawn through body in the shape of a pentagram, as was the Iron pentacle. At each point, "Sex deepens into Love" and a violet flame alights at our crown. "Pride deepens into Law, or True Will," and a ruby flame alights at our right foot. "Self deepens into Knowledge," and a topaz flame alights at our left hand. "Power deepens into Power," and an emerald flame alights at our right hand. "Passion deepens into Wisdom," and a sapphire flame alights at our left foot.[5]

The priestesses closed the ritual by "grounding" the energy we raised and bringing us back to the present. "Grounding" was a calming process that brought us out of the realm of visualization and meditation into the concrete reality of our presence in a group of people sitting around a hotel conference room. As part of our return to ordinary reality, we "released" Brigid and the elemental powers of fire, air, water, earth, and spirit that we had invoked— we bade them good-bye. Knight asked us to return from the "astral" plane to our bodies, to touch the earth, notice the boring hotel carpet, and remember where we were. Finally she shared a Buddhist blessing with us: "We dedicate the benefit of this act, and all acts, to the complete liberation and supreme enlightenment of all beings everywhere, pervading space and time, so mote it be. May the benefit of practice, ours and others', come to fruition ultimately and immediately, and we remain in a state of presence."[6] Then we all let out a loud "AAAAAAAAHHHHH!" in order to spread the benefit of the ritual throughout the world.

Knight, like many other Neopagans, has found ways to harmonize her spirituality with work in the world. She lives in the San Francisco Bay area, where she is a massage therapist and founding member of the band Pandemonaeon. "Her private practice uses art, music, and dance to tap the mythic powers of the psyche," says her promotional flyer.[7] The Iron and Pearl Pentacle visualizations that we went through were Knight's versions of rituals she learned as an initiate in Feri Witchcraft. Her flyer explains that "Feri is an ecstatic tradition of Witchcraft first developed and taught by Victor Anderson. It is characterized by a fierce, wild spirit and non-specific gender identification. Its training is rigorous and its initiates are skillful, well-rounded magick users with a strongly developed sense of self and personal ethics." The tradition is based on the visions of its founder, Victor Anderson

(1917–2001), and most participants in this tradition trace their lineage back to him. It has influenced many other branches of Neopaganism, especially through the writings, rituals, and activism of Starhawk, a priestess well known in Neopagan circles and even in the larger culture, who was trained by Anderson.

In *Drawing Down the Moon*, her groundbreaking study of Neopaganism, journalist Margot Adler wrote of her encounter with Victor Anderson that, "his was the only story I heard that was clearly from the land of faery." Anderson told Adler that when he was around nine he met an old woman who told him that she was a Witch. As a child he had become almost completely blind and remained blind throughout his life, but nevertheless he witnessed a ritual involving a god and goddess. He came across the old woman sitting in the middle of a circle in the woods, and he took off his clothes and experienced a "sexual initiation." He recalled that "'We seemed to be floating in space. . . . I heard a voice, a very distant voice saying "Tana, Tana." It became louder and louder. It was a very female voice but it was as powerful as thunder and as hard as a diamond and yet very soft. Then it came on very loud. It said "I am Tana." Then, suddenly, I could see there was a great sky overhead like a tropical sky, full of stars, glittering brilliant stars, and I could see perfectly in this vision, despite my blindness. The moon was there, but it was green.'" He saw that they were on the edge of a jungle and that out of the jungle a male figure was approaching them: "'A beautiful man. There was something effeminate about him, and yet very powerful. His phallus was quite erect. He had horns and a blue flame came out of his head. He came walking toward me, and so did she. I realized without being told that this was the mighty Horned God. But he was not her lord and master or anything like that, but her lover and consort. She contained within herself all the principles and potencies of nature.'" Soon after the appearance of the god and goddess, the darkness vanished and Anderson was back in the circle with the old woman, who showed him how to use herbs in ritual and bathed him. Then he put his clothes on, went back to his house, and slept.

Anderson worked with a magickal group in Oregon that held rituals according to the phases of the moon until World War II, when the group disbanded and he married Cora, one of its members. Cora had been raised in the southern United States and brought her knowledge of that region's "folk magic" to the ritual practices she and Victor shared, which were also shaped by Hawaiian Kahuna traditions and other influences. They later initiated a young man named Gwydion Pendderwen, who incorporated Celtic material, especially Welsh mythology, into the tradition they had founded. Like many

Neopagan organizations that allow members to personalize their teachings, Feri—also spelled "Faery" or "Faerie"—was shaped and changed over time by the individuals who became involved with it. This individualistic tradition is one important example of the ways in which New Age and Neopagan traditions incorporate a variety of different spiritual paths and religious traditions into their practices. In Sharon Knight's Grail ritual, for instance, Feri blends Celtic mythology and Buddhist compassion with traditional Witchcraft symbols of the circle and pentagram. According to one Feri practitioner, the various branches that are taught by different teachers, who trace their lineage back to Victor and Cora Anderson, have incorporated sources as diverse as Sufism, American Indian traditions, Mesopotamian mythology, Greek mythology, Santeria, and Basque mythology, among others.[8]

In a eulogy for Anderson on The Witches' Voice Web site, Neopagan Penny Novack observed that much of the national Neopagan culture was influenced by him and Cora: "In teaching, they created a huge pool of talented, intelligent Witches and Pagans whose huge body of work has deeply influenced the entire nation. Within this dynamic fountain of creative force which has fed and lifted the psyche of those whose lives' paths followed the Old Religion, were all the arts plus philosophy and healing."[9] The Feri tradition has its own set of deities and rituals that overlap with other Witchcraft traditions in some ways and are unique in other ways. According to one teacher, "Feri witches commune with their gods, not as archetypes, but as living beings," and "Feri training commonly revolves around doing visualization and meditation."[10] Starhawk, a Neopagan leader and author of some of the most popular Neopagan books, was initiated in the Feri tradition and wrote this version of its creation myth:

> Alone, awesome, complete within Herself, the Goddess, She whose name cannot be spoken, floated in the abyss of the outer darkness, before the beginning of all things. As She looked into the curved mirror of black space, She saw by her own light her radiant reflection, and fell in love with it. She drew it forth by the power that was in Her and made love to Herself, and called Her "Miria, the Wonderful."

> Their ecstasy burst forth in the single song of all that is, was, or ever shall be, and with the song came motion, waves that poured outward and became all the spheres and circles of the worlds. The Goddess became filled with love, swollen with love, and She gave birth to a rain of bright spirits that filled the worlds and became all beings.

But in that great movement, Miria was swept away, and as She moved out from the Goddess She became more masculine. First She became the Blue God, the gentle, laughing god of love. Then She became the Green One, vine-covered, rooted in the earth, the spirit of all growing things. At last She became the Horned God, the Hunter whose face is the ruddy sun and yet dark as Death. But always desire draws Him back toward the Goddess, so that He circles Her eternally, seeking to return in love.

All began in love; all seeks to return to love. Love is the law, the teacher or wisdom, and the great revealer of mysteries.[11]

Myths like this one and rituals like the Iron Pentacle create the impression of a tradition rooted deeply in time and history, yet with a contemporary focus on self-knowledge and personal experience. Both aspects are central to Neopagan and New Age religious life. These religions are eclectic at heart, blending old and new, the visionary and the concrete, dance and music, foreign and indigenous cultural practices to meet the needs of late twentieth- and early twenty-first-century people.

# CHAPTER TWO

# Introduction to the Religious Worlds of Neopagans and New Agers

Diana was born in 1953, one of the generation now known as the "baby boomers." She remembers having unusual experiences as a child that frightened and fascinated her and worried her parents. She saw fairies in the woods and played with an imaginary friend. But her mother thought demons possessed her and insisted on taking Diana with her to the evangelical church she regularly attended. As Diana puts it, all the magic was forced out of her. When she left home she stopped attending church and lived a secular life for a few years, avoiding both Christianity and alternative religions. When she was in her mid-twenties, an astrologer told her that she possessed psychic gifts, so she took out books on Witchcraft and crystal healing from the public library. As she read and remembered her childhood experiences, her spiritual life was reinvigorated. She joined a Wiccan coven and began attending workshops on psychic healing. She regularly went to a hypnotherapist who helped her explore her past lives. Diana now describes herself as a Wiccan interested in shamanism who is part of the larger Neopagan community. She signs e-mail petitions about environmental issues and is a registered Democrat, but is not otherwise politically active. Diana's current spiritual work is focused on coming to terms with a past episode of sexual abuse by a relative when she was thirteen and on maintaining a healthy balance among work, spirituality, and personal life.

Gary was born in 1965 to parents he labels "hippies" who lived on a commune for a couple of years but later divorced. His mother joined the Krishna Consciousness movement (the Hare Krishnas) and his father became a lawyer. He remembers accompanying his parents to a Lakota sun dance one summer and being fascinated rather than disturbed at this ritual that involved body piercing and endurance. In college he took courses on American Indian religion and participated in workshops at a New Age center, where he learned to meditate and read people's auras. Every summer he went to the Burning Man festival, a gathering of artists, musicians, computer programmers, and curious reporters and others that takes place on Labor Day weekend in the Nevada desert and includes collective rituals involving thousands of participants. After graduating from college, Gary became a massage therapist; he now works in a building in Santa Fe, New Mexico where his neighbors are psychic healers and past-life regressionists. Gary believes a new age of enlightenment is under way and that his work helps others to participate more fully in it.

Stories like Diana's and Gary's are common among Neopagans and New Agers, who see their lives as journeys to greater self-awareness and spiritual advancement.[1] For them the path of personal spiritual progress is central to life and is the best way to effect changes in the world around them. But it is hard to say that anything is typical of the New Age and Neopagan movements, which have been from the start diverse and individualistic. Participants include teachers, househusbands, librarians, accountants, lawyers, factory workers, farmers, and artists. A disproportionate number are baby boomers who express their generation's disenchantment with traditional religious options and desire for self-fulfillment and personalized religious worlds. Exceptions will be found for almost any generalization that can be made, so categorizing participants in these movements is a near impossible project.

But there are common trends and concerns that can be found in most, if not all, Neopagan and New Age communities. For instance, New Agers and Neopagans draw on similar techniques to explore and transform the self. Although their gods and spirit helpers are highly diverse, they contact them in ritualized settings. Some of the entities they honor exist on a separate plane of reality, while others are extraterrestrials with special messages intended to improve human life on this planet. New Agers and Neopagans usually believe that individuals are responsible for their own spiritual lives, but they also seek out guides and religious specialists through ritual groups, weekend workshops, and professional-client relationships. They consult astrologers and tarot cards, the *I Ching* and other divinatory techniques for guidance in life choices and to further self-knowledge. They appropriate the spiritual riches of other religious cultures, including Tibetan Buddhist, Hindu, Taoist, Egyptian, American Indian, and even some Christian beliefs and practices. They put statuettes of the Buddha or Hindu or Egyptian deities on their home altars alongside objects such as pentacles, candles, crystals, and goddess figurines.

Most of them believe in reincarnation (rebirth—the continuity of the soul through many lives) and *karma* (derived from the Hindu belief that the condition into which each soul is reborn is the result of good or bad actions performed in previous lives), and they look to past lives to help them understand the present. In order to heal wounds from the past and past lives and to live more fully in the present, New Agers and Neopagans engage in holistic healing practices such as herbal therapies, aura cleansing, psychic healing, and massage and other types of body work. Healing practices tend to be focused on cleansing and purifying the self and healing old and new physical and emotional wounds. The goal is to enable the practitioner to participate in developing a more peaceful, tolerant, healthy, and spiritually enlightened society.

The stories at the beginning of this chapter share common themes with other accounts of how men and women became New Agers and Neopagans, yet there are thousands of other stories of people who joined these movements through different avenues. Both movements emerged in the 1960s from the counterculture but also drew on a long American tradition of alternative religious practice and the teachings of British Witches, magicians, and theosophists. They were also shaped by the cultural milieu of the 1960s and 1970s, and especially the social movements that were picking up steam in those decades: feminism, environmentalism, the sexual revolution, and the pan-Indian movement. Emerging New Age and Neopagan communities were significantly influenced by the American encounter with Buddhism from the 1950s on and by the influx of Asian religious teachers when immigration restrictions were lifted in 1965. Many New Agers and Neopagans came of age at a time when the convergence of these and other historical forces encouraged new religious movements to flourish. By the end of the twentieth century, New Age and Neopagan cultures had expanded to include a vast Internet presence and voluminous book sales by mainstream presses as well as obscure cottage industries, and it is often through Web sites and books that spiritual seekers discover them.

## Popular Culture and the Media

Participants often first encounter New Age and Neopagan cultures through books and popular media and then begin to seek out information on the Internet or from people and bookstores in their local communities. Although Neopagans and New Agers share some goals and practices, the ways they discover and pursue their new religious identities can be quite varied. They often have unusual experiences in their youth, such as seeing fairies or predicting future events, followed by a period of spiritual seeking and an encounter, often years later, with a book, teacher, or small group that affirms their early experiences. Neopagans are more likely to find information on the Internet, have a longstanding interest in mythology, or read Starhawk's *Dreaming the Dark* and *The Spiral Dance* as their introduction to the tradition. New Agers often consult holistic health practitioners or psychic healers as a last resort for an ailment that has not responded to any other form of treatment. Or they might pick up a copy of a book such as actress Shirley MacLaine's spiritual biography, *Out On a Limb* (1986), as their first introduction to the New Age. This book, later made into a televised miniseries, brought New Age ideas and the practice of trance channeling into the homes of many Americans. MacLaine describes a spiritual journey that takes her to trance channeler J. Z. Knight, who speaks for Ramtha, an "enlightened being" who told her he was last incarnate about 35,000 years ago and is a member of an enlightened brotherhood that watches over humanity. MacLaine's success is one of many examples of the popularization of New Age ideas once relegated to the radical fringe of the American religious landscape.

No longer to be found in the dusty corners of occult bookstores, New Age and Neopagan titles are readily available for browsing in megastores. Many branches of Barnes and Noble include New Age sections with hundreds of titles, and these same books are available for speedy order via Amazon.com and other Internet sources. How-to Witchcraft books by Neopagan authors share the shelves with titles on crystal healing, psychic readings, tarot cards, astrology, and even vampires. What was once secret and obscure knowledge transmitted through private covens or other small groups that could only be found by word of mouth or in sessions between psychic healers and their clients is now readily available to anyone in or near a good-sized city or with access to a computer and modem.

The Seth books (the first was published in 1972), the predictions of a spirit channeled by Jane Roberts; *A Course in Miracles* (revelations channeled by Helen Schucman and published in 1976); and *The Celestine Prophecy* (1993) by James Redfield are popular books that first exposed many readers to New Age ideas about different realms of consciousness, disembodied beings, and a coming social transformation. These were best-sellers (the series of Seth books together sold more than a million copies) and created large followings that included discussion groups and workbooks to help individuals absorb and work with the truths and wisdom they believe the books contain. *The Celestine Prophecy* opens with the disappearance of a Peruvian manuscript that contains nine important insights that humans must grasp as they enter "an era of true spiritual awareness." The first insight is that "in each of our lives occur mysterious coincidences—sudden, synchronistic events that once interpreted, lead us into our true destiny."[2] This sense of synchronicity appears in many New Age and Neopagan accounts of individuals' spiritual paths and is one aspect of the tendency in both groups to view life as a spiritual journey that is constantly unfolding before the truth-seeker. They also demonstrate the significant impact of publishing and the Internet on New Age and Neopagan religion. Videos, audiotapes, compact discs, and Web sites offer further information to supplement the books. The Celestine Prophecy Homepage includes opportunities to network with people nearby, the journal of the page owner's journey to Peru, links to "The New Civilization Network," and links to people who are experimenting with sending healing energy on the Internet.[3] The Course in Miracles Web site lists study groups throughout the world; links to a retreat center in Temecula, California; offers a daily lesson that can be played on the computer; and includes an online catalogue where the "Course" is available in nine languages. The catalogue also includes "workbook lesson cards," Helen Schucman's poetry, audiotapes, and videotapes. These books and the study groups and spiritual pilgrimages they inspired have also spread New Age ideas to a much broader public that may include participants with other religious affiliations.

Neopaganism has also captured media attention and a Web-savvy following. Hollywood films such as *The Craft* (1997) made rituals such as casting a circle (by the adolescent witches in the film) familiar to the general public. Even though a Wiccan served as a consultant for the film, some Neopagans criticized it for sensationalizing and trivializing their religion. The movie was released at a time when New Age and Neopagan book sales were booming, and it contributed to these sales. Neopagan author Silver Ravenwolf's *Teen Witch* is a popular title at Amazon.com, and its follow-up "Teen Witch kit" was released in August 2000. Teenage reviewers give the book raves and the kit less enthusiastic reviews on Amazon.com: "If you're a teen who has already studied your Buckland and Starhawk, if you own your own athame and cauldron, if you're part of a Wiccan family, this kit is not for you. If you're a younger kid, if you live somewhere with no occult supply stores, if your parents don't mind you taking your money to the bookstore but won't take you somewhere where you can get your own pentacle necklace, if it means a lot to you to have something 'officially witchy' in your personal space—this kit can be fun."4 High school and college students probably account for a large percentage of the growth of Neopaganism in the early twenty-first century.

The Internet has played an important role in popularizing these traditions and making them accessible to seekers everywhere. Web sites for New Age authors and Neopagan organizations abound and are designed to guide the uninitiated who are surfing for information on the strange religion they heard about in the news or elsewhere. The Web site of the Covenant of the Goddess, a national ecumenical Neopagan organization, includes resources for teenagers, families, and solitary practitioners as well as schedules of events taking place throughout the country. Communities like Findhorn (Scotland), Omega (New York), and Esalen (California), that have shaped the development of the New Age movement, host Web sites that include decades of history, biographies of their founders, statements of their spiritual missions, descriptions of workshops and retreats, and photo tours of their grounds and building projects. Sites for Neopagan communities like Circle Sanctuary and the Church of All Worlds have similar content, with the addition of resources on religious freedom and religious persecution, such as Circle's "Lady Liberty League."5 Neopagan Internet discussions have been in existence since the early 1990s, a reflection of the disproportionate technoliteracy among Neopagans. Such groups remain one of the important ways that practitioners, especially young Neopagans, stay in contact with others who share their spiritual concerns.

## Defining Neopaganism

A quick survey of Web sites and popular book titles suggests that Neopagan practices highlight the centrality of the relationship between humans and nature and reinvent religions of the past, while New Agers are more interested in transforming individual consciousness and shaping the future. Because the Covenant of the Goddess is eclectic and inclusive, it provides a good starting point for defining Neopaganism. With its goals of inclusiveness and egalitarianism, it is a good example of how American historical and social forces shaped the emergence of new religions in the 1960s and 1970s. According to the COG Web site, "Wicca, or Witchcraft is the most popular expression of the religious movement known as Neo-Paganism. . . . Its practitioners are reviving ancient Pagan practices and beliefs of pre-Christian Europe and adapting them to contemporary life."[6] The result is a religion that is both old and new, "traditional" and inventive.

As this mention of the rapidly increasing numbers of Neopagans suggests, they are everywhere, and not all of them dress in long black capes and dangling pentacles. In fact, the term "Neopagan" covers a wide variety of beliefs and traditions that include re-creations of ancient Celtic Druidism (a British organization of sun worshippers who gathered in sacred groves), Wicca or Witchcraft, ceremonial magic, and neoshamanism (revivals of ecstatic journeys into the spirit world in indigenous and pre-Christian cultures). In Europe, contemporary Pagan organizations usually claim a lineage that is ancient and unbroken, often tied to nationalism and ethnic pride. American, British, and Australian "Neopagan" communities differ in that they are self-conscious revivals created to be egalitarian, individualistic, and, in the American case, influenced by currents of apocalypticism and social change movements.[7] This book focuses on American Neopaganism, and especially its place in American historical and cultural contexts.

The various forms of Neopaganism in the United States share a desire to revive ancient pre-Christian nature religions. In the process of creating new religions in the cast of old ones, Neopagans borrow from American Indian and other available religious cultures. Neodruids often learn ancient Celtic languages and focus on their roles as caretakers of the woods. Neopagans who are intrigued by specific ancient cultures look to Tibetan, Greek, Roman, and Egyptian pantheons. They find ritual texts, usually in translation, and fashion their practice after mythological stories, such as the descent of the goddess Persephone into the underworld. Neopagans dressed as Aphrodite and Dionysus may put in appearances at Neopagan festivals, where rituals encourage participants to explore divine archetypes from ancient pantheons of deities. Neopagans' current images of god and goddess emerged from nineteenth-century British folklore and literature and were influenced by the armchair anthropology of scholars like Sir James Frazer, author of the sweeping *Golden Bough* (1890), and Robert Graves, author of *The White Goddess* (1966). New Agers and Neopagans tend to be tolerant of eclectic uses of other cultures' myths and traditions, but borrowing from American Indian religions has been controversial. Some Neopagans, for instance, argue that "white people" should only borrow myths and deities from their "own" cultural heritage, such as Witchcraft or ancient Druidism of the British Isles.

Witches form the largest religious culture under the Neopagan umbrella and include at one extreme separatist feminist Witches who worship a great goddess in women-only covens and at the other, traditional Gardnerian Witches who worship a god and goddess together, claim to have the oldest lineage, and pass down their rituals from teachers to students who are instructed to perform them in exactly the same way. Gardnerian rituals emphasize the dual nature of divinity in the form of a paired god and goddess. In twenty-first century America, however, traditional Witchcraft characterizes a minority. An increasing number of Witches are men or women who call themselves "eclectic Witches" or "Wiccans" and borrow from British traditional Witchcraft as well as from a variety of other religious cultures, such as African Yoruba or ancient Egyptian. Witches are sometimes trained and initiated through covens, but they can also be self-taught or guided by correspondence courses and books like Raymond Buckland's *Complete Book of Witchcraft* (1986), which includes lists of ritual tools, directions for making ritual robes, simple explanations of Witchcraft's moral principles, and guidelines for basic rituals. Do-it-yourself Witchcraft has to some extent replaced traditional covens that included several levels of initiation. Another popular title is Starhawk's *The Spiral Dance* (1979), which encourages individuals to tailor their rituals to suit personal needs and preferences and includes sections on herbal charms, chants, blessings, spells, and myths. Witches have only a few beliefs that most of them adhere to; these include "The Wiccan Rede: An it harm none, do what you will," and "The Law of Threefold Effect," the belief that any action a person commits will return to them threefold. These beliefs are also held by most Neopagans—ceremonial magicians and Druids, for instance—who, like Witches, have origins in early twentieth-century British occult groups.

Ceremonial magicians, another important community of Neopagans, are more likely to turn to late nineteenth- and early twentieth-century occultists for inspiration, especially the writings of British occultist Aleister Crowley and the Edwardian occult group, the Golden Dawn, which included Irish writer William Butler Yeats among its members. Where ceremonial magicians emphasize their Golden Dawn heritage, Witches identify with the work of English civil servant Gerald Gardner, whose novel *High Magic's Aid* (1949) and pseudo-anthropological study of a coven, *Witchcraft Today* (1954), are founding documents for contemporary Witchcraft. Ceremonial magic also draws heavily on kabbalah, a Jewish mystical tradition. Ceremonial magicians may blend these traditions with their own interests in religious cultures as diverse as Haitian Vodou and Tibetan Buddhism, while others stay within the bounds of organizations like the OTO, or Ordo Templi Orientis, which Crowley joined in 1913 and eventually became head of, and which involves lengthy study and specific rites of initiation.

Although organizations like the OTO and Gardnerian Witchcraft offer structured guidelines for their members and levels of initiation modeled on the secret societies of the Freemasons, many Neopagans choose to create their own spiritual practice by drawing on information from a rich array of teachers and traditions, and practice alone instead of in groups. Hierarchical structures were common in the earliest Neopagan groups and still character-ize some contemporary communities, but more typically they are loosely structured and egalitarian ritual groups. Elders are acknowledged for their wisdom and experience, but not viewed as all-powerful. "Everyone is a Star," proclaims Elf Lore Family literature welcoming Neopagans of all faiths to festivals in southern Indiana. One of the ways American Neopagans adapt religious traditions from the past and other cultures is to make them more democratic and inclusive, and this is particularly evident in the new rituals they create.

For Neopagans, ritual is the touchstone of religious identity and com-munity. They honor the cycles of nature with rituals at new and full moons and on eight seasonal festivals, including the solstices and equinoxes. New Agers also sometimes hold rituals on solstices and full moons, but their cal-endars are less consistent and many of them do not mention these holidays in their books or Web sites. Neopagan rituals are specific to each particular community and individual, but tend to be focused around the seasons and lunar cycles. Regular rituals are often conducted in small groups for any number of purposes, including healing and personal spiritual growth. They are usually held in circles and facilitated by ritual leaders who explain the purpose of the ritual, invite deities or spirits to be present, monitor the group's energy, and end the ritual in such a way that everyone returns to a normal state of consciousness. Ritual spaces are generally oriented in rela-tion to the four cardinal directions and feature altars that hold statues of deities and symbols of water, air, fire, and earth. Neopagans also periodically hold rituals to mark life passages, including death rites, baby blessings, and marriage vows. Rituals and festivals for seasonal celebrations include retellings of ancient myths, theater, ritual performances, music, feasting, and storytelling. Rituals link the human and celestial worlds and celebrate the cyclical movement of life and death and the changes of the seasons.

Terminology is an issue in the Neopagan community, and many mem-bers do not like the label scholars have given them. They prefer to call themselves "Pagans" to designate the continuity between their practices and those of ancient and indigenous cultures, or they locate themselves in specific traditions, such as "Gardnerian Wiccans." Many Neopagans object to being identified with the New Age movement or defined under the New Age umbrella. They make clear distinctions between their religion and New Age, which they criticize for being too focused on money and "white light," by which they mean that New Age positive thinking is too simplistic. As one Witch puts it, "New Age stuff is, to me, all white-lite and airy-fairy. It's escapism, fantasy, living in a dream world."[8] On the other hand, New Agers often do not like being identified with Neopagans, especially flamboyant gothic Witches and ceremonial magicians dressed entirely in black. Neopagans and New Agers reject stereotypes, which are shallow and often inaccurate representations of the depth and diversity within these religions. And because their spirituality or religious identity is highly personalized, they do not believe that labels capture its richness and complexity. In fact, they share more than they would appear to at first glance. Their common historical origins in nineteenth-century religious movements and the ways they were shaped by the 1960s counterculture will be explored in the next two chapters. They also have a similar orientation to the world, such as a tendency to privilege internal over external authority and experience over belief, and a focus on self-exploration as the best route to truth and knowledge. For these reasons, scholars generally group the movements together. But the desire of many Neopagans to revive ancient traditions is not shared by most New Agers, who are more concerned with ushering in the future.

### Defining the New Age Movement

Like "Neopaganism," "New Age" is an umbrella term that encompasses multiple beliefs and practices. New Agers are committed to the transformation of both self and society through a host of practices that include channeling, visualization, astrology, meditation, and alternative healing methods such as Reiki (laying on of hands to help the body use its own energy to heal) and iridology (using the eyes to diagnose illness). New Agers share with other Americans an interest in angels, miracles, and psychic phenomena such as clairvoyance, but they combine such beliefs with other elements, such as Asian religious traditions, the human potential movement, American Indian beliefs, and holistic healing practices. Trance channelers, psychic healers, therapists specializing in past-life regression, and holistic health practitioners are usually situated in New Age culture. Instead of monthly or weekly ritual groups, like covens, in which Neopagans commonly participate, New Agers are typically more comfortable in specialist-client relationships. And far more than Neopagans, New Agers tend to emphasize spiritual and physical healing to facilitate the shift to a new level of consciousness.

For New Agers, self-growth techniques and physical healing practices are based on the assumption that positive thinking most effectively produces change. They believe that salvation comes through the discovery and culti- vation of a divine inner self with the help of techniques that can be learned from books and workshops as well as spiritual teachers. In addition to posi- tive thinking, they emphasize the idea that negative experiences are illusory and that it is within human ability to change them to positive ones. New Agers believe that tapping one's own psychic powers is at the root of both physical and psychological healing, and the techniques they use to do so are varied and diverse. Because holistic thinking stresses the continuities among all planes of existence, everyday activities like eating food take on cosmic sig- nificance, blurring the boundary between sacred and profane. New Agers also range widely in the extent of their participation in healing and dietary practices. Some form intentional communities that provide models for an emerging planetary culture that conforms to New Age ideals. Some live their beliefs day in and day out within the general culture, while others may attend one New Age workshop a year and meditate at home.

New Agers say that divine power dwells in as well as outside humans and the natural world. Understanding the interconnectedness of all things makes it possible to heal some aspects of human lives and culture that are frag- mented by false dualities. This aim sometimes turns into explicit social criti- cism of institutions and trends that have isolated people from one another and from other living things. Because they believe in interconnectedness and the unlimited potential of human consciousness, many New Agers think hu- mans have a special responsibility to the rest of the planet. Sometimes this view is accompanied by an understanding of the earth as a living being (called the Gaia hypothesis) put forth by scientists James Lovelock and Lynn Margulis. New Agers who take their global responsibilities seriously counsel against personal and social fragmentation and encourage planetary healing and holistic thinking. They often position themselves in opposition to other religious traditions by criticizing scientific and religious reductionism and being more open to feminism, personal freedom, and nonduality (overcoming the false division between matter and spirit). Their goal is to create an alternative society that will eventually replace the one we live in.

New Agers inherited the belief in continuity between matter and spirit from the western metaphysical tradition that includes Transcendentalism, Swedenborgianism, Christian Science, New Thought, Theosophy, mesmerism, spiritualism, and dowsing (using a divining rod). Nineteenth-century spiritual healing traditions emerged out of a system of beliefs that scholars have called "metaphysical" or "harmonial" religion. The central teachings of harmonial religion—that humans and the universe are ultimately one, that they are interconnected and the divine is not outside the world but within human beings as well—has been taken up by the New Age movement. Nineteenth-century figures like Ralph Waldo Emerson (1803–1882) and Helena Blavatsky (1831–1891), the founder of Theosophy (a religion blending Asian and western thought), were proponents of the harmonial view. They also introduced Asian religious teachings into American thought, another aspect of this earlier stream that plays a central role in the lives of New Agers.

Like interest in Asian religions, channeling, one of the most popular New Age practices, can be traced back at least to nineteenth-century America, when spiritualist mediums conveyed messages to the living from dead relatives and spirit guides. Channeling in the form of spiritualism declined in popularity by the end of the nineteenth century but continued to attract a small following well into the twentieth. By the 1970s, channeling was again on the rise. Typically, a client seeks out a trance channeler (medium) when wondering what happens after death, worried about a specific ailment, or looking for spiritual guidance. This medium, who can be male or female, then contacts the spirit world and conveys messages from a spirit guide. When Shirley MacLaine published her popular autobiographical account of the spiritual journey that led her to the "icons of the new age"—J. Z. Knight and the entity Ramtha—channeling was again in the public eye.[9] Ramtha's popular teachings sum up New Agers' self-realization goals: "Ramtha . . . allows us the vision, the hope, the desire to become all that we can become, which is unlimited probability."[10] Channeled entities and spirit guides embody the future, and for this reason New Agers look to them as models of human potential.

Another way that New Agers develop and practice their beliefs is through psychic readings. Whereas in channeling, a spiritual being communicates through a human medium, psychic healing relies on the powers of the individual to see into the future and to diagnose illnesses, sometimes in consultation with spiritual beings. Psychics lead their clients on journeys of personal transformation and prescribe cures for their illnesses. They sell their skills in most American cities today, and many, though not all of them, are New Agers. New Age psychics tend to help clients work toward self-transformation and healing rather than predicting future events, and this marks the difference between psychic reading as a skill and as part of a belief system. Psychic healers draw on their own personal powers or work with the help of power animals and spirit guides. They also have a long history on the American religious scene. Probably the best known and most influential American psychic healer was Edgar Cayce (1877–1945), whose teachings are still widely disseminated through the Association for Research and Enlightenment that he founded in 1931. Like spirit guides, psychics serve as mediators between different levels of reality. They have the ability to see and hear in the spirit world and to bring back messages and information for other humans. And they are recent players in a stream of religiosity that dates from the nineteenth century and continues in the twenty-first.

Interests in indigenous cultures and ancient civilizations as well as extraterrestrials, yoga, and meditation blend together in New Age culture, and these topics are taught through centers and groups with names like "Aquarian Research Foundation" and "Spiritual Frontiers Fellowship." At some holistic health centers, New Age philosophy exists side by side with Reiki energy work, color therapy, creative movement classes, and yoga workshops. Every year, Omega Institute offers hundreds of seminars and workshops on body work and spiritual growth from eastern and western traditions. In 2004 these include "The Heart of Yoga," "Soul Survival," "A Gathering of Shamans," "The Six Realms of Tibetan Spiritual Tradition," and "The Feminine Face of God." Numerous other centers like Omega exist across America and offer a similar cornucopia of spiritual and healing practices, workshops, and training sessions.

Annual spending on workshops and seminars of this kind, channeling, self-help businesses, and alternative health care was $10 to $14 billion at the end of the twentieth century. An estimated 12 million Americans are involved with New Age activities, although they may also participate in other religious organizations.[11] These numbers testify to the extent to which religious ideas put forward by the New Age movement have attracted attention. But self-identified New Agers are not the only ones who visit channelers and crystal healers. Christians, Buddhists, atheists, and Jews may also participate in practices dubbed "New Age" without risking their religious identities. Just as New Agers borrow indiscriminately from other traditions, so others may sample their meditation retreats and channeling sessions. Because religious efficacy is measured within rather than by an external standard, no one can judge, they say, what is best for another person.

## Spiritual Eclecticism

New Agers and Neopagans alike tend to emphasize the self over external authority, and this is due in part to the explosion of information available on the Internet and in bookstores that makes it seem unnecessary to rely on religious elders, though they are still sought out for their ritual experience, charismatic presence, and detailed knowledge of specific traditions. Spiritual eclecticism and the focus on individual needs link New Agers and Neopagans in a common religious project. The process of self-exploration through consciousness-shifting techniques, such as meditation and visualization, is similar whether a spirit guide communicates through a human teacher or a priestess speaks for the goddess. Both offer ways to deepen self-knowledge and transform self and society. As Starhawk says of the exercises and rituals included in her book *The Spiral Dance*, "It is not, however, meant to be followed slavishly; it is more like a basic musical score, on which you can improvise." Neopagan and New Age religious practices are flexible and can be personalized to fit individual needs. This is in part because of how they understand the relationship between human and divine. Starhawk argues that the goddess who guides human beings dwells in the earth and in the world around us: "We can open new eyes and see that there is nothing to be saved *from*, no struggle of life *against* the universe, no God outside the world to be feared and obeyed; only the Goddess." The goddess looks at "each of us unique and natural as a snowflake, each of us her own star, her Child, her lover, her beloved, her Self."[12] This means that the self has all the necessary resources for spiritual advancement, and that the divine is within as well as without. It is a view echoed by many other Neopagans and New Agers, but it also accounts in part for the diversity of religious identities among them.

Neopagans and New Agers tend to emphasize newness, creativity, imagination, and invention over tradition, creed, established doctrine, and institutionalized religion, but they also claim ancient traditions as their heritage. New Agers borrow certain aspects of pre-Christian and indigenous cultures to model the future, but their ways of mixing and matching beliefs and practices are decidedly new, even though they were shaped by the history of alternative religious practice in the United States. Likewise, Neopaganism did not emerge directly from ancient pagan cultures, even though a few Neopagans would argue that their religion descended through the centuries from a pre-Christian goddess religion. According to scholarly consensus, there is no direct lineage from ancient goddess cultures to Neopaganism. Contemporary Pagans ("pagan" was originally a term that referred to non-Christians or country dwellers) are "Neo" in the sense that they are revising and updating what they can learn from ancient traditions to meet their needs today. They believe that in some aspects of life ancient cultures have much to teach us, such as respect for the earth and maintaining a balance between humans and nature. Neopagans and New Agers tend to romanticize ancient and non-Christian cultures that they think possess solutions for a culture gone awry. They search for alternatives to the gods they were raised with by looking to Asian and American Indian religions or distant galaxies, and they claim that spiritual beings from other cultures are more accessible to humans than the god of western monotheistic religions.

## *Spiritual Beings*

For some New Agers and Neopagans divine power is personified by a great goddess or the planet Gaia, and for others divinity is polytheistic—assorted deities are available to help and teach humans. They may be seen as spirits, gods, or goddesses representing the forces of nature or anthropomorphized into archetypes that represent particular aspects of human personality such as the "wild man" or the "trickster." Many Neopagans and New Agers are familiar with the writings of Carl G. Jung (1875–1961) on dreams and archetypes and incorporate his ideas into their belief systems. Practitioners in both groups are likely to reject monotheistic understandings of deity, except for those Neopagans who worship one great goddess and New Agers who remain nominally Christian or Jewish and believe in one all-powerful god. New Agers are more likely to understand the universe itself as divine or assume that god is everywhere and, more important, in everyone, a perspective that scholars label "pantheism." Some New Agers downplay divine power (their books may not mention deities at all) and prefer to focus inward, while others center their religious practice around interaction with spirits.

Making contact with spirits is a frequent occurrence in many New Age and Neopagan communities. New Agers attend channeling sessions or speak with spirit guides in meditation and Neopagans communicate with their deities through home altars and group rituals. Spirit guides may be conceived of as separate entities, as they were by nineteenth-century spiritualists, or may be identified as part of the self, sometimes called the "higher self," a spiritual aspect that is wiser than the ego. New Agers are more likely to be attracted to spirit guides who claim to belong to ancient races or say they are bringing messages from civilizations on other planets. Seth, an entity channeled by trance medium Jane Roberts during the 1960s, told Roberts that he had experienced many lifetimes and eventually became "an energy personality essence no longer focused in physical reality."[13] Roberts expresses a common assumption among Neopagans and New Agers that the self has multiple layers: "we have a supraconscious that is as far 'above' the normal self as the subconscious is 'below' it. . . . It may be that Seth is the psychological personification of that supraconscious extension of my normal self."[14] But she acknowledges that Seth may be what he says he is: part of an ancient entity. New Agers believe that, regardless of their origins, beings like Seth are here to help humans understand themselves and evolve in ways that will lead to a more peaceful world. "Seth," for example, says that the purpose of his communication to humans is to provide a "means by which people can understand themselves better, reevaluate their reality, and change it."[15] The relationship between humans and spirits is described differently within the New Age and Neopagan movements, but in almost all instances, spiritual beings are approached for help with everyday concerns, like finding jobs and lovers, as well as spiritual growth and global healing.

Spiritual beings also come into humans' lives without being asked, and their presence can be disruptive. Most trance channelers are surprised to be contacted by disembodied spirits and undergo major life changes in their new role as medium. J. Z. Knight says that her life of "dinner parties" and "hybrid roses" was interrupted by the completely unlooked-for appearance of Ramtha, an ancient entity, at the end of her bed one night.[16] The founding of the Findhorn community in rural Scotland is another famous example from the history of the New Age movement of spirits initiating contact with humans. In 1964 Peter Caddy, his wife Eileen, and their friend Dorothy Maclean started a garden on a barren, sandy peninsula in northeast Scotland. They believed that their spiritual paths had led them to this particular spot, a place of special powers. The spirits asked them to do things that Maclean and the Caddys thought impossible, and the three of them struggled in poverty for months before the Findhorn garden began to thrive. They were guided by "God," understood as a universal spirit who spoke directly to Eileen Caddy, and by plant "devas" that told them how to nurture their garden. By following the devas' instructions, Maclean and the Caddys grew miraculously huge vegetables and a host of herbs and flowers that should never have been able to flourish in this inhospitable area. They gave credit to organic farming techniques, hard work, the sacred power of the land, and their spiritual path. According to Maclean, "God is an indwelling presence, the core of what I am and what everything is."[17] She regularly contacted the Carrot Deva, the Pea Deva, and other plant spirits with questions about how to care for the plants and came to understand that the devas were angelic figures and representations of "the life force."[18] Ten years later, Findhorn had become a well-established New Age community and pilgrimage destination with an extended network of people to garden and run workshops and conferences that have attracted New Age luminaries and spiritual seekers from around the world. In 2003 Eileen Caddy still lived at the much-expanded Findhorn site and presided as a spiritual guide for the community. Many American New Age teachers and authors have visited and stayed at Findhorn, the most prominent being David Spangler, New Age author and founder of the Lorian Association of "spiritual futurists" (with Maclean and fifteen others in California in 1974; it later relocated to Washington). According to the association's Web site, its "work is based on exploring and articulating . . . emergent new paradigms of spirit." Both Spangler and Maclean continued to communicate with spiritual entities after they left Findhorn. A project that was apparently initiated by spiritual beings became one of the founding New Age centers for spiritual exploration, attracting participants from around the globe and sending its former students off to establish their own New Age organizations.

Like Maclean and the Caddys, other Neopagans and New Agers enjoy intimate and highly personalized relationships with spiritual beings. The influential Neopagan teacher and writer Starhawk stresses this point:

> Our spirituality is based on experience, on a direct relationship with the cycles of birth, growth, death, and regeneration in nature and in human lives. We see the complex interwoven web of life as sacred. . . . To us, Goddesses, Gods, and for that matter, archaeological theories are not something to believe in, nor are they merely metaphors. An image of deity, a symbol on a pot, a cave painting, a liturgy are more like portals to particular states of consciousness and constellations of energy. Meditate on them, contemplate them, and they take you someplace, generally into some aspect of those cycles of death and resurrection.[19]

Most Neopagans would agree with Starhawk's assessment, as would many New Agers, though for some belief—not just experience—plays a more important role than Starhawk admits. Because these movements are decentralized and have no founding text or teacher, participants vary greatly in how they understand their interactions with the gods and spirits. For some the gods are part of an elaborate belief system, but for others they are, as Starhawk suggests, rooted in practice and experience. In both movements, spiritual beings can be images that "take you someplace" or friendly guides leading seekers on spiritual journeys, but what they have in common is being accessible to humans and humanlike themselves.

## Ways of Practicing

Communicating with spiritual beings in another reality is one type of religious practice, but there are others as well, and they can take place in collective or individual settings. Neopagans and New Agers may belong to organized communities and ritual groups with clear leaders or rotating facilitators, or they may attend an occasional weekend workshop on, say, shamanic drumming or crystal healing to learn specific techniques from acknowledged experts. Both groups have in common a belief in other levels of reality, such as the "astral," that are accessible to humans who are searching for powerful spiritual experiences and meaning in their lives. This astral level or spirit world can be reached through techniques learned from books and teachers. Meditation sessions, theatrical rituals, psychic readings, and workshops on healing through sound vibrations are a few of the many methods available for self-exploration. Many New Age and Neopagan practices are private rituals that individuals conduct in their homes, while others are large group experiences, such as Neopagan festivals, holistic healing fairs, and weekend workshops and conferences. New Agers hold retreats focused on spiritual growth and Neopagans gather in covens and ritual groups to work magic, also focused on journeying inward to see knowledge and wisdom as well as calling up power to send out to others or incorporate into oneself. Neopagan rituals and events tend to be more elaborate and theatrical than New Age gatherings. Neopagans may also conduct personalized rituals focused on an altar at home and keep their religious identity completely secret. New Agers are more likely to conduct their religious lives in publicly recognizable places such as learning centers or offices advertising their services. Neopagans rarely put out shingles naming what they do, and their rituals are more likely to be attended by people who found them through word of mouth rather than in newspapers or on health food store bulletin boards. Levels of commitment exist on a spectrum from daily meditation and ritual work to an occasional weekend away at a New Age retreat or Neopagan festival. "What works best for an individual" is the constant response of Neopagans and New Agers when asked how to go about living as a Witch, shaman, healer, or medium. The consensus seems to be that the practices for changing one's consciousness can be myriad, with no one right way for everyone.

Neopagans and New Agers reject institutionalized religion because they believe in personalized religious practice. For the same reason, they often choose alternative healing practices instead of seeking relief from conventional medicine. Holistic healing coexisted with alternative religions as a stream of beliefs and practices before being taken up self-consciously by the New Age movement in the early 1970s. One of the earliest New Age journals, *East West* (later it became *Natural Health*), started in 1970 and for the next two decades ran articles on such varied topics as macrobiotic diets, yoga, spiritual healing, and using essential oils to heal illness. Techniques of self-transformation commonly involve emotional or physical healing; for example, at New Age retreats, workshops on self-exploration may be followed by workshops on healing touch or meditation, visualization, crystal therapy, or hypnotherapy. Spiritual autobiographies bring order and meaning to healing experiences as they are transmitted and circulated through New Age networks.

Not all holistic healing practitioners consider themselves "New Age," but most share New Age assumptions about the intimate connections among body, mind, and spirit. Participants in closely related new religious movements such as Neopaganism also make use of many holistic healing and self-development techniques. New Agers might take advantage of a number of services and practices such as Reiki, iridology, and macrobiotics (a special vegetarian diet) with the goal of healing body and spirit. They are more likely than people of other faiths who adopt one or more of these practices to see them as components of an evolved lifestyle that is part of a growing change in planetary consciousness. Vegetarian and vegan diets, massage therapy, herbal healing, crystal therapy, and fasting are all ways of caring for and manipulating the body to maximize health and prevent disease. These practices can be done on one's own with the help of the many books available or by consulting practitioners who specialize in one or more therapies. New Agers and holistic healers hope that a new body and mind will facilitate and accompany a transformed heaven and earth.

### Earth Religion and Sacred Geography

Although New Agers and Neopagans focus their religious practice on the self, they are also concerned for the natural world and the deities that embody forces of nature. Their attitudes toward nature run the gamut from radical environmentalism to sacred journeys around Mount Shasta. Neopagans say they practice ancient nature religions and New Agers do not, though they often have a vision of the future that is earth-centered. An important element of Neopagan theology that also characterizes some New Age views is the belief in immanence, the idea that divinity permeates the world around us and runs through other humans, the earth, and all living beings. Deities are typically identified with forces of nature—the earth goddess Gaia is one example—and the four elements, earth, air, water, and fire, are almost always invoked in Neopagan ritual work. Another popular Neopagan deity is the god Pan, who emerged as an archetype in mid-twentieth century Britain and was incorporated into the magickal subculture in the form of a "horned god" paired with a goddess derived from Artemis and other Greek deities.[20] Many Neopagans continue to interact with the god and goddess, while others have returned to Pan in his Greek form. Morning Glory Zell, one of the co-leaders of the Neopagan Church of All Worlds, traces Pan to his Homeric origin: "Our classical imagery of Pan is derived from the 'Homeric Hymn to Pan,' celebrating the rustic god whose home was in remote Peloponnesian Arcadia. The poet evokes the god as he wanders woodland glades with dancing nymphs." Zell sees Pan as the original god of nature. She tells her readers that on Mount Olympus the gods named him "Pan, from *pas*, 'all.' Scholars of Alexandria believed that Pan personified the natural cosmos. Our word *pantheism* is derived from that idea, that all Nature is God and that God is all Nature."[21] Some New Agers may also identify nature with deity, but they are more likely to focus on humans than on earth, to identify with Pan as a part of the self but not ask him to join their rituals. New Age rituals rarely include tributes to deities, but Neopagans call Greek, African, Egyptian and other gods into their ritual space and put statues of them on their altars.

Because of their close identification of deity with nature, urban Neopagans might keep images of Pan on home altars to bring nature into the city, but they also travel to the woods and establish nature sanctuaries to honor their gods. Several Neopagan organizations have created retreats and sanctuaries, where stone altars and ritual circles can be constructed in the woods to facilitate interactions with the natural world. Circle Sanctuary in southwestern Wisconsin is a prominent Neopagan organization that bought land in the 1980s specifically to set aside for the enjoyment of the Neopagan community as a retreat from the outside world. Gatherings and other ritual events held there include caring for the land, planting, and learning about local edible plants and healing herbs. Lothlorien in southern Indiana was also established as a Neopagan retreat, and, like Circle, is open to people of all faiths as long as they are tolerant of others. Named after novelist J. R. R. Tolkien's land of the elves, the Neopagan Lothlorien is envisioned as a magical place where spiritual beings are free to roam and accessible to humans who treat the land properly. Nature sanctuaries are one of the ways that Neopagans put their religious ideas into practice, because they are set up to facilitate the relationships between humans and other sentient beings.

When Neopagans act as caretakers and stewards of the land, they embody an alternative response to environmental problems that does not require social and political activism. That said, some environmental activists practice a green religion that is very close to and borrows from Neopagan theology. Some Earth First! members who are radical environmentalists involved in spiking trees and setting up tree sits to prevent logging in old-growth forests are likely to share the Neopagan belief that nature is imbued with spirit, and this is what fuels their activism. Famous tree sitter and radical environmentalist Julia Butterfly Hill, who made the national news for her two-year tree sit in a coastal redwood called "Luna," believed her action was justified because "majestic ancient places, housing more spirituality than any church, were being turned into clear-cuts and mudslides."[22] Butterfly Hill saw the woods and humanity as part of "the Universal Spirit." Radical environmentalist Peg Millett likewise became involved with environmental protests and civil disobedience out of the conviction "that the earth and all the creatures were sacred."[23] Like New Agers and Neopagans, these environmentalists act from the conviction that humans are part of a web of life that includes trees and animals. Destruction of other living beings, they say, destroys us all. The ideas of interconnectedness and immanence have clearly spread beyond New Age and Neopagan communities into the broader culture.

New Agers tend not to make nature as central to their religious identity, although they hold certain places to be sacred. Two of the most popular New Age sites in the United States, Sedona, Arizona and Mount Shasta, California, are striking for their natural beauty and attract many tourists as well as New Age pilgrims. Mount Shasta (14,162 feet tall) is the focus of many myths and stories circulated among New Agers. First and foremost is the idea that the last remnants—beings and cities—of a lost and ancient culture—Lemuria or Atlantis—are buried beneath the mountain. People tell of seeing Lemurians mysteriously appear and disappear around the mountain. Some also tell of mysterious lights, angel-shaped clouds, and spaceships over Mount Shasta. New Agers believe these places are sites where energy vortexes occur. They define vortexes as places on earth where spiritual power is concentrated, and they travel to these sites, including Mount Shasta, Sedona, and places in South and Central America such as Machu Picchu. Shasta Vortex Adventures is an organization in Mount Shasta City that offers "An Insight Hike and Bike Tour," "A Guided Vision Quest," "A Peak Experience Retreat," and "a Sacred Site Tour to connect with the many spirits of the mountain." According to psychic healer Ashalyn, who runs the organization, Mount Shasta is known "by many worldwide as a powerful energy vortex," and her tours are designed to allow participants to "reconnect with the healing and nurturing qualities of nature . . . in a beautiful, peaceful, inspiring environment."[24]

Neopagans occasionally make pilgrimages to sites of power, more likely to Stonehenge in Europe than to Sedona. Neopagans emphasize their identification with ancient cultures, while New Agers stress that power spots have special energies. New Agers travel to such sites in the hope that their consciousness will be altered, but Neopagans prefer to harvest herbs from the land and talk to the earth's spirits in ritual circles. Each culture sees the proper relationship between humans and nature somewhat differently, and this difference in part accounts for their diverse visions of the future.

## Living for the Future and Looking to the Past

Perhaps the most important distinction between New Agers and Neopagans is that New Agers tend to look toward the future, when a new age of expanded consciousness will dawn, while Neopagans look to the past for inspiration in order to revive old religions and improve life in the present. An annual Neopagan gathering called Rites of Spring hosts a "Medieval Feast" during which medieval music is played and festivalgoers are served by "wenches" dressed in period costumes. Some men and women become Neopagans because they are interested in historical reenactment and may be involved with the Society for Creative Anachronism (SCA), a medieval reenactment organization. Interested in authenticity, Neopagans may perform Egyptian rites based on ancient texts, dress like Renaissance mages, or engage in Yoruba divination, replicating the original as best they can. In 1993 large numbers of Neopagans attended a festival in Nashville, Tennessee to honor the goddess Athena, whose statue there is the largest indoor statue in the western world, according to a report in the Neopagan magazine *Green Egg*. They reconstructed ancient Greek games and held a ritual to pay tribute to Athena.[25] Even though New Agers borrow from indigenous and pre-Christian cultures, they are rarely interested in reviving these religions in the present. Instead they create paradigms for the future that may be inspired by ancient cultures.

In 1987, large numbers of New Agers around the country gathered at power sites, believing they would usher in a new era marked by a collective shift in human consciousness toward unity, love, and peace. When New Age prophet Jose Arguelles predicted that the Harmonic Convergence of August 16 and 17, 1987 was to be the dawning of a New Age, thousands of believers flocked to Mount Shasta; Machu Picchu, Peru; Chaco Canyon, New Mexico; England's Stonehenge; and Sedona, Arizona. A week before the event *Newsweek* reported that "So many people have already gathered at California's Mount Shasta that the U.S. Forest Service has issued a bulletin asking other New Age voyagers to stay home."[26] One curious observer reported from the Harmonic Convergence gathering at Mount Shasta that he saw "African drumming, Buddhist shrines, Native American sweat lodges, tarot cards . . . " (Michael Roesch, "Harmonic Convergence," www.siskiyous.edu/shasta/fol/har/). Arguelles, a Mexican-born art historian, writer, and artist, came up with the idea through his interpretation of the Mayan calendar, which he described in *The Mayan Factor* (1987) and other writings. Tens of thousands of people around the world, who heard about the event from friends or read about it in New Age newsletters, participated in rituals and meditations on the appointed time of the convergence.

For both New Agers and Neopagans, a new era characterized by personal growth and social transformation is on its way, but New Agers tend to be more preoccupied with the details of the idea while Neopagans view it in the abstract. A popular New Age/Neopagan festival called Starwood, held every summer in southwestern New York State, celebrates the complementary but opposite interests of the two movements. The focus on consciousness is symbolized by the name of Starwood's sponsor, an organization called ACE—the Association for Consciousness Exploration. The fifteenth annual Starwood program decribes the festival's origins in 1981 as "the first interface festival between the New Age Movement/Futurism and the Magickal Movement/Medievalism." Starwood's list of workshops gives a sense of the diversity of this eclectic gathering of around a thousand people: 146 workshops were scheduled over the five days of Starwood 1999 and ran simultaneously from 9:30 in the morning until 6:00 in the evening. They covered a variety of healing traditions: "Finding the Healer Within," "Sound Vibrational Healing," and "Crystal Healing," as well as body work: "Tai

Chi," "Ritual Dance," "Introduction to Massage," "Yoga for Couch Pota-
toes," and "Body-painting." Mythological and religious topics were also part
of the program: "Voodoo of New Orleans," "Rhythms and Cultures of the
Nile," "Greek Paganism Today," "Witch's Sabbat," and "The Howling
Dervish" (Sufism) were a few of the many offerings. Alternative lifestyle
topics—"Polyfidelitous Relationships" and "Spiritual Midwifery" are two
examples—and several drumming workshops filled out the schedule. Rituals
and concerts made up most of the evening programs. Other Neopagan festivals focus on specific traditions such as Druidism and Wicca, but Starwood
strives to be as eclectic and inclusive as possible, and this in part accounts for
the overlap of New Age and Neopagan interests.

The offerings at New Age and Neopagan events reflect their visions for
the future, which in most cases are multifaceted and include methods of personal growth and relating to other people, alternative family structures,
healthier approaches to the environment, and respect for other cultures. The
Institute of Noetic Sciences, a New Age organization founded in 1973, has

> the twin aims of fostering research on consciousness and exploring its
> relevance to human affairs. As we have grown over the last twenty-two
> years, we have watched people around the world also growing—indi-
> viduals awakening to a more profound understanding of themselves,
> and groups creatively finding ways to link our social, ecological and
> spiritual visions through action. To broaden awareness of these changes,
> we are reporting on people, projects, trends and ideas that embody a
> blend of action and awareness and give us renewed hope for the earth.
> They may be, we think, signs of a world awakening.[27]

The language of awakening and enlightenment characterizes much New
Age literature. Like other religious people, New Agers believe that they are
in the vanguard, taking up roles as spiritual leaders in a society severely un-
evolved in the realm of consciousness. New Age writer Shakti Gawain suggests that many who "are now on consciousness journeys began this lifetime
by following the path of the material world, but at some point we have sensed
that other alternatives exist, and we have begun our spiritual reawakening."[28]
New Age language can be both hopeful and apocalyptic because practitioners believe old ways of being in the world are doomed, but they look to the
future with anticipation.

New Agers and Neopagans base their religious lives on providing and
accessing what they see as much-needed alternatives to available religious
options. They believe that their special role is not to maintain tradition,

though there may be some who try to do this, but rather to change self and society. On issues from gender roles to politics, they believe that humans should interact in different, and, to their minds, healthier ways. Wiccan priestess Judy Harrow affirms that "the very meaning of magic, of changing consciousness in accordance with will, is people taking charge of their own inner lives." Because they begin with the assumption that the self is sacred or divine, they place the responsibility for change with each individual. Even when it is social and political structures that need changing, the self and not the institution is the agent and locus of change.

New Agers' and Neopagans' approaches vary. "Many people feel that there is something drastically wrong with the world and the way they have to live in it," according to Neopagan author Marian Green, whose book *Magic for the Aquarian Age* (1983) offers visualization and divination exercises aimed at personal transformation. She argues that the world can be changed, "and made the beautiful place of peace and plenty many of us dream of." In her view, "By changing our point of view, by developing our own inner skills, each of us can learn to shape the world into the perfect planet everyone yearns for."[29] According to Green and other Neopagan and New Age authors, destructive ways of relating to one another, ongoing interpersonal and global violence, and environmental devastation are some of the ills that need to be addressed as personal healing takes place. That said, it is important to point out that such beliefs do not necessarily lead to social and political activism. New Agers and Neopagans participate in a range of activities. On one end of the spectrum is the entirely private pursuit of transformation in which one consults information in books and on the Internet for guidance. At the other end is involvement with public protest actions such as the Neopagan group march as a "living river" at the World Bank meeting protests in Ottawa in 2001 and a group of Witches' "earth-based blessing" with other religious groups at the School of the Americas Protest in Columbus, Georgia the same month.[30] Some Neopagans and New Agers thus publicly challenge the American status quo while others focus on making personal changes.

### Studying New Religious Movements

The Neopagan and New Age religions are new movements that draw on, but radically revise, older religious and cultural traditions. All world religions of today were once new movements. Christianity, for instance, began as the Jesus sect, one of many new religions to emerge in the ancient Mediterranean world. It borrowed from but altered Judaism and other religions of the time. Like early Christianity, new movements of the 1960s and 1970s arose in opposition to established religious options and tended to focus around charismatic leaders. For this reason and because of their smaller size, social scientists called them "cults." But by the 1970s, "cult" had developed a derogatory meaning as Americans responded to what many saw as the threat of new religious movements that were taking young people away from the established churches. New Agers and Neopagans have often been "countercultural," choosing not only unusual religious options but also a variety of unorthodox dietary and health practices such as vegetarianism and holistic healing. Because new religious movements are often viewed suspiciously by the general public and more established religions, scholars are frequently forced into the position of defending them against anticult tactics and charges of brainwashing.

Neopaganism and the New Age movement developed as conscious alternatives to existing religions and as revisions of older traditions, but they did not form around a single charismatic leader. Rather, from the beginning they were decentralized. People gathered together for rituals or to hear the messages of trance channelers, but groups quickly splintered and new ones surfaced. Unlike in other new religions, such as the Unification Church and the Rajneesh movement, no one person emerged as leader and authority and there was no founding document or universal moral code. Neopaganism and the New Age movement inherited the outlook of other decentralized religions that flourished in the eclectic religious atmosphere of the mid-nineteenth century.

# CHAPTER THREE

# Early Varieties of Alternative Spirituality in American Religious History

At the beginning of the twenty-first century, New Age channelers transmitted messages from "ascended masters," advanced beings in the spirit world willing to help humans, and contemporary Pagans called to ancient Egyptian spirits in their rituals. These and many other current religious practices have their origins in nineteenth-century religious movements that built on a stream of alternative beliefs present in North America since colonial times. This alternative tradition had no code of conduct, central doctrine, single sacred text, organized body, or central leadership. Instead, it was a loose network of overlapping beliefs and practices that scholars have variously dubbed "metaphysical religion," "the alternative reality tradition," "harmonial religion," and "shadow culture."[1] This stream of religious thought and practice became more popular and widespread in the mid-nineteenth century. Some expressions of it were fairly short-lived while others, like Christian Science and the Church of Jesus Christ of Latter-day Saints (the Mormons), grew into major denominations, leaving behind their occult roots as they became institutionalized ("occult" refers to secret or hidden knowledge). Other movements, such as Spiritualism, updated their occult origins with Christian elements, but remained small and marginalized. The complex story of the many figures and movements that made up this alternative world of astrologers, psychics, mental healing, hypnotism, water cures, and the like shows that the "New Age" and "Neopaganism" are not as new as they might at first seem.

Characteristics of the New Age and Neopagan movements, such as salvation through the discovery and knowledge of a divine inner self and the continuity rather than separation of matter and spirit, have been present for centuries in the occult tradition. These new movements self-consciously updated and synthesized older streams of religious thought and practice. The roots of both New Age and Neopagan religions reach back to early modern European occult traditions that took on new forms in the American context, even though the movements' direct origins were in the 1960s counterculture. This chapter will trace the ways in which a loose collection of beliefs and practices were shaped by social, religious, technological, and economic forces in the nineteenth century into diverse religious movements. Many of these movements and their teachings became permanently embedded in the American religious landscape and then later influenced the spiritual life of the 1960s counterculture.

Nineteenth-century occult religions built on popular beliefs and practices that had long existed on American shores. Practitioners of magic, astrology, and divination were found throughout England and Europe in the sixteenth century. According to historian Jon Butler, "The laity obtained magical charms and amulets from 'wise men' and 'wise women' to keep away disease. They patronized astrologers who predicted the future, explained the past, and cured illnesses. They accepted the existence of witches as a way to explain unexplainable things."[2] Christianity coexisted with these other belief systems in the lives of most laypeople in the American colonies. Colonial historian David Hall describes the overlapping beliefs and practices in the era's religious culture as "worlds of wonder" and argues that in the lived religion of ordinary people Christianity was not nearly as monolithic as many historians once assumed.[3] In the colonial period, occult practitioners included both educated members of the elite and illiterate healers who learned their lore through word of mouth and apprenticeship—a democratization of religious life that would also characterize nineteenth-century occultism. Some of the practices that were current in colonial times, such as astrology and divination, are common among New Agers and Neopagans today. Americans have always looked to the alignment of stars and planets to guide their lives, to read future events in this world as reflections of celestial realities, and to predict good days to harvest crops, sail, marry, and conceive.

Even though colonists brought along many traditions from their old to their new homes, the transmission of magic and the occult to America was made difficult by religious and political leaders' goal of creating a Christian country and the absence of the Old World's magical landscape. A sacred geography of shrines, enchanted woods, and magical springs was important to occult traditions in England and Europe, but similar sites were slow to emerge in the newly settled land. Indigenous people of the Americas inhabited a land imbued with supernatural powers and marked by sacred places, but American Indian sacred sites only became important to New Age and Neopagan religious practice from the 1960s on.

Christian and occult practices were not always separated in the colonial period because most colonists moved through both worlds; nevertheless, they often came into conflict. Upper-class men, including ministers, looked to learned traditions such as Jewish mysticism and Renaissance alchemy to understand the world around them. But over time the disapproval of orthodox religion and the rise of rationalistic science resulted in declining interest in the occult among the educated. By 1680 a folklorization had taken place, by which astrology and divination survived among the poor but were abandoned by the elite. Skepticism about the efficacy of astrology and other magical practices increased, as did Christian criticism of them, but almanacs were still published and many people continued to consult astrologers and diviners.

Controversy surrounding practices that involved contact with supernatural powers characterized the relationship between Christianity and the occult tradition in every century of American history. Colonial critics disapproved of blending Christianity and astrology and saw magic as evil and demonic. Evidence from Salem's 1692 witch trials indicates that although occult practices were illegal and kept hidden in the colonies by the end of the seventeenth century, they were nevertheless widespread. Accused women were often fortune-tellers, astrologers, or "wise women" who were knowledgeable about herbs and other healing methods. Witch trials were an attempt by the elite to suppress such activity, but even after the trials were over, belief in witches and occult practices survived in large segments of the population. Controversy about the occult tradition is most clearly seen in the writings of the Mathers, a family of Puritan theologians and ministers. Increase Mather's *Essay for the Recording of Illustrious Providences*, written in 1684, focused on "wonders" that provided evidence of the hand of God in the world, but Mather took pains to distinguish them from suspicious miracles and magic.[4] Increase's son Cotton Mather (1663–1728) wrote several essays criticizing the resilience of occult practices that he thought to be dangerously blasphemous and the result of colonists' attempts to cure diseases through illegal means. In *Angel of Bethesda*, a medical essay, Mather complained that "the search for health turned New Englanders from a pursuit of wonders to an invocation of miracles and, hence, to the Devil and diabolism."[5] But the educated classes of the seventeenth century did not always side with critics of the occult. After 1720 more recent immigrants from

Europe to the colonies introduced new sources of occult practices into the population. Many educated people, including ministers, were widely read in magic and alchemy, and some blended Christianity and astrology.[6] But if they were interested in such subjects, they usually kept that interest to themselves. As a result, most occult practices disappeared from widespread public view and approval during the eighteenth century and resurfaced with a vengeance after the War of 1812. In a period when the new nation was undergoing cataclysmic changes, there was an outburst of interest in alternative traditions accompanied by new religious movements that are the most important antecedents of contemporary Neopagan and New Age religions.

## The Nineteenth-Century Spiritual Hothouse

Scholars of the historical period roughly between the War of 1812 and the outbreak of the Civil War in 1860 typically describe these fifty years with inflated language: "a spiritual hothouse," " a seething cauldron," "a highly unstable atmosphere," "the storm center," "the antebellum American assault on limits," "religious enthusiasm," "freedom's ferment," and "religious anarchism."[7] In the decades that followed the War of 1812, communal experiments that rejected traditional marriage arrangements, séances in which spirits spoke through adolescent girls, hypnotic trance healings, cures using water baths, herbal healing, homeopathic medicine, interest in yoga and meditation, and many other new religious and health practices that built on the older occult tradition all had their day. Ralph Waldo Emerson (1803–1882), who participated in and observed many of the new movements of his era, wrote, "We are all a little wild here with numberless projects of social reform. Not a reading man but has a draft of a new community in his waistcoat pocket."[8] This exciting period was brought about by a number of different forces that included economic, technological, social, and religious change.

Antebellum America, specifically the years from 1812 to 1860, provided a "hothouse" atmosphere for religious creativity and social experimentation. Social and economic forces contributed to the movement of people across the land and facilitated the spread of new religious ideas. In this tumultuous time experimental religious communities came and went and millenarian expectations (either of Christ's second coming or of cataclysmic change) permeated the air: "These were the peak years of the market revolution that took the country from the fringe of the world economy to the brink of commercial greatness. They were also (not coincidentally) years of intense religious excitement and sectarian invention."9 The growth of cities enabled crowds to gather around popular speakers and to attend demonstrations where religious and political ideas were exchanged. In unprecedented numbers that would not be matched again until the 1960s, middle-class Americans experimented with lifestyle changes that included shifting gender roles, changes in diet and clothing, and a wide variety of unusual religious practices.

Industrialization and urbanization greatly increased social mobility and at the same time generated uneasiness as old ways of being in family and community were called into question. New opportunities for women to work outside the home raised questions and concerns about gender roles in the new middle-class society. Debates over the proper constitution of the family, appropriate sexual mores, and the meaning of social class accompanied the rise of the market society and were played out at Spiritualist events and in other collective arenas of religious meaning making. New waves of immigrants from Europe challenged the dominance of a Protestant worldview and irrevocably changed the cultural landscape of nineteenth-century America. A burgeoning middle class that was a ready audience for the masses of printed material now available due to changes in printing used newsletters and journals to spread information and debate the relative merits of new healing techniques and religious ideas. The building of railroads and the opening of the Erie Canal in 1825 made travel easier across the Northeast and elsewhere, and the Gold Rush spurred westward movement.

All of these changes were powerfully felt in New York State, where some of the most significant new religious movements of the time had their start. A "psychic highway" followed the Erie Canal through New York west of the Catskills and the Adirondack Mountains.10 Towns like Rochester and Utica became important urban and religious centers, especially as religious revivals spread like wildfire across the region, so that the area came to be known as the "Burned-over District." Radical publications and speaking circuits spread the news of innovative religious and healing techniques that were accessible to men and women, rich and poor. The Burned-over District provided fertile ground for prophets and visionaries. For instance, the region gave birth to early Mormonism and Spiritualism, which would eventually develop in completely different directions, one toward institutionalization and the other toward decentralization, one to eventually downplay its miraculous and visionary origins, the other to enshrine them. Mormonism became a large and politically powerful religion while Spiritualist practices dispersed into the culture at large and were not popularly manifested again until twentieth-century channeling.

The outbreak of Christian revivalism, or the Second Great Awakening (1800–1830), was responsible for the wildfire of spiritual enthusiasm that swept across the country and reached its highest point in the Burned-over District. Ironically, Christian revitalization helped to spur interest in the many alternatives to Christianity that followed in its wake. Revivals and revivalist rhetoric encouraged widespread optimism about human nature, belief in social progress, and expectations of the millennium, understood either literally as the thousand-year reign of Christ or more generally as a time of utopian peace and plenty. Religious excitement was tinged with urgency, and the proliferation of prophetic voices urging change in everything from exercise to the afterlife fed expectations of cataclysmic events.

Joseph Smith (1805–1844), the founder of Mormonism, was one of many prophets to appear in the excited religious climate of the Burned-over District. Smith's parents were interested in visions and dream interpretation, and one of the family's friends was a magician and fortune-teller.[11] Smith, like other New Yorkers of the time, was interested in treasure hunting—looking for buried gold. This was often done with a divining rod. Divining or "dowsing" is one example of the ways an alternative reality tradition was carried on in America across a landscape increasingly sacralized by European Americans. Smith also had a penchant for other occult practices and in 1821 had a vision of God's messenger, "Moroni." When he started proclaiming God's message given him by Moroni, he won over increasing numbers of believers, some of whom followed him westward. By that point he had also established himself as a successful healer, but in the midst of his success Smith was charged with fortune-telling and treasure seeking and found guilty of using a "seer stone" for fraudulent purposes.[12] Smith's run-in with the law suggests that many occult practices were still illegal in the mid-nineteenth century, even if they were widespread.

In the turbulent religious climate of the 1820s and 1830s Smith was one of many prophets and visionaries making end times predictions and forming new communities. Many Americans thought that the Second Coming of Christ was at hand, and by the 1840s some of these people gathered under the leadership of prophet and visionary William Miller (1782–1849), who set several dates for this event. Millerites were disappointed when Christ did not come, but later many of them joined a group that eventually became the Seventh-Day Adventists. Not everyone expected sudden and miraculous changes to bring on the millennium. Most revivalists did not take their expectations to the extreme of date-setting; rather, they focused on individual transformation and social change as avenues through which to gradually usher in the millennium on earth.

Nineteenth-century evangelical Protestants also looked toward a new millennium, but for most of them it was to take place on earth through the perfection of human society and human religiosity. Revival preachers like Charles Grandison Finney (1792–1875) created new expectations of salvation and provided the methods necessary to get there. Finney and other revivalists preached that human nature was basically good, not evil, and that all individuals were capable of spiritual transformation and eventual salvation. This optimism and emphasis on personal experience became a basic assumption underlying mid-nineteenth century alternative religious movements.

Social, political, and health reform movements flourished in the atmosphere of millennial expectation and interacted constantly with spiritual healing regimes and religious concerns. The reformist agenda was initiated by a transformed social and economic landscape and revivalism's emphasis on the ability of humans to direct their own lives and to perfect the world around them. Puritan and other brands of Calvinist teaching about predestination, the view that God's plan for every human was set in stone, were challenged by the emphatic belief of revivalist preachers that men and women could shape their own destinies. While many Americans joined evangelical revivals, others took this message of self-determination to heart and looked for redemption through social and personal reforms that were often at odds with Christian doctrine.

Occult beliefs that had gone underground resurfaced and were adopted by an emerging middle class looking for ways to exercise its newfound social power. In the nineteenth century, American occult religion became popular again and blended with European imports like Mesmerism and Swedenborgianism to flourish in movements such as Transcendentalism, Spiritualism, the Theosophical Society, and New Thought, all of which influenced and are reflected in New Age and Neopagan religions. The prevailing cultural mood made it possible for men and women of the most humble origins to become religious leaders and sought-after healers and speakers. The idea that humans could understand and manipulate supernatural forces through occult means had been manifested in colonial times in wise men and women and in the alchemical manipulations of the elite. But in the nineteenth century popular and elite religious agendas converged in the context of a middle class that was literate and willing to experiment with techniques that had become increasingly disreputable in the previous century. This emerging alternative religious tradition taught that there was a correspondence between the natural and divine worlds and assumed that the self was sacred. Occult beliefs about correspondence and harmony between humans, the natural world, and the heavens existed from colonial times on. Historian Sydney Ahlstrom describes "harmonial religion" as a tradition that "encompasses those forms of piety and belief in which spiritual composure, physical health, and even economic well-being are understood to flow from a person's rapport with the cosmos."[13] This approach sought to connect humans with the world and the divine powers surrounding them. Harmonial religion is also the outlook that characterizes New Age and Neopaganism and is based on the understanding that harmony exists between human and cosmos, spirit and matter; that they are not separate or distinct.

Mesmerism was the first harmonial religious movement in North America, and it influenced most of the alternative religious and healing traditions that emerged in the nineteenth century. Mesmerism was wildly popular in the nineteenth century before it was recast into Spiritualism, hypnotism, New Thought, and other new religious and therapeutic forms. Mesmerists believed in a universal occult energy, an invisible magnetic fluid flowing between planets and other heavenly bodies, Earth, animals, plants, and humans. They taught that spirit and matter are not separate; humans, nature, and the divine are all connected. Anton Mesmer (1734–1815), the founder of this movement, was an Austrian physician and astrologer whose ideas were brought to America by several of his adherents and spread by traveling demonstrations that opened people's minds to the possibilities of mental healing. Mesmerist healers went into trance states from which they could diagnose and advise treatments for illness. Mesmer's teachings (particularly his 1779 dissertation on animal magnetism) led to the belief that healing could be accomplished by manipulating the fluid that permeated all things. This view influenced Spiritualists and other Americans who came to believe in the unity of all existence. It was the vehicle by which nineteenth-century men and women were introduced to and carried forward the occult tradition in America, transmuting it into a popular religious tradition that cut across gender and class lines. Interest in mesmerism and other trends of the day was spread by nineteenth-century mass media and speaking circuits.

Two important figures in the nineteenth-century alternative religious tradition encountered mesmerism in the turbulent 1830s and 1840s. Phineas Parkhurst Quimby (1802–1866) was directly responsible for the lineage of mental healing that led to the formation of Christian Science and several other religious groups that have endured into the twenty-first century, while

Andrew Jackson Davis (1826–1910) is the one person most identifiably responsible for formulating and then publicizing the worldview of Spiritualism. In 1838 the famous mesmerist Charles Poyen stopped in Belfast, Maine to give a demonstration at the local lyceum (lecture hall). Quimby, a young clockmaker, was in the audience that day and was inspired to investigate mesmerism. He quit his job and followed Poyen from town to town, becoming adept at mesmerist demonstrations, putting his assistant into trances during which the assistant would read people's minds and prescribe treatments for illness. Newspapers followed Quimby's successful career and word spread of his abilities, ensuring that crowds would gather whenever he appeared.

Over time Quimby began to doubt the theory of animal magnetism and to suspect that cures were successful because patients believed they would be. This simple revision of mesmerism would have a significant impact on the metaphysical (meaning "mind-only," beyond the physical) tradition in America, which in turn would shape the New Age and Neopagan movements. Influenced by the ideas of Swedish mystic Emmanuel Swedenborg, Quimby eventually changed his practice to mental healing through visualization (using mental imagery to achieve a desired goal, such as healing). He quit the lyceum circuit, which demanded constant traveling and public demonstrations, and set up a healing practice in Portland, Maine. Like many other alternative healers of his time, he was suspicious of both orthodox medicine and established churches, yet often referred to Christianity in his teachings.

Quimby promoted the idea that humanity's natural state was health and that disease was caused by mental disturbance, an understanding widely shared by mesmerists and Spiritualists, among others. Quimby's healing methods were simple. He sat down with patients and sensed clairvoyantly what was wrong with them, after which he explained his theory on the origins of disease. Patients were sick, he told them, because they *believed* they were. Then he visualized the patients as healthy and encouraged them to see themselves that way. Quimby's work established psychic healing and visualization as key elements of the alternative religious tradition. Because of his focus on the powers of the mind, Quimby decided that visions at Spiritualist séances, which were common during the time he worked as a healer, came about because of participants' beliefs and not the actual presence of spirits. His theory of illness was founded on hopeful notions about human progress and belief in the possibility of harmony in both personal and social life in the present rather than in some future millennial period. Like other nineteenth-century healers, Quimby offered "a tool for healing and restoring sick societies as well as sick bodies."[14]

Along with Anton Mesmer, Emanuel Swedenborg (1688–1772) was an important correspondence theorist and exerted the most influence on Quimby and other healers and religious visionaries. Swedenborg was one of the "most widely read authors of the nineteenth century in American popular culture even though he attracted less attention during his lifetime."[15] His writings brought together liberal religion with scientific and social trends of the mid-nineteenth century, laying the groundwork for the rapid growth of Spiritualism. In his classic *Religious History of the American People*, historian Sydney Ahlstrom gives Swedenborg an important place in American religious history:

> Of all the unconventional currents streaming through the many levels of American religion during the antebellum half-century, none proved more attractive to more diverse types of dissenters from established denominations than those which stemmed from Emmanuel Swedenborg. His influence was seen everywhere: in Transcendentalism and at Brook Farm [one of many nineteenth century communal experiments], in spiritualism and the free love movement, in the craze for communal experiments, in faith healing, mesmerism, and a half-dozen medical cults; among great intellectuals, crude charlatans, and innumerable frontier quacks.[16]

Swedenborg was the son of a Swedish theologian who spent the earlier part of his life engaged in scientific research before he turned to religion. His father healed people with prayer, laying on of hands, and casting out spirits.[17] Swedenborg's own scientific investigations encompassed chemistry, astronomy, and anatomy before he gradually turned to explorations into his own consciousness. Around the year 1745, at the age of fifty-five, Swedenborg experienced a spiritual crisis during which he had nightmares and visions, culminating in a vision of God. According to poet William Butler Yeats's account, "he was sitting in an inn in London, where he had gone about the publication of a book, when a spirit appeared before him who was, he believed, Christ himself, and told him that henceforth he would commune with spirits and angels. From that moment he was a mysterious man describing distant events as if they were before his eyes, and knowing dead men's secrets."[18] Swedenborg believed that God had chosen him to interpret the Bible and, in order to facilitate his knowledge of Christian scripture, would allow him to travel through spirit worlds, heaven, and hell. Swedenborg then embarked on a spiritual quest and practiced clairvoyance and astral travel (traveling in spirit to other planes of existence). He threatened and angered the church with the argument that God is immanent, not transcendent, and the scientific community with his belief that God exists. Swedenborg argued that the natural world was divine and that divine knowledge could be found within the self. His teachings influenced English poet and reformer William Blake and American Transcendentalists like Ralph Waldo Emerson, and laid the theoretical groundwork for alternative healing practices such as homeopathy and osteopathy. Swedenborg was sure that "the Creator in his divine providence, while allowing sickness and the multitude of human ills, yet provided for their cure by concealing remedies within the world of nature."[19] His scientific background and religious experience came together in the belief that God communicated to humans through nature, a view later elaborated in the writings of Emerson and Henry David Thoreau (1817–1862). Swedenborg's writings affirmed the occult tradition's emphasis on correspondence between the human and divine worlds and between the self and God. He introduced many of the ideas that were disseminated through Spiritualism, Theosophy, and New Thought and shaped the New Age and Neopagan movements.

Swedenborg was also one of the first popular writers of the nineteenth century to self-consciously synthesize science and religion. Throughout the mid-nineteenth century, these writers overlapped and borrowed from each other, even while scientists tried to discredit many new religious movements. Alternative religious and healing traditions took root in America in an era when science, medicine, and religion were being loosely combined in some belief systems and rigidly separated in others. The New Age movement today likewise borrows the language of science and works to bring itself into alignment with scientific theories just as it tries to fit scientific discoveries into its own philosophical frameworks. Neopagans, who tend to reinvent ancient religions, are less concerned with scientific validation.

The New England Transcendentalists, and especially Ralph Waldo Emerson, further developed Swedenborg's theory of correspondence and the idea that all individual souls were part of a world soul, the "oversoul." Transcendentalists thought that individuals should look within for their salvation and should strive to understand the harmony existing between self and universe. Like contemporary New Agers and Neopagans, they gave the mind power to change the world. Emerson and other Transcendentalists drew from a wide range of philosophical and religious sources, including Asian religious teachings and Swedenborg's writings, and became involved with the popular psychology and alternative religious practices of their day.

Emerson was active on the lyceum circuit, where he encountered mesmerists, Spiritualists, abolitionists, and health reformers. Emerson's second wife was interested in alternative medicine; diet fads were part of life at Transcendentalist communities such as Brook Farm; Thoreau studied yoga and Native Americans; Margaret Fuller, editor of the Transcendentalist magazine *The Dial*, used a phrenological publisher; and Emerson and Fuller read the *Bhagavad Gita* and other Asian texts.[20] Transcendentalists spoke and wrote about inner experience and inner journeys, describing the inner world in topographical terms, thus anticipating twentieth-century New Age and Neopagan narratives of self-exploration. Emerson said that the inner self is an "unfathomed sea of thought and virtue," a depth to be plumbed, if never entirely known.[21] He wrote of the importance of self-knowledge and the futility of organized religion to help individuals to acquire it: "what good are religious dogma and the priestly caste if divinity truly lies within?"[22] Emerson and the Transcendentalists clearly expressed popular ideas in literary form. Among other views, they shared a suspicion of institutions and orthodox religion with Spiritualists, mesmerists, and alternative healers. After the Civil War, Transcendentalism declined as a movement in its own right, but its ideas became part of an alternative culture characterized by religious eclecticism and interest in correspondences between nature and the divine.

## Mediums, Healers, and Radical Reformers Meet at the Lyceum

If Transcendentalists furthered Swedenborg's understanding of harmony between humans and the natural world in their writings, then Spiritualism put these ideas into a form of practice that is an important antecedent to New Age channeling and Neopagan spirit possession. Spiritualism, the most popular and widespread new religion of the mid-nineteenth century, came directly from Mesmer's and Swedenborg's teachings. Spiritualist mediums performed in private houses and on stage, contacting the spirits of deceased loved ones and other spirit guides who gave them messages for the living. Although examples of belief in spirits and spirit communication were already present in America, Spiritualism as a movement began in Hydesville, New York on March 31, 1848, when three young sisters in the Fox family heard rappings in a bedroom of their family's old farmhouse. The news media and word of mouth spread their story, and the Fox sisters began appearing publicly to transmit messages from the spirits. Their appearances initiated an era in which mediums, especially young women, were popular and common.

Five years after Phineas Quimby's encounter with mesmerism, another young man was well on his way to blending mesmerism and Swedenborgianism into a religious platform. In 1843 mesmerist J. Stanley Grimes passed through Poughkeepsie, New York, where he put a local cobbler, Andrew Jackson Davis, into a trance. While in trance, Davis received messages from Emmanuel Swedenborg and other spirits of the dead. He later believed that the truths he received were communicated by spirits, and he became Spiritualism's most important spokesman. Davis believed that spirits could take on temporary bodies that were like projections: "The images are made of a substance drawn from the medium who loses weight, and in a less degree from all present, and for this light must be extinguished or dimmed or shaded with red as in a photographer's room. The image will begin outside the medium's body as a luminous cloud, or in a sort of luminous mud forced from the body, out of the mouth it may be, from the side or from the lower parts of the body. . . . One may see a vague cloud condense and diminish into a head or arm or a whole figure of a man, or to some animal shape."[23] Like other nineteenth-century popularizers of new religious and health techniques, Davis traveled the lyceum circuit in order to win converts to his new faith. By 1849 Spiritualism had spread across the continent to major cities like New Orleans, Chicago, and Cincinnati, and west to California as well. It was a movement mostly composed of white, Anglo-Saxon, middle-class former Protestants, though numerous African Americans found an affinity for Spiritualism as well.[24] By 1851 more than 150 Spiritualist circles were active in New York State alone, and by 1854 at least ten Spiritualist publications were circulating nationally. At the movement's height in 1855, participants in some aspect of Spiritualist practice numbered one to two million in a population of twenty-five million. Many famous people attended Spiritualist demonstrations, including Harriet Beecher Stowe, James Fenimore Cooper, Abraham Lincoln, and Mary Todd Lincoln. Spiritualism fit the mood of the time with its democratic inclusiveness, the opportunities it offered women, the comfort it gave to people who had lost loved ones and could not find solace elsewhere, and the evidence it provided for the immortality of the soul.

As it became a national religious pastime, Spiritualism developed two modes of practice. The first was the home séance, often conducted by adolescent girls and young women, who were expected to maintain a certain amount of Victorian domesticity regardless of the women's rights ferment happening in public arenas. Professional mediums, on the other hand, traveled the countryside offering public séances and medical examinations. This was an important avenue by which middle-class women could venture outside the home while remaining in a relatively passive, and thus somewhat acceptable, role as mediums who voiced messages from wiser beings.[25] Spiritualist practices included rapping, séances, levitation, displays of floating spirit bodies, trance writing, and table tipping. Many mediums used an object called a "planchette," a heart-shaped piece of wood that rolled across surfaces, similar to the device used with present-day Ouija boards. Practitioners believed the planchette responded to the presence of spirits through the body of the medium, who placed her fingers on it in order to transmit messages from the spirit world. In this and other ways, mediums' bodies provided evidence to support people's faith in the continuity of life and afterlife.

Spiritualists often attended funerals, where they comforted grieving family and friends by relaying messages from recently departed spirits telling those left behind that all was well in the afterlife. Spiritualists wore white at funerals to symbolize their hopefulness about life after death. Andrew Jackson Davis exhorted people to "robe yourselves with garments of light to honor the spirit's birth into a higher life!"[26] Spiritualist mediums also took from mesmerism the idea that a person in trance could heal disease, and they prescribed medicines and herbal concoctions.[27]

The eclecticism of mid-nineteenth century Spiritualist gatherings and publications is similar to that of New Age magazines today, with their variety of unorthodox religious and healing practices. Spiritualists participated in a network of loosely connected beliefs and practices that included social and political reform movements as well as dietary and other health fads. In fact, the spirits themselves preached a reformist agenda: "The spirits, it was thought, had rapped their approval of women's rights, abolition, labor reform, communitarianism, health reform, marriage law reform, and occasionally 'free love.'"[28] In the 1890s Spiritualist Lois Waisbrooker agitated for the reform of marriage and sexual mores and was called a "she Abraham Lincoln." Waisbrooker believed that Spiritualism allowed her to see beyond conventional morality because she was "no longer sitting in the shadow of reflected light, but clothed with the sun, with direct power."[29] She explained in her book, *The Occult Power of Sex,* "that the magnetic forces that made spirit communication possible also powered the sex drive that drew men and women together."[30] She linked sex and religion and viewed her "struggle to emancipate human beings from uncongenial marriages and sexual relations and her struggle to emancipate souls from the dogma of conventional religion as one and the same."[31] Other nineteenth-century men and women also invoked the messages of spirits to support marriage reform and free love and to agitate against social ills.

Spiritualist publications argued for better treatment of American Indians, abolition of capital punishment, prison reforms, and higher wages for workers.[32] The *Banner of Light*, a major Spiritualist publication that ran from 1857 to 1907, exhorted Spiritualists to attend to social ills and included directories that listed phrenologists (who interpreted the contours of the skull as indicators of mental faculties and character), magnetic healers, herbalists, aura readers, mediums, astrologers specializing in Egyptian religion, and doctors offering such treatments as massage, therapeutic baths, laying on of hands, and electrical therapy.[33] This exchange of ideas and practices was facilitated by large public gatherings like Spiritualist conventions and lyceums that featured antislavery and women's rights speakers, and visionary ideas and prophetic figures, allowing many nineteenth-century men and women to dabble in new faiths and fads. Spiritualism was a point of origin for other nineteenth-century movements that would affect the development of the New Age and Neopagan movements: New Thought through mental healer Phineas Quimby and the Theosophical Society through Madame Helena Blavatsky (discussed in the next section).

One of the most significant twentieth-century metaphysical religious traditions to influence New Age beliefs had its beginnings in the nineteenth century in the writings of Emerson, Mesmer, and Swedenborg and in the healing work of Phineas Quimby, and came to be known as New Thought. It also colors Neopagans' attitudes toward healing, though to a lesser extent. During the twentieth century Theosophy and Spiritualism became less prominent, but their metaphysical teachings dispersed throughout American religious culture and were carried on by New Thought.

New Thought emerged as an identifiable movement in the 1890s and described an attitude toward mind and body that would characterize the New Age movement to come; both put responsibility for health and illness on the individual. New Thought's main influence was through its publishing. Ralph Waldo Trine's *In Tune with the Infinite* (1897) sold over two million copies.[34] New Thought differed from Spiritualism and Theosophy in that it did not involve spirits or otherworldly masters. It also rejected occultism; Quimby taught that hidden secret knowledge was another illusion of the mind and an impediment to health. He encouraged his followers to pursue health and prosperity by taking a positive attitude toward life and dispelling negative thoughts and emotions. Visualization, usually accompanied by meditation and relaxation, was the most commonly used technique.[35] Quimby and his followers emphasized the impact of an individual's spiritual health and will power on their body. Mental healing practices were democratic and universal in that they were available to everyone, and this democratization was an important part of New Thought's nineteenth-century legacy. Some healers and teachers felt they should help people harness their mental powers for the purpose of healing, while others used the power of the mind to move proactively through the world seeking financial success.[36] The tension between these different goals would later trouble New Agers and Neopagans as well.

One of the most important sites for disseminating new ideas was the lyceum, or lecture hall; the word was originally a Greek term for the grove or garden where a philosopher walked back and forth when he spoke to his students.[37] The American lyceum movement began with Josiah Holbrook's 1826 plan for an educational forum for sharing scientific and cultural knowledge.[38] By 1834 some three thousand lyceums were established across the country and featured many famous speakers, including abolitionist William Lloyd Garrison, former slave and famous orator Frederick Douglass, Ralph Waldo Emerson, and Henry David Thoreau. Speakers discussed women's rights, temperance, and slavery. Following the lyceum model, gatherings of other kinds also took place in socially and geographically mobile antebellum culture. Camp meetings and tent revivals were the Christian counterparts to Spiritualist conventions, and Theosophist salons were more selective, smaller gatherings for the exchange of ideas. Lyceums and Spiritualist conventions helped to spread the word about social problems and informed participants of the latest treatments for physical ailments. Lyceum speakers and audiences were usually involved with Spiritualism and other religious experiments of the time. Frederick W. Evans, an important Shaker elder from Mt. Lebanon, New York, traveled to some Spiritualist conventions; he was one of many examples of the overlap between Spiritualists and nineteenth-century communitarian groups.[39] The Shakers, also called the United Society of Believers in Christ's Second Appearing, lived communally in "families" of celibates and shared all property in common, and were in the midst of "Spiritualistic revivals" around the time of Spiritualism's emergence on the alternative religious scene. The Shakers practiced ecstatic ritual dances and believed in male and female aspects of the divine, pacifism, and "the power of spirit over physical disease."[40] Young Shaker girls went into trances where they saw visions of angels and dead members of their natural and Shaker families.[41]

Health reform was also promoted on lyceum stages and in the pages of Spiritualist publications. New and radical hygiene practices spread rapidly during the 1830s and 1840s, carried along by optimism, a democratizing spirit, and a desire for reform of body and society. Health reformers borrowed from ancient traditions, such as the work of Galen (a second century

C.E. Greek physician), and incorporated Mesmer's and Swedenborg's understandings of health and illness. Like the flourishing of New Age religion alongside holistic healing, Spiritualism was often part of an entire regime of alternative strategies intended to shape the individual into a new kind of person and in this way contribute to social progress.

Dietary reform was also popular in the middle of the nineteenth century, and many Spiritualist gatherings included advocates of vegetarianism as well as abolitionists and temperance campaigners. One of the key figures in this reform movement was Sylvester Graham, a Christian who marketed a vegetarian, whole-grain diet to his contemporaries (graham crackers were named for him). Nineteenth-century middle-class men and women were optimistic about the power of human beings to shape their own destinies, and a healthy body was part of their agenda.

At lyceums and in Spiritualist publications, health and political reform agendas coexisted with healing practices also based on the idea of correspondence. Homeopathy and phrenology were two popular nineteenth-century healing methods debated at lyceums and featured in Spiritualist publications. Homeopathy, developed by Samuel Hahnemann (1755–1843) in Germany, was the first therapy regime to become part of America's alternative culture.[42] It involved administering minute doses of a remedy (that in healthy people would produce symptoms similar to the disease) in an effort to stimulate the body's natural defenses; by the end of the twentieth century, it had secured a place in the field of alternative healing. Phrenology, originally called craniognomy, was developed by Franz Joseph Gall (1758–1828), a medical student in Vienna. Phrenologists diagnosed personalities based on the shape of the skull. For instance, they thought that the character trait of "ideality" was "situated nearly along the lower edge of the temporal ridge of the frontal bone. . . . It is essential to the poet, the painter, sculptor, and all who cultivate the fine arts. . . . A great deficiency of it leaves the mind in a state of homeliness or simplicity. . . . The organ is larger in civilized than in savage nations."[43] Phrenology's theory that bumps on the surface of the head could be used to read the essence of personality died out, but has parallels in New Age interests in reflexology and iridology, both of which similarly exemplify the theory of correspondence.

Chiropractic and osteopathic medicine also had their origins in mesmerism and Swedenborgianism. They developed out of the same optimism, democratization, and suspicion of the orthodox medical tradition, which critics aligned with orthodox religion. Alternative healers complained that orthodox or allopathic medicine saw the body as prone to disease and its natural state something to fight against, while they believed the body's natural state was health. Samuel Thompson (1769–1843), one of the earliest promoters of a system of natural health treatments, developed an alternative medical practice that incorporated steam baths and herbs. D. D. Palmer (1845–1913), the founder of chiropractics, was a grocer in Iowa involved with mesmerism and Spiritualism before he developed his own healing system. Palmer opened a magnetic healing office in Burlington, Iowa. He held to mesmerism's belief in energy flowing through the body, but added his own insight that disease was caused by blockages of this energy along the spine. Andrew Taylor Still (1828–1917), the founder of osteopathy, which focuses on proper body alignment to prevent and cure disease, was also influenced by Spiritualism and advertised himself as a "magnetic healer" before developing his own system.[44]

From the nineteenth century on, American religious history included a stream of eclectic alternatives to institutionalized health care and religion. Spirit communication had become an important component of this tradition and featured a century-and-a-half-long lineage of psychics, healers, and channelers; some of the most recent wrote best-selling New Age books such as Jane Roberts's *Seth Speaks* (1972) and Helen Schucman's *A Course in Miracles* (1976).

### Spiritual Masters and Asian Religions

As the alternative health tradition took shape, other new religions branched out from Spiritualism. Most important to the evolution of ideas that would become central to the New Age movement, such as spiritual masters and the astral plane, was the Theosophical Society, founded in New York in 1875 by Helena Petrovna Blavatsky (1831–1891). Like contemporary Neopagans and New Agers, Theosophists looked to the past and to ancient cultures for truth and wisdom, hoping that through their reinvention of those cultures and revival of ancient myths and rituals they would usher in a new age of enlightenment. Like Transcendentalists, Theosophists saw harmony between physical and spiritual realities and believed in the interconnectedness of humans, other living things, and the planets. In blending Asian and Christian religions, Theosophists established a model of American religiosity that was to become much more widespread when the New Age movement took off in the late 1960s and 1970s. Fascination with past and foreign cultures, including Asian religious teachings, would become an important characteristic of New Age and Neopagan religions. Theosophists were responsible for spreading Hindu and Buddhist beliefs in reincarnation (rebirth—the continuity of the soul through many lives) and *karma* (the belief that the condition to which each soul is reborn is the result of good or bad actions performed in previous lives, and that actions now have consequences for future lives) among Americans. In *The Secret Doctrine* (1897) Blavatsky explained that,

> That which is part of our soul is eternal. . . . Those lives are countless, but the soul or spirit that animates us throughout these myriads of existences is the same; and though "the book and volume" of the physical brain may forget events within the scope of one terrestrial life, the bulk of collective recollections can never desert the divine soul within us. Its whispers may be too soft, the sound of its words too far off the plane perceived by our physical senses; yet the shadow of events that were, just as much as the shadow of events that are too come, is within its perceptive powers, and is ever present before its mind's eye.[45]

Theosophists also began a publishing enterprise and published a Theosophical translation of Indian philosopher Patanjali's yoga sutras that was the first mass-produced version available in the West.[46] Theosophists wrote and spoke about ancient wisdom, promoted Asian beliefs, and held rituals that challenged other religious communities.

In 1876 Theosophist Baron Joseph Henry Louis Charles de Palm's funeral made headlines for its "pagan" elements because it included an Egyptian dirge and affirmed the harmony between humans and the cosmos. De Palm had asked Colonel Henry Olcott, who was his executor and one of the founders of the Theosophical Society, to conduct the funeral "in a fashion that would illustrate the Eastern notions of death and immortality" and then to cremate his body.[47] Cremation was controversial at the time and De Palm's was the first in America to be publicized. Olcott spoke at the funeral that preceded it and clarified the intent of the Theosophical Society "to study the history of ancient myths and symbols, religions and science, the psychological powers of man, and his relations with all the laws of nature."[48] Like other nineteenth-century new religious movements, Theosophy supported a range of religious expression and lifestyles that included important rites of passage such as funerals as well as social reforms.

Olcott and Helena Blavatsky, the founding members of the Theosophical Society, first met through a Spiritualist family in New York State. In 1874

Olcott, a lawyer from New York City who was interested in many of the fads and trends of the mid-nineteenth century, read a newspaper story about spirit activity at the Eddy family's farm in Vermont. He went to the Eddy farmhouse to witness these supernatural events, then wrote them up in articles published in the *New York Sun* and the *New York Daily Graphic*. Helena Blavatsky, who was born in the Ukraine but emigrated to New York City, read Olcott's accounts of spirits from different cultures appearing at the Eddys' and decided to meet Olcott at the farm. Blavatsky and Olcott quickly discovered their common interests and began holding salons in New York City to discuss and practice their own esoteric brand of spirit communication.

Blavatsky and Olcott felt that their movement was superior to popular manifestations of occult religion, particularly Spiritualism. In a letter to Cornell professor and Spiritualist Hiram Corson, Blavatsky insisted that her interest in Spiritualism was "not through the agency of the ever lying, cheating mediums, miserable instruments of the undeveloped spirits of the lower sphere, the ancient Hades. My belief is based on something other than the Rochester knockings [of the Spiritualist founders, the Fox sisters], and springs out from the same source of information that was used by Raymond Lully, Pico della Mirandola, Cornelius Agrippa, Robert Fludd, Henry More, etc., etc., all of whom have ever been searching for a system that should disclose to them the 'deepest depths' of divine nature and show them *the real tie which binds all things together*."[49] Blavatsky and Olcott's gatherings were self-consciously elitist and included New York gentry—lawyers and doctors, for example. Blavatsky believed that supernatural messages were from advanced beings that she called the "mahatmas" or "ascended masters," rather than spirits of the dead. These beings inhabited a spirit world where they evolved separately from humans. The idea of such spirits, who can be contacted through certain ritualized techniques and are available to help humans in their own spiritual journeys, became an important theme in the alternative tradition from Blavatsky through the New Age movement.

Like many of her contemporaries, Blavatsky encouraged self-exploration and self-improvement. She argued that an individual's life is a "grand cosmic drama in which one was working to uplift one's essence from body to astral body to soul to spirit—away from the groveling animals and up towards the 'Masters' who had united their spirits with the imperishable and indescribable Absolute."[50] Like her counterparts in Spiritualism and mental healing, Blavatsky believed in the ultimate harmony between human and divine rather than in a transcendent deity outside the world, and she promoted the idea that humans could, using the proper techniques, come to know the divine. In its early years the Theosophical Society focused on explaining and critiquing Spiritualism, but later its focus shifted to Asia.[51] Theosophy's popularity grew slowly until Blavatsky incorporated Asian thought and religion in *Isis Unveiled* (1877). In her book she attempted to show that all western knowledge was originally derived from Asian wisdom. Theosophists' interest in Asia and teachings about ascended masters and other levels of reality like the "astral plane" were absorbed into the New Age and Neopagan movements.[52]

Theosophists borrowed from religious beliefs and practices current in the mid-nineteenth century, but some of them also addressed social problems of their day. While Blavatsky focused on the inner life, Olcott emphasized the ways in which the Theosophical Society would help to usher in utopian social reforms alongside personal transformation. Blavatsky's contributions to Theosophy have been the most influential on New Age and Neopagan spiritualities, especially the former, which borrowed the idea of ascended masters. For Neopagans the legacy of the Theosophical Society is the revival of European magical traditions. Many Neopagans incorporate in their belief system the elite tradition of European occult magic embodied by Renaissance figures such as Marsilio Ficino and Pico della Mirandola, who blended Hermeticism and the kabbalah (Jewish mysticism), and the Rosicrucian movement that started in seventeenth-century Germany and later developed into Freemasonry. Ficino and Mirandola belong to what some scholars call Western Esotericism, a tradition that includes the gathering and transmission of knowledge about astrology, alchemy, hermeticism (based on texts thought to be of ancient Egyptian and Greek origin) and the kabbalah (Jewish mysticism). This tradition dates back to late fifteenth-century Europe and continues through the work of Eliphas Levi, a French occultist who lived in the mid-nineteenth century.[53]

Another English occult organization that was particularly important in the development of Neopaganism was the Hermetic Order of the Golden Dawn, a ritual magic group formed in England in the 1880s that drew on Levi's work. The Golden Dawn was a relatively small and elite group, including for a time the Irish poet William Butler Yeats and the controversial occultist Aleister Crowley, whose writings influenced many Neopagans. The Golden Dawn shared with Theosophy an emphasis on communication with advanced spirit beings and an interest in ancient Asian and Egyptian beliefs, the kabbalah (Jewish mysticism), and Renaissance alchemical writings.[54] The order's secret rituals were later made public by a former member, Israel Regardie, who published a thick book called *The Golden Dawn* that eventually made its way into the homes and temples of many Neopagans. The Theosophical Society and the Golden Dawn helped transmit Western Esotericism to a new generation when they contributed to the emergence of the New Age and Neopagan movements.

In addition to the European alchemical traditions and the writings of Mesmer and Swedenborg, the Theosophical Society incorporated Asian religious traditions into its practices, especially the doctrines of karma and reincarnation. Like the Transcendentalists, Theosophists helped familiarize a broad range of people with Asian beliefs. The influence of Asian traditions in the United States became more widespread at the end of the nineteenth century and the beginning of the twentieth because the American public was exposed to Asian religious teachers such as Swami Vivekananda (1862–1902) at the World's Parliament of Religions, a feature of the Columbian Exposition in Chicago in 1893 that took place in a "White City" built expressly for the event. Cultures from around the world were displayed for crowds of European Americans who were fascinated with the exotic East. Up to this point only small groups of intellectuals had read Asian classics like the *Bhagavad Gita* or the works of Emerson and Blavatsky. The World's Parliament of Religions introduced a broader public to Asian religious thought. A few years afterward, in 1897, Vivekananda established an American Vedanta society that taught the unity of all religions and gained members from New Thought and Theosophy. Adherents spread a form of Hinduism that was palatable to westerners because it focused on cultivating inner divinity and taught that truth was universal. Traveling swamis began to give public talks on astrology and other subjects. Their legacy would be taken up by Asian religious teachers who came to the United States after President Lyndon Johnson lifted immigration bans in 1965.

By the end of the nineteenth century, religious excitement had died down as alternative religious practices were institutionalized or increasingly seen as private concerns. But beliefs and practices that would serve as the heart of the New Age movement were now part of American culture. Alternative healing methods and psychic mediums would continue, and prophets and visionaries, while no longer on the front pages, would continue to gather people around them to form new religions. Harmonial or metaphysical religion had a firm hold on the American imagination and continued to attract many Americans until its second burst of popularity in the second half of the twentieth century.

Since the nineteenth century, the alternative tradition has held an ambivalent position in relationship to Christianity. Many New Agers and Neopagans today follow their nineteenth-century counterparts in valuing the historical figure of Jesus and Christian teachings, but criticizing institutionalized churches for being dogmatic and intolerant. Nineteenth-century Theosophists, for example, were anti-Christian, while later Theosophical organizations tried to link their teachings with Christianity. Even though harmonial traditions have their own specialists, they typically emphasize the ability of individuals to experience the divine without relying on the intervention of priests or ministers. For this reason, many people looked to Christian texts but not to established churches for guidance, even as they dabbled in mesmerism and mental healing.

At the end of the nineteenth century New Thought had established an informal network of healers. Quimby's success as a Swedenborgian teacher and healer led directly or indirectly to the formation of several new religions. Phineas Quimby healed Mary Baker Eddy (1821–1910), the founder of Christian Science, and she later borrowed many of her ideas about mental healing from him. Although Eddy herself was influenced by Spiritualism, participated in séances, and shared some basic assumptions with Spiritualism, such as the continuity of spirits after death, she rejected mediumship and the reality of the physical body, emphasizing spirit only. Quimby also healed Warren F. Evans (1817–1889), one of the founders of New Thought. New Thought and Christian Science gave rise to other religious traditions that overlapped with much of what is considered New Age today, especially faith in the power of the mind to heal illness. Eddy's student Emma Curtiss Hopkins (1853–1925) founded her own independent Christian Science seminary in 1886. Hopkins's students in turn founded the Church of Religious Science (in the 1920s) and the Unity School of Christianity (in 1889), both of which had branches across the United States by the beginning of the twenty-first century.

### Occultists and Psychics in the Early Twentieth Century

Astrology, psychics, channelers, and self-help literature were resources for healing and self-transformation that Americans turned to throughout the first half of the twentieth century.[55] Historians of religion do not discuss this period with the same inflated language and fascination as they do the mid-nineteenth century, and in many ways it was a quieter era for alternative religions. But several new and important trends appeared in the 1920s and 1930s—most notably, accounts of UFO sightings and interest in the lost ancient civilizations of Atlantis and Lemuria—and converged with the nineteenth-century religious legacy. The period between the First and Second World Wars was particularly fruitful for new homegrown religions, in spite of or perhaps due in part to the Great Depression of the late 1920s and 1930s. By the beginning of the twentieth century, occult religious practices were no longer marketed by a public culture of prophets, visionaries, mediums, and unorthodox healers who made the news headlines. Smaller followings congregated around specific charismatic figures who drew inspiration from beliefs and practices made popular in the nineteenth century. Much of the information that was once spread through speakers' circuits and Spiritualist newsletters was disseminated by way of book publication. The Theosophical Press was particularly successful in spreading Asian religious teachings. In the early twentieth century the Theosophical Society became successfully institutionalized and continued to publish works devoted to promoting esoteric knowledge and Asian religious thought. Other teachers and writers who influenced alternative spirituality in the first half of the twentieth century and beyond were psychologist Carl G. Jung (1885–1961) and spiritual leader Gurdjieff (1866?–1949). Jung's theory of archetypes continues to influence New Agers and Neopagans today, as do the spiritual techniques that Gurdjieff taught could enable anyone to reach enlightenment.

After the Civil War, Spiritualism declined in numbers and significance, but Spiritualist churches nevertheless remained part of the American religious landscape into the twenty-first century. They experienced a temporary surge in membership immediately after World War I, as a nation of families mourned those lost in war and, like their nineteenth-century counterparts, turned to Spiritualism for comfort. With the exception of the Shakers, nineteenth-century communal experiments did not endure into the next century nor appear prominently until the new communal movements of the 1960s and 1970s. Mesmerism in its nineteenth-century form disappeared, but the practice of putting people into trances continued in modern hypnotherapy. The various health reforms and alternative healing practices, especially homeopathic and chiropractic medicine, continued to gain adherents in the twentieth century and then, like alternative religions, again experienced a boom in the 1960s. While the occult tradition was no longer in the public eye, many Americans still sought religious options outside of established churches and consulted unorthodox healers. Two prime examples of the turn to alternative religious and healing practices in the 1920s and 1930s were the teachings of psychic Edgar Cayce (1877–1945) and the I AM movement, a synthesis of nineteenth-century alternative traditions founded by Guy Ballard (1878–1939).

At the same time that New Thought religions were forming in the opening decades of the twentieth century, individual psychics developed loosely organized followings of their own. These psychics anticipated New Age belief in spiritual healing and promoted self-transformation. Some, like Edgar Cayce, also combined metaphysical beliefs and Asian religious thought with Christianity. In his approach to healing Cayce picked up on many of the ideas developed by Theosophy and Spiritualism, especially the blending of Asian religious beliefs like reincarnation with Christian teachings. Cayce had a lasting impact on New Age religion, and his legacy continued in the form of the Association for Research and Enlightenment (ARE), based in Virginia Beach, Virginia and founded in 1931, which still disseminates his teachings. By 1970, ARE had grown to 12,000 members and by 1981, to 32,000.[56] Cayce's books gained considerable popularity through the 1960s and into the beginning of the twenty-first century. New Agers and other Americans were drawn to his writings on ancient civilizations, past lives, and remedies for a wide variety of physical and psychological afflictions.

Cayce was dubbed the "sleeping prophet" by journalists because he went into a deep trance and successfully diagnosed illnesses and prescribed healing remedies. Like many other religious figures in the alternative reality tradition, Cayce underwent a spiritual and healing crisis during which his clairvoyant gifts became apparent. He was at first reluctant to assume the role of healer and doubted his own abilities, but over time he came to believe his powers were a gift from God. At first Cayce gave "healing readings," but after an encounter with a Theosophist in 1923, he began giving "life readings" that included references to karma and reincarnation. His readings also mentioned other practices that would become central to the New Age movement from the 1960s on, such as crystals and the ancient civilization of Atlantis.[57] Accounts of such lost civilizations, usually provided by psychics and channelers, were widely circulated in American religious subcultures of the early twentieth century. For example, former Theosophist and founder of Anthroposophy Rudolph Steiner's book *The Submerged Continents of Atlantis and Lemuria* was published in the United States in 1911.[58] Steiner (1861–1925) defected from Theosophy with a majority of German Theosophists who joined his Anthroposophical movement (which blended Rosicrucian, Christian, Theosophical, and occult thought and stressed the natural accessibility of divine wisdom), but his books influenced American

Theosophists who read them in translation. Anthroposophy survived Hitler's attempts to disband it and became well established throughout Western Europe and in the United States through Waldorf schools (schools that integrate sensual experience of art and music with more traditional curricula to nourish children's bodies and minds), architecture, art theory, and biodynamic farming.

Like Cayce and Steiner, Alice Bailey (1880–1949), a psychic and founder of the Arcane School, was influenced by the Theosophical Society and adopted the Spiritualist practice of mediumship. Bailey established the Arcane School to promote the program set forth by beings she channeled called the "Great White Brotherhood," a group of spiritual masters that included a Tibetan teacher. In the tradition of Helena Blavatsky, she saw herself as a messenger who was directed to write down and spread the teachings of spiritual beings or "masters" who communicated with her while she was in a trance state. Bailey was responsible for popularizing the terms "New Age" and the "Age of Aquarius."[59] Like Cayce, she believed in karma and reincarnation as well as some aspects of Christianity. They set the standard for New Age channelers and described a world populated by disincarnate spirits, spirit guides, devas, and angels that continues to attract Neopagans and New Agers.

In the early decades of the twentieth century the center of new religious ferment shifted from Boston and New York to California.[60] Theosophy's American center was by that time on the West Coast, and many of the most widely publicized new religious movements had their start in the West. The "I AM" movement, an important example of early twentieth-century California eclecticism, was founder Guy Ballard's synthesis of nineteenth-century alternative traditions. Ballard, a former medium and hypnotist, was also an effective self-promoter who took advantage of new technologies, such as radio advertising, to spread his religion, which was founded in the 1930s. The "I AM" movement borrowed many Theosophical teachings; for instance, Ballard told of his encounter at Mount Shasta, California, with an "Ascended Master," Saint-Germain, an important figure in Helena Blavatsky's pantheon of advanced spirit beings. Ballard also borrowed from the Rosicrucians, Asian religions, Christianity, and the Spiritualist tradition of large public demonstrations during which spirits communicated with an audience. According to Ballard, Saint-Germain had chosen him as a mouthpiece through which to communicate with humanity. Ballard and his wife Edna emphasized healing, especially with the aid of cosmic beings that spoke and worked through them. Like nineteenth-century mediums before them and New Age channelers to come, Cayce, Bailey, and Ballard all served as channels of communication between the human and spirit worlds.

Early twentieth-century channelers and psychics were antecedents of the New Age movement, but Neopaganism also descended directly from early twentieth-century esoteric phenomena, such as the Order of the Golden Dawn and the Rosicrucians. AMORC (Ancient and Mystical Order of the Rosae Crucis), one early Rosicrucian group, was founded in New York City in 1915 and moved to San Jose, California in 1928. Like early twentieth-century Theosophists and New Thought adherents, the Rosicrucians were numerous and loosely organized, and their beliefs overlapped with those of many of their contemporaries. AMORC claimed not to be a "religion" but assumed that the universe was created by a god that had a plan for humans; members taught techniques to bring into being mental images of health and happiness. Rosicrucian teachings built on the Renaissance occult tradition or Western Esotericism, as did the rituals of the Golden Dawn. One of the major organizations to carry on the teachings of Victorian occultist Aleister Crowley and the Golden Dawn in the United States was the Ordo Templi Orientis (OTO) lodge, founded in Los Angeles in the 1930s. When Neopagan groups emerged out of the religious ferment of the 1960s, they looked for inspiration from esoteric organizations like Theosophy and the OTO that were eclectic and interested in reviving ancient traditions.

Other isolated phenomena of the early twentieth century had an impact on the alternative religious tradition and would later shape New Age and Neopagan beliefs. During the 1930s popular tales of rural paganism and satanism circulated, an unfortunate pairing that has continued to confuse outside observers. UFO sightings occurred in the first half of the twentieth century but were not widely publicized or popularly believed until the late 1940s and 1950s. The late 1930s also saw the beginnings of the human potential movement, which flourished in the 1950s and helped direct the spiritual thrust of the 1960s counterculture. Norman Vincent Peale's first major book on this subject, *You Can Win*, was published in 1938. All of these elements would eventually burst on the popular religious scene in the 1960s when the alternative tradition again became the fodder of reporters and a target for critique by Christian churches.

# CHAPTER FOUR

# The 1960s Watershed Years

In 1961, Robert Heinlein's science fiction classic *Stranger in a Strange Land* was published and *Black Elk Speaks,* an account of the life of a Lakota medicine man, was reissued in paperback and became "the current youth classic."[1] Both books would have an impact on the generation of men and women who would become Neopagans and New Agers. The first 1960s Neopagan groups looked for ancient and indigenous cultures on which to model their rituals, but they also took ideas from science fiction. New Agers too were attracted to stories of distant worlds and enchanted by the myths and rituals of American Indians. During the 1960s patterns of American religiosity inherited from the nineteenth century were pushed to new imaginative dimensions by the (mostly young) men and women who made up the counterculture. Beginning with several important phenomena of the 1950s, such as social and demographic changes, the UFO craze, and the Beat movement, this chapter charts the forces responsible for the emergence of communities and loosely structured networks of people who by the early 1970s could be identified as New Agers and Neopagans.

Nineteenth-century beliefs and practices such as channeling and reincarnation resurfaced during the late 1950s, surged in the popular imagination during the 1960s, and were shaped by social forces that converged in these two decades. Social and cultural upheavals initiated religious and cultural trends such as the human potential movement, the feminist movement, the rise of ecological awareness, and the turn to nonwestern religions, all of which also influenced New Age and Neopagan spirituality. Personal and planetary healing and self-transformation, defining characteristics of New

Age and Neopagan religions as they developed in the 1970s and 1980s, took on heightened importance during the 1960s and appeared in the writings of important leaders, gurus, and modern-day prophets and the communities they spearheaded. Key figures of the 1960s counterculture and early New Age movement, such as psychedelic guru Timothy Leary and spiritual teacher Ram Dass, as well as important channelers like Helen Schucman developed followings in the '60s and '70s. Beginning in the 1960s and continuing into the twenty-first century, New Age and Neopagan interests coalesced around particular people, books, institutes, retreats, communes, and centers; some of these lasted, others were short-lived. What emerged out of this period was a loosely connected network of individuals and communities that proceeded to grow into a more mainstream movement over the following two decades.

## Postwar America and the 1960s Spiritual Boom

After World War II the United States underwent rapid social transformation, unregulated industrial growth, and economic expansion. Following years of war and economic depression, the late 1940s and 1950s were characterized by significant increases in national production and per capita income.[2] Demographic shifts accompanied economic and industrial expansion as masses of people moved from rural areas to urban centers, a trend that had been ongoing for decades but reached its peak in the 1950s. The postwar years were marked by a new prosperity that resulted in an expanding middle class and larger families. By the mid-1950s, 60 percent of all Americans had income at levels considered middle-class, compared to only 31 percent in the 1920s. This shift meant that larger percentages of the U.S. population had cars and discretionary income.[3] At the end of the 1940s and into the 1950s the average age of marriage and motherhood fell, fertility increased, and divorce rates declined for the first time in more than a hundred years.[4] The so-called "baby boomers," a generation that would found and support first the countercultural movement and then New Age and Neopagan communities, were born between 1946 and 1964.

Along with these other changes, Cold War patriotism in the face of atheistic Communists initiated a postwar religious revival. Christianity was established, both formally and informally, as America's civil religion during these years. For instance, no organized opposition spoke out against the 1954 addition of the words "under God" to the Pledge of Allegiance. Church building and church attendance were on the rise during the decade or so after the end of World War II. In 1957, for instance, polls showed that 96 percent of Americans gave specific church affiliations. All of this would change by the end of the 1950s as people began to seek new spiritualities.

However, the phrase "the way we never were," the title of Stephanie Coontz's historical look at nostalgia for the "traditional family," could be broadened to denote the entire decade. The 1950s had a shadow side lurking beneath its Christian veneer and the clean and upbeat television programming that symbolized the ideal American culture many people associate with these years. Looking back nostalgically on the '50s has been an American pastime for decades, but "beneath the polished façade of many 'ideal' families, suburban as well as urban, was violence, terror, or simply grinding misery that only occasionally came to light."[5] Youth movements stirred at the edges of the façade, and by the end of the decade, Beat generation poets had made a striking entrance on the literary scene and psychedelic drugs were about to be promoted among young people willing to experiment. These two examples suggest that trouble was brewing because some American youth were not satisfied with the promise of affluence and a future shaped by middle-class Christian values.

The 1960s are seen as watershed years for religious experimentation, but much of what occurred in that decade emerged out of streams of belief and practice already in place on the American religious landscape by the 1950s: channeling, psychic phenomena, Theosophical beliefs, and mental healing, for instance. But most of these practices were not popularized or publicized until a host of other changes that accompanied and facilitated the 1960s birth of many new religious movements, including Neopaganism and New Age. The most significant examples of new events in the 1950s that fed the alternative religions of the 1960s were interest in UFOs, the Beat generation's eclectic Asian religiosity, and early signs of the emergent psychedelic drug culture. These phenomena reveal a different story of the 1950s, characterized by spiritual seeking and discontent with available religious and lifestyle options.

Aldous Huxley, a writer interested in religious mysticism, experimented with mescaline in the 1950s and published an account of his experiences in a 1954 book, *The Doors of Perception*, in which he wrote,

> The mescaline experience is without any question the most extraordinary and significant experience available to human beings this side of the Beatific Vision. To be shaken out of the ruts of ordinary perception, to be shown for a few timeless hours the outer and inner worlds, not as they

appear to an animal obsessed with survival or to a human being obsessed with words and notions, but as they are apprehended, directly and unconditionally, by Mind at Large—this is an experience of inestimable value to anyone.[6]

It was clear to readers of his book—many men and women who would become involved with the counterculture of the 1960s—that "the inner planes of reality . . . could now be directly known, seen, and experienced on the streets of a new world, in part with the help of magic potions known to the wise."[7] Psychedelics would become one of the main routes by which young people in the 1960s explored their inner selves and envisioned new religious options. Huxley's early descriptions of altered states of consciousness helped to refocus attention on personal experience and his discussions of the parallels between psychedelics and religious experience helped to direct his readers to new religious worlds.

Whereas psychedelics were the tools of inward exploration as an end in itself, Norman Vincent Peale's "positive thinking" program advocated inner growth as a means to external success. Mental healing was reinvigorated in the 1950s by the popularity of his self-improvement techniques. Peale, who had written books on "positive thinking" for over a decade, became wildly successful when he published *The Power of Positive Thinking* in 1952. Peale's advice for self-improvement emphasized the power of the mind: "A primary method for gaining a mind full of peace is to practice emptying the mind. . . . I mention it now to underscore the importance of a frequent mental catharsis. . . . The formula is: (1) PRAYERIZE, (2) PICTURIZE, (3) ACTUALIZE."[8] Peale's optimism legitimated the desire of middle-class Americans in the 1950s for increasing affluence and emotional comfort. His program built on that stream of harmonial religion in the nineteenth century that taught people they could achieve health and happiness by following the proper techniques. Certainly the ethic of self-reliance in Peale's writings carried over into the 1960s, but optimism such as his was in sharp decline among many Americans by the end of the '50s. If Peale was at one end of the 1950s spectrum as the prophet of middle-class positive thinking, then the Beat poets were at the other as vocal critics of what that middle class represented. Both were important in the development of the counterculture and thus had an impact on New Agers and Neopagans, who would emerge from a generation of baby boomers looking for religious alternatives.

Beat poems and novels highlighted the spiritual crisis of postwar America and emphasized the quest for self-knowledge. In his social critique of the

1950s published in 1956, cultural critic Paul Goodman identified the Beats as resisters of the status quo: "balked in their normal patriotism and religious tradition, the Beats [sought] pretty far afield for substitutes . . . red Indians or feudal Zen Buddhists."[9] The Beats' response to what they believed was a spiritually impoverished culture was "to heighten experience, and get out of one's usual self."[10] Jack Kerouac's *The Dharma Bums* (1959) was the fullest expression of this quest and detailed the exploits of Kerouac's fictionalized friends and acquaintances, especially Japhy Ryder (a thinly disguised portrayal of Buddhist poet Gary Snyder), a quintessential Beat who meditates, studies Zen Buddhism, and travels to Japan to live in a Buddhist monastery. The narrator, Kerouac's character, accompanies Japhy on a backpacking trip that includes meditation breaks:

> We went over to the promontory where we could see the whole valley and Japhy sat down in full lotus posture cross-legged on a rock and took out his wooden juju prayer beads and prayed. That is, he simply held the beads in his hands, the hands upsidedown with thumbs touching, and stared straight ahead and didn't move a bone. I sat down as best I could on another rock and we both said nothing and meditated. Only I meditated with my eyes closed. The silence was an intense roar. From where we were, the sound of the creek, was blocked off by rocks. . . . When I opened my eyes the pink was more purple all the time. The stars began to flash. I fell into deep meditation, felt that mountains were indeed Buddhas and our friends.[11]

The characters in the novel and the people they were modeled after exemplified a self-determined search for meaning that incorporated personalized interpretations of Buddhism and showed the way for subsequent self-styled truth seekers.

While the dharma bums' search was largely internal, UFO fanatics of the 1950s looked outside the self and beyond the planet for meaning. Widespread fascination with UFOs dates to the summer of 1947 when Kenneth Arnold, a U.S. Forest Service employee sent to look for a downed plane in Washington State, saw nine brightly lit, spherically shaped flying objects near Mount Rainier. Reports of unidentified flying objects existed in earlier decades, but this was the first sighting to gather widespread public support (and to generate considerable controversy). Arnold's story was picked up by the Associated Press and circulated by the national news media. Stories of other sightings appeared in the years following Arnold's experience and were also controversial: "Many contactees emerge with heightened psychic abilities and spiritual awareness, only to face harassment, ridicule and scorn from 'nonbelievers.'"[12] Some people recalled being abducted and abused, while others believed that aliens were benevolent beings come to guide and protect humans, sometimes by delivering messages through human channels. George King, an Englishman who was influenced by Theosophy, founded the first UFO religion, the Aetherius Society, in 1956 in London, then moved it to Los Angeles in 1959.[13] *The Urantia Book*, a document channeled through Wilfrid Kellogg (1876–1956), a trance channeler, beginning in the early twentieth century, provided evidence for other inhabited worlds; it was published in 1955.[14] The popularity of UFOs in the 1950s marked the beginning of widespread interest in other worlds in America's alternative or occult tradition.

Psychic healers like Edgar Cayce, prophets of positive thinking like Peale, faith in otherworldly salvation, experimentation with psychedelics, and disaffected Beats looking East were a few of the many popular movements in the 1950s that coalesced with older alternative religions like Theosophy and spiritualism as well as with 1960s social movements. By the 1960s assumptions about progress and unprecedented growth—"technocratic society," to borrow a phrase from one of the most astute sixties observers, Theodore Roszak—resulted in a pervasive sense of national failure and dislocation. Science and technology seemed frighteningly unbounded to many people, and the atomic bombing of Hiroshima demonstrated to all Americans the real possibility of human extinction. Enthusiasm about UFOs and space exploration (the Soviet Union launched Sputnik, the world's first space satellite, in 1957) spurred interest in American scientific developments. There was a widespread cultural sense that science was the cure-all, yet events like the Cuban missile crisis in 1962 also underscored its dangers. Many of the material and cultural changes of the 1960s had interesting parallels in the mid-nineteenth century and both eras were above all times of unusual religious creativity. Changes in communications media in the mid-nineteenth century and again in the 1960s made information more accessible and exposed people to new ways of being in the world. Television and photojournalism (*Life* magazine in particular) brought the Vietnam War and unfamiliar Southeast Asian cultures into American living rooms. Photos of Buddhist monks setting themselves on fire and soldiers returning home brought Asian religious worlds to the awareness of many Americans, building on the Asian presence that was already here. The first moon landing in 1969 brought about increased awareness of other planets and a sense of humanity's relative insignificance in the vast universe. Key events like these affected a generation of young people who responded to the times by joining a diverse range of religious movements, including Neopagan and New Age.

### The Counterculture and the Personalization of Religion

The context for the 1960s counterculture from which Neopagan and New Age movements emerged can be approached from many perspectives. The following list is just one of many ways to tell the story, beginning with some important dates:

1961: *Stranger in a Strange Land* and *Black Elk Speaks* are published; Esalen Institute is formed; Richard Alpert (Ram Dass) and Timothy Leary experiment with LSD.

1963: President John F. Kennedy is assassinated.

1965: J. R. R. Tolkien's *Lord of the Rings* U.S. paperback edition is published; Helen Schucman begins channeling what will become "A Course in Miracles"; Asian immigration quotas lifted; U.S. military involvement in Vietnam officially begins.

1967: Church of All Worlds and Feraferia, two important Neopagan groups, are founded.

1968: Martin Luther King Jr. and Robert Kennedy are assassinated.

1969: U.S. astronauts land Apollo 11 on the moon.

1970: Student protesters at Kent State are shot and killed by National Guardsmen.

While New Age and Neopagan assumptions about the self emerged most directly out of shifts in American religiosity that took place during the 1960s, in other ways they were continuous with the alternative tradition of the nineteenth and early twentieth centuries that included spiritualism, psychic readings, Theosophy, and mental healing. Even when world events did not appear so promising, the self remained a source of optimism. The assumption that it could be shaped and changed, key to many nineteenth-century religious and healing movements, was expanded and enriched with a host of new self-improvement technologies like meditation and yoga. New Agers in particular, and Neopagans to a lesser extent, taught that salvation was possible through the discovery of a divine inner self. The youth culture of the baby boomers—the counterculture—came to be "grounded in an intensive examination of the self, of the buried wealth of personal consciousness."[15] Religious seeking in the 1960s was "the quest for personal fulfillment. . . . Everyone had to compose his or her own story; autobiography threatened to displace history as a dominant way of making sense of things."[16] The counterculture celebrated synchronicities and claimed to reject linear time, ordinary reality, and history: "There was attention to signs and omens, the portent of simple actions, the importance of dreams and hallucinations."[17] Some took the divine self to be their goal, while others allowed that the discovery of divinity within helped them connect to other beings and to the greater universe.

Along with other new religions, the New Age movement and Neopaganism emerged during a "radical turn in religion and morals that took place during the 1960s."[18] One aspect of this turn was a cultural shift toward understanding the self as a commodity to be created and presented.[19] Self-expression and "personal autonomy" were central to the 1960s counterculture and resulted in "a progressive democratization of personhood" and a search for individualized religion.[20] Family relationships, diet, fashion, and exercise were all areas in which "good" and "bad" were measured by their effects on self-knowledge and personal growth.

As they created the self anew, Neo-Pagans and New Agers continued to play out the search for personalized religion that was integral to the counterculture. This replaced the importance of a community of others and institutional authorities. The 1960s moral authority for most Americans was increasingly located in the self rather than in family, church, or nation.[21] Involvement in church life was normative until the social revolution of the 1960s resulted in the "third disestablishment" of institutionalized religion,[22] in which secularization and personal religious seeking displaced denominational affiliation and institutional commitment. "If one scans any of the underground weeklies," noted one observer of the period, "one is apt to find their pages swarming with Christ and the prophets, Zen, Sufism, Hinduism, primitive shamanism, theosophy . . . every manner of mystery and fakery, ritual and rite [is] intermingled with marvelous indiscrimination."[23]

During the 1960s, many young people made more personalized religious commitments, rejected the religions of their parents, and looked suspiciously at institutions in general and religious ones in particular. Neopagan festival communities and important organizations like the Church of All Worlds originated in the 1960s counterculture and exemplify changes in the relationship between religion and self-identity that took place during that decade. Historian of religion Robert Ellwood observed that beginning in the 1960s, "external religious authority is widely rejected in favor of one's right to find a religion that meets one's own perceived needs."[24] According to social scientific research, the tumultuous decade influenced many people to take a more eclectic approach to spirituality.[25]

Probably the most insightful outside observer of 1960s countercultural concerns was a young history professor, Theodore Roszak. His book *The Making of a Counterculture: Reflections on the Technocratic Society and Its Youthful Opposition* (1969) situated the countercultural movement of the 1960s, and especially its spiritual aspects, in a particular configuration of social and historical forces. Roszak described the many sources from which the counterculture drew inspiration, such as Asian religions, backward-looking European and American romanticism, certain forms of psychiatry, anarchist social theory, the absurdist dada movement in the art world, and American Indian lore.[26] This eclecticism also meant that many men and women shopped around for spiritual paths that worked for them. They consulted psychics and channelers, ate vegetarian meals with the Hare Krishnas, and read Timothy Leary's *The Politics of Ecstasy* (1968) and Tolkien's *Lord of the Rings*.

While television increased exposure to new ideas, many young people believed that technological changes were destructive and preached about moving back to nature and simpler lifestyles. Baby boomers had benefited from the economic boom of the 1950s, but they were not sure they wanted to claim that heritage: "the orthodox culture they confront is fatally and contagiously diseased. The prime symptom of that disease is the shadow of thermonuclear annihilation beneath which we cower. The counterculture takes its stand against the background of this absolute evil."[27] Young people were ambivalent about the many technological changes that were under way in the 1960s. Space technology and weapons of mass destruction were in the background of protests against what American society had become because the counterculture rejected the "high gods" of science and technology. Roszak predicted that opposition to the dominant society would continue as long as young people "reject reductive humanism, demanding a far deeper examination of that dark side of the human personality which has for so long been written off by our dominant culture as 'mystical.'"[28]

Many other writers of the time agreed with this assessment of the counterculture's spiritual motivations. Radical activist Abbie Hoffman went by the pseudonym "Free" in his account of the 1960s, *Revolution for the Hell of It*. Free explained that "the myths of America are strong and good but the institutional machine is a trap of death."[29] If technocratic society rejected myth and ritual, he suggested, then of course the counterculture should embrace these elements of human experience, reclaiming ancient shamanism and looking to nonwestern cultures for wisdom and guidance. Sociologist Andrew Greeley, another observer of the '60s counterculture, likewise noted, "the communes, rock music . . . hallucinogenic drugs, the *I Ching*, tarot cards, astrology, witchcraft, the Meher Baba cult, etc., are an attempt to reassert meaningful community in ecstasy in a rationalistic, hyperorganized world which had assumed, in keeping with the tenets of the conventional wisdom, that man could dispense with all these elements."[30] Although many political radicals in the counterculture were atheists who believed that dabbling in astrology had nothing to do with real social and political change, others pointed to the many ways that spirituality and politics worked together to create an alternative culture. Writers and artists of the time advocated blending the two, as in this poem by Julian Beck:

> *it is 1968*
> *i am a magic realist*
> *i see the adorers of che*
>
> *i see the black man*
> *forced to accept*
> *violence*
>
> *i see the pacifists*
> *despair*
> *and accept violence*
>
> *i see all all all*
> *corrupted*
> *by the vibrations*
>
> *vibrations of violence of civilization*
> *that are shattering*
> *our only world*
>
> *we want*
> *to zap them*
> *with holiness*
>
> *we want*
> *to levitate them*
> *with joy*

*we want*
*to open them*
*with love vessels*

*we want*
*to clothe the wretched*
*with linen and light*

*we want*
*to put music and truth*
*in our underwear*

*we want*
*to make the land and its cities glow*
*with creation*

*we will make it*
*irresistible*
*even to racists*

*we want to change*
*the demonic character of our opponents*
*into productive glory.*[31]

This kind of rebellion was not designed to further distance oneself from the enemy, but to transform the enemy as well as the self, through both spiritual revolution and political action. Poet Diane DiPrima explored the same issue in "Revolutionary Letter #7":

*but don't get uptight: the guns:*
*will not win this one, they are*
*an incidental part of the action*
*what will win*
*is mantras*
*the sustenance we give each other*
*the energy we plug into*
*(the fact that we touch*
*share food)*
*the buddha nature*
*of everyone, friend and foe, like a million*
*earthworms*

*tunneling under this structure*
*till it falls*[32]

Both poets voice the widespread view that revolutionary social change could be accomplished through spiritual means and changes in consciousness. Countercultural men and women came up with imaginative forms of opposition to social institutions that were drawn from both science fiction and backward-looking medievalism. If the present was bankrupt, then past cultures and future worlds were the best sources of inspiration for new communities. New Agers, and especially Neopagans, looked optimistically to the past as a source for constructing a better future. "The past," observed historian of religion Robert Ellwood in his study of spirituality in the 1960s, "was of help in the counterculture's quest for legitimation and authority," in part because it was seen as the locus of truth. In the 1960s and 1970s, "The theme of nostalgia dominated popular culture: nostalgia for times past, for places either remote or undisfigured by technology, for family, and for the experience of community."[33] Typical of this idealistic quest was "romantic neo-medievalism" exemplified by the popularity of Tolkien and of Lerner-Loewe's musical *Camelot*.[34] College students wore buttons proclaiming "Frodo Lives" and put up posters of Middle Earth in their rooms.[35] Also characteristic of the 1960s romantic "backlash" against rationalism was renewed interest in witchcraft and supernaturalism.[36] One example of the popularization of all things occult was the *Dark Shadows* television soap opera, which ran from 1966 to 1971 and depicted a family "involved with everything that made up the sixties spiritual counterculture. They did astrology and tarot cards, witchcraft, the *I Ching*."[37] For many young people, the esoteric and the ancient were attractive and led to Neopagan efforts at reclaiming the witch and the Druid.[38] Astrology and tarot evinced the romanticized past of a simpler, more harmonious world. But most significantly in relation to Neopaganism, the ethos of the past was "thought to be close to the earth and the cycles of nature which Neopagans see as the central metaphor of their cosmology." The elevation of nature as divine presence and the turn to the past as a source of inspiration date at least to the English Romantic poets like Wordsworth and Keats, who looked nostalgically to ancient Greece as an example of humans living in harmony with nature and the gods. Neopaganism is a recent take on a literary tradition characterized by the desire to return to a time when religion was supposedly less dogmatic and institutionalized and more in tune with the natural world.

## Utopia in This and Other Worlds

Science fiction and futurism as well as nostalgic fantasy were popular in the 1960s. Robert Heinlein's *Stranger in a Strange Land* would became the basis for one of the first Neopagan religions in the United States, the Church of All Worlds (CAW). One Neopagan fan of the genre argued that "Science fiction/fantasy readers tend to think of things in terms of the galaxy as a whole . . . rather than think in a local or national sense."[39] In 2002 the Church of All Worlds was still going strong and still guided by its original founder. According to its Web site, "The CAW is the first Pagan Church founded in the US. It was incorporated in 1968 by Oberon Zell-Ravenheart and recognized by the IRS in 1970. Zell-Ravenheart read *Stranger in a Strange Land* by Robert Heinlein and was so inspired by the vision of a Nest—a close-knit group seeking a deep knowing of each other—that he brought his vision alive with the CAW." The church began in 1961 when a group of high school students met to discuss the philosophical novels of self-sufficiency written by Ayn Rand and the work of human potential psychologist Abraham Maslow. A couple of these students formed a smaller group called "Atl" and read Timothy Leary and other authors popular with the counterculture. One of these students was Zell-Ravenheart. From its founding, the CAW was "dedicated to the celebration of Life, the maximal actualization of Human potential, and the realization of ultimate individual freedom and personal responsibility in harmonious eco-psychic relationship with the total Biosphere of Holy Mother Earth."[40] The focus on human potential and personal freedom was from the beginning at the heart of the Neopagan movement. And like many Neopagan groups to come, CAW saw nothing inconsistent with living in harmony with nature on this planet and being fascinated by other worlds. For many young people in the 1960s such literature provided useful models for creating new lifestyles and beliefs at a time when many Americans were desperately seeking alternatives to their parents' religious and lifestyle choices.

Religious seekers in the 1960s also looked within for truth and wisdom. Other techniques to explore consciousness, such as meditation, grew in popularity and earned a permanent place in the New Age and Neopagan movements. Healers and psychics had incorporated hypnosis and visualization in their treatment of patients since the nineteenth century, when mesmerists traveled the countryside. But in the 1960s these older techniques were updated and revised because of contact with Asian religious beliefs and practices. Meditation was incorporated into a wide variety of religious practices. Human potential workshops, witchcraft covens, communal gatherings, Zen retreats, and new movements like Transcendental meditation and Krishna Consciousness that followed Asian teachers all incorporated meditation. Meditation centers and weekend workshops were established, and many communes also made meditation part of their daily routine. Some people practiced alone while others sought out communities or retreats that would encourage and guide them.

The decade of the 1960s was characterized by contradictions; this was particularly clear in the tension between personal autonomy and desire for community. Many spiritual seekers rejected any structured group setting while others looked for guidance from experienced teachers. An important development early in the decade that contributed to the New Age emphasis on healing and self-transformation within group settings was the human potential movement. Psychologists like Abraham Maslow (1908–1970) and organizations like the Esalen Institute in Big Sur, California (founded in 1961 by Michael Murphy and Richard Price, thirty-year-old Stanford graduates with psychology degrees) encouraged the process of self-actualization that was to become central to the New Age movement—the phrase "do your own thing" was coined at Esalen. It has as its mission "the exploration of what Aldous Huxley called 'the human potential,' the world of unrealized human capacities that lies beyond the imagination."[41] Murphy had lived in an ashram in India, and his spiritual interests were complemented by Price's therapeutic focus. According to Price: "In 1960, the basic model Michael had, after his year at the Aurobindo ashram, was something more spiritual and searching, while my interests are what I call therapeutic and clinical. . . . The two ideas there were a good match: a spiritual model coupled with a place to help people at various levels of emotional difficulties." Esalen workshops often incorporated world religions with various kinds of therapy and bodywork. Gestalt therapist Fritz Perls (1894–1970) was an important figure in the institute's early history and a good example of the focus on self-examination. Perls's Esalen sessions encouraged exploration of inner worlds and asked participants to dramatize personal conflicts by speaking with voices from different parts of the self.

Weekend retreat centers like Esalen were to some extent a withdrawal from the political scene. Communes made this disengagement permanent as men and women moved "back to the land" to live in accordance with their ideals. One of the earliest 1960s communes was Millbrook, in New York, "both ashram and research institute, where Timothy Leary and his family moved in 1963 to further his experiments with psychedelics."[42] The communal "deluge" was well under way by 1967, "the Summer of Love," and continued through the early 1970s.[43] One of the most famous Northern California communes was Morning Star Ranch, which exemplified the blending of spiritualities common in the counterculture. Inhabitants of this Sonoma County ranch practiced Christianity alongside yoga and meditation. Some communes were "Jesus movement" (evangelical Protestant hippies); others, like the Krishna Consciousness community New Vrindaban in West Virginia, were based on Asian religious teachings. Most communal experiments of the 1960s had a religious component, even if it was eclectic and loosely defined. Countercultural men and women envisioned communes as model alternatives to the society they had rejected, and alternative spiritual practices were part of their vision.

The Farm, a commune started in Tennessee by refugees of the Haight-Ashbury counterculture in San Francisco, was one of the longest-lasting examples of a 1960s spiritual community in practice. "It was rooted in prototypical hippie spirituality and religiosity, espousing a unique faith that drew from the deepest insights of all the world's major religious traditions. . . . It was steeped in rural idealism. . . . It had a charismatic leader who was a veritable archetype of the hippie philosopher. . . . Members took vows of voluntary poverty and dedicated themselves to helping the poor of the third world . . . they also unabashedly used marijuana and natural psychedelics and regarded getting high as an essential implement in their spiritual toolbox."[44] The Farm began during the 1960s as a study group in San Francisco organized by Stephen Gaskin, who became the commune's spiritual leader. Gaskin drew from a wide range of world religions and "compared the world's spiritual teachings to a deck of old-fashioned computer punch cards (envelope-sized cards that contained data in the form of holes punched through them). All he was doing, he said, was picking up that pack of cards and holding it up to the light; where the light came through, where all the religions had punched their holes in the same places, were the universal truths."[45] Groups of men and women searching for spiritual alternatives or teachers to guide their meditation practice gathered around charismatic figures like Gaskin.

At the same time that communitarians retreated from the public realm, important social movements emerged that would influence the development of New Age and Neopagan traditions. What is now labeled Second Wave feminism challenged traditional gender roles and pushed men and women to examine internalized sexism and to play with social assumptions about gender. The American Indian Movement and the Black Panthers brought injustices done to American Indians and African American separatism into the awareness of many Americans. They also exposed the general public to their cultural and religious traditions. The popularity of *Black Elk Speaks* is one of many examples of widespread fascination and involvement with American Indian cultures in the 1960s. Many young people looked to American Indian traditions for alternative lifestyles, and this was to shape New Agers' and Neopagans' subsequent turn to and incorporation of indigenous peoples' practices into their own rituals and belief systems. In Ram Dass and Paul Gorman's book, *How Can I Help?* one of the stories included is a memory: "I went as a representative of the hippie community of San Francisco to meet the Hopi Indian elders to arrange a Hopi-Hippie Be-In in Grand Canyon. We wanted to honor their tradition and affirm our common respect for the land. As you can guess, this was during the sixties."[46] The desire to share in native peoples' perceived harmony with nature became a common theme of the 1960s counterculture and in 1970s Neopaganism and New Age communities. However, Indians, then and now, were ambivalent about middle-class white people appropriating their traditions, and indiscriminate borrowing by New Agers and Neopagans continues to be controversial.

One of the religious trends of the 1960s that generated and continues to cause controversy has been New Agers' attraction to places sacred to Indian peoples, especially Mount Shasta in Northern California and Sedona, Arizona. Struggles over sacred sites date to the earliest presence of Europeans on the North American continent, but white people's religiously motivated *attraction* to such places did not become common until the 1960s. People of mostly European descent lost their connection to the land of their ancestors with the immigrant generation and only gradually discovered places of power in their new homes. In part, nostalgia for beliefs of the past and attraction to exotic traditions was a yearning for sacred places now absent. New Agers acted to fill this need by resacralizing the landscape with a combination of indigenous myths and stories of UFOs and ancient lost civilizations like Lemuria. Nineteenth-century dowsing, for instance, resurfaced in New Age interest in ley lines, lines of power crisscrossing the earth.

The turn to places where ancient cultures found power is one of many methods by which the counterculture rejected the suburbs and cities of a society they believed had gone mad. Sedona's importance as a New Age site began as early as the 1950s and then grew in the 1960s, largely because of the energy of Mary Lou Keller, a hatha yoga teacher interested in many New Age practices, who helped other groups get established in Sedona, among them Eckankar, the Rainbow Ray focus group, and her own Sedona Church of Light.[47] A variety of New Age interests converged at this small town, including interaction with American Indian sacred sites through medicine wheels, beliefs in UFOs and extraterrestrials, "hot spots" (especially powerful places where energy lines supposedly converge), myths of ancient civilizations, psychics, and channelers. But both Sedona and Mount Shasta became central in contests over meaning as U.S. Forest Service concerns, American Indian access rights, and New Age desire came into conflict at these sites.

Borrowing from Asian religions has not generated the same level of controversy. New Agers and Neopagans have borrowed indiscriminately from Asian traditions, in part because of the availability of Asian religious texts and the presence in the United States from 1965 on of religious teachers from Asia. Some of these teachers founded their own new religions based on Hindu and Buddhist texts and teachings that overlap considerably with ideas of the New Age movement. A.C. Bhaktivedanta Prabhupada (the founder of the Krishna Consciousness movement, or the Hare Krishnas), Bhagwan Shree Rajneesh, Swami Muktananda, and Maharishi Mahesh Yogi (the founder of Transcendental Meditation) are a few of the most famous examples. Concepts of reincarnation and karma, already familiar to Theosophists and Transcendentalists, entered common parlance during the 1960s, even outside the counterculture. An excellent example is Ruth Montgomery's best-selling *Here and Hereafter*, published in 1968. Montgomery was interested in the work of Edgar Cayce, and like him tried to bring together eastern and western teachings, such as meditation practice and Christian prayer. In her foreword Montgomery explains that "the purpose of the book is to emphasize the deep spiritual values to be derived from knowing oneself."[48] The book details several cases of people who recalled past lives, one of them being Edgar Cayce, who believed he had also lived in ancient Egypt.

Movement back and forth between India and the United States deeply enriched the alternative tradition in America. Some European Americans made themselves over into teachers of Asian wisdom. They studied and traveled to India to look for and then live with Indian gurus, returning later to the United States to share what they learned. Foremost among these was Baba Ram Dass (born Richard Alpert). Ram Dass's *Be Here Now*, published by the Lama Foundation in 1971, was one of the first of many books to explain techniques for meditation. In it, Ram Dass describes his life as a driven but successful social scientist at Stanford and Harvard who drove elegant sports cars and oversaw a large office staff. At Harvard he directed the Center for Research in Personality; down the hall from his spacious offices was a converted closet that had been given to Timothy Leary. The two colleagues began spending time together; before long, Leary was experimenting with psychedelics and gave

Ram Dass (then still Richard Alpert) psilocybin (a hallucinogenic derived from a fungus). Wanting to share their powerful psychedelic experience and explore its variations, they gave psilocybin and LSD to many other people as well. Over time, however, Alpert found these psychedelic "trips" unsatisfying because they were temporary. As he put it, "it was a terribly frustrating experience, as if you came into the kingdom of heaven and you saw how it all was and you felt these new states of awareness, and then you got cast out again, and after 2 or 300 times of this, began to feel an extraordinary kind of depression set in."[49] In the early 1960s he came across the *Tibetan Book of the Dead* and was struck by the similarities between states of mind described in the book and his own psychedelic experiences. Many of his friends, including Leary and Beat poet Allen Ginsberg, had gone to India, so Alpert decided to make that journey as well. He sought out various religious teachers, visited Hindu temples and a Buddhist monastery, began learning yoga postures, and finally met a teacher, with whom he studied before returning to the United States. Underlying Ram Dass's descriptions and other New Age approaches to meditation is the assumption that meditation changes consciousness and that such change can bring about healing and spiritual growth. Meditation may also involve contact or interaction with spiritual entities. As the practice encourages consciousness to separate from the physical body, meditators feel that they move into another plane of existence, sometimes called the "astral." It is on this level of consciousness that individuals access spirits, have visions, and discover psychic skills like clairvoyance, all of which became important to Neopagan and New Age religious practice.

If science fiction expanded imaginative frontiers into space, then the emerging drug culture of the 1960s that Ram Dass dabbled in opened the "doors of perception," to borrow Aldous Huxley's phrase, through which inner worlds could be explored. Huxley's *Doors of Perception* and books on psychedelics published in the 1960s by Timothy Leary and others were tremendously popular within the counterculture. Many accounts of psychedelic experimentation during this era emphasized the extent to which drug experiences were religious and not purely recreational. Because of this focus, psychedelic drugs certainly played a part in the emerging New Age and Neopagan communities, which advocated expanded consciousness and self-knowledge. Inward journeys, central to both religions, were for many people initially facilitated by psychedelic experiences. Most New Agers and Neopagans today do not advocate drug use as part of their practice, but as these traditions developed in the 1960s, drugs opened the way for inner exploration and self-transformation.

Timothy Leary's biography suggests that psychedelics played a tremendous role in shaping an attitude toward consciousness and the self that was to become central to the Neopagan and New Age movements. Leary was the prophet of psychedelics throughout the 1960s and until his death in 1999; even very late in his life, he gave a public talk at a Neopagan festival in New York. Among other influences, experimentation with psychedelics led Leary and others to approach spirituality as a journey inward though a kind of geography of the psyche. After Alpert and Leary lost their Harvard jobs for giving LSD to undergraduates (it was legal at the time and they were running clinical tests, but had been told not to include undergraduates), Leary moved to an estate in New York called Millbrook that was owned by wealthy brothers who were the grandsons of Andrew Mellon and heirs to the Mellon family fortune. Millbrook became a commune of sorts and the heart of a revolution in consciousness brought about by psychedelics. Leary, like Huxley before him, saw the drugs as tools for spiritual growth. In the opening lines of his *The Politics of Ecstasy* published in 1968 Leary reports, "Once upon a time, many years ago, on a sunny afternoon in the garden of a Cuernavaca villa, I ate seven of the so-called sacred mushrooms which had been given to me by a scientist from the University of Mexico. During the next five hours, I was whirled through an experience which could be described in many extravagant metaphors but which was, above all and without question, the deepest religious experience of my life."[50] Like many other writers adopted by the sixties counterculture, Leary described psychedelically induced spiritual experience as an alternative to the dominant culture:

> When you turn on, remember: you are not a naughty boy getting high
> for kicks. You are a spiritual voyager furthering the most ancient, noble
> quest of man. When you turn on, you shed the fake-prop TV studio and
> costume and join the holy dance of the visionaries. You leave LBJ and
> Bob Hope; you join Lao-tse, Christ, Blake. . . . To turn on, you need a
> sacrament. . . . A sacrament flips you out of the TV-studio game and
> harnesses you to the 2-billion-year-old flow inside."[51]

"Turning on" was a commonly used 1960s phrase that referred both to the use of psychedelic drugs and more generally to the opening up of one's consciousness to change.

Opening their minds to new possibilities also made many young people willing to believe in aliens and spirit beings, which relayed messages through human channels in the 1960s just as they had to Edgar Cayce, "the sleeping prophet" of the 1930s. These messages were very different in content than those found in organized churches of the time. They spoke directly to a generation of young people who were disenchanted with institutionalized religion and searching for alternative paths to salvation. Channeling, a feature of the alternative spirituality tradition since nineteenth-century spiritualist demonstrations, surged during the 1960s and became a cornerstone of the New Age movement. One of the most successful, if reluctant, channelers was Helen Schucman (1909–1981), a psychologist and daughter of a Theosophist, who received and recorded about 1,200 pages of channeled material between 1965 and 1973. These messages from Schacman's "inner voice," sometimes designated in the text as Jesus of Nazareth, were published as *A Course in Miracles* by the Foundation for Inner Peace in 1976; it provided a series of lessons that combined Christian and Asian religious beliefs in a program that aimed to teach forgiveness and inner peace.

Channeling requires bodies—either divested of spirits or with a consciousness willing to subordinate itself temporarily—through which spirits can speak. But also significant in the 1960s was the revival of attention to diet and physical healing as methods of self-transformation, reminiscent of the various popular healing techniques of the nineteenth century. New diets that included macrobiotics, vegetarianism, and organic foods, to name just a few, became popular. The 1960s return to the body also included a celebration of sensuality and evoked memories of childhood interactions with nature. Esalen was the first community of the 1960s in which spiritual seeking was accompanied by bodywork of various types, including massage therapy. The sensual experience and freedom of being naked was a feature of Esalen's hot tubs, some communes, and other countercultural gatherings. A relaxed attitude toward nudity carried over into the Neopagan movement and to a lesser extent into New Age communities. Nudity has been optional at most Neopagan festivals (where it is called "skyclad") and required for many small Wiccan rituals. It was a statement of health as well as a social protest against and alternative to the dominant culture's attitudes toward the body.

Sensual experience, nudity, and childlike play were central to the countercultural ethic and extolled by 1960s poets and writers.[52] Performers and announcers at Woodstock, for instance, constantly referred to the audience and themselves as "children." In *The Greening of America*, Charles Reich, a law professor at Yale during the turbulent 1960s and early 1970s, argued that "young people were finding new self-affirmation and a reaffirmation of childhood ideals."[53] Reich understood their widespread use of psychedelics as a method of increasing awareness and sensitivity to the world around

them, often resulting in a turn to nature as "the deepest source of consciousness" accompanied by "a desire for innocence, for the ability to be in a state
of wonder and awe."[54] The year 1967 (in which early Neopagan communities Feraferia and the Church of All Worlds were founded) marked the
height of 1960s optimism and innocence, according to sociologist Todd
Gitlin, who claims that "days of rage" followed, with the deaths of concert-
goers at Altamont in 1969 and the murders of Kent State students by National
Guardsmen in 1970. In his analysis of 1960s writers, Morris Dickstein identifies a pervading belief that individuals can shape reality at will and that the
most effective sources for social change are individuals, not institutions.[55]
Many commentators on the legacies of the 1960s agree that these goals failed
and that disillusionment characterized the late 1960s.

Like the counterculture's "sense of wonder at nature," Neopagan festivals later evoked a similar sense of wonder and enchantment, while both
Neopagans and New Agers tended to focus inward, on the inner child as part
of the landscape of the self. The partnership of spiritual and physical exploration that was widespread in the 1960s shaped New Age and Neopagan attention to healing and self-transformation.

Interest in American Indians, ancient Egyptian mythology, science fiction and fantasy, Asian religions, past lives, astrology, aliens, yoga, macrobiotics, explorations in consciousness through psychedelics or meditation, and
communal living were gradually incorporated into movements that are now
recognized as New Age and Neopagan religions. Neopaganism can be dated
to the founding of the Church of All Worlds and Feraferia in 1967, although
it has roots in Victorian magical groups like the Golden Dawn and Gerald
Gardner's books on witchcraft. Rosemary and Raymond Buckland brought
Gardnerian witchcraft to the United States from England, founding their
coven here in 1964. The New Age movement became publicly aware of itself
in the 1970s as a blend of the human potential movement in psychology and
the 1960s counterculture's lifestyle of personal exploration. Added to these
elements were the "light groups" in England that discussed the prophecies of
a new age in the works of Theosophists Blavatsky and Bailey. The important
British New Age community of Findhorn grew out of one of these groups.
Theosophist and channeler David Spangler spent several years in Findhorn
and returned to the United States in 1973 to form a New Age community in
Wisconsin. New scientific ideas, best represented by physicist Fritjof Capra's
best-selling *The Tao of Physics* (1965), also contributed to the emergence of
the New Age movement by combining western scientific theories with eastern religious thought.

During the 1960s and early 1970s the New Age dual emphasis on self-transformation and planetary healing was expressed in the writings of important leaders, gurus, and modern-day prophets as well as in the lives of the communities they spearheaded. They all helped to configure free-floating ideas and practices into a recognizable movement. The teachings of spokesmen for the New Age like David Spangler and Ram Dass were popular in the counterculture of the 1960s and early 1970s, but were not in the general public's awareness. By 1987 the Harmonic Convergence, promoted by Jose Arguelles, and Shirley MacLaine's televised miniseries *Out on a Limb* further spread New Age ideas in the mainstream of American culture. Key among them was the belief that alternatives to the medical model of healing were available for mind and body, and holistic healing converged with New Age spirituality. Healing became a central focus of many Neopagan rituals and a major source of income for New Age psychics and channelers.

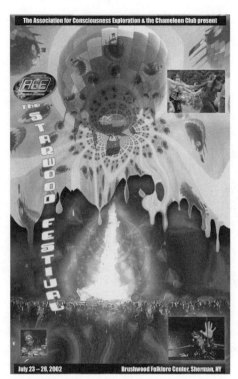

2002 Starwood Festival poster. Courtesy of
Starwood Festival

Priestess Morning Glory of the Church of All Worlds makes a ritual offering
to the Goddess. Courtesy of Oberon & Morning Glory Zell/Mythic Images

A circle dance at the Neopagan Green Spirit festival. COURTESY OF SELENA FOX/CIRCLE SANCTUARY

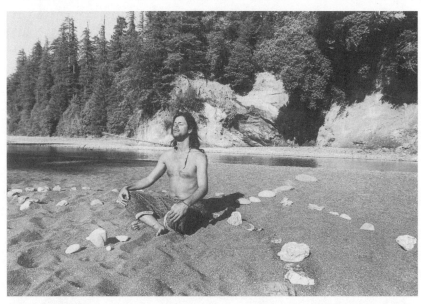

Earth First! member "Sundog" meditates in a medicine wheel of rocks on the banks of the Eel River in Northern California. AP PHOTO

A practitioner of mesmerism puts his client into a trance.

Texas Wiccans celebrate the spring equinox.

Morning Glory (priestess) and Don Jon deClese (priest) at the Nashville Panathenaia. COURTESY OF UBERON & MORNING GLORY ZELL/MYTHIC IMAGES

Actress Shirley MacLaine, author of popular New Age books *Out on a Limb* and *Dancing in the Light,* at her home in Malibu, California in 2000. AP PHOTO

Feminist priestess Z. Budapest, author of *The Holy Book
of Women's Mysteries.*   COURTESY OF Z. BUDAPEST

Gerald Gardner, the founder of contemporary Witchcraft and author of *Witchcraft Today*, at
a wishing well.   COURTESY OF WWW.GERALDGARDNER.COM

Psychic and alternative healer Edgar Cayce.
COURTESY ASSOCIATION FOR RESEARCH AND
ENLIGHTENMENT, INC.

Hippies celebrating the summer solstice at Golden Gate Park in San Francisco in 1967.
AP PHOTO

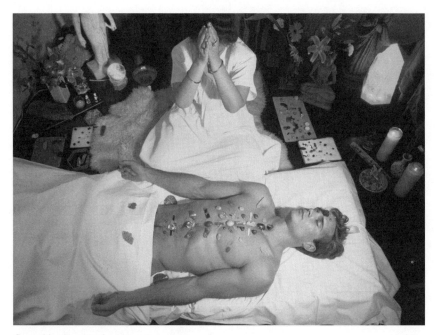

Crystal healing ritual. STONE, GETTY IMAGES

Reiki healing session. COURTESY OF MELINDA RODRIGUEZ, ANGLEZONE.ORG

A group of people drumming at the New Age Ehama Institute. CORBIS

Neopagan organization Circle Sanctuary's maypole dance. COURTESY OF
SELENA FOX/CIRCLE SANCTUARY

**Church of All Worlds handfasting ritual.** COURTESY OF OBERON & MORNING GLORY ZELL/MYTHIC IMAGES

**Altar to Isis at an Isis temple in Geyserville, California.** COURTESY OF OBERON & MORNING GLORY ZELL/MYTHIC IMAGES

Center for the New Age in Sedona, Arizona. COURTESY CENTER FOR THE NEW AGE, SEDONA, AZ

Mount Shasta in Northern California. COURTESY NASA

Aetherius Society UFO believers conducting a prayer ritual.  COURTESY THE AETHERIUS SOCIETY

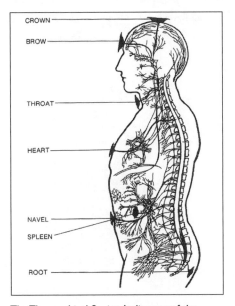

CROWN

BROW

THROAT

HEART

NAVEL

SPLEEN

ROOT

The Theosophical Society's diagram of the seven chakras.  © THE THEOSOPHICAL SOCIETY IN AMERICA

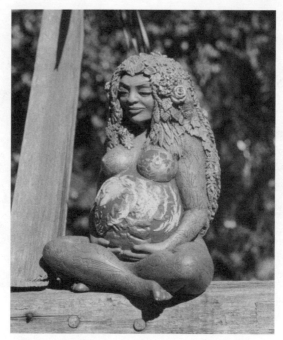

Oberon Zell-Ravenheart's Millennial Gaia goddess figurine.
COURTESY OF OBERON & MORNING GLORY ZELL/MYTHIC IMAGES

Popular Neopagan deity, the
Greek god Pan.

*Part Two*

CHAPTER FIVE

# Healing and Techniques of the Self

At Pagan Spirit Gathering 1993, several hundred people gathered in a large ritual space for the "Village Meeting." Festival organizers made announcements about the day's events and then called for everyone to visualize healing energy going out to those in need. We were asked to send energy to a woman in the hospital with a broken clavicle and to another woman who was pregnant and had planned to be at the festival, but had to stay home, close to the hospital, because her water bag was hanging out of her cervix. Then other names of people in need of healing were called out from the circle. Later that evening, men and women had separate rituals. In the women's ritual three priestesses called on the goddess in each of her three aspects: "maiden, mother, and crone." Women were told they could call to the god silently if they wanted to. The priestesses then enacted a brief performance where they modeled a "healthy mother-child relationship" in the center of the circle. The priestess playing the crone told us, "If your childhood was a bowl of shit instead of a bowl of cherries, respirit it." And she reminded us that as adult women, we are our own "magical mothers." After they closed the circle, a "bubble priestess" blew bubbles to make a portal through which we all passed, after being offered shells for healing if we needed them.

As these examples suggest, healing is a common focus of Neopagan and New Age ritual life, and a ritual's emphasis can vary from healing the planet to healing the "inner child," a part of the self that may carry childhood wounds. Lisa, a Neopagan healer, believes that "the act of healing—be it spiritual healing, emotional healing, the healing of one's own self-esteem as well as the healing of the physical body—is at the root of all magickal disciplines. In many Western ceremonial traditions, magicians work to heal the relationship between the soul and the Universe and in Wicca there is healing of the earth as well as the more conventional healing of the physical body."[1] Neopagans and New Agers tend to agree that one's own healing work must come before healing the planet and other people. According to one Witch, "any occult path is a process of self-healing, of the pursuit of personal wholeness; so that will naturally also be the emphasis of the occultist's or Witch's actions on behalf of other people."[2] Repairing wounds from one's own past and reaching out compassionately to help others heal are seen to go hand in hand. For this reason Witches and Neopagans of all kinds seek out and provide alternative healing methods, such as aura cleansing, herbal remedies, acupuncture, and massage. New Agers are also likely to emphasize the importance of personal healing to global transformation, and to see it as a precondition for ushering in the New Age.

## Constructing a Healing Tradition

Neopagans and New Agers construct healing traditions by blending techniques from anthropological studies of shamanic rites and ancient medical texts with healing traditions from India and China. They seek out American Indian medicine men and take workshops with Peruvian healers. They learn about the properties of herbs and roots and study the teachings of psychics like Edgar Cayce. Healing practices contribute to Neopagans' construction of a historical tradition of marginalized people. Sam, who calls himself a Witch, agrees that healing is "important work . . . I think the origin of the Craft I most resonate to is our forebears who were the herbalists, medicine people, healers and midwives, not the temple religionists. So I learn about edible and medicinal herbs, massage, and often work healing magic of one sort or another."[3] Many Neopagans locate themselves in a lineage of healers and magic practitioners. In his how-to guide, *Buckland's Complete Book of Witchcraft*, Wiccan author Raymond Buckland suggests that contemporary Wiccans are carrying on the tradition of witches as herbal healers: "traditionally Witches have a great knowledge of herbs and their healing properties." He provides a list of herbs to treat common ailments and encourages Witches "as natural healers" to become psychologists, dietitians, and students of anatomy and physiology.[4] Medicine and religion go together for many Neopagans and New Agers, an integration that they believe characterized ancient and indigenous cultures.

Like contemporary Witches, New Agers do not work in a vacuum. They contextualize their healing practice with reference to other psychics and spiritual healers, and if they are channelers, to spirit beings. They also place themselves within traditions of alternative healing and see their special role as bringing about change in the present using ancient techniques. Because they find western medicine lacking, New Agers look to the healing practices of nonwestern cultures. New Agers and Neopagans typically believe that what is missing in western healing practices can be discovered in Asian and indigenous traditions of healing, so they mine available resources on Chinese medicine, shamanic healing, ayurvedic (Indian) medicine, and American Indian herbology. They may claim these traditions for their own when, for example, they turn to American Indian shamans to learn about healing techniques, just as Neopagans claim to be carrying on the legacy of medieval witches: "identification with tribal shamanism holds immense appeal because it conjures up romantic images of sweat lodges, ancient tribal wisdom, and control of mystical powers."[5] In *Planetary Herbology: An Integration of Western Herbs Into the Traditional Chinese and Ayurvedic Systems*, herbalist Michael Tierra describes the ignorance of western herbalism when compared to thousands of years of research and practice behind Chinese and ayurvedic systems of herbal healing.

New Agers and Neopagans look to other cultures for knowledge and legitimacy because they do not have any centralized organization, such as the AMA (American Medical Association), to turn to (although most agree that this is a good thing). Many of them are self-taught; others apprentice with well-known herbalists and psychic healers, or take courses through prominent New Age institutions or occult bookstores. Psychic Francine Bizzari, who practices faith healing and aura and past life readings, was visited by the spirit of her mother, who encouraged her to share her psychic gifts with others. She also consulted the Edgar Cayce Institute (ARE, the Association for Research and Enlightenment) in Virginia Beach, where she was told to further develop her psychic skills with an experienced teacher. After taking a class with a local teacher, she began seeing clients for various kinds of divination as well as healing.

For Bizzari, healing involves cleansing the afflicted person's aura (the subtle energy field around a person's body) using a process that she says removes negative energy. For this purpose she again turns to another authority and uses "holy ashes that she has secured from a mystic practicing in India. . . . She blesses the afflicted person and rubs the ashes on the affected areas. At one of her ritual healings, a woman with a sizable lump on one of her legs came up to the stage. Bizzari put the ashes on the swollen area and claims that the woman awakened the next morning to discover that the lump had vanished."[6] Although Bizzari does not belong to a group such as a coven or an organization such as the Neopagan Circle Sanctuary or the New Age Mind-Body Institute, she does not work in isolation. She places her work as a healer in the tradition of Edgar Cayce, and feels legitimated by the organization that promotes his teachings. But she also draws legitimacy from an ancient and foreign culture in the form of the Hindu mystic's ashes.

Neopagans and New Agers often mix the old with the new. Neopagans turn to European wise women and herbalists of the Middle Ages in their search for an authentic tradition, but they may also be guided by spirit beings of the land where they live. New Agers look to American Indian and Asian cultures for healing techniques, but they also believe that channeled spiritual entities and extraterrestrials advise them. In her work as a healer, Rosemary Altea, author of the *New York Times* best-seller *The Eagle and the Rose* (1996), draws on the wisdom of her spirit guide and "constant companion," an Apache shaman named Grey Eagle.[7] The many channeled entities described in anthropologist Michael Brown's study of contemporary channeling included John the Essene from biblical times, a sixteenth-century Irish pickpocket, a Nubian priest from 1300 B.C., a financial advisor to the pharaohs of ancient Egypt, and beings from distant galaxies. New Age and Neopagan spiritual healing draws on a long and ancient tradition that also includes nineteenth-century chiropractors and osteopaths, who used physical manipulation and herbal treatments to effect healing, and psychics like Edgar Cayce, whose widely varied prescriptions for a range of ailments continue to exert a significant influence in the New Age community. These religious ancestors lend legitimacy to a new movement. Channelers and spiritual healers update and imaginatively blend together archaeology, science fiction, anthropology, messages from spirits, psychic readings, and ancient wisdom to meet the needs of the present.

### Person and Cosmos:
### Historical and Philosophical Foundations of Spiritual Healing

By the 1970s the alternative or holistic health movement had become a network of healers shaped by the 1960s counterculture so that it emphasized changes in consciousness as well as healthy lifestyles. This movement was one aspect of a much larger trend in the 1970s and 1980s that included the emergence of the New Age movement. *The New Holistic Health Handbook: Living Well in a New Age*, published by the Berkeley Holistic Health Center in 1985 (first edition in the mid-1970s), provides an overview and reveals holistic health's close connections with New Age. The book's preface discusses the importance of connections between inner and outer worlds, person and society, human and earth. Holistic health means treating the whole person, notes editor Shepherd Bliss, an approach that has gradually won over many medical practitioners. One of the main shifts from the first edition of the handbook is the inclusion of more medical doctors as authors. In one chapter, David Teegarten, a family practice physician with an M.D. from Stanford Medical School, describes how the experience of healing his own severe back pain changed his view of illness and health. Since that experience, he says, he has come to see the interconnectedness of body, mind, spirit, and world:

> The healing process depends greatly on spirit and on interpersonal relationships. Both holism and general systems theory emphasize the underlying interdependence in the universe. It is healing to be in touch with our spirit and the spiritual process in the world. It is healing to acknowledge, through our behavior and values, our interdependence with people, the community, the environment and the world.[8]

Other physicians who come to this perspective often turn to alternative healing methods when all other treatments have failed.

Holistic health reflects the basic values of the New Age and Neopagan movements, especially in its focus on interconnectedness and its view that the self mirrors society. Starhawk's writings clearly show the Neopagan parallels with holistic healing, as do the writings of many New Agers. In *Dreaming the Dark* and *The Spiral Dance*, Starhawk discusses the ways in which inner life is shaped by society and transforming the self can also transform the world. She instructs readers that "to heal ourselves, to create sustainable culture, we must consider how to meet our needs: the needs of the individual body and of the larger earth-body that encompasses us all."[9] Starhawk and other Neopagan and New Age writers stress the connection between personal and social malaise. They believe that an unsustainable culture is perpetuated by unhealthy individuals who feel isolated from others and carry wounds from past traumas. Holistic healing, then, means taking care of the self and the world, because one cannot be healthy without the other.

Healing practices reveal some of the shared characteristics of New Age and Neopagan cosmologies. In the tradition of nineteenth-century alternative healers, Neopagans and New Agers understand humans to be connected to the rest of the universe in subtle ways. They also turn to the scientific views of contemporary authors to illustrate and defend their understandings. Many New Age books refer to the "new physics" of Fritjof Capra's *The Tao of Physics* (1975) and Gary Zukav's *The Dancing Wu Li Masters* (1979) to give credence to the belief in subtle energy fields. Both authors draw parallels between an emerging paradigm in physics and Asian philosophical and religious understandings of the world, especially the idea of a unifying energy that permeates the universe. Zukav translates the Chinese phrase for physics, *wu li*, as "patterns of organic energy." One of the most significant contributions of the new physics to the New Age movement is its support for the existence of universal patterns and the role of human consciousness in constructing reality. According to Zukav, "Something very exciting is happening. Physicists have 'proved' rationally that our rational ideas about the world in which we live are profoundly deficient."[10] To New Agers the new physics suggests that every element of the universe—human, plant, mineral, animal—is connected. Thus, no action occurs in isolation, but has the potential to influence everything else. Neopagan healer Annette Hinshaw explains it this way: "Think of the universe as a single, highly interconnected body of related energies . . . we may think of the earth as Gaia, a single consciousness in which we are one form of cell. . . . Once you bring this unity and interconnectedness into a comprehensible model, it is a small step to accept that all you have to do to send a healing to another being is to focus on that being."[11] For those New Agers and Neopagans who do not believe in an all-powerful deity, the new physics concept of interconnectedness offers a meaningful way to understand how things happen in the world around them.

New Age and Neopagan healing methods share the assumption that energy forces connect all beings. Sending healing energy, or "nonlocality," as M.D. Larry Dossey calls it, is one of the most common approaches to healing others from a distance. Nonlocal healing can be done in large groups, but also through private prayer and meditation, and it can include healing for specific people or more generally for "the planet" and "future generations." Selena Fox of Circle Sanctuary in Wisconsin has held a monthly healing ritual for years. Anyone can send a request for healing along with a ribbon as an offering to represent their request. Instructions on Circle's Web site specify the kind of ribbon and describe what will happen when Circle receives the ribbon and request: "We will first place them on our healing altar in our temple room so that you will begin receiving spiritual healing support immediately. Later, more healing will be sent your way during the ritual in which your ribbon is added to the sacred Healing Hoop outdoors at Brigid's spring."[12] Fox includes three types of healing in the ritual—self-healing, healing others, and planetary healing—that can be channeled in various ways, "including meditation, laying-on of hands, visualization, dance, chanting, rattle shaking, drumming, and crystal work. But whatever the ritual technique we use, the power behind our healing is the same—the power of Love, which is the greatest magic there is."[13] This list of possible techniques is typical of Neopagan and New Age eclecticism. Both movements avoid orthodoxy: there is no one right way to do things, and whatever works, as long as it is done with "love" or positive energy, is generally tolerated.

### Self-Healing and the Role of the Healer

A common approach to healing among Neopagans and New Agers is the ritual or workshop that involves some kind of internal process intended to heal emotional wounds from the past as well as current psychological problems and physical ailments. During these healing sessions "energy work" is not directed outward to others in need, but rather is internalized to make changes within the self. The "womb ritual" at the Neopagan gathering Rites of Spring was this kind of rite. Open to men and women, it focused on a guided meditation during which participants were asked to recall emotional and physical traumas from their pasts. The workshop culminated in a rebirthing process during which each participant passed through a "vagina" formed by the others, who created a difficult passageway by linking arms and holding tight as the person being reborn tried to move through. At the end of the ritual everyone discussed what, if anything, had changed inside them.

Neopagan festivals and New Age retreats often include rituals and workshops geared toward inner transformation, such as "Pagan Meditation: The Inner Work of the Old Ways," "Guided Shamanic Journey," and "Metamorphosis: An Approach to Addressing Prenatal Patterns and Means of Change." ELF Fest 1991 held a "Descent of Persephone" evening ritual that included a blindfolded journey into dark woods to encounter the "goddess within." The ritual facilitator instructed every participant to bring a small token of some aspect of their lives they wanted to cast away, and they were given a chance to do so later in the ritual. In turn, they were given a coin to symbolize what they brought out of the underworld to enrich and transform their lives. As participants moved through various stages of the ritual, they were acting out internal emotional struggles over relationships, work, abuse in their pasts, and sickness. Neopagan and New Age rituals heal by external-izing suffering and loss and helping individuals to process painful aspects of their lives within a supportive group setting.

Another common type of healing practice in New Age and Neopagan communities is the healer-client relationship. The healer may possess one or more special gifts, such as therapeutic touch or clairvoyance, that he or she draws on for diagnosis and/or healing. Ananga, a scientist and university professor as well as an accomplished healer, describes his approach:

> I sit quietly by the subject, relax, and open my mind up to the forces around me. There is a great and wonderful power there, call it anything you like. I invoke this with prayer and envisage it channeling down through the top of my head and spreading through my body. I gently touch the sufferer with finger tips of both hands and envisage the force travelling down my arms' and into the other's body. If I know the pain source I try to see within my mind the contents of the cells in the affected area being affected by the force, mitochondria absorbing positive en-ergy, etc. . . . A tingling starts in my fingertips and a strange but pleasant feeling begins in the palms of my hands. I let the process proceed until I get the feeling it is enough . . . the whole process usually takes just min-utes, I withdraw my hands and extend thanks and that's it.

Ananga described himself as "a reluctant healer" who only slowly became convinced that his healing touch had an effect and that "the solid rock of sci-ence I'd stood on for years was highly porous."[14] His comments echo the ex-periences of many spiritual healers who were unsure at first of their own gifts, or what they perceived to be "unscientific" techniques.

One important distinction between Neopagan and New Age healers is that Neopagans usually, though not always, are adamant that no money should exchange hands where healing is concerned. New Agers are much more likely to charge for their services in typical provider-client relation-ships, and Neopagans who make their living as chiropractors, acupuncturists, or massage therapists usually also charge a fee, whereas those who do psychic readings, for instance, usually do not.

Some Neopagan and New Age healers believe that the efficacy of their practice comes from the gift of being able to travel to the spirit world and speak with spirits. New Age healer Rosemary Altea, in *The Eagle and the Rose*, shares stories of the clients she healed by talking to their departed loved ones in the spirit world and consulting her spirit guide. A colleague brings to her a young man who has repeatedly attempted suicide. By traveling to the spirit world and speaking to his mother and grandmother, she discovers that his suffering is a direct result of his mother's bitterness toward his father. Repeatedly hearing the message that men are evil, he hates himself, but when Altea tells him what she discovered about his past, she sets him on a path to recovery. The "casebooks" she lists in her books describe her problem-solving approach to healing. By speaking with spirits of dead loved ones, she finds the hidden stories behind her clients' problems. Like rituals that allow participants to transform painful past experiences, Altea provides a narrative framework in which her clients come to understand and heal wounds from the past.

## Illness and Its Causes

Neopagans and New Agers believe that minor ailments are a sign of larger afflictions, including isolation from other people, the earth, and spiritual truth. Neopagan writer and healer Kenneth Deigh believes that many people experience a "wound of separation, of alienation from our essential and primordial Self. It constantly reminds us, at a level so deep that we can rarely hear it consciously, that we are alone. . . . My own life work has been about healing this wound, and about helping others to heal as well."[15] According to Deigh, the key to healing this wound is self-knowledge that allows us to discover "the place where we are all One. This is where we begin to explore real connectedness. On the inner planes this is done by connecting with nonordinary entities. On the outer planes, by practicing stillness with like-minded people."[16] Like many other New Age and Neopagan healers, Deigh stresses the importance of connecting with others, which can be done through ritual and in healer-client relationships. Gatherings like festivals, retreats, weekend workshops, and channeling sessions facilitate healing by bringing together like-minded people.

Theories of the causes of illness are varied among New Agers and Neopagans, but tend to be of two kinds. The first derives from the nineteenth-century alternative healers who believed that people become ill when the body's natural energy flow is blocked. The blockages can have many different causes, but frequently they are seen to result from trauma and abuse in childhood, a common theme in many Neopagan and New Age workshops and rituals. For those who see illness this way, "We have the greatest healing effect on the world when we allow the life force to move through our own bodies. Our power comes not simply from what we say or do. Rather, our words and actions are vehicles for our life energy. What really transforms is the life force moving through us."[17] No one agrees on the best way to remove the blockages, so New Agers and Neopagans use such self-treatments as herbs, yoga, ritual, fasts, and special diets, or they seek out Reiki practitioners and other healers who move energy around by laying their hands on people's bodies.

Others see illness as a symptom of "spirit out of place . . . caused by spiritual and emotional imbalance."[18] At its extreme, this view holds the individual responsible for his or her illness. Seth, a disembodied entity channeled by psychic medium Jane Roberts, believes that we create our own illnesses: "We form physical reality as a replica of our inner ideas. . . . You create your own difficulties. . . . What we are supposed to do, then, is change our mental attitude, search ourselves for the inner problem represented by the symptoms, and measure our progress as the symptoms subside."[19] According to Seth's messages, transcribed by Roberts's husband, physical illness and pain are "communications from our inner self" that are telling us to look within for the root of the problem.[20] Many people locate the origin of their search for self-transformation in an illness or trauma caused by a serious accident or struggle with substance abuse, while others changed their lives when they first picked up a book that shook their taken-for-granted world, such as Shirley MacLaine's *Dancing in the Light* or the channeled teachings called *A Course in Miracles*. It makes sense to many New Agers that if illness is caused by spiritual imbalance, or "spirit out of place," then healing should be accomplished through spiritual means.

Another important way that illness is understood is as a challenge that humans can meet productively. According to the editor of *The New Holistic Health Handbook*, disease is "an important feedback message to be dealt with consciously as part of the life process, not as a victimization by a hostile nature."[21] In this view, suffering and inner chaos provide opportunities for personal growth. Psychologist Jean Houston, co-director of the Foundation for Mind Research, claims that "we live in self-created chaos to hasten our own meeting with ourselves." In workshops and classes Jean always asks her students what she calls "the great and terrible question, 'where and by whom were you wounded? What or who is trying to be born in you from that wound?'" For many New Agers and Neopagans, what they can make of past and current crises determines the extent of their healing and self-growth. Workshops, seminars, and rituals as well as consultations with spiritual healers and body workers can only help along a process that must be carried out by each individual. Wounds and traumas almost become an expectation. Participants in healing workshops are encouraged to dig deep into their pasts, and if they do not find anything that needs healing they may be seen as self-deluded. Most New Agers and Neopagans view contemporary American culture itself as deeply troubled and assume most of us have been affected by the problems around us. From this perspective poverty, violence, power imbalances, and environmental devastation are reflected in the suffering of individual lives. If suffering is then alleviated and given meaning on a personal level through a healing process, society can also be changed.

## Alternative Healers and the Medical Establishment

In their recognition of the need for connection and community, holistic and spiritual healers understand the causes of illness differently from standard medical practitioners. But New Agers and Neopagans do not always reject the medical approach, and increasingly work in tandem with it. According to the famous "Witch of Salem" Laurie Cabot, "magic and medicine should and can work hand in hand."[22] But since the nineteenth century a great divide has existed between western orthodox medicine and alternative healing practices. As the medical establishment became increasingly institutionalized in the early twentieth century, a stricter boundary was drawn between accepted techniques and unorthodox practices such as herbal treatments and healing methods involving unseen energies or spirits.

Alongside the emergence of the New Age movement in the 1970s, medical practice changed to include alternative therapies like acupuncture and prayer. Typically, medical doctors addressed specific symptoms and viewed the body as a machine whose parts could be fixed to keep the whole functioning smoothly. But gradually some physicians questioned the limitations of this approach to healing and, often through their own personal experiences of illness and suffering, came to agree with the New Age view that body, mind, and spirit are interconnected. Small numbers of physicians concluded that illness could not always be explained through mechanical metaphors, that emotional and spiritual factors in illness were as important as physical ones. Some psychiatrists were more willing to support alternative therapies, but it took physicians who identified with the most scientific aspects of medicine, such as surgeon Bernie Siegel, to shift medical thinking in new directions during the 1980s and 1990s. Additionally, they began to encounter (as a result of immigration changes from 1965 on) physicians from India and China, where alternative healing techniques are common. Siegel was the most highly visible physician to come on the New Age scene in the 1980s. His observations of self-healing in cancer patients led him to believe in such "miracles." His book *Love, Medicine and Miracles: Lessons Learned About Self-Healing from a Surgeon's Experience with Exceptional Patients* (1986) instructs readers that miracles come about by "finding your authentic self and following what you feel is your own true course in life."[23] Siegel describes numerous cases of healing facilitated through touch, prayer, relaxation, and visualization techniques, or sharing emotions with other people. Throughout the book he argues that the mind and emotions have powerful effects on physical health, and that healing is best accomplished not by the individual alone, but in partnership with physicians and support groups. We need others, agrees Edward C. Whitmont, M.D. in his book, *The Alchemy of Healing*, because "our capacity for healing ourselves is limited" and other people "provide us with human channels of energy, bridges to the Self-field." For Whitmont, healing is part of human existence because "we wound our earth, we interfere with its vital functioning and, as our consciousness of self and world gradually increases, we also strive to heal these wounds."[24] In the decade and a half following Siegel's groundbreaking book, other physicians changed their thinking about the meaning of health and illness.

Other books by medical doctors include Larry Dossey's *Recovering the Soul* (1989) and *Reinventing Medicine: Beyond Mind-Body to a New Era of Healing* (1999). As the title of the second book suggests, Dossey, like many New Agers, looks to the coming of a new era, which he calls "Era III." He believes that Era I was characterized by "mechanical medicine," the dominant medical paradigm since the nineteenth century, followed by Era II, "Mind-Body Medicine," which developed out of studies of "psychosomatic diseases" in individuals. Era III, however, deemphasizes the individual and promotes an understanding of consciousness as energy that links people together. Dossey began to develop his theories of the different eras when he experienced a sequence of dreams over several days. He had an unusually vivid dream about the young son of one of his colleagues at the hospital where he worked. The following day he watched in shock as the dream came true: "It was as if the world had suddenly decided to reveal a new side of itself, for reasons I could not fathom."[25] Consequently, he investigated research being done in scientific and medical settings on the connections between mind and body, and over time he became a visionary and prominent healer blending orthodox medicine with spiritual healing.

Many New Age thinkers agree with Dossey that human beings are evolving through stages of spiritual development that shape their views on medicine and healing. Peg Jordan, health author and former health reporter for radio station KTVU in San Francisco, reports on "seven shifts" that separate the New Age from previous eras. One of these is the shift from allopathic medicine (a symptom-treating approach) to "integrative healing," another label for a holistic approach in which body, mind, spirit, and earth are seen to be intricately connected.[26] Views of this type are common among New Agers, but not as typical of Neopagans, whose interest in reviving ancient religions necessitates a less evolutionary idea of history. Although New Age healing techniques borrow from ancient cultures, they are seen as part of an evolving new age of consciousness that will carry humans into the future.

Self-healing and the shift from orthodox to alternative methods can take several different forms among New Agers and Neopagans. The first is a sudden conversion experience or rift between the old and new self, often brought about by a healing crisis. Many New Agers, and less typically Neopagans, describe such an experience that then sets them on a healing trajectory and results in major life changes, such as choosing a new profession or moving to a different part of the country. The conversion event sets in motion the second type of healing experience, which is a long process of self-transformation that involves not simply getting rid of physical symptoms but profoundly altering one's sense of self and place in the world.

But not everyone in American society is ready for these shifts. Controversies over alternative healing treatments have plagued the New Age movement from the start. By the beginning of the twenty-first century, alternative healing traditions had gained a foothold in the medical establishment, just as New Age ideas had become more prevalent in the broader culture. However, orthodox medical wisdom about health and illness still prevailed in major hospitals and in most medical practices across the United States. Web sites for New Age organizations like the Association for Research and Enlightenment ask readers to check a disclaimer stating that they are not seeking medical help before they enter the "health pages," which include descriptions of different therapies Cayce prescribed for specific ailments. Controversies about the medical application of herbal remedies have resulted in charges of practicing medicine without a license, and the Federal Drug Administration (FDA) has been urged to submit herbs and supplements to the same kinds of rigorous testing required for drugs. Alternative healers exercise caution where legal liability is concerned, and New Agers and other Americans seeking alternative healing are sometimes surprised when they are persecuted for following religious and philosophical positions that are not widely accepted.

Social scientist Fred M. Frohock details many examples of persecution in his book *Healing Powers*, including the case of Caleb Loverro. Like many alternative healers, chiropractor Joseph Loverro believed that the body heals itself if any interference in the body's energy flow is removed. When his son Caleb was diagnosed with leukemia, he and his wife initially cooperated with the chemotherapy prescribed by their pediatrician, but then discontinued it because they felt the side effects were damaging their son and further weakening his system. They also objected to the ways in which Caleb's treatments were the same as for all other patients with leukemia; no effort was made to tailor them to his individual needs, as an alternative healer would do. In consultation with a naturopathic doctor, they tried a macrobiotic diet and homeopathy. But the original physician overseeing Caleb's case was concerned when the parents told him what they were doing and contacted county officials. The parents were arrested for child endangerment and their son put into state custody. Charges were later dropped and their son returned home when the Loverros agreed to bring him in for regular chemotherapy treatments. This dispute, like many others involving the treatment of minors, is about different understandings of health and illness and different views of reality. Following Siegel's and Dossey's alternative approaches to illness, other physicians adopt alternative therapies while they continue to advocate appropriate use of standard medical approaches. New Agers who seek to replace established medical traditions with spiritual healing continue to find their choices challenged on legal and moral grounds.[27] Even with the support of some physicians, spiritual and other alternative forms of healing continue to arouse suspicion and opposition.

## Healing Techniques

Because they see illness as a blockage of life force and a symptom of spiritual malaise, New Agers and Neopagans design healing techniques to help the spirit as well as the body. A host of possible treatments includes herbs and tonics, personal and group rituals, and visits to specialists in such methods as crystal healing and body work. New Agers and Neopagans try sound, art, crystal, and color therapies as well as Reiki (a Japanese technique of laying on of hands), Feldenkrais (gently changing habitual movements), rolfing (body work involving manipulation of deep tissue between bone joints), and yoga. New Agers carry on the belief of Edgar Cayce and others that the body can heal itself. According to the health page of Cayce's Association for Research and Enlightenment's Web site,

> Our cells' ability to renew and regenerate themselves is the most fundamental of universal laws and, according to the readings [Cayce's com-

munications during trance], is the first principle of spiritual forces. Our bodies contain within them the pattern to be whole and are continuously trying to achieve that pattern. Far from being a passive victim to disease, the human body can rally its healing forces and repair itself with more vigor than the world's best-trained medical team. . . . Healing requires "attuning each atom . . . to the awareness of the divine that lies within each atom, each cell of the body."[28]

Most New Age and Neopagan healing techniques function under this assumption that humans contain within themselves the power to heal and that health is their natural state; they just need help to return to it.

For example, using the aura to diagnose and treat illness is a common approach among Neopagans and New Agers. In *Buckland's Complete Book of Witchcraft*, Raymond Buckland discusses herbal healing and auric healing in his ritual instructions for Wiccan students. Reminiscent of nineteenth-century mesmerists who identified what they saw as magnetic energy running through all living beings, Buckland defines the aura as "the electrical magnetic energy that emanates from the human body" and is also present in plants and animals. Buckland instructs his students to do auric healing by visualizing a certain color of light around the person. He links specific colors with specific problems: "to invigorate you'd use grass green. To inspire, yellows and oranges. . . . For someone with a nervous headache, see their head surrounded by violet or lavender light." He also gives instructions for color healing (using colored glass or plastic), gem therapy (using precious and semiprecious stones), and pranic healing (directing the body's life force to afflicted sites of the body).[29] In Buckland's view, Witches should be familiar with some of these healing techniques and prepared to draw on their knowledge to help others in need.

A common stereotype of New Agers is of "crystal-gazers," but New Agers and Neopagans take their crystals seriously. Crystal healer Daya Sarai Chocron believes that "we are now living in an era of great cleansing and purifying for everyone. . . . The crystals and stones are the catalysts that bring about the purification."[30] Crystals and gemstones come in different colors that can be applied to specific ailments and for some healers are related to astrological signs. New Agers also use "chromotherapy" (color therapy) with auric or crystal healing to clear blockages in the energy flow through the body that they believe cause ill health. After learning about healing from her experiences with trance channelers J. Z. Knight and Kevin Ryerson, Shirley MacLaine wrote that, "we can all learn to heal ourselves simply by visualizing colors. Each color has the power to set loose higher vibrations in our consciousness that can heal ailments of various parts of the body: blue for the problems in the throat, orange for the liver, green for the heart, yellow for the solar plexus and so on." New Agers believe that the universal white light of spiritual energy enters humans through their auras and spreads into the seven *chakras* (the Hindu term for spiritual energy centers in the body), each identified with a different color: "Red, orange, yellow, green, blue, indigo, and violet thus correspond to the seven *chakras* located along the spinal column. Any technique that can aid us in activating the proper flow of light through our various *chakras* can thereby stimulate the healing process."[31]

New Agers and Neopagans who follow holistic healing practices respond to illness with a mix of physical and spiritual techniques. They may address short-term physical suffering such as a broken bone or head cold by combining alternative therapies with visits to medical doctors. Short-term healing does not necessarily involve soul-searching work, but rather the direct application of herbs, crystals, flower remedies, therapeutic touch, etc. Janet Farrar, co-author of *The Life and Times of a Modern Witch*, suffered from recurrent shoulder pain that was cured after her coven performed a healing ritual for her: "We sat in the Circle, and Stewart [her husband] put his hands on the painful part. Two other coven members put their hands on Stewart's back, with more behind them with their hands on the couple's backs. We used this 'pyramid' to pour power through Stewart into Janet. The pain ebbed and ceased, and did not recur."[32] Even though this hands-on healing ritual was directed at a specific problem, it is one of many stories shared among New Agers and Neopagans that shore up their belief in healing energy and the efficacy of collective ritual work.

Blocked energy can be released through visualization and meditation, or may require other treatments such as massage or acupuncture. Shirley MacLaine describes her visit to an acupuncturist who explains this view: "Your body is holding certain memories that you need to release. I will place the needles at meridian points that will facilitate the release. . . . Every cell in your body is holding the energy of experience, not only from this lifetime, but from every lifetime." The acupuncturist consults her spirit guides, who instruct her on how to proceed. As the needles go in, MacLaine experiences mild pain. The acupuncturist feels some scar tissue and asks MacLaine about it. The scar tissue was located where she had a cancerous growth removed some years before. Then the acupuncturist suggests that the scar tissue might have caused the cancer rather than vice versa: "the growth probably came as a reaction to a memory the body was still holding in that area. The body remembers everything. The soul imprint is on every single cell in the body. We carry the memory into each incarnation and those memories need to be resolved and cured if we are to go on to a higher enlightenment."[33] She uses the needles to help the body remember and thus releases the trauma associated with old memories. Once the needles are in place, MacLaine goes into a state of deep relaxation and allows pictures to come into her mind. Many different images come to her, including several of her mother, but she also sees a crystal pyramid in what she guesses is the ancient civilization of Atlantis. The image of a storm then comes to her and she learns that in a former lifetime she could control the weather but had abused her power. Healing techniques of this sort help Neopagans and New Agers to explore past lives as well as to deal with current problems. As in MacLaine's case, therapeutic responses to physical ailments may raise spiritual and emotional issues.

The Farrars' and MacLaine's healing stories suggest that ritualized therapies and ritual experience are conducive to healing. Rituals allow people to separate from daily routines and experience altered states of consciousness. One significant, though not hard and fast, difference between New Age and Neopagan healing rituals is that Neopagans are more likely to mark sacred space and include props and costumes. They pay careful attention to creating a safe and consecrated space in which ritual work can be done. The priest, priestess, ritual facilitator, or individual celebrant (if the ritual is done alone) will cast a circle by calling in deities and/or the powers of the four directions. Neopagans typically invoke the elements associated with each direction (west/water, north/earth, east/air, and south/fire). Many American Wiccans and Neopagans have adopted Starhawk's version of a circle casting described in her classic, *The Spiral Dance*. For the direction of south, for example, she suggests the following:

> *Hail, Guardians of the watchtowers of the South,*
> *Powers of Fire!*
> *We invoke you and call you,*
> *Red Lion of the noon heat,*
> *Flaming One!*
> *Summer's warmth,*
> *Spark of life,*
> *Come!*
> *By the fire that is Her spirit,*
> *Send forth your flame,*
> *Be here now!*[34]

The priest, priestess, or ritual participants address the powers of the other three directions in a similar fashion, reciting a prepared text or improvising.

Neopagans believe that casting a circle creates a protected space where energy and power are concentrated and more easily channeled into ritual work. Incense, candles, salt, a chalice of water, and gestures made with wands, swords, or the *athame* (ritual dagger) may be included in the circle casting. Often a ritual bath or purification with salt water is done beforehand. Once the circle is cast and the space made sacred, ritual participants have the feeling of being outside ordinary space and time. As Starhawk sees it, sacred space is "'between the worlds' of the seen and unseen, of flashlight and starlight consciousness, a space in which alternate realities meet, in which the past and future are open to us. . . . Within the circle, the powers within us, the Goddess and the old Gods, are revealed."[35] For Neopagans, sacred space facilitates contact with divine powers, whether these are seen as aspects of consciousness or separate spiritual entities. When participants are in this space, accompanied by divine beings, healing begins.

Because of the influence of feminism and the predominance of women in many Neopagan groups, rituals often address the suffering caused by rape and sexual abuse. Such rituals usually provide "a womb-like space in the center of the circle, an attempt to find ways to affirm the goodness of the body, and awareness that complete wholeness is rarely if ever achieved instantaneously."[36] Stories of healing wounds from physical or sexual violence abound in New Age and Neopagan communities where women are prominent participants. Margot Adler facilitated a workshop on defining "Witch" at a Pagan festival and later received a letter in the mail from one of the participants, a woman named Oreithyia, describing the kinds of rituals that define "Witch" for her. She explains that women join in circles "to celebrate the turn of the seasons; to pour handfuls of rich, brown earth over a map of nuclear waste dumps, missile silos, and power plants" and goes on to describe a ritual designed to heal, cleanse, and comfort a woman who had been raped:

> Women who have sat together, pained and fierce, calling the wind, asking Her aid, sweeping up, in great gentle swirls the dirt and degradation and fear clinging to the woman in that circle's center, the woman who, three days before, had been attacked on the mid-afternoon country roadside as she jogged along. Again and again the wind came up, the house fairly sang with the force of it moving through the gaps in the clapboard siding; the women sang the wind's song to add to their strength. It was a howl of pain, a howl of mourning. It moved and grew.

It became a song of fury, an Amazon battle call, the sound of the sacred axe swung round and round to turn the tide. The sound, and the constant evocation, invocation, incantation of the one who, for this night, in this place, for this purpose, wrapped herself in indigo, taking on the mask of the dark Mother.

For many Neopagans, a "dark goddess" is one aspect of divinity, a force of anger and power that is available to give women strength and to make them feel empowered in disempowering situations. She is sometimes pictured as Kali, a fierce Hindu goddess who wears skulls around her neck, a part played during this ritual by one of the participants. Oreithyia explains how the gathering healed and cleansed the woman in the center:

> Together, the wind and the Women and the dark One, together they lifted off layer upon layer of filth. Together they called to the woman who was at its center, together they forged the fury and the love that coursed through the pain, transforming what had been rendered numb back into wholeness and self-respect. What had been broken they began to heal. The power for the healing rested where it belonged, in the person of she who must be healed. The ritual went on a while longer. There was tea for the woman in the center, and soft, strong arms to hold her. More than one breast to rest against. More than one set of hands to rub her back, massage her shoulders, catch her tears, see her safely to sleep.[37]

Although the collective presence of the group and the aid of the goddess they called generated the energy for the ritual, in the end power was returned to the victim. New Agers and Neopagans look to healers and spiritual beings outside the self to help them unblock or redirect healing energy, but they usually bring ultimate responsibility for health back to the individual. Neopagans point out that in this, they diverge from religions like Christianity that place ultimate responsibility with God (although some New Agers and Neopagans also believe that an outside force or god has an effect on health and illness). The ritual Oreithyia described set in motion a powerful and transformative experience and then grounded it in the familiar comforts of tea and touch. The healing process was helped along by sacred space, a cathartic performance involving a deity, and the support of a group to channel and focus the energy raised.

Ritual space, altars, ritual tools, participants dressed as deities, mediums channeling entities—all of these offer a way to leave the everyday world and participate for a time in another reality. For Neopagans and New Agers, these ritual elements are tools available to people who want to make changes in their lives. It is in the space and time of the other reality that participants say their healing process begins or something in their life shifts. Rituals often mark the beginning of a spiritual journey or become episodes in a larger narrative of healing.

## Healing Narratives

In the process of healing mind and body, New Agers and Neopagans construct narratives of the self, ordered accounts of how they came to be who they are now and explanations for the troubles in their lives. They share stories of how healing has reversed the effects of past suffering and moved them along in their journey of transformation.

In his extensive interviews with psychics, social scientist Fred Frohock observed that "the standard opening in psychic narratives usually involves the healer as a gifted or extraordinary child." The biographies and memoirs of psychics and spiritual healers suggest that many of them went through some kind of crisis before they were able to draw on their gifts. They may have had their first psychic experiences as children but were afraid to tell anyone. Reluctant to admit that they had healing powers, they kept silent for fear of being ostracized or ridiculed. Psychic healer Edgar Cayce exemplified this pattern: he suffered from debilitating headaches for many years, and in a trance state he diagnosed and prescribed a treatment for his own illness. Like some New Age healers, at first he did not take credit for his success. He saw himself as an instrument for energy or "God" to work through, just as channelers believe that they are the mouthpieces for other beings and that the information that comes through their mouths is not really theirs. At first Cayce was hesitant to help other people and to take responsibility for curing them because he did not trust himself. He consulted neighboring physicians and had them compare his diagnoses to their own. And he occasionally wondered whether his gifts came from God or the devil. But people came to him as a last resort and over many years his confidence grew, in part because he had successfully treated his own health crisis.

Anna, who holds public channeling events in upstate New York, also went through a major health crisis on her way to becoming a successful medium. After graduating from college she experimented with several alternative religions, including two New Thought religions: the Church of Religious Science and the Unity Church. She also learned to meditate and read several of Jane Roberts's Seth books. She had constant health problems, including severe allergies that almost killed her at one point. Her doctors told her there was nothing they could do: "They said that I should move to the desert and live in a stainless steel trailer." So Anna said to "the God-head . . . 'Either heal me or take me because I can't stand living like this' . . . and that night I totally surrendered. When I woke I knew that there was eternal life." After this experience her allergies cleared up. Anna believed that beings called "The Wise Ones" had come to her during the night, so she developed her channeling practice to help others by transmitting messages from these beings.[38] In New Agers' and Neopagans' autobiographical narratives, experiences of this sort sometimes marked the beginning of a journey of personal growth and healing on a deeper level after the immediate problem was solved. The crises described by New Agers often involve the dynamic of doubt and surrender, a characteristic of religious conversion narratives in many other traditions.

In their stories of illness and healing, Neopagans and New Agers stress the centrality of self-knowledge. They say that the inner realms of the self are the locus for healing work. Healing stories describe pulling apart the self and putting it back together. The work may be done with both spiritual (visualization and meditation) and physical (massage therapy or acupuncture) techniques, but it is always a kind of archaeology that involves excavating the inner landscape and exploring its previously hidden facets. This understanding of self is shaped by psychoanalytic views of layered selves and mystical traditions that emphasize searching within to find god or enlightenment. Neopagans and New Agers say that during or because of this excavation process, lasting changes come about in their lives. According to anthropologist Don Handelman, "Radical personal change, self-transformation occurs when the person takes himself apart (or is taken apart), thereby opening the way to possible reconfigurations of existential being, of selfness."[39] The belief that everyone needs to engage in this tumultuous process makes New Age healing somewhat different from nineteenth-century alternative healing. For New Agers and other Americans who came to adulthood during the consciousness-raising days of the late 1960s and 1970s, the needs of the self come first, and individual health is a benchmark for the health of society. Although the self is seen as part of an interconnected world, there is also a sense that "the healer inside us" is empowered to make the healing process work, as in the ritual for healing rape described earlier. Other people and spiritual beings can offer support, but ultimately the healing process must work within the sick or suffering person.

New Age and Neopagan healing techniques, then, usually involve a journey of self-exploration. If the self is pulled apart and explored, if self-growth comes from taking life's challenges and using them as opportunities for self-transformation, then the story of that transformation is of great importance. New Agers and Neopagans share accounts of how they explored and reconstituted the self, and these contribute to their healing work and create richness in their religious lives. According to Neopagan author Marian Green, "the magical journey of inner exploration" maps "an uncharted country."[40] New Agers and Neopagans believe that consciousness is infinite and that the land within can never be completely covered or completely known. As spiritual teacher Shakti Gawain puts it, "the journey of consciousness is a spiral. We move in cycles, but each cycle takes us to a deeper level."[41] The discovery of divinity within the self, of spirit guides, of deity or ultimate truth may play a part in the journey. Gawain goes so far as to preach "disarmament" of the self, which she understands to be a "nation-state."[42] For her, everything that exists outside can also be found within. To address violence in society, violence in the self must be recognized and explored.

Because illness challenges one's sense of identity and undermines one's reality, healing narratives provide coherent form for the chaos of illness and suffering and weave together fragments of the past, which may include past lives as well as childhood in the current lifetime. New Agers and Neopagans recall stories of past lives in ritual, under hypnosis, through the messages of channeled beings, and in dreams. Memories are reconstructed to fit healing narratives as individuals understand the past through the lens of the present.[43]

Neopagans and New Agers believe that self mirrors society. According to Don Handelman, "healing does the repair and synthesis of the world, the renewal of entropy, the re-articulation of social relationships—and also does all of these analogously within the 'microcosm' of the person."[44] The ancient tradition of correspondences, of harmony between micro- and macrocosm that was promoted by Emmanuel Swedenborg and his philosophical grandchildren, such as the New Thought movement, is shared by the New Age and Neopagan communities and clearest in the area of healing practices. Holistic and spiritual healers often assert that the balance of the world hinges on personal health. Only by effecting the changes in consciousness necessary for a new kind of future can humans make any kind of progress. Marina Raye believes that "We must do the profound inner homework of healing our emotions for our personal evolution and for raising humanity's collective consciousness. Every issue that we process and heal on an individual level produces transformative change on a planetary level."[45] The New Age, then, requires both personal growth and planetary healing; if that age has already arrived, then healing work is one of its most appropriate components.

# CHAPTER SIX

# "All Acts of Love and Pleasure Are My Rituals"

## Sex, Gender, and the Sacred

Due to the influence of two important historical movements—feminism and sexual liberation—Neopagans and New Agers often focus on gender and sexuality as sites where healing and personal/social transformation are most needed and can be most effective. They believe that in our troubled contemporary culture, everyone is damaged and needs to be repaired, and nowhere is this more true than in these areas. They diagnose and offer remedies for the historical causes of gender inequality and sexual repression. Because New Agers and Neopagans believe that Christianity has debased sex and the body and made them sinful aspects of human experience, they elevate sexuality in all its forms. Because they believe rigid gender roles and traditional religions are responsible for much of what is wrong between men and women and within each person, they have formed religious communities that offer ways to transform thinking about gender and sexuality. Their rituals and healing practices explore gender dynamics and aim to change imbalances of power and abusive behavior. Workshops and rituals exploring masculinity and femininity, celebrating sacred sexuality, healing sexual wounds, and overcoming destructive gender conditioning are common at Neopagan and New Age events.

Since the emergence of the New Age and Neopagan movements in the 1970s, gender roles and sexuality have become increasingly important sites of self-growth and spiritual exploration. The sexual liberation movement of the 1960s aimed to make sex a healthy and open aspect of human experience; Neopagans and New Agers took it one step further by placing sexuality in the realm of the sacred. They have reconstructed histories of ancient goddess-worshipping matriarchies, borrowed sacred sex techniques from Tibetan Tantric traditions, embodied gods and goddesses in ritual, and reclaimed roles previously seen as negative, such as the "sacred prostitute." This experimentation included much creative thought and practice but also led to confusion, especially as masculinity and femininity were disconnected from biological sex. A world of possibilities opened to participants in these new communities, but so did the potential to make mistakes. Along the way, many Neopagan and New Age groups discovered that the full realization of human potential was not immediate but entailed long, hard work. They do this work because they believe that healing the self through changing practices and perceptions of gender and sexuality will bring about broader changes in socialization and gender politics. They are convinced that the transformation of the body, sexuality, and gender roles is a precondition for the transformation of society.

Festivals, weekend workshops, ritual groups, and classes offer alternative spaces in which Neopagans and New Agers can explore more deeply the varied meanings of masculinity and femininity and can transform their understandings of gender and sexuality. The types of events offered at large, eclectic Neopagan festivals such as Starwood in western New York (organized by the Association for Consciousness Exploration), Rites of Spring in western Massachusetts (sponsored by Earthspirit Community), and Pantheacon in the San Francisco Bay area (sponsored by Ancient Ways store) suggest the diverse approaches to sex and gender issues in the Neopagan community. At these festivals, workshops on Norse deities or a more specific topic like "Pan-Germanism and the Nazi Use of Runes" compete for time with "Pansexuality—Out in the Open." Gay and straight marriages or handfastings are performed and "Radical Faeries" (participants in a gay Neopagan community) may hold their own camps and meetings. Gay and lesbian couples walk around holding hands and displaying affection as freely as heterosexual couples in the broader society. At Esalen and Omega institutes, weekend workshops have included topics such as "Celebrating the Gay Male Spirit," "Holistic Sexuality: Integrating Sex and Spirit," "Getting the Love You Want for Gay and Lesbian Couples," and "Women and Power: Bringing Balance to the World."[1] The goal of these events is to establish tolerant communities that model healthy patterns of sexuality and spirituality and support equality between the sexes.

For many men and women, Neopaganism and the New Age movement allow for more sexual freedom than they have experienced in other religions. For some, this was part of the attraction to and an important benefit of alternative religions. Neopagan Airique recalls that

Being gay and Catholic never mixed well. Christian teachings turned my parents and families from me. . . . I knew that I could not belong to a faith that did not accept me for who I was. Wicca holds no such prejudices. The duality of the anima/animus, goddess/god in every person does not allow for the restrictions of society. I'm solitary because for the moment I'm too busy finishing grad school to find a coven or group to work with/learn from. . . . I was very strongly drawn to fairy tales and mythology as a child, became very disillusioned with patriarchal/Christian culture in my twenties, always loved the outdoors (grew up camping and hiking with my family), so I suppose the best way to briefly describe my journey towards paganism is through the eco-feminist route.[2]

Many gay and lesbian Neopagans have been disillusioned about religion and felt there was no place for them. They describe finding Neopagan and Wiccan communities as coming "home" and discovering "family." Neopagan and New Age groups typically welcome people who have been uncomfortable in other religious settings, including sexual minorities. But this was not always the case. Gavin and Yvonne Frost were among the first influential Wiccan teachers in the United States, and they believed that homosexuality had no place in Wicca.[3] In the 1970s, many influential Neopagans maintained that Wicca and other forms of Neopaganism were fertility religions that depended on the polarity of the goddess and her male consort. Feminism and the struggle for gay rights challenged this heterosexual emphasis.

By the late twentieth century, most Neopagan and New Age writers and organizations encouraged men and women to explore other cultural approaches to gender and sexuality as part of their journey of self-transformation. For example, they may blend Christian ideas with Asian mysticism and worship of ancient Celtic deities in a framework that they believe is more sexually liberating and inclusive. Marianne Williamson, a spiritual teacher who spreads the channeled message of *A Course in Miracles*, says, "Our sexual impulses become canvases onto which we extend our love or project our fear. When sex is of the Holy Spirit, it is a deepening of communication. . . . The Holy Spirit uses sex to heal us; the ego uses it to wound us. . . . It is only when sex is a vehicle for spiritual communion that it is truly loving, that it joins us to another person. Then it is a sacred act."[4] Here Williamson expresses the blend of Christian and New Age ideas that characterizes *A Course in Miracles*. Disenchanted with Christianity, some New Agers and Neopagans choose not to reject the entire tradition, but redeem certain aspects of it. For example, Mary Magdalene, who in traditional Christian iconography is portrayed as a prostitute, is reclaimed by some New Agers and Neopagans as an independent woman; others attempt to reclaim the Holy Spirit as a sacred universal energy. For some, though, Christianity is beyond redemption.

As the feminist movement of the 1970s picked up momentum, women began leaving organized religions and searching for alternative forms of spirituality. By 1979, scholar of religion Naomi Goldenberg observed that, "The feminist movement in western culture is engaged in the slow execution of Christ and Yahweh."[5] Unlike those Christian and Jewish feminists who remained within their traditions, Goldenberg predicted that "no feminist can save God" because feminists are searching for new forms of authority: "We can picture public power held by a woman or a group of women, shared by both sexes, or rotated between the sexes. These more fluid concepts of hierarchy are certain to affect our view of God."[6] Because they criticized Christianity and Judaism for their oppression of women and the absence of women from leadership roles, the alternative spiritual tradition in America was one of the few places to turn. Many feminists felt that organized religion was completely bankrupt and sought to create their own spiritual practices. They were eager for sources, and when archaeologists and art historians began publishing their work on ancient goddess-worshipping cultures, the timing was perfect. In the occult and metaphysical stream of thought and practice, spiritualist mediums and religious visionaries like Helena Blavatsky and Mary Baker Eddy had found a voice and gathered followers. So again, beginning in the 1970s, channeling and psychic healing, as well as other practices that had long been available to both men and women, grew over the next four decades into the popular and widespread Neopagan and New Age religions, in which women are now established as powerful and important.

Neopagan and New Age religions offer leadership opportunities for women who feel called to be priestesses and healers and for those who want to found their own covens and spiritual growth centers. Psychic healer Katy Crystal felt oppressed by "the patriarchal language" and expectations of the church she grew up in. She wanted to become a minister but because she was a woman she was not encouraged, so she finally "found her calling" as a leader of workshops on feminist spirituality and psychic healing. From the 1970s on, many women made a place for themselves in alternative religions where they shaped emerging woman-centered religious communities.

More important, women founded or play prominent roles in some of the most important organizations. Many New Age and Neopagan groups are founded and led by women, and many psychic healers and other New Age healing practitioners are female. Women run occult bookstores, facilitate large public rituals, perform as Neopagan musicians, lead sacred journeys at

Mount Shasta, and organize psychic fairs and festivals. Two of Findhorn's three founding figures were women. Two of the most famous New Age channeled teachings, the Seth material and the *Course in Miracles*, were channeled through female mediums, Jane Roberts and Helen Schucman, respectively. Chain bookstores like Barnes and Noble carry hundreds of New Age and Neopagan titles, many if not most authored by women. The spiritual leader of Circle Sanctuary is Selena Fox and the most public face of Neopaganism is Starhawk. Even though the Church of All Worlds was founded by Oberon Zell, his wife Morning Glory Zell is equally prominent at gatherings and in print.

## Spiritual Feminism and the Myth of Ancient Matriarchal Goddess Religions

Neopagans and New Agers make use of whatever tools are available to them and borrow from the sources at hand—foreign cultures, the ancient past, science fiction, even Christianity and Judaism. But the key to the transformation of gender roles they advocate was the emergence of stories about ancient goddess-worshipping matriarchies. Beginning in the 1970s, New Agers interested in human potential and Neopagans looking for ancient ways of being religious discovered the research of archaeologists and revisionist feminist historians that reconstructed a woman-centered past. One of the most successful summaries of this work was Riane Eisler's *The Chalice and the Blade* (1987), which in five years sold approximately 181,000 paperback and 24,800 hardcover copies.[7] Eisler tells the story of ancient matriarchies (or what she calls "partnership societies") that were destroyed by "dominator societies" ruled by men.

This history—or "herstory"—served as both a feminist critique of traditional history and a new model for ritual and social organization in the Neopagan and New Age communities. In an effort to reclaim a feminist past, separatist spiritual feminists developed women-only rituals and celebrations for lesbians and other women looking for a spiritual place of their own. The American Neopagan community then incorporated some of the ideas of these women's circles, or what a few of them called "sister's circles," and at the same time developed men's rites. One of the most influential of these conscious reclaimings of women's rituals was brought into being by Zsuzsanna Budapest, a Hungarian exile who founded the Susan B. Anthony coven in Los Angeles in 1971 and whose books were widely read by women seeking new religious models. Budapest's early writings describe a past during which women's mysteries were held to honor ancient goddesses. She summarizes the story of ancient goddess worship this way: "In the olden times. The Goddess had many groves and wimmin served her freely and in dignity. The Goddess' presence was everywhere, and her wimmin knew her as the eternal sister. The patriarchal powers burned down her sacred groves, raped and killed her priestesses, and enslaved wimmin. Her name was stricken from history books, and great darkness of ignorance descended upon womankind."[8] This and other, similar versions of the defeat of goddess-worshipping matriarchies formed part of the mythology of goddess feminists and shaped Neopagan attitudes toward gender and history.

Budapest called for women-only covens and rituals because she believed women needed a spirituality to call their own and one that allowed them direct access to their creator and source of spiritual power: "In the time of the Matriarchies, the craft of wimmin was common knowledge. It was rich in information on how to live on this planet, on how to love and fight and stay healthy. . . . The remnant of that knowledge constitutes the body of what we call 'witchcraft' today. The massive remainder of that knowledge is buried within ourselves, in our deep minds, in our genes. In order to reclaim it, we have to open ourselves to psychic experiences in the safety of feminist witch covens."[9] To further women's reclaiming of their own spiritual tradition and because she felt they needed their own book, Budapest wrote *The Holy Book of Women's Mysteries*. Many women bought and used her books and attended her circles in order to learn how to creatively design their own goddess-based spiritual practices. As a result of the popularity of writers like Eisler and Budapest, ancient goddesses from many eras and cultures have been adopted by Neopagans and incorporated into their ritual lives. Some of the most frequently referenced are a Near Eastern "Great Goddess" (a monotheistic counterpart to the Christian and Jewish God); Greek and Roman deities such as Persephone, Demeter, Athena, Aphrodite, and Artemis; and the Hindu goddess Kali.

Like other 1970s feminists, Budapest was influenced by a variety of different sources, including a classical upbringing, her sculptor mother, a house full of books, and particularly the writings of the poet Robert Graves and the classicist Jane Ellen Harrison. Budapest's ideas were subsequently supported by feminist scholars like the archaeologist Marija Gimbutas, who argues in *The Goddesses and Gods of Old Europe* (1982) that artifacts from excavations in Europe and the Near East indicate that goddesses were worshipped in ancient Europe around 6500–3500 B.C.E.[10] Even before Gimbutas's feminist interpretation, archaeologist James Mellaart had argued that evidence from a site in Turkey showed that women played central roles in a peaceful goddess-worshipping society that occupied this area from 6500 to 5650 B.C.E.[11] During the 1980s and 1990s many books were written about goddesses and subsequently incorporated into Neopagan rituals and New Age personal growth workshops. Altars to the ancient Mesopotamian goddesses were set up at Neopagan festivals and goddess tours to Crete and Glastonbury, England drew feminists interested in reclaiming ancient goddesses as part of what they saw as a more positive historical tradition for women. Influential works by feminists attempting to reconstruct ancient goddess-worshipping cultures include Merlin Stone's *When God Was a Woman* (1976) and Carol Christ's *The Laughter of Aphrodite* (1987). Stone speculated from the basis of art historical evidence what goddess religion might have been like. Feminists following this lead sought archaeological and textual evidence to construct an inspirational history with an aura of academic respectability.

Feminist writers responded to the explosion of interest in goddesses in other ways as well. Neopagan priestess Starhawk's efforts to develop woman-centered myths and rituals were shaped by the feminist movement of the 1970s and 1980s, an era when early advocates of goddess religion attempted to incorporate Jungian psychology with feminist goals for women's empowerment. Interest in archetypes and myths among psychologists led to the publication of books by Jungian analysts Clarissa Pinkola Estes and Jean Shinoda Bolen. Estes's book, *Women Who Run with the Wolves* (1992), tells many stories of "wild woman" archetypes available for women who want to liberate aspects of the self that they feel have been repressed by a society that only gives them limited roles. "Wild woman is the health of all women," Estes writes; she is "the innate, instinctual Self."[12] Bolen's *Goddesses in Everywoman* (1984) and *Crossing to Avalon: A Woman's Midlife Pilgrimage* (1994) link mythical accounts of goddess religion to women's rites of passage. In *Crossing to Avalon* Bolen explores the Grail myth from Arthurian legend as an example of the women's mysteries that she believes became lost as Christianity overcame ancient religions where a goddess reigned. She encourages women to remember, reinvent, and bring into the present the ancient rites of a goddess-centered society: "Somewhere in our souls, women remember a time when divinity was called Goddess and Mother. When we become initiates into women's mysteries we then come to know that we are the carriers of a holy chalice, that the Grail comes through us."[13]

Bolen also explores the ways in which women's experiences, such as giving birth, are ancient feminine mysteries that contemporary women can reclaim. Bolen observes that "pregnancy was an initiatory experience that changed my body, shifted my consciousness, taught me surrender, and was the beginning of the dawning awareness of the physical, psychological, and spiritual demands and gifts that would come through being a mother."[14] Many Neopagans and New Agers follow her lead in affirming that bodily experience can become a method of expanding spirituality and the body a source of spiritual knowledge and power.

According to these authors, pregnancy, labor, delivery, and breastfeeding are ways that women embody the goddess in the biological events of their lives: "A pregnant woman would know that she shares in the essence of the Goddess as creator, who brought forth all life from her own body."[15] Bolen's view of breastfeeding as a sacred act is reflected in the section of her book called "Deepening the Experience of the Mother: Breastfeeding as Sacred Communion." She also interprets menstruation as something positive in the chapter on "Women's Experience of the Blood Mysteries." Here she imagines how a goddess-centered society would view the onset of menses: "Blood would be held in awe. This blood would mean that she could now become fertile, that she could be like the Goddess or the earth, and life could come forth from her."[16] Bolen and other goddess feminists seek to transform what they see as destructive and disempowering images of body and self by identifying women with the divine and ancient myths. In this way, female bodies are made sacred and women use their bodily experiences as initiations, transforming their identity as they move from one stage of life to another.

Fiction writers responded to and promoted the interest in ancient goddess-worshippers by fictionalizing the efforts of feminist archaeologists and art historians who tried to reconstruct a history of societies ruled by goddesses. They imagined what ancient goddess-worshipping cultures might have been like as a way to inspire modern women's imaginations and provide ideas for rituals. Starhawk's influential books about ancient and contemporary goddess worship and the novels of popular feminist writers like June Brindel, author of *Ariadne*, and Marion Zimmer Bradley, author of *The Mists of Avalon*, describe the various forms of power, including sexual power, that might have been available to women in the service of goddesses.

An aspect of the ancient matriarchy myth that struck a chord with Neopagans was the practice of ritual sex in the goddess's name, especially "sacred marriage" and "sacred prostitution," imagined to be important and sacred sexual roles for women. Although its historical accuracy is questionable, the myth of a sacred marriage between a priestess embodying a goddess and a man embodying a god that is promoted by these authors represents for many of their readers a mythical time when sex was holy and female sexuality was celebrated in partnership with men. In Starhawk's description of the sacred marriage between Inanna and Dumuzi, she stresses the importance of the pleasurable union between male and female participants. In one section of her book *Truth or Dare* called "All Acts of Love and Pleasure Are My Rituals," she describes their sacred marriage, a ritualized sexual experience in which the priestess becomes goddess and the priest becomes god.

Breathe. See the full moon rise above the temple terrace. Hear the drums and voices of the procession: he comes, bringing rich offerings, cattle and grain, milk and fruit to fill the storehouse. You will be filled. He ascends the stairs, he comes up. Moonlight glints on bare arms. The women dance, arms upraised to the moon, hips curving, as the drums beat and the chants rise in the night air.

You ascend. The drums call you. Your shoulders shake; your feet pound out the rhythm. The women sing the courting songs. On the high wind a voice calls out:

"She has called for it! She has called for it!"

"She has called for the bed!" the people answer with one throat.

"She has called for the bed of heart's delight!"

"She has called for the bed!"

The drums beat faster. A sweetness rises in you. You are Inanna's priestess; she fills you. You are Dumuzi's priest; in you he swells. You find each other; you can't remember who you are, only that you are a living vessel of honey, only that touch is fire, is sweet cool water, only that you can pour yourself out like rich, creamy milk, a foam that pours over the people, over the herds and groves and fields and soaks into the living loam.

And so life is renewed.[17]

Translations of Sumerian tablets from the late fourth and third millennium B.C.E. have allowed goddess worshippers to imagine such a ritual. Starhawk claims that these texts testify to the celebration of male and female fertility in an era when people "called the Goddess and God to take possession of priestess and priest and so enacted the renewal of the world through the life-sustaining power of the erotic."[18] She argues that the Sumerian sacred marriage cycle exemplifies a society based on "power-within" that was gradually replaced by a society based on "power-over" that is to blame for our current problems, especially troubled relations between men and women. For New Agers and Neopagans, this is a crucial distinction in the project of creating a future society or new age of enlightenment and equality. In the search for alternative models to twentieth-century gender roles, particularly gendered religious roles, the past is one of the few sources available, especially an imagined past of ancient goddess-worshipping cultures in which women were politically and religiously powerful.

For most goddess-worshipping feminists, this must be a pre-Christian past because Christianity is cast as the villain in their reconstructed history. For example, feminists and Neopagans blame Christianity for the execution of thousands of women and men charged with practicing witchcraft in early modern Europe. Some of them call this chapter in the story of ancient matriarchies "The Burning Times," which is the Neopagan version of the Holocaust. A common Neopagan refrain that places current persecution and prejudice in the context of a mythic history is "Never Again the Burning Times." In 1968 members of a feminist organization in New York known as WITCH (Women's International Conspiracy from Hell) wrote a manifesto in which they claimed that Witchcraft was the religion of pre-Christian Europe: "Its persecution in the early modern period had therefore been the suppression of an alternative culture by the ruling elite, but also a war against feminism, for the religion had been served by the most courageous, aggressive, independent, and sexually liberated women in the populace. Nine million of these had been put to death."[19] In *The Spiral Dance*, her first book on goddess religion, Starhawk argues that Christians perverted the goddess's rituals of pleasure just as they transformed the horned god of the witches into the devil. Similarly, she and many other goddess feminists argue that the witches persecuted in early modern Europe were representatives of an ancient goddess-worshipping tradition. They were midwives and wise women who knew how to heal with plants and potions and worshipped a great goddess. According to this view of history, these "witches" were effectively wiped out by the Christian church. Contemporary Witches claim that the "devil" represented in the texts of Christian witch hunters was actually a fertility god and consort to the goddess of "the Old Religion."

Historians of the period and other scholars point out that nine million is completely inaccurate and refute the Neopagan myth of goddess religion survivals. Their evidence suggests that many streams of magic, literature, mythology, and folk religion were blended into the first British Witch covens of the 1950s.[20] But historical validity is eclipsed by the power that the myth of ancient goddesses and the "Old Religion" hold for some contemporary Neopagans. Like all emerging religions, Neopaganism derives its authority from tradition and the past, but not all Neopagans argue for the historical reality of ancient matriarchies and a European pre-Christian religion of witchcraft. Instead, many believe that the psychological power of these myths is what makes them useful. Historical authenticity also seems less important for New Age authors like Jean Shinoda Bolen, who are clear that the mythical reality, not the historical one, is what is important in constructing new images of deity for women.

In her novel *The Mists of Avalon*, feminist author Marion Zimmer Bradley recounts a tale about the persecution and suppression of the goddess's rituals by an increasingly misogynist and patriarchal form of Christianity. Underlying the rituals and myths created by Bradley and other goddess feminists is the influence of arguments (now discredited by the academic community and many Neopagans) made by British anthropologist Margaret Murray in *The God of the Witches* (1933) for the survival in Britain of "the Old Religion." Starhawk and other Witches believe they are the figurative, if not the literal, descendents of the fictional goddess worshippers. Bradley's novel vividly evokes the tradition goddess feminists and Neopagans are trying to revive in their rituals and workshops. At the heart of her story about the goddess and her priestesses of Avalon is the rite of the sacred marriage. Bradley imagines how rituals that celebrated the positive power of women's fertility and the partnership between men and women gave way to Christian rituals of guilt and expiation, which she sees as negative. The sacred marriage that takes place among other kinds of "sex magic" and fertility rites on the Neopagan holiday Beltane (May 1) is both marriage and initiation for the man and woman who take part in it by becoming goddess and god.

Jean Shinoda Bolen believes that Bradley's book had an impact because so many women identified with the story:

> The book strikes a chord in many women. We feel as if we are hearing something about our past about which we have no memory, and then when we are reminded, we feel in our bones that it is true. . . . Somewhere in us, we know of a time when this feminine principle prevailed, a time of the Goddess, of the sacredness of sexuality and fertility, of our link to the earth. Somehow we know that there once were priestesses, healers, and wisewomen who were keepers of knowledge.[21]

The theme of "remembering" is frequently mentioned in feminist writing on goddesses, and *The Mists of Avalon* is one creative example of how myth and story are presented as a recollection of the past, a fictionalized history. In this novel the paradigmatic union is between the virgin priestess Morgaine and her half-brother Arthur, soon to be king of England. Both characters are brought to the spring rites (on the Neopagan holiday of Beltane) without having seen each other since they were young children, and in the dusk of evening they do not recognize each other amid the festivities. Painted and bedecked with flowers, Morgaine encounters Arthur in a cave after he, in the role of the young king stag, has killed the older king stag. He comes to her with the blood still fresh on him from the deer whose horns will crown next year's young stag. During the initiation/marriage all thought of their individual identity vanishes in the enactment of what they consider to be a timeless ritual. Here, as in Starhawk's ritual for Inanna, the female priestess becomes the goddess and suppresses her human identity:

> Now it is the time for the Goddess to welcome the Horned One—he was kneeling at the edge of the deerskin couch, swaying, blinking by the light of the torch. . . . She had to guide him. I am the Great Mother who knows all things, who is mother and maiden and all-wise, guiding the virgin and her consort . . . dazed, terrified, exalted, only half-conscious, she felt the life force take them both, moving her body without volition, moving him too, guiding him fiercely into her, till they were both moving without knowledge of what force gripped them.[22]

In horror, at daybreak Arthur and Morgaine recognize each other as brother and sister. Although Morgaine tries to reassure Arthur, "We are in the hands of her who brought us here. . . . We are not brother and sister here, we are man and woman before the Goddess, no more,"[23] in her private thoughts she shares the despair he expresses about what they have done. That the influence of Christianity, rather than anything inherent in the worship of the goddess, causes them both to experience guilt and shame is made clear throughout the novel. On her return journey to Avalon, Morgaine remembers stories of the Virgin Mary told to her by her childhood priest, and she feels shame at her own impurity and about incest, while at the same time she recognizes that shame and guilt are incongruous with her training as a priestess of the goddess. Throughout the novel Morgaine struggles with this tension. Bradley echoes Starhawk's contention that the goddess's rituals should be performed in the name of pleasure, including sexual pleasure made sacred by the presence of the divine in the priest and priestess.

Another way that Neopagans imaginatively re-create ancient goddess-worshipping cultures is by reclaiming the image of the sacred prostitute, whose role is to sacralize sexuality for visitors to the goddess's temple. She is not seen as a victimized woman abused by men for sexual gratification, but rather as a priestess of sexual mysteries, teaching and sharing sexual power with men (and sometimes women) who come to her. The Cretan world of the priestess Ariadne in June Brindel's novel of that name exists at the time of transition from goddess-centered worship to a patriarchal society. Ancient rituals to honor the goddess have been ignored and King Minos refuses to sacrifice himself to her as he is expected to do by tradition at the end of his year-long reign. The ancient custom challenged by Minos, which Ariadne seeks to revive to appease the goddess, dictates that the king must die so that the natural cycle of decay and renewal will be restored. This belief echoes the Wiccan view of the wheel of the year in which the male deity dies in winter and rises again in spring. According to goddess feminist Merlin Stone's retelling of the myth, in Minoan Crete the "young god was always subject to the goddess—he was the instrument of her fertility and is shown in humble and worshipful attitudes."[24] Stone speculates that ancient Crete was a matriarchy in which women ruled over men. In Brindel's novel, as Ariadne learns about the old rituals suppressed by Minos, she begins to invoke and then becomes possessed by the goddess: "I am She that is Mother of all things. . . . At My will All things grow and fill the universe, Die and are renewed. . . . All are with My womb."[25] Brindel writes in the appendix to *Ariadne* that she wanted to "recapture the old psychology" through the voice of a young woman who grew up believing that a "Great Mother Goddess" existed and that "she herself, the queen and high priestess, was the visible embodiment of the Goddess."[26] For Starhawk and other goddess worshippers, such fictionalized accounts of ancient goddess-centered cultures provide myth and history that was wanting in their own religious upbringing.

Although they have provided many women with creative ways to reimagine their spirituality, goddess feminists have also come under attack. They want to create a woman-centered religion, but others may experience this goal as narrow or repressive. Salome, a Neopagan from Cincinnati, recalls her own sexual healing in which an important experience was the sexual freedom of Neopagan festivals, but she also notes the confusion that may accompany such freedom. She noticed a dichotomy between lesbian separatists and the straight community. Gays and lesbians were very welcome at festivals and she appreciated that, but as a woman who identified as bisexual she felt that others tried to force her into one category or another: "One woman asked me at the last festival, 'Are you family?' meaning are you gay? I said, 'Well, it depends on how you define "family,"' and she said, 'Oh, you're bisexual.' I find it easier to find same-sex dates in mainstream society than I do at festivals because people have such hang-ups about the goddess, that the goddess is the only way. I believe in god and goddess. There are a lot of people who want to ignore the male side of everything."[27] During the 1990s, Neopagan festivals began to incorporate bisexuals and transgendered people and were at the forefront of the broader social trend, especially on university campuses, to recognize "queer" or "lgbt" (lesbian/gay/bisexual/transgendered) people. This trend promoted inclusivity and allowed for more fluid understandings of sexual identity.

Men have accused goddess worshippers of reverse sexism; transgendered people disallowed by a few woman-only groups have charged that they are discriminatory; some heterosexual women in lesbian-dominated feminist groups have felt uncomfortable; archaeologists and historians of the ancient world have dismissed arguments for ancient goddess-worshipping matriarchies. Nevertheless, feminist spirituality remains a powerful force in the New Age and Neopagan movements and according to participants, has brought much positive change in their lives. Cynthia Eller, a scholar who has researched feminist spirituality, is sympathetic to the goal of liberating women from oppressive religious institutions, but she makes the most succinct criticism of what she calls "the myth of ancient matriarchy": the problem is replacing a patriarchal hierarchy with a matriarchal one. She believes this move repeats the same kind of imbalance that women criticize in social institutions dominated by men. But the women Eller studied represent one segment of the New Age and Neopagan populations. Others have taken a different approach. For their gatherings and religious practices they try to create alternative images and rites for men and women that do not replicate the problems that plague other religions. New rites of passage in Neopagan and New Age communities strive to celebrate men's and women's different life changes and at the same time express egalitarian views of gender relations.

## New Rites of Passage for Men and Women

Rites for healing the damage done to sexuality and gender identity and rites that honor and celebrate love relationships, sexual expression, life passages, and bodily experience are creative ways that New Agers and Neopagans try to realize their hopes for a transformed world. Such rituals work with gender and sexuality in a variety of ways in order to consciously provide alternatives to other religious options. Healing from rape and abusive or unhealthy sexual relationships is a common focus, as are rituals and guided meditations that explore gendered aspects of the self. New Agers experiment with psychological and emotional aspects symbolized by different goddesses, while Neo-pagans create theatrical rituals with ancient deities and encourage partici-pants to act out sexual abuse or try on different gender identities. Men wear skirts and gowns for some Neopagan rituals and at festivals; New Age men explore the feminine within but are less likely to wear dresses. New rituals are intentionally designed to replace outdated rites or to fill in gaps where Amer-icans have no tradition to turn to.

Creating new rites of passage is more at the heart of Neopagan religion than New Age communities, though this distinction is never hard and fast. Rites of passage are an important way that Neopagans celebrate embodied life changes and create religious community. In covens and at festivals, they honor the passing of one phase of life and the entrance into another, often with their chosen family rather than their birth family as witnesses. The goal is not simply to help a person celebrate significant life changes but also to strengthen the community. Neopagan leaders believe that "Ritual affirms the common patterns, the values, the shared joys, risks, sorrows, and changes that bind a community together. . . . A living community develops its own rituals to celebrate life passages and ease times of transition, to connect us with the round of the changing seasons and the moon's flux, to anchor us in time."[28] Neopagans have created new rituals and reinvented old ones around pregnancy and birth, marriage, puberty, and death.

Rites for women are much more common than rites for men, in part be-cause of the tremendous popularity of images and stories of goddesses and the disproportionate influence of the feminist movement on New Age and Neopagan communities. The men's movement has had less impact and, some would argue, was less necessary to correct the balance weighted heavily to-ward men in most American religions. According to feminist priestess Ruth Barrett, women's rituals are a way to "connect with the life force" and take "the initiative to consciously evolve ourselves." She calls these rites "Women's Mysteries," defined as "ritualized celebrations honoring the rites of passage of women's lives." For Barrett, "Women's Mysteries are the es-sential physical, emotional, and psychic rites of passage women experience by having been born into a female body. These include the five mysteries of birth, menstruation, birth/lactation, menopause, and death, which are women's ability to create life, sustain life, and return our bodies to the Source in death. Women's mysteries celebrate the Earth's seasonal cycles of birth, death and regeneration, and women's likewise cyclical nature."[29] Rose, a Neopagan priestess, planned to give birth at home; a couple of weeks before her due date, she invited her midwife and other female friends to her home for a "blessingway," a term Neopagans borrowed from a Navajo healing tradition. The women went out to a sacred circle behind Rose's house. The midwife called to the four directions, summoning the special powers of each. Rose, in the center of the circle, was given a foot-washing ceremony. One at a time, the women each sprinkled an herb that held special meaning for them into the water. They gave a gift of power to mother and baby, a strength that they themselves possessed, which they described out loud to her. While they were doing this Rose channeled a song, which she then taught to everyone. At the end of the ritual the women sang, danced, and shared a feast.

Gatherings like this generate new religious understandings of female roles and life experiences. Women-only rituals allow women to gather and celebrate shared experiences. Neopagans honor biologically based experiences and transitions and at the same time say that biology is not destiny, that some women may choose not to give birth and that all choices are valid. A wide range of views on the link between biology and gender exists in both Neopaganism and the New Age movement. Some believe that biological sex carries with it certain strengths, so that for instance, women are celebrated for being nurturing mothers. Other Neopagans and New Agers prefer to see such behavior as disconnected from biological sex and available to all male and females equally. In her study of Reclaiming, a Witchcraft coven in San Francisco, theologian and anthropologist Jone Salomonsen observes that "There is a constant tension in Reclaiming between the radical extremes of these viewpoints: Goddess as mystical symbol, equally important to women and men, versus Goddess as birthing, female lifeforce; gender as structuring and meaning-making metaphor versus sexual difference as ontological reality."[30] Some New Agers and Neopagans promote androgyny as a third type of gender identity. One channeled being speaking through a human medium argued, "It is time for male/female balance to come to the fore. We talk to many beings about androgyny, which we find to be an exquisite state . . . you are either in a male or female body, but you are not purely male or female. You are a third type."[31] Both of these views express the desire to affirm and make positive those aspects of gendered behavior that they believe have been repressed or seen as evil, such as homosexual relationships, women celebrating their sexuality outside of marriage, and men choosing more traditionally feminine roles. Personal freedom and individual choice tend to be valued, although they sometimes give way to dogmatic notions of political correctness. Nevertheless, the prevalence of women-only rituals testifies to the extent to which many women feel their experiences have not been honored and valued in the broader society.

Regardless of their position on this larger ideological issue, New Agers and Neopagans feel that women-only workshops and women-only spaces for rites of passage and healing rituals for rape and abuse are practical because they allow more freedom of expression and facilitate a deeper level of sharing. Some Neopagans and especially Neopagan women have created initiation rites for adolescents that they complain are unavailable elsewhere in American culture. They believe that negative views of the body and sexuality are taught to young children and particularly to adolescents, and that the way to change this is to offer a different perspective. Starhawk tells the story of how her coven created a ritual to celebrate the first menstruation of a member's daughter:

> We prepared for months, making her a special robe upon which each of us embroidered some symbol of power. On the appointed day we took her and her mother down to the beach. We tied them together with a silver cord and asked them to run. They ran together as fast as the mother could run; then we cut them apart and the daughter ran on alone. We then went to a friend's house and joined other women in a hot tub. Thirteen of us, all women, spent the afternoon telling Bethany the stories of how we had become the women we were. Each of us gave her a special gift. We dressed her in her robe, formed a circle around her, and chanted her name to empower her.[32]

Later they went into the house, where male friends had created a feast of red foods, and the men also gave her gifts. Starhawk's description of the first menses ritual appears on her well-known Web site, where it provides a model for other communities looking for alternative rites of passage for their adolescents.

Old women, mothers, and adolescent women are each celebrated in unique ways. Many Witches and other Neopagans believe in the "Triple Goddess" of maiden, mother, and crone (wise old woman) that originated with the first Neopagans in mid-twentieth-century England. But many other goddesses have also been called upon as models for women to follow in their own lives and as an affirmation of the different life stages women go through and the roles they fill. According to historian Ronald Hutton, the idea of the Triple Goddess has its origins in the work of early twentieth-century British scholars Jane Ellen Harrison and Sir James Frazer, whose writings were consulted by the earliest Neopagans. Cambridge University classicist Harrison described a Great Earth Mother of prehistoric Europe who was worshipped in three aspects: "The most important of these were Maiden, ruling the living, and Mother, ruling the underworld; she did not name the third." Harrison's colleague Frazer came to believe that prehistoric Europeans worshipped a double goddess, as suggested by the Greek myth of Demeter and Persephone.[33] The idea of the Triple Goddess that most directly influenced contemporary Witches was further developed by Edwardian occultist Aleister Crowley in 1929:

> For she is Artemis or Diana, sister of the sun, a shining Virgin Goddess; then Isis-initiatrix, who brings to man all light and purity, and is the link of his animal soul with his eternal self; and she is Persephone or Proserpine; a soul of double nature; living half upon the earth and half in Hades . . . and thirdly she is Hecate, a thing altogether of hell, barren, hideous and malicious, the queen of death and evil witchcraft.[34]

Finally, argues Hutton, poet Robert Graves provided the most direct link to Neopagan theology of the goddess in his book *The White Goddess* (1948), which tells of a Triple Moon Goddess who is Maiden, Mother, and Crone.[35] Graves "took Harrison's imagery of three aspects, and related them to the waxing, full, and waning moon, to represent the One Goddess most potently as bringer of life and death, in her forms as Maiden, Mother, and Crone."[36] In this case something old was made anew to meet the needs of contemporary British and American Neopagans trying to construct a tradition rooted in pre-Christian religions but relevant to twentieth-century people. But the Triple Goddess offers more than a deity with ancient credentials; she embodies and thus gives value to the stages of women's lives. Although in many Neopagan traditions she is paired with a god, either she is dominant or they are partners—she is never seen as subservient. Starhawk affirms that "The Goddess is Mother, Crone, Lover, as well as Virgin." For Neopagans and other goddess feminists, the deity is expansive, not restrictive, and encompasses women's multiple roles.

The revaluing of women's bodies at all stages of life and the identification of the feminine as divine have made possible many of the new rites of passage Neopagans have created. Sociologist Wendy Griffin describes a ritual she observed in 1991 during a weekend gathering of sixty women camping in the mountains. The ritual was held on the full moon and, as she watched, a procession of priestesses walked along a mountain path toward women gathered in anticipation.

The priestesses paused in the south, and then I noticed the enormous shadow thrown against the hill. It is Diana [Roman goddess of the hunt] who comes behind them. Rationally I know it is Hypatia [one of the priestesses], but I also "know" it is Diana. A heavy green cape is swept over her shoulders and matches her baggy pants. Her huge breasts are bare, and her chest is crossed with the leather straps that holds her cape and the quiver of arrows on her back. She carries a large bow and her face is hidden behind a mask of fur and dry leaves. Deer horns spring from her head. There is no face, not a human one anyway. . . . The Goddess pauses between the torches and fits an arrow to the bow. She draws it back and with a "twang" shoots it into the darkness. The sound is a catalyst. We are released like the arrow and begin to cheer.[37]

The priestess later told Griffin that she "manifested that part" of her that was identified with Diana. "Other images of Diana are all sexualized from a male point of view, kind of a scantily clad Playboy bunny in the woods. But when she came walking up and I realized who she was, it was really different. It was really kind of overwhelming and shocking. But after the initial shock, she was Diana. This was a female who radiated power with her body and costume." Diana is usually identified with the maiden aspect of the Triple Goddess, but clearly "maiden" does not mean young and weak. Neopagans redefine the archetypes and leave them open to personal interpretation by the women who look to them for guidance.

Cynthia Eller describes another ritual involving the Triple Goddess, this time honoring the crone or wise woman. Feminist spiritualists gathered at a camp on the shores of a lake in Maine to celebrate three women who had passed their fifty-sixth birthday. All the women who had already become crones formed a circle in the middle of a room and were surrounded by two circles of women who had not yet reached that age. The crones talked about how their lives changed as they became older. The group characterized out loud with one word what each decade of their life meant to them ("miserable marriage," "lesbianism"), ending with only one woman in her seventies left in the circle. Then they gathered in circles again, with the three women to be croned in the center:

Each crone describes what she likes about being older: being more at home with herself, not caring what people think of her, having the freedom to love whom she will. Then the official croning begins: Each woman in turn is presented with a "stole," a chain of braided ribbons that the crones in camp have been wearing around their necks as a token of honor off and on throughout the weekend. They are also given a "crone stone" to symbolize the weight and solidity of the wisdom they have gained over the years. The presentations are made by personal friends, who preface the gifts of stole and stone with stories of how they met and what this woman's friendship has meant to them. Several daughters of the new crones are present, and as their mothers receive the symbols of cronehood and acknowledge them, they sit beaming and proud. When all three presentations are made, the larger circle begins to call out to the crones, saying, "I thank you for your wisdom," "I thank you for your strength," "I thank you for your beauty."

The ceremony is closed with singing, as a storm that has been brewing outside finally lets loose with wind and lightning, thunder and rain.[38]

New Agers celebrate images of goddesses and gods as well, but they tend to focus on metaphors and archetypes instead of rites, particularly the extent to which they lead to inner growth and transformation. New Agers do not emphasize ritual sex or ritual nudity and do not believe in the symbolic union of goddess and god embodied by priest and priestess that is sacred to Witches. They are more likely to take a mythological or Jungian approach that explores male and female archetypes, such as Bolen's work on women's bodily experiences and the Grail, Estes's book on the wild woman archetype, poet Robert Bly's writing on gender roles in *Iron John* (1990), or Sam Keen's men's movement classic, *Fire in the Belly: On Being a Man* (1991).

Keen's and Bly's writings inspired the men's movement of the 1990s and encouraged New Agers and Neopagans to explore masculinity and celebrate the variety of male gods that men can look to as models. Bly's book presents the warrior as empowering for men and divorced from negative connotations of aggression and violence. He argues that because American society lacks rites of passage for men, they need to reclaim and invent them. In *Fire in the Belly* Sam Keen analyzes the oppressive messages men receive when they are growing up, which he calls "the wounds of the warrior psyche," and constructs liberating models of masculinity to replace them. Bly's and Keen's approaches have inspired many men's events and have also influenced New Age and Neopagan gatherings, so that workshops and rituals on men's issues and for men only coexist with woman-centered activities.

Pagan Spirit Gathering, an annual summer festival, has included men's as well as the more common women's rituals. Many Neopagans and New Agers also look for male images of the divine that offer alternatives to the Christian and Jewish God. Anticipating the objections of feminists who want to dispense with male deities entirely, Starhawk claims that the horned god represents "positive" male characteristics. She imagines him to be a "God of love . . . his sexuality is fully *felt* in a context in which sexual desire is sacred, not only because it is the means by which life is procreated, but also because it is the means by which our own lives are most deeply and ecstatically realized."[39] Yet it is not just the man and woman, priest and priestess of the ritual, who are transformed by the sacred marriage between god and goddess; Witches believe that the external world is also affected by the erotic magic of the ritual. Starhawk claims that the male and female aspects of humanity are united in the marriage of goddess and god, and so too are all opposites united and the cyclical motion of the natural world sustained. Wiccan priestess Judy Harrow believes in

> willed human transformation. . . . And that means that I affirm that men can do the hard work of repairing cultural damage. Many have, in a movement complementary to feminism . . . . Traditional role models are not just factually incorrect. They are wrong. They hurt people, and therefore they are contrary to the Wiccan Rede ["An it harm none, do what you will"]. The association of men with culture and intellect and women with nature and instinct, has historically been the rationale for keeping women, "barefoot, pregnant and in the kitchen." . . . Mother Nature didn't make us that way. It's our upbringing that pushes each of us into living from only half our potential.[40]

Feminists and men's movement leaders both argue that established patterns of socialization have been oppressive and limiting. All men and women, they say, need to heal old wounds and change how they live before they will be free to explore their full potential as human beings.

The men's and women's movements support a kind of psychological polytheism that allows them to discover and invent deities that express parts of the self. Pantheacon, a Neopagan convention held in 2003, included sessions on "Mystery and the Masculine: Connecting to the Male Divine" and "Liturgy for Chiron the Centaur as Sage." New Age and Neopagan men have followed feminist strategies in borrowing images of deities from ancient cultures that they believe had healthier views of masculinity. For instance, Sam Keen suggests that Dionysus embodies a playful wildness: "Dionysian man adds 'passion' to the definition of manhood. While Apollo counsels 'everything in moderation,' the wild man advises us that 'the path of excess leads to the place of wisdom.' . . . He encourages us to 'follow our bliss' and explore the deepest desires of our being."[41] Like goddess feminists, Keen believes ancient cultures offer more diverse models for masculinity and allow men to explore their human potential without being subject to rigid male ideals like the emotionless warrior. One of the most popular images among Neopagans is that of the Greek god Pan. According to Neopagan Morning Glory Zell, "Pan is a proud celebration of the liberating power of male erotic energy in its purest and most beautiful form. . . . Pan is the Father, the Lover, the Son, the Brother and the Friend.[42] His message to us today is to trust our bodies and love our erotic animal energy." Just as the Triple Goddess presents women with multiple forms of divinity, Pan and other male deities embody new forms of masculinity.

Men's rites have been more slowly accepted than women's and sometimes receive mixed reactions at large Neopagan festivals. Neopagan ritual leader Peh described the "male mysteries" that took place at a festival he attended. He explained that the ritual planners built on Bly's ideas about the male warrior and hunter. Peh played the role of the stag. But he said that others at the festival were uncomfortable with the celebration of male roles, and "after it was over there was a conflict [with] the woman who was the priestess of the main ritual that night. . . . She wanted the men to go around and do this, and the women to go around and do that. Now shame on her for being so uptight and shame on the people who pushed that button. There was a guy who said, 'Well, I'm female-identified, can I be with the women?' And his partner was saying, 'I'm male-identified, I really want to be in the male circle.'" Peh was frustrated that the problem was blamed on the men's ritual: "I guess they decided that it got our testosterone up too much."[43]

Peh believed that the influence of feminism and goddess worship made it difficult for men to explore various aspects of masculinity. He explained that "There's a male apology and that seems to be more the current now than the acceptance of male power. To them, in order to achieve balance and harmony between the male and female, the male has to be toned down. That's not the way I'm going to do it. In order for there to be balance between male and female, there has to be recognition, maybe an empowerment of the warrior, among themselves; better to allow it and accept it."[44] He designed a men's initiation for young men in his local Neopagan community that aimed "to reclaim what we have given up to be in this culture" and included flint knapping, making coal from plants, fire starting, and beer making. In men-only and women-only spaces, New Agers and Neopagans say they feel free to explore aspects of femininity and masculinity shaped by biology and culture. Their work with gender and sexuality is often done in sex-segregated spaces, but it also involves mending and strengthening the spiritual aspects of relationships. According to Sam Keen, men's relationships often fail because of their inability to access their own emotions. Through inner exploration using myths and archetypes, he believes emotional healing will occur and their potential to love and be loved will grow.

## Sex and Spirituality

Because Neopagans see sexuality as something sacred and New Agers believe it is an area for expanding human potential, they look for ways to explore the connection between sexuality and spirituality. In general, Neopagans and New Agers tend to be tolerant if not actively supportive of sexual diversity. Trance channelers David and Sasha Johnson cautioned an audience of New Agers: "Sex is an energy. From this point of view there are no value judgments and there are no morals and no ethics about sex. What we're working towards here is unconditional acceptance of your own sexuality and, of course, unconditional acceptance of everyone else's sexuality." David added that all forms of sexuality "provide a soul with useful lessons."[45] On one end of the spectrum of diverse choices is celibacy used to channel sexual energy into spiritual practice, while on the other end is polyamory (multiple lovers) within a spiritual community. Starhawk believes that sexuality is sacred in many forms because it is the "direct expression of the life force . . . seen as numinous and sacred. It can be expressed freely, so long as the guiding principle is love. Marriage is a deep commitment, a magical, spiritual, and psychic bond. But it is only one possibility out of many for loving, sexual expression."[46] According to Witches and other goddess worshippers, sacred sexual rituals ensure the balance of natural cycles and the movement of life embodied by the priestess or initiate who becomes the goddess in one of her different phases. From this perspective, the human body, and especially sexual expression, is the cosmic or divine force that powers the movement of the universe.

Neopagan and New Age communities are likely to encourage both men and women to feel comfortable in their bodies, to see the body as sacred and beautiful, a site for healing and a source of power. Jean Shinoda Bolen argues that "The Goddess makes the body and life sacred, and connects us to the divinity that permeates all matter."[47] This emphasis comes in part from the feminist movement's critiques of oppressive body images in the media and valuing the beauty in bodies of all sizes and all ages. Neopagans from their origins in 1950s England have often participated in rituals without clothes, or "skyclad," and most Neopagan festivals are clothing optional. However, anthropologist Tanya Luhrman observes that in the five covens she studied, nudity was not equated with sexuality: "The nudity is also usually well-contained within the circle. The coven I joined would disrobe just before the ritual, and another instituted separate 'changing rooms' for men and women to disrobe and robe before the ritual."[48] For Neopagans the body, like the rest of the world around us, is sacred. One of the ways it becomes divine is through identification with nature, and so Neopagans and New Agers often stress the connection between body and sacred earth: "We are reclaiming the experience of the sexuality of the Earth, resacramenting that feeling as well as the human body and the sensitivity. A willingness to experience through every pore of the skin and not be intimidated by sensation. Lying down in the water, lying down in my canyon in the sands, is lying in the arms of a lover. By returning to the lover Earth, I am returning to myself."[49] In this passage body and earth become one, and for Neopagans and New Agers, there is rarely a strict boundary between them.

Starhawk sees the oppression of women, the persecution of Witches, and the destruction of the earth as profoundly interconnected. Her rituals present a vision of society in which connections among women, nature, and sexuality are celebrated. She believes that elevating what has been devalued in our culture and creatively remembering all the women who were tortured for being witches or for resisting their given social roles will allow us to heal the wounds of the past and look toward a future where women and nature are revered. Starhawk argues that myths invented by goddess worshippers are part of a history and language outside and opposed to images used by "patriarchal culture" to maintain social order. Her construction of new rituals proceeds on the assumption that the ritual texts we use must be in line with the kind of future we envision: "nothing does change unless its form, its structure, its language also changes." To work magic, Neopagans begin by making new metaphors, and earth as body is a popular and powerful one.

Neopagans and New Agers do not believe that all cultures have debased sexuality and nature. Some of the most powerful metaphors incorporated into their beliefs about and practices concerning sexuality have come from Buddhist and Hindu Tantric traditions of Tibet and India, grounding their interest in working with sexual energy in ancient Asian traditions. The Neopagan festival Rites of Spring included workshops on "Tantric Ecstatic Breath Ceremony" and "Tantric Polarity—Healing Our Sacred Sexuality." The Breath

Ceremony was described in this way: "Breathe the Breath of the Goddess, awakening the sacred snake of Kundalini, purifying and opening your vessel to the Divine Chalice. Breathe the Breath of God, and fill with the light of manifestation. Bathe in the ecstasy of their Sacred Union. In this Snake magic tantric ceremony be prepared to move through what stands between you and ecstasy." Neopagans and New Agers borrow the Asian concept of kundalini as an energy that flows through the spine and chakras. Here again the body is a source of power. The divine comes into the human body and the human taps into the divine, or what is seen as the sacred power of the universe. The "Tantric Polarity" workshop was based on the assumption that "tantra teaches us to shift our perceptions and see the divinity of our partners and to know our own."[50] Tantra offers techniques to better integrate sacred or divine energy into one's body. This and other methods of bringing together sex and spirituality exemplify the New Age idea of divinity in everyone.

Like the many other beliefs and practices that Neopagans and New Agers borrow, Tantric practice means something different to them and takes place in a different context than it would for Tibetan Buddhists and other Asian practitioners. New Agers and Neopagans encounter Tantrism as one of many spiritual practices or as a way to learn sexual techniques that incorporate a spiritual dimension, rather than an all-encompassing practice. For instance, in March 2003 the Toltec Center of Creative Intent in Berkeley, California offered a six-week intensive series on "Dark Shakti: Reclaiming Female Sexuality and Power." Women were invited to "transform sexual wounds, patterns and belief systems while working through inhibitions in a safe, supportive, women-only environment. . . . Discover how healing and growing your sexual strength expands your creativity and freedom in the world." New Age Tantric workshops usually involve different kinds of breath work and moving energy around in the body. The "Dark Shakti" workshop was to blend "tantric practices, trancework, ritual, movement and breath to help women emerge into sexual freedom and ecstasy."[51] The New Age magazine *Voice of the New Earth* advertised "Sacred Sexuality: An Introduction to Tantra for Women" and "Evoking Divine Passion: Women's Tantra," a workshop in which participants were told that they would "Experience the joys of Tantra, expand your capacity for intimacy. Enjoy breathing practices, imagery, sacred dance, and heartfelt rituals that deepen your connections and reclaim your sensual nature. Learn to move kundalini, heal your sexuality, activate ecstatic states."[52] Like other kinds of healing, sexual healing for New Agers and Neopagans is necessary for sexual and spiritual growth. And like other aspects of the self, sexual experience and identity are seen as holding nearly unlimited potential. New Age writer Shakti Gawain believes that American society is moving toward a revolution in relationships of which Tantric practice is one aspect. Tantra is part of her spiritual journey and her religious identity, her path and her spiritual name: "I am committed to a Tantric path—the journey which takes us through the deep, dark, unknown places in life, into the light of self-realization. In the Tantric tradition, Shiva and Shakti represent the male and female, seeking wholeness through their union."[53] Neopagans and New Agers adopt models like these as a conscious alternative to the sexual values they learned in other religions or in secular society.

The turn to alternative models of sexuality in other cultures has contributed to the belief among Neopagans and New Agers that sex is a sacrament—an act that is sacred and special, identified with rather than divorced from spirituality. For instance, Starhawk describes the connection this way: "Sexuality is sacred because it is a sharing of energy, in passionate surrender to the power of the Goddess, immanent in our desire. In orgasm, we share in the force that moves the stars." Neopagan writer Carl Jones suggests that "Only if we allow ourselves an inner quietness can we hear the sweet wooing of sexual ritual's voice and taste her loveliest fruit: that utterly consuming, embracing feeling of being submerged in an oceanic experience and bathing in the mystical waves of that thoroughly unintellectual thing we call love . . . sexual magic . . . reflects a spiritual realization of mystical experience born in an appreciation for the power and joy inherent in sexual expression."[54] Sexual experience is an opportunity for worship of what is sacred in the self and in the other person.

Some Neopagans connect this experience specifically to the Asian understanding of chakras in the body. Carl L. Weschcke's instructions for "Tantric Occultism" in the magazine *Gnostica: Esoteric Knowledge for the New Age* describe the benefit of Tantric practice as the opening of the chakras: "Every orgasm, in Tantra, causes the chakras to open, to 'click' for a moment. Every ecstatic experience represents an opening of the chakras. The more joy that can be experienced, the more the chakras are opened up."[55] Psychologist and popular New Age writer Caroline Myss explains the connection between sex and the second chakra: "Sexuality and all of our attitudes toward it are patterned in the second chakra. . . . Sexual eroticism is a form of spiritual and emotional liberation as well as physical liberation. Why spiritual? Erotic pleasure is, by nature, 'in the moment,' an encounter in which we drop most of our physical boundaries in order to enjoy the full measure of human contact. Explored without shame, erotic energy can elevate the human body and spirit into sensations of ecstasy, at times producing altered states of consciousness." Myss echoes the views of many New Agers and Neopagans as she describes the ways in which "kundalini energy" rises up through the seven chakras of the body. She explains that some mystics learn to channel sexual energy "to rise up the spine and culminate in a spiritual union with the Divine" and in this way reach altered states of consciousness.[56] Like the recreation of ancient cultures where priestesses served the goddess through sexual rites, borrowing Asian models provides a method of blending sex and spirituality and justifies Neopagan and New Age sexual experimentation.

The Neopagan Church of All Worlds has been one of the most vocal supporters of diverse sexual expression. Morning Glory Zell, one of its founders, presents workshops on "polyamory," a term she says she coined to refer to structured relationships with multiple partners at Neopagan festivals, one of which she called "A Bouquet of Lovers." Church of All Worlds member Michael Aluna believes that "panfidelity" is one antidote to the isolation and alienation that individualism breeds in the lives of many Americans. In "Panfidelity: Sacred Sex, Deep Ecology, and Human Destiny," he argues that living in community is an essential development in our evolution: "We must create sustainable communities or die. It is that simple. It seems likely that nuclear families will soon coexist with multi-adult living groups, or intentional extended families. Such 'expanded families' or 'pods' will consist of networks of intimate friends who may or may not live together, and for whom the possibility of sexual involvement with each other is open."[57] And essential to these communities is "sacred ritual," because "Rituals work at a level of consciousness far deeper than the merely rational and verbal level. . . . They bond us to each other, and align us with the cycles and rhythms of both our inner and outer nature."[58] Neopagan writer Deborah Anapol also equates multiple relationships with spiritual growth and human evolution:

> Intimate relationships at their best are a path to higher consciousness and greater self-knowledge, largely because of the valuable feedback or mirroring effect one receives from a beloved. Having more than one partner at a time not only increases the available quantity of feedback, it also makes it harder to blame your partner for the problems you might be creating in the relationship . . . the challenges of exploring new ways of relating intimately are no less demanding than those faced by the intrepid explorers who sailed over the edge of a supposedly flat world.[59]

New Agers and Neopagans often equate inner with outer journeys, and this is particularly true in the area of sex and spirituality.

Like authors Bradley and Brindel, modern-day Witches and other goddess worshippers imagine the sacred marriage in such a way that it becomes transformative for them. Contemporary sacred marriage rituals can be used to initiate followers into the goddess's "mysteries" as well as to "work magic." Witches interviewed for Janet and Stewart Farrar's study of contemporary Witchcraft described occasions for the practice of contemporary "sex magic." The Farrars asked interviewees from North America, Australia, Europe, and Britain how—assuming belief in the centrality of male-female polarity is shared by most Witches—sex comes into their rituals. Respondents confirmed that that they included the Great Rite—ritualized intercourse, often between priest and priestess—in their religious practice. For most, "the Great Rite may take two forms—'actual,' involving intercourse, or symbolic, in which the union of the male and female principles is symbolised by the insertion of the athame (ritual knife) into the chalice to bless the wine."[60] Several people told the Farrars that the "actual" form was most often used on special occasions, "particularly ones concerned with the basic elemental forms of the natural environment."[61] Margot Adler explains that "the idea behind the 'Great Rite' is that a woman who, through ritual, has 'incarnated' or *become* the Goddess, and a man who, through ritual, has 'incarnated' or *become* the God—in other words, two people who have drawn down into themselves these archetypal forces, or, if you will, have allowed these forces within them to surface—can have a spiritual and physical union that is truly divine." However, in her study of contemporary Neopagans, Adler reports that many covens do not use actual sexual rites.[62]

The actual ritual is also sometimes used in ceremonial magic rituals and Wiccan handfastings, a form of marriage. However, unlike the imagined rites of ancient Britain, handfastings often take place to formalize relationships that have already been established. In the fictional rites no one "'gives away' the bride. Like her groom, she comes to it as a free human being, nobody's property but her own."[63] Contemporary Witches and other Neopagans elevate sexuality, but this does not translate into promiscuous sexual behavior. "Sex magic" is not some kind of free-for-all orgy but is most frequently enacted in a structured ritual setting by couples who are already involved in a relationship. One of the Farrars' respondents put it this way: "sexual union between the male and female, which creates the ultimate power, should only be raised between people who actually love each other and have emotional bonds. . . . I think it's important that there should be both a mental and a physical link between those who are participating in 'sex magic.'"[64] Sexual freedom is important to many Neopagans because they believe that sexuality is both natural and sacred, but "freedom" is translated to mean the right to choose a homosexual relationship, to have multiple lovers, to be celibate, or to commit to a monogamous heterosexual relationship.

New Agers and Neopagans believe that changes in gender roles and sexual identity symbolize a shift from the Piscean (ruled by the male or father) to the Aquarian (ruled by the female or mother) Age. As Shakti Gawain sees it, "humanity has gone through a time of expressing its male energy, which achieves, explores, gets things done." Now, she says, people are "becoming aware of their female energy, the part of us that wants to merge, make whole, and heal."[65] Health author and journalist Peg Jordan also believes that humanity has been moving into a more "feminine" age at the end of the twentieth and beginning of the twenty-first centuries, characterized by a shift from "the Conquering myth to the Regeneration myth."[66] She suggests that this change has come about because "this pool of energy has been permeated by enough feminine spirit to transform consciousness in a massive way." New Agers believe that the evolving planetary society will be characterized by the return of the feminine or goddess archetype as a corrective to centuries of male domination. New Age teacher and writer (and advisor to then First Lady Hillary Clinton) Jean Houston observed in 1996 that the feminine mind was becoming dominant: "The tide of consciousness was rising, and feminine sensibility and potential were becoming critical to human survival. . . . The noosphere or global mind field . . . is coming closer, and essential to its development is clearly the rich mindstyle of woman, now ready to emerge everywhere after centuries of gestation in the womb of preparatory time. Herstory, rich and fecund, is coming into the light."[67] If the future will take feminine form, it will also be modeled on a particular construction of the past, on goddess-worshipping societies that were conquered by patriarchal ones. Like goddess feminists, Houston draws on the work of James Mellaart, Marija Gimbutas, and Riane Eisler to imagine the revival of an ancient "partnership model" between men and women. Like many New Agers, she looks toward the future with optimism and excitement. Rites of passage to honor the stages in men's and women's lives, exploration of various forms of masculinity and femininity, tolerance of sexual diversity, the celebration of sexuality as sacred, all exist in this vision of a future "Aquarian Age" populated by transformed men and women.

# CHAPTER SEVEN

# The Age of Aquarius

Although the idea of a New Age was popularized by Alice Bailey in the early twentieth century, the term had been around at least since the American Revolution before it was used self-consciously by Theosophists like her who believed a "master" would come to enlighten humanity and usher us into a new age.[1] The concept picked up relevance as the 1960s counterculture looked toward the Age of Aquarius as a utopian future of peace and equality. Movements aimed at social and personal transformation that emerged or were given new meaning in the 1960s continue to shape New Age and Neopagan religions. Ideas about the expected new era vary among Neopagans and New Agers, just as they ranged in the 1960s from social revolution to communal escape from society. But most agree that it will include a changed dynamic between men and women, healthy diet, holistic healing practices, and peacefulness.

Along with and related to holistic healing and feminist restructuring, environmentalist concerns are seen as key in bringing about the transformation of society. Many New Agers and Neopagans believe that an ecologically viable relationship to the natural world will characterize the future age, when humans will live more harmoniously on earth. Some also believe the earth itself, a living being that has been ill used by humanity, will bring about cataclysmic changes, while others expect a gradual dawning of enlightened consciousness among large numbers of people to usher in the New Age. Goddess religion will emerge from a "Great Purification," claim some observers, borrowing a phrase from Hopi prophecy: "Look at the freak weather phenomena all around us . . . Mother Nature is beginning to take things into her own hands."[2] In their desire to shape the future through healing the body, instituting balanced gender roles, creating or rediscovering rituals and sacred spaces, transforming consciousness, and caring for the environment, New Agers and Neopagans get involved in social and environmental activism as well as inner work.

## Apocalyptic Thinking and the Aquarian Age

One of the ways new religions attract members is by holding out an opportunity to shape the future and to play a part in creating a new heaven on earth. Like their conservative Christian counterparts, some New Agers and Neopagans have an apocalyptic vision. They approach the Age of Aquarius in mythological terms by turning to ancient Hopi and Mayan prophecies and astrological theories. Historian Catherine Albanese explains that "in astrological thinking the stars symbolized not only the life paths of individuals but also the quality of time in general. In many cases an astrological 'dispensationalism' prevailed, and astrologers claimed to read the coming of different eras in the stars." According to Albanese, the Age of Aquarius, "an early name for the New Age, became a symbol for the consciousness that New Age people believed would replace old and outworn beliefs." Some astrologers spread the theory that when the sun entered the constellation of Aquarius on the day of the spring equinox, the Aquarian Age would arrive. Albanese points out, however, that although "according to strict astrological charting the Age of Aquarius would arrive some 300 years after the last decades of the twentieth century, the concept—like astrological belief in general—became an important ingredient in the New Age."[3] New Agers turned the idea of an imminent astrological shift into an apocalypse characterized by chaos and suffering that they believed would lead to an era of peace or a new age characterized by "Aquarian consciousness."

These views are based on an ancient system of predicting future events and understanding the present in relation to the positions of planets. In astrology the heavens are divided into twelve zodiac signs named for the constellations. The signs stay the same, but the constellations move in cycles. Each lines up with its corresponding sign for a little over 2,000 years, and the entire cycle takes over 25,000 years to complete. The so-called Piscean Age has lasted for about the 2,000 years during which the Piscean sign and constellation have been in alignment. The next alignment will be the sign and constellation of Aquarius, but precisely when the Aquarian Age will begin or whether it has already begun is open to interpretation, because no one is really sure when the Piscean Age began and exactly how long it has lasted. Many astrologers predict that the transition from one age to the next will be a time of chaos and cataclysm, while others believe the shift will be more gradual. They also stress the role of individuals in shaping the nature of this transition.[4]

Neopagan author Marian Green points to the individual as a source of power in the astrologically determined New Age: "We are changing from the astrological age of Pisces, in which people acted like schools of fish, all following the same rules and the same patterns of life, to the new age of Aquarius. Aquarius is usually shown as a man with a water pot, pouring out a stream of water. This symbolises individuality."[5] Because astrology is a source of knowledge and guidance that both Neopagans and New Agers turn to, they share similar beliefs about the Age of Aquarius. Marilyn Ferguson, author of *The Aquarian Conspiracy*, also sees the shift to the age of "Aquarius, the waterbearer in the ancient zodiac, symbolizing flow and the quenching of an ancient thirst."[6] Ferguson's book, published in 1980, describes a network of "Aquarian conspirators" who emerged in the late 1970s as a result of the convergence of "the social activism of the 1960s" and the "consciousness revolution" of the early 1970s when "social transformation resulted from personal transformation—change from the inside out." Ferguson explains that she chose the term "Aquarian" to give a positive note to the "conspiracy" that she feared might be understood as something negative. "I was drawn to the symbolic power of the pervasive dream in our popular culture: that after a dark, violent age, the Piscean, we are entering a millennium of love and light."[7] Not only has the preceding age been violent, but some New Agers and Neopagans argue that violence is the only way to bring about change.

Many New Age teachers and writers imagine that a global cleansing or purification is necessary before the New Age can take place. New Age visionary and Ojibwa Indian Sun Bear describes prophecies from different eras and different cultures in his book *Black Dawn, Bright Day: Indian Prophecies for the Millennium That Reveal the Fate of the Earth* (1992). "Be aware," he says. "There is always a warning." Sun Bear believes that chaos will grow first in cities, where diseases and earthquakes will wreak havoc: "there will come a time of great destruction to the Earth. The wise people will know what to do and will move in a sacred manner to make the changes necessary for their own survival and for the survival of others. Those who do survive will be the people who have studied the prophecies and have learned how to hear the Earth."[8] He assumes that a violent cleansing of the planet is necessary because "too many humans have become out of balance on the Earth Mother." Those who remain afterward will "relearn the language of nature," and Sun Bear and other New Age teachers are ready to show them how.[9] In one of his books Sun Bear provides maps of safe places to live and lists of supplies to help survive a cataclysmic event. If the apocalypse is necessary, and many New Agers believe it is, then humans should prepare to live differently as they transition from one age to the next. People will learn new ways of existing more harmoniously on the planet, he predicts, and "will share the same level of consciousness, found in their own individual ways."[10] His comment captures an important aspect of the New Age view: in the future, global unity will prevail without the sacrifice of individuality and personal freedom.

Many Neopagans also believe that the utopian society they envision will only be possible after a cataclysm. Witch Laurie Cabot expresses a popular belief that the earth is a goddess who will initiate the purification process: "The earth must adjust herself to the problems that human life has created for her. The great Titans of the earth are waking up to take part in this cleansing: fires, earthquakes, volcanoes, storms, droughts, floods. . . . But even the end of the earth may not be a disaster when viewed from the perspective of the All. We just don't know. At best we must heed these events as messages from the earth to reform our ways and live in harmony and balance with the earth and her many communities."[11] Cabot and others who look for a violent purification of the planet have little sympathy for humans because they believe that people have lived destructively on the earth and have brought this fate on themselves. Although unlike New Agers, they rarely focus on this topic during their rituals and festivals, Neopagan authors identify it as an underlying concern. In "What Next? Alternative Community in the Next Millennium," Neopagan Jim Cairo predicts that "the entire Earth will be thrown into a cultural Cuisinart set at high speed. The past will be gone, the present will be a jumble, and the future will be uncertain. . . . Group living arrangements, extended families, the legal redefinition of the family—our very concept of what it means to be human—will all be changed. This will be an exciting time for those of us experimenting with new-yet-old forms of alternative communities."[12]

New Age and Neopagan workshops on pansexuality and healing masculinity and femininity are part of this preparation for a transformed future. New Agers and Neopagans also prepare for basic survival when chaos comes. Most of them do not spend much time imagining the details, but a few think in concrete terms about the consequences of a global apocalypse. When I first met P. J., a member of the Neopagan Elf Lore Family, she told me that she thought of ELF's nature sanctuary, Lothlorien, as a safe place to escape to when "everything falls apart." New Agers are typically more inclined than Neopagans to describe the shift to the Aquarian Age in violent terms. Whatever they think about the apocalypse, both religions advocate new ways of living on the planet and think they have the best models for a viable future.

With the transition to the Age of Aquarius comes the displacement of truth and wisdom from church authorities to individual interpretation and personal experience, emphasized among New Agers and Neopagans alike. New Age writer Marianne Williamson predicts that "in the 'end days' we will not escape the horrors of the world through vehicles that soar into outer space, but through vehicles that soar into inner space. Those vehicles are our healed minds."[13] Church of All Worlds spiritual leaders Oberon and Morning Glory Zell believe the current global situation is dire, but that individuals can have an effect on the future: "it will truly take a miracle to reverse such global destruction. The only thing that can save us is a total and electrifying change of consciousness. Nothing short of a worldwide realization of our planetary awareness will bring home the desperation of our plight. We must activate our Gaian identification so that we regain our shattered empathy with the Spirit of Nature. We must become one with the Earth Mother in order to feel Her pain/our pain and make it stop before the cancer we have become reaches terminal phase."[14] According to these writers, a change of consciousness is not only to bring about self-growth but also to ensure planetary survival.

Neopagans and New Agers often speak as though they are in the vanguard, an elite who will trigger the shift into an Aquarian Age through personal revolutions in consciousness. Metaphysical writer Laverne E. Denyer emphasizes a common New Age theme, the impact of personal change on the cosmos: "when our thoughts reach critical mass, they will quickly spread beyond our personal contacts through the web to everybody. . . . We have connecting bands of energy that link us all emotionally, mentally, psychically, and even physically."[15] Channeler Bryan Wood's spiritual allies, "the Clan," advised him that "the restructuring of your society must begin with the restructuring of your personal life. Focus on changing your own life to celebrate your own uniqueness in a way that makes you happy, and society will follow suit."[16] These New Agers see themselves as part of an advanced group whose consciousness has evolved beyond the rest of humanity. There will be those who have a "grander vision of the future and those who are blind to anything but the past"; those who have "made love to life . . . will soon give birth to a new century."[17] New Age author Marina Raye expects a violent transformation brought about by select individuals: "We represent the transformative power of lightning, burning away the old realities and re-birthing ourselves, and all of humanity."[18] At once both cathartic and painful, the apocalypse can be brought about by New Agers themselves in their de-sire to transform self and society.

If an evolved group will lead the way into a utopian future, everyone else will be left to a different fate. In "The Calm Before the Storm," Neale Don-ald Walsch's contribution to *Solstice Shift*, a collection of New Age thinkers' assessments about the future, he describes the current global condition of humanity as "a tale of two planets." In his view, the consciousness revolution will be exclusive; not everyone will belong to the Aquarian future. In a ver-sion of apocalyptic thinking that bears a striking resemblance to that of con-servative Christians who believe the Rapture will remove true Christian be-lievers from the tribulations of earth, leaving everyone else behind to suffer, Walsch predicts that "there will be the planet of the 'haves' and the planet of the 'have nots,' the home of the hopeful and the home of the hopeless, the world of believers and the world of nonbelievers."[19] In this way some New Agers affirm their unique role in history and their place in the future. They are the enlightened ones who will advance the course of evolution. Joe, one of the participants in a metaphysical group that Melinda Bollar Wagner stud-ied in the 1970s, who teaches a "Metaphysics of Death" class, believes that people who are enlightened will have a different experience at death than the unenlightened, and when the New Age comes, will be separated from the masses: "The enlightened would be allowed to reincarnate on earth, and the unenlightened would not . . . those who had already embarked on their path to spiritual growth would come to lead others, and to serve as examples to others, as the turmoil concomitant with the change from the Piscean to the Aquarian Age reached its peak."[20]

Joe's understanding falls in line with the teachings of Earlyne Chaney, founder of the New Age group Astara that Joe joined. Chaney believes that "numerous changes are to transpire in the minds of men, [and then] there will be a slow swing toward mysticism, and a gradual awakening of conscious-ness as humanity en masse begins to turn from darkness to light."[21] In his study of New Age sacred sites, religious studies scholar Adrian Ivakhiv calls this approach "ascensionism"; it is characterized by a dualistic view of the world in which forces of light, often embodied by ascended masters who speak through human channels, are contrasted with forces that hold back human potential: "The evolutionary potential of humanity is often modeled on the motif 'ascension' to higher levels or dimensions of existence." Ascensionist or dualistic literature—popular in the New Age movement and less common among Neopagans—"makes frequent use of quasi-scientific language to describe the 'higher frequencies,' 'vibrations,' 'light quotients' and 'energy bodies,' energy shifts and DNA changes, that are said to be associated with this epochal shift."[22] New Agers sometimes borrow from scientific discourse in an attempt to make their theories seem more plausible to a secular world and to demonstrate their place among the elite who will lead society into the new era.

However, New Agers and Neopagans assume that joining the elite is really just a matter of choice: you don't buy status, and you're not born with it. Anyone can pay for workshops and channeling sessions or attend Neopagan festivals that teach the skills and share the knowledge people need to evolve into the next age. Many events are open to the public, and individual Witches, astrologers, psychics, and channelers sell or donate their services in cities throughout the United States. These religious movements do not aggressively seek converts and believe that individuals are on their own spiritual paths. If people are meant to discover Witchcraft or to seek personal guidance from, say, the channeled entity Seth, then they will, and if not, then they will have other lifetimes in which to progress spiritually. Nevertheless, New Agers in particular are very publicity conscious. They advertise in yellow pages or newsweeklies and leave their free newsletters in hotel lobbies and bookstores. New Age and Neopagan Web sites give contact information for groups and individual teachers throughout the country and offer online courses, so that everyone who is ready and willing can join them. But ascensionism is just one of many strands of thought about the future; there are New Agers and Neopagans who do not share its exclusivist views.

### Utopian Communities and the Next Generation

For many New Agers and Neopagans, social or global upheaval is not necessary to produce the Aquarian Age; it has already arrived or will come gradually. Influential New Age writer David Spangler criticizes the belief in sudden transformation, especially if the transformation is outside the efforts of individual humans, because he thinks this is too much like the expectation of Christ's second coming. He believes the shift is a gradual one through which the New Age will offer "a greater state of individual freedom of soul and consciousness to embody and express more fully the unique configuration of sacredness that each of us represents." "At the same time," he writes, this freedom will include "a greater awareness of our participation in larger wholes, from our families on up to all of humanity and beyond, to the community of planetary and cosmic life itself."[23] In his introduction to the memoir of Findhorn founder Peter Caddy, Spangler writes that "the challenges of the late twentieth century demand that we reimagine our future and that we are daring in making changes personally and collectively to shape a more compassionate tomorrow . . . at least if we want angels and not rough beasts to define what our future will be like. We must dare to be skilled visionaries."[24] Many New Agers and Neopagans would agree that the Age of Aquarius has already come to pass and humans must work to bring their personal lives into alignment with this global shift. In order to do this they must undergo a personal initiation that may be difficult and painful.

Spangler envisions the New Age as one of an evolved "earth-consciousness," but he warns that "the spirituality of the earth is more than a slogan. It is an invitation to initiation, to the death of what we have been and the birth of something new."[25] This kind of apocalyptic thinking is on a personal, not a global level, and involves psychological rather than material destruction and rebirth. In the minds of New Agers and Neopagans, the coming of the Aquarian Age is initiatory. The transition to a new age will involve suffering and healing, intense personal examination and introspection, and significant changes in relationships with other people and with the planet. Their vision is utopian in its hopefulness about human potential and the belief that everyone has the resources within to transform themselves and the ability, if they choose, to access spirit guides and other spirit beings for aid.

One of the ways Neopagans and New Agers choose to bring their lives into alignment with or to prepare for a planetary shift is by creating and participating in communities. Intentional spiritual communities offer models for the future and allow New Agers and Neopagans to craft a visible alternative to the society they criticize, to live the teachings of their religions, and to make material their beliefs. Some believe that urban areas offer the best sources for new ideas and the necessary population to spread New Age visions, while others look to rural farmland or wilderness and believe that living close to nature is preferable. One Neopagan told journalist Margot Adler that "The breakdown of Piscean culture and the developing of Aquarian culture is occurring in the big cities. Aquarians gravitate there because they are freer to develop there."[26] Networks of New Agers and Neopagans meet in urban areas throughout the United States for public festivals and gatherings, rites of passage, healing rituals, group meditation, and other community events.

On the other hand, New Agers gather in naturally beautiful and out-of-the-way places like Sedona, Arizona and Neopagans create nature sanctuaries in rural locations. Gaia's Oasis, a nature sanctuary in the Sierra Nevada foothills of Northern California, was founded by its owners to "be a place of deep connection to the earth, where we can heal ourselves of the wound of separation from nature and so participate in the earth healing herself."27 Stone mandalas near Sedona and shrines in the woods of Neopagan nature sanctuaries are ways of inscribing beliefs on the land and of interacting with spirit entities that live there. These sanctuaries offer peaceful retreats to urban dwellers who visit on weekends or ongoing live-in communities for those who have left urban life.

Two and a half miles north of San Francisco, Harbin Hot Springs is a "New Age Growth and Spiritual Center" established by the Heart Consciousness Church in 1975. A curving road leads through the Northern California coastal mountain range along dry hillsides spotted with valley oak trees and mountain laurel. Harbin lies in a chain of hot springs in Lake County, one of California's oldest known areas of human habitation. The area was an ancient site of worship for the Pomo people, and after they had been pushed out by settlers, many health spas sprang up there during the nineteenth century. In the 1880s invalids traveled by stagecoach to "Harbin Hot Springs Health and Pleasure Resort," and some of the structures on the site date to that era. The springs are channeled into several pools of varying temperatures that are clothing optional, and massage and acupuncture are available on site, as is a juice bar. People camp or stay in the lodge for a quiet retreat and to participate in workshops of varying lengths on topics such as "Kundalini Yoga," "Sufi Dancing," "Tantric Massage for Lovers," and Unconditional Dance." But there is also an established live-in community that runs the guest services and takes care of the land. According to Harbin's Web site, the Heart Consciousness Church hopes to "seed a New Age Society" with this community living on the land as a model for the future: "We are a springboard for the creation of a New Age society. . . . Our New Age point of view is defined as the common thread contained in the Human Potential Movement, the Holistic, Natural Movement, and universal spirituality. We identify ourselves so completely with this point of view that we call it a religion and ourselves a church. For what is religion, but what we resonate with most deeply, and try to manifest consciously?" The church is run by a network of small groups that make decisions by consensus and emphasize respect for individual spiritual

expression and mutual learning: "The common thread of these three movements is experienced differently by each member, and we are gentle in defining it. Clearly these elements stand out: growth; wholeness; health; related-
ness; loving support and sharing; a universal, all embracing view; organic
process seen as essence; and the essential value, not only of all parts of the environment, but of each part of each person."[28] The community welcomes
people who want to contribute to the realization of these goals and offers ritual activities and other events to the general public.

Utopian visions of community are common at Neopagan and New Age
gatherings, where activities are tailored toward a hoped-for future even
though the gatherings are temporary communities. Sometimes they develop
into committed and permanent communal situations. One of the first Neopagan organizations to hold a large eclectic festival was the Boston area–
based Earth Spirit Community; they rented a rural site owned by the YMCA
for their festivals year after year. Eventually a core group of people involved
with Earth Spirit, including founder Andras Arthen, decided that they
needed to acquire rural land in order to actualize a vision he had of living in
community closer to nature. Staring into a fire one night when he was camping in Maine, Arthen pictured the following scene:

> Nestled among the rolling hills of western Massachusetts there is a place
> bounded by streams, with woods of hemlock, of maple and of birch, and
> stretches of green meadow with apple trees and berry bushes and gar-
> dens with flowers of many kinds. Atop a hill, a fire blazes inside a ring of
> stones, its sparks cavorting across the midnight sky to join the twinkling
> canopy of stars. Drums pound, voices sing, shadows dance; a large black
> dog watches with unblinking eyes. A slender, tall and branchless tree
> stands all alone, sheathed in an intricate web of many-colored ribbons.
> Dawn stirs awake, a hawk flies overhead. This place is home to a family,
> to a community of people linked together not by blood but by belief in-
> spired by the power of ancient ways to build a bridge of hope and of in-
> tent toward the future. And to this place many people come—to learn,
> to teach, to heal, to build, to change and shape, to dream. Seeds sprout,
> gates open; the glowing tendrils of a shimmering web reach out across
> the land to other places, to other beings, seeking kinship, seeking balance
> restored. The gurgle of the streams carries a song; the trees join with the
> wind in atavistic dance; the standing stones, with measured, silent voices
> tell a story older than humankind, older than time itself. The call is sent,
> the ancient powers come.[29]

Twenty-five years later, Andras reported on Earth Spirit's Web site that the vision was realized: "I am happy to report that, since last Fall, a group of us has been living in community at Glenwood Farm, in the hills of western Massachusetts, a place that looks and feels strikingly like the one I saw in the fire so long ago. The land encompasses 130 meadows and woods, with a few streams, a pond, and several buildings."

Many of these model communities in the woods and mountains have multiple functions, often combining educational space with ritual sites. Harbin is a retreat center and tourist attraction as well as a spiritual community. Earth Spirit's land is home to a fledgling community and not yet a teaching center, but Arthen's vision suggests it will eventually be put to many other uses. In southern Indiana another Neopagan community put their ideals into action by combining a spiritual community, teaching center, and environmentally conscious living on the land. In the 1980s the Elf Lore Family acquired 100 acres of old farmland and woods and let nature take its course, although they maintain several trails and a large field for gatherings. They named the sanctuary Lothlorien after Tolkien's land of the elves in *The Lord of the Rings*. Lothlorien was conceived as a "nature sanctuary, survival education center [and] woodland meeting grounds," according to ELF literature. ELF combined ritual activities for Neopagans with alternative energy workshops, and built composting toilets and solar-powered buildings. They offer workshops in herbal healing using native plants and planted trees. "Chanting isn't enough," claims one ELF publication, "unless we actively engage ourselves in REGREENING, the environmental crisis will continue to grow . . . go beyond apocalypse and actively plant the planet." Planting is a major enterprise as well at Annwfn, a site in Northern California near the city of Ukiah that is owned by the Church of All Worlds. According to its Web site, CAW's tree-planting organization, "Forever Forests," works to care for and replant the land. In the early 1990s ELF publications called for "econauts" to make self-sustaining "bioshelters" on the land and to "make the quantum leap . . . integrating permanently into the 'post apocalyptic dreamtime.'"[30] Here again the idea is that the shift is mental, a change of attitude, rather than physical, like earthquakes and floods. In their own homes as well as at festivals, many New Agers and Neopagans put in practice their environmentalist visions of the future. In a broad sense, the goal is "planetary consciousness" shared by a global community in harmony with the natural world: "The Gaia hypothesis seeks not only one world culture and a united consciousness among humans, but a deep reverence for life and a consciousness of oneness with it."[31] For some this kind of oneness is best realized by creating sanctuaries and rural communes where those who are inclined can find a home and city-dwellers an escape from hectic urban life.

Neopagan and New Age communities have expanded to include participants in all phases of life, especially children and the elderly, to whom they paid little attention when they organized gatherings in the 1970s and 1980s. Current visions of community include the next generation, new ways to live in families and to raise children that are in harmony with their religious beliefs but also protect their families from ostracism. In 1999 sociologist Helen Berger estimated "conservatively that 82,600 children are being raised in Neo-Pagan families throughout the United States."[32] Only a minority of Neopagan and New Age families choose to live in isolated rural communities. Most are well integrated into society even if at the same time critical of it. They pay taxes, go to school and work, take their children to after-school sports and other activities, and volunteer in their neighborhoods. But their religious practices are often quite different from those of their neighbors. For those who choose to live within mainstream society, meditation rituals, rites of initiation, and seasonal celebrations can be at odds with the traditions of people who live around them. Tensions over children are often at the heart of Neopagan and New Age conflicts with the broader society and within their own communities.

Neopagan festivals, for instance, started in the late 1970s and early 1980s to serve a community largely composed of young adults without children—many of whom participated in the 1960s counterculture and were searching for and experimenting with alternative lifestyles and new forms of spirituality. As this first generation aged, had families, and started bringing them to festivals, they were forced to adapt to a new challenge—how to incorporate children into their communities. Family-oriented events and family festival spaces were created to address these new community needs. Starwood instituted a "Kids Village" for preteens and "co-op childcare" for small children.[33] At one Rites of Spring festival, children participated in the main ritual by blessing the sacred circle with their singing and bell-ringing; one young girl even played the part of the maiden goddess.[34] Festival organizers developed children's workshops on ancient myths and mask-making and created rites of passage for adolescents. Still, the organizers faced complaints from within their communities as well as from neighboring ones. Some parents complained about the noise of late-night drumming that was keeping their children awake, while others claimed that the drumming lulled their children to sleep. But they also had to face the charges of outsiders who saw festival nudity and Witchcraft rituals as evidence of a culture of child abuse.

For this reason, parents concerned about custody issues sometimes choose to stay at home and practice their religion privately. Neopagans have increasingly added children's activities to their gatherings and placed resources for teenagers on their Web sites in order to provide the next generation access to knowledge that will encourage them to imagine their own communities for the New Age.

Elders as well as children are honored in New Age and Neopagan communities. As a large cohort of Neopagan leaders is aging and watching friends age and die, there has been increasing discussion of Neopagan nursing homes and green burials. One Neopagan Web site discussed "Pagan burial grounds" as a way to extend the beliefs of an ecologically friendly religion into dealing with death. What better way to nurture the next generation, suggests the author, than by "creating beautiful Sacred Groves—intentionally planted forests made up of memorial trees marking where our physical remains are. . . . Do we want our memorial place looking very much like a golfing green? Most cemetery plots do not allow trees to be planted over the dead. We need to create ecocemeteries, and Pagan burial grounds where the wildlife habitat is expanded and augmented, where Memorial Trees are planted and we may thereby give back to the Mother."[35] Here values of interconnectedness and reciprocity are extended into the final transformation of self in this lifetime.

## Social and Environmental Activism

In order to shape the future, Neopagans and New Agers turn outward as well as inward; they care for the well-being of their local communities and families as well as the health of the planet. The sense that individual transformation has to happen before society can change prevents some from making activist commitments. One New Age author who believes that activism is part of the work of individual transformation notes that "Just as the world is at a great turning point, so is the consciousness movement. Rather than following a transcendent path and withdrawing from the world, we must commit ourselves to the transformational path and take responsibility for changing the world."[36] Historian Catherine Albanese observes that "the New Age social ethic has been an environmental ethic . . . from the early days of the movement, New Age people have—in keeping with the theory of correspondence—linked the well-being of their lives to the well-being of the world."[37]

Popular Neopagan author and long-term activist Starhawk exemplifies the marriage of religion and activism. In 2002 during the World Trade Organization meeting protests in Seattle, Washington, Starhawk was one of a group of Neopagans arrested and detained for nonviolent resistance. Starhawk helped with the nonviolence training conducted weeks in advance. She joined the efforts there to shut down the meeting and was arrested. Over the Internet she sent an "Open Letter to the Pagan Community" describing some of the ways that magic helped at the protest: "We were, of course, working magic on every level, from rituals we offered before the action to a meditation on shared intent that Margo Adair taught us, to the trancework some of us did in our own circles, to the WTO spell (an ice sculpture that melted throughout the ritual) we had as an altar at the Spiral Dance" (the Spiral Dance usually involves a large group of people linking hands and dancing in a spiral). After Starhawk and hundreds of other nonviolent protesters were arrested and taken to jail, she turned to magic to help herself and them deal with that experience: "We worked magic in jail, as well. We sang songs, told stories, shared meditations, and learned to ground and call on the elements. About fifty of us held an impromptu ritual while waiting in a holding cell for arraignment and later danced the spiral dance. We practiced the art of changing consciousness at will . . . a depth of almost radiant happiness like a pure current in a roiling river that I could tap into whenever my spirit started to flag." She also suffered a severe case of bronchitis while in jail and was again helped by the ritual work she and her friends engaged in:

In one of our rituals, my friend Willow had invoked the Green Man and reminded us that oxygen is his breath and he is everywhere. When I lay in my airless, torturously overheated cell at night, coughing and feverish and struggling to breathe, I could call upon him through such air as there was and visualize the cool, moist scent of the redwoods by my home. I'd close my eyes and see the ancestors marching with us in great rivers, turning the tide. And I could feel a depth of strength in myself that I didn't know I had. It was the most powerful initiation I've ever experienced. Why did we do it? I did it because I am a Pagan and a Witch. I know that in the vast, broad Pagan world out there, we don't all share the same politics—but I think there are some core things that we do share and the WTO touches all of them. We worship nature. The WTO is part of a global attempt to elevate profit as a value that supersedes nature or any other value.[38]

The integration of ritual and activism is a particular focus of Starhawk's work. She and other Neopagans and New Agers who believe that all things are interconnected want to promote an ecologically viable future through changing consciousness and acting in the world.

Environmental activism is important to many Neopagans because they believe that if the New Age is to come peacefully, then the planet—"Gaia"—must be healed and protected. According to Neopagan priestess Vivianne Crowley, the British Neopagan Dragon environmental group "conducts magical healing rites at threatened natural sites" and a similar group in New York City called the "Gaia group" focuses on "ecological magic." Crowley applauds these efforts because she believes that "earth healing rituals raise awareness of environmental issues and those who take part in them are generally encouraged to take action on the material as well as on the magical plane to further their ends."[39] Famous "Witch of Salem" Laurie Cabot believes that environmental issues provide the most appropriate opportunities for good works: "Witches will speak out for the rights of the earth. Our voices will be among the loudest, calling all people to live in balance and harmony with the communities of plants, animals, and minerals. . . . Witches of the future will pioneer new ways for individuals to scale down their needs and live lighter, touching the earth more gently."[40] When Neopagans and environmentalists in Northern California came together to fight a timber harvest plan, they met at the site of the proposed harvest next to the river they were trying to protect. They had a rattlesnake in a bucket because it appeared in a friend's driveway the day of the protest, as an omen, they speculated. They had given up trying to find justice for the forest through official channels. And so they chose another approach—to bring about change through ritual action:

> So we gather in the woods to claim this forest as sacred space, to charge our letters, our petition, our phone calls, with magic, that extra something that may shift the structures just a bit, create an opening for something new. We sing, we chant, we make offerings, we claim this land as sacred space. We dare to call upon the ancestors although we recognize ourselves as the inheritors of stolen lands. Out of these contradictions, out of our willingness to listen, to guard the soil and the trees and the rivers, to cherish each other and the love that arises from our history of everyday work and quarrels and our common song, we intend to conjure back the salmon, the ancient groves, the community of those indigenous

to this place. We draw spirals in the dirt. We have feathers, yarn, a shell: our altar. We release the snake from her bucket. She is beautiful, the scales on her back glistening in diamond shape, her tail crowned with many rattles. . . . When we go, she will coil her body into a spiral and remain, a fitting guardian for this land. . . . This is how it works: someone has a vision that arises from a fierce and passionate love. To make it real, we must love every moment of what we do. Impermanent spirals embed themselves in asphalt, concrete, dust. Slowly, slowly, they eat into the foundations of the structures of power. Deep transformations take time. Regeneration arises from decay. Si se puede! It can be done.[41]

For Neopagans who hold a cyclical view of time and history, decay is hopeful. The signs of ecological catastrophe are horrific, but they are not cause for despair. Just as Neopagans celebrate Samhain, a festival of harvest and honoring the dead, so they see the abuse of "Mother Earth" as a disaster that can yield positive change.

Most Neopagans and New Agers are not involved with activism to the extent that Starhawk is; nevertheless, many of them try to live in ways that they believe will benefit society as well as enrich their own lives. Sometimes this translates into public activism, but it can also mean participating in local changes that contribute to the future. In *The Power of the Witch* Laurie Cabot tells her readers to engage in "good works," to volunteer in their communities, plant trees, take meals to the poor, and help people in nursing homes plant gardens. In civic protests, city life, temporary festival communities, and rural communes, New Agers and Neopagans attempt to live out their dreams of a new age. But as they voice their concerns in public and materialize their visions of the future through communal living, they become more visible to other Americans who do not understand or disapprove of their beliefs and practices.

## Oppositions and Controversies

Like all religions, and especially new ones, the New Age movement and Neopaganism have experienced controversies within and tensions between their beliefs and those of their neighbors. These controversies have tended to come from two very different sources: conservative Christians and American Indians. For conservative Christians, both Protestant and Catholic, the issue is the "satanic" threat they believe is posed by New Agers and Neopagans; for Indians it is cultural borrowing (or "stealing," depending on one's perspective).

During the decades following the 1960s, as Neopagans and New Agers made countercultural concepts central to their religious identity and lifestyle, opposition to their vision of an Age of Aquarius grew. New Age parenting guides and Neopagan workshops for teens were seen by another emergent movement—conservative Protestant evangelicalism—as dangerous portents for American society. What New Agers saw as an exciting promise for the future, conservative Protestants (and Catholics to some extent) understood as a threat to their own very different plans. Since their beginnings, both Christianity and these new movements have believed in social transformation and tended to think in apocalyptic terms. But for conservative evangelical Protestants the expectation of a violent apocalypse, during which true believers would be taken away in the "Rapture" while everyone else was left behind to suffer, became central. New Agers might share similar assumptions about a cataclysm that an enlightened elite would survive, but they were as likely to see the millennium as a gradual and peaceful transformation.

Christian concerns about the New Age movement were voiced from its first emergence in the 1970s through the opening years of the twenty-first century. The resultant controversies are ongoing struggles for the shape of the future, spiritual wars in which both sides believe their cultural survival is at stake. In March 2003 the London *Guardian* reported that "the Catholic hierarchy has underlined its opposition to New Age spirituality with a 100-page document urging its flock to resist the lure of cranky, holistic 'experimentation.'"[42] Neopagans who have for years been trying to get the Vatican to apologize for the witch-hunting that Catholics spearheaded in sixteenth-century Europe were outraged by this latest offense and spread the outcry internationally over the Internet.

While denominations like the Unitarians and Universalists have welcomed Neopagans and New Agers to use their meeting places and some Christian theologians have expressed beliefs similar to those of New Agers and Neopagans, conservative Protestant Christians have attacked them as evil and demonic. For instance, in 1999 ministers and members of Congress were in an uproar when they discovered that Fort Hood in Killeen, Texas, the largest U.S. Army base, had sanctioned its first Wiccan group two years earlier and created a space for Wiccans to worship: "Christian groups were calling the base and threatening to stage a march in town and disrupt the rituals, forcing the Army to beef up security around the campsite." Since then, observes one reporter, "witch skittishness" has spread as far as Washington, D.C. "Please stop this nonsense now," Rep. Robert L. Barr Jr. (R-Ga.) wrote to Lt. Gen. Leon S. Leponte, the commanding officer of Fort Hood. "What's next? Will armored divisions be forced to travel with sacrificial animals for Satanic rituals? Will Rastafarians demand the inclusion of ritualistic marijuana cigarettes in their rations?"[43] Local ministers long opposed the Wiccan presence at Fort Hood: "Everyone thinks they're such sweet, lovely people," said the Rev. Jack Harvey, who runs the Tabernacle Baptist Church in Killeen, but "God says, 'Suffer not a witch to live.' . . . We would like to see them saved, but God doesn't change his mind." According to an article in the *Salt Lake Tribune*, "Paul M. Weyrich, radio talk show host and president of the Free Congress Foundation, has called for Christians to boycott the Army until it "withdraws all official support and approval from 'witchcraft.'" He was joined in his call for a "recruiting strike" by other Christian conservative groups, including the Christian Coalition, the Traditional Values Coalition, and the American Family Association.[44] Conservative Protestants have attacked Neopagans and New Agers on other fronts as well, especially morality. Evangelical and pro-life activist Jay Rogers maintains a Web site that equates abortion and Witchcraft. In his article "Child Sacrifice in the New Age: Salem's Witch Cult and America's Abortion Industry," he describes the growing presence of Neopagans and New Agers on the American religious landscape as the "paganization of our culture" and calls for Christians to "Engage in spiritual warfare against demonic forces. . . . God has a prophetic company of men and women who are destined to go forth in the spirit and power of Elijah to confront wickedness and change our nation!"[45] Christian antagonism toward New Age and Neopagan communities comes from the conviction that it is a Christian's mission from God to fight these alternative belief systems.

Much of the conservative Christian antagonism toward Neopagans and New Agers hinges on their perceived influence over children and adolescents. Conservatives believe that control of their children and the shape of the future depend on purging New Age "humanism" from their schools and neighborhoods. "Satan wants our kids, and we just can't let him have them," says one of the parents in Frank Peretti's *Piercing the Darkness*, a fundamentalist best-seller and fictional story of a supposed satanic plot to take over a small-town school district. In this novel a Christian reporter discovers that a sinister New Age institute called Omega has supplied a New Age curriculum to public schools, resulting in most of the students being possessed by demons. Satanic forces attacking the school further their campaign by accusing a teacher at the local Christian academy of child abuse. Not only are the teacher's children taken away by a social worker who participates, along with many of the teachers, in meditation and visualization groups sponsored by

Omega, but also the very survival of the Christian academy is threatened. "Angelic" warriors come to aid the Christian teacher, a young minister and the reporter. The reporter discovers a curriculum that includes a variety of New Age practices: "all the usual humanist, cosmic stuff: collectivism, global consciousness, altered states, relativism." Peretti depicts the New Age movement as a vast and corrupt organization whose members are controlled by an army of demons. Aimed specifically at vulnerable children, this demonic conspiracy reads more like something dreamed up by organized crime.

In contrast, Johanna Michaelsen's Christian parenting manual *Like Lambs to the Slaughter: Your Child and the Occult* describes New Agers as well intentioned but nevertheless damned. According to Michaelsen, most channelers, astrologers, and witches are not intentionally evil, but the consequences of following their teachings and practices are always devastating: "In a kind of roundabout way, New Age religion has a point: 'All paths lead to the same place.' That is true. All their paths do lead to the same place, and if Jesus is right about it, *you don't want to go there!*"[46] Michaelsen believes that the New Age conspiracy to take over public education began with influential American philosopher John Dewey's brand of humanism and is being continued by New Age advocates of personal transformation: "once the religious philosophy of humanism became firmly entrenched in our society, the stage was set for the next logical step: the introduction of *cosmic* humanism which today we know as the New Age Movement."[47] Michaelsen's concern about New Age or "humanistic" techniques focuses on the use of meditation and visualization to help children "get in touch with their inner selves" and find their "inner guides." According to her and other conservative Christians, the only hope for safeguarding children from "the Aquarian conspiracy" is to get them away from the influence of secular humanism and the New Age by getting them out of the public schools.

Christian attacks on Neopagan and New Age religions are interpreted by both sides as part of an ongoing spiritual war. Michaelsen urges parents to take control of their children's lives by destroying all objects connected to occult practices, to make them renounce all friends who remain interested in the New Age movement, and to "put on God's armor." If parents disregard this warning and refuse to fight for their children, "many will be lost in the battle."[48] According to these authors, parents must educate their children about and protect them from the dangers of New Age and Neopagan beliefs and practices. Christian writer Roger Elwood's book *The Christening* carries a warning on its title page: "Note from the publisher: Scripture is clear that in the last days there will be an increase in occult practices and spiritual phenomena. It behooves every person to be aware of the dangers and adequately equipped for spiritual warfare."[49] Christian author Angela Hunt warns her readers that the teachings of the New Age movement are "nothing more than humanism done over in flashy colors, with celebrity endorsements, center around the words of the serpent to Eve: 'In the day ye eat thereof, then your eyes shall be opened, and ye shall be as gods, knowing good and evil.'"[50] These warnings specifically targeting New Agers and Neopagans provide fuel for their neighbors' determination to banish "evil" from their communities, as in the case of Fort Hood.

Neopagans are more likely to become involved in religious freedom campaigns because they are more likely to be targeted for persecution. Neopagans, for instance, may dress in black and wear pentacles, easily associated with devil worship. New Agers rarely wear black or anything that could be associated with satanism, so they are less likely to draw this kind of attention and are not as easily attacked by people who do not understand their religious ways. Because of persecution, Neopagans have established national networks to advocate for religious freedom, organize for environmental causes, and spread information about social and political issues.

Circle Sanctuary founded the Lady Liberty League in 1985 to "provide information and networking assistance to individuals and organizations concerned with religious freedom issues pertaining to Wiccan ways, Paganism, and other forms of Nature religions." The league's spring 2003 report includes news of a Wiccan priestess suing her county because she was not allowed to offer a prayer at the beginning of the county supervisors' meeting when other religious leaders were; a Wisconsin prison chaplain who is facing opposition from local Christians trying to get her fired; support for parents dealing with child custody issues; and a class action lawsuit to win Neopagan prison chaplains access to inmates on Death Row. The Lady Liberty League also sponsors a Prison Ministries Task Force and a "child custody issues specialist."[51] Its Web site and other Neopagan sites such as The Witches' Voice (www.witchvox.com) provide up-to-date news on religious freedom issues. Although Neopagans defend Witchcraft as an earth religion that values women's contributions and teaches ecology and good morals, most outsiders, especially Christians, do not see it that way.

The anticult movement, which flourished in the 1970s and 1980s, also condemns New Age and Neopagan organizations. Anticultist agendas sometimes overlap with those of conservative Christians, but many anticultists are secular people who find certain aspects of new religious movements, or as they prefer to call them, "cults," to be threatening and dangerous. This kind of negative attention from the broader society has often been a problem for New Age groups that developed around a charismatic leader, such as Elizabeth Clare Prophet of the Church Universal and Triumphant (CUT). CUT's leadership and direction are based on Prophet's spiritual authority rather than on the inner guidance of each member. Prophet claimed to be receiving messages from advanced spirit beings that told her to leave society and form a community in rural Montana to await the coming apocalypse. In their subordination of individual vision and experience to the demands of a leader, such organizations are not typical of the New Age movement. However, they share nineteenth-century origins in spiritualism and Theosophy and the influence of the I AM movement of the 1930s that derived many ideas from Theosophy. They hold in common many New Age beliefs, such as the existence of ascended masters who speak through human channels and say they will lead the world into the New Age.

The other major area of controversy concerning New Age and Neopagan religions is their borrowing of rites from American Indian traditions. *In the Light of Reverence*, a film released in 2001, focuses on controversies over American Indian sacred sites, including the conflict between the Wintu tribe and New Agers at Mount Shasta. According to Wintu oral history, the Panther Meadows area of Mount Shasta with its freshwater spring has been a sacred site for thousands of years, a place where their ancestors came to be healed, to gather herbs, to perform ceremonies, and to revisit their myths of origin there on the mountainside. New Agers also visit the sacred site of the Wintu, who are offended by the nudity of some of these visitors. They complain that New Agers trample on the herbs Wintu people have traditionally gathered every summer in Panther Meadows and are otherwise disrespectful of their traditions. A group of New Agers who came to the spring to drum and dance were interviewed for the film; while they do not seem ill intentioned, they appear to have no idea why anyone is upset. "But it's natural," one of them says in response to the Wintus who were offended by nudity. Native poet Wendy Rose accuses New Agers and Neopagans of being "white-shamans" and "plastic medicine men" who represent the final thrust of colonialism conquering and co-opting Indian spirituality.[52]

Neopagans and New Agers hold widely divergent opinions on this contentious issue, as do American Indians. Some New Agers and Neopagans respond by taking a hands-off approach to American Indian traditions, turning toward African, Asian, and ancient European cultures instead, all of which are less contested. Others, however, believe that spiritual practices are universal, share common origins, and are not specific to particular cultures, and are thus available to everyone. A. Lizard, a participant on the listserv Pagan Digest, believes that in a global culture all traditions are up for grabs: "Use your dream catchers in good health. There are plenty of Native Americans using 486 based PCs made in Taiwan right now, and the fact that the i486 chip or a Taiwan assembly plant largely come from non-Native American cultural origins doesn't affect their usefulness to their Native American user base in the least. A tool is a tool is a tool. The question isn't who invented it, it is DOES IT WORK FOR YOU???"[53]

Native scholar Joe McGeshick claims that most of the American Indian medicine men he talked to were amused rather than troubled by white-shamans, and that the most virulent attacks were coming from Indian academics insecure in their own identity.[54] Martina Looking Horse, a Lakota activist, not an academic, however, feels that cultural borrowing threatens the very existence of Native traditions: "Our religion is being bought and sold by the *wasicu*; objects sacred to the Lakota can be found in any store. . . . Prophets for Profit . . . will take a ceremony, one they know nothing of, and sell to some poor unsuspecting soul. . . . Some will claim knowledge of the old ones and of old ancient medicine, or claim to have visions. . . . I think these people are just hallucinating."[55] Nora Bunce, a Cherokee woman, agrees: "the New Agers do not do a good job of representing the beliefs of my people. They steal ceremonies and parts of the belief that they choose without permission, without knowledge. They bastardize them and re-package them [to] sell to the public."[56] Several American Indian Web sites include statements and declarations that urge people not to borrow their traditions, and one even has a list called "New Age (and Other) Ripoff Sites."[57] These issues of cultural identity and the appropriation of other cultural idioms will continue to be problematic as Neopaganism and the New Age movement spread around an increasingly interconnected world.

### The Internet as Twenty-first Century Spiritual Hothouse[58]

An important factor in the growth and accessibility of New Age and Neopagan religions is the popularity of the Internet and online religious communities, such as listservs, where religious knowledge and expertise are shared and rituals may even be performed. The New Age is also an electronic age of online communities, sacred Web texts, virtual rituals, church Web sites, and online organizing for religious freedom. The New Age and Neopagan movements have put the resources of the Internet to use in spreading information and building community. While they may turn for help to ancient deities of the past and romanticize primitive cultures, they keep up with technological advances, spread prophetic teachings, and promote their version of the future online as well as in books and magazines, through public gatherings like holistic health conventions open to everyone, and public Spiral Dances and other rituals.

Neopagans were disproportionately represented on the World Wide Web in its early years. This is probably due to the fact that many of them work in computer-related fields and were drawn to this medium of communication because they were afraid to disclose their religious identity in public. The Internet serves a number of different purposes for Neopagan and New Age communities and in turn has shaped the movements in different ways. It is above all an accessible source of information about religious practices that are often demonized; it allows individuals to learn about these religions at a level they are comfortable with. This may include reading information on Web sites about basic beliefs and practices they can try alone at home or participating in online communities through listservs and online rituals. Finally, the Internet is a way to contact real people, to read about the latest activities of favorite authors, and to keep track of events at institutes like Omega and Esalen. The Internet is also a quick and anonymous way to find a local astrologer, channeler, Wiccan study group, drum circle, men's gathering, etc. Large and publicly acknowledged organizations such as Circle Sanctuary, Covenant of the Goddess, Church of All Worlds, and the Institute of Noetic Sciences offer information and services.

Many Neopagan and New Age Web sites also include goods for sale, such as books, ritual supplies, suggestions for seasonal rituals, information about festivals and other public gatherings, current astrological predictions, and summaries of recent news stories. The Witches' Voice, a popular Neopagan site for news stories and information about a wide range of Neopagan traditions, maintains one part of the site for "Pagan Passages: The Circle Dance of Life" that "celebrates births, deaths, handfastings and other rites of passage related to the online Witch community." When Feri tradition founder Victor Anderson died in 2001, an announcement of his death and his biography were posted, along with eulogies from his students and other Neopagans who felt deeply affected by his death. The Internet made it possible for Neopagans across the country who had been influenced by Anderson's teaching or had known him personally to mourn him together.

The Internet has become a powerful means of spreading news through the national and international Pagan community. News about cases of persecution and harassment and calls for financial and magickal support are spread rapidly through Neopagan Internet networks. In 1996, when Wiccan Kerri Patavino was arrested and charged with sexual assault and ritual objects from her home were removed as evidence, the media ran scandalous headlines about "witches and sex orgies." But with Internet postings, e-mail, and phone calls, Neopagans organized a defense fund for Kerri and asked everyone to write letters explaining their religion to the media and the governor. When Representative Bob Barr attacked Fort Hood's inclusive policies toward Wiccans, Neopagans turned to the Internet for news stories and contact numbers for further information and to volunteer in the protest. When Starhawk was jailed after the WTO protests in Seattle in 1999, her missives were widely distributed through informal networks of Internet users as well as Neopagan listservs. As early as 1995, and probably earlier, the Internet was being used by many Neopagans to spread news of rituals and events. For instance, Archdruid and Neopagan spokesman Isaac Bonewits sent out an announcement for a large-scale ritual on July 4, 1995. He encouraged "Pagans, as well as Ceremonial Magicians, New Agers, and all others concerned with freedom in our country—especially religious freedom—to cast spells this July 4th." Bonewits explained that he and some other Neopagans in the Washington, D.C. area "consecrated" the statue of the "Goddess of Liberty that stands atop the Capitol Building":

> We consecrated it to serve as a channel for that Goddess to affect all those who work in that building, as well as in the White House, the Supreme Court, and all the rest of the national government, to make them work for *genuine* freedom and liberty. . . . This July 4th, and every July 4th from now on, I will perform a ritual to reinforce that consecration and warding. . . . CAW and other Pagans in the Washington DC area [will] create a magical lens to focus all the blessings and prayers that the rest of us will be generating. . . . I encourage American citizens everywhere in the world to join me at any time from noon to midnight EDT.[59]

Virtual rituals like this one have become a way for geographically isolated Neopagans or those who want to maintain their anonymity to still participate in a religious community. This example suggests an important aspect of New Age and Neopagan belief: that individual actions have an effect on a national or global scale. Bonewits and other participants in this ritual were concerned with the impact of many people turning their attention toward this particular end. Some New Agers also make use of the Internet as a ritual tool: "Self-described cybershamans propose that the Net's virtual space can be manipulated much as a tribal shaman controls the visionary space of trance." Another group of participants in an online discussion "proposed that the Net could serve as an electronic Ouija board that would allow them to reestablish contact with the entity Seth."[60] Like channeling entities, the Internet is a disembodied way of communicating that extends religious practice beyond the body and expands ritual space into the virtual and otherworldly realms.

The Internet also includes virtual communities, sites where people interact with like-minded others online. And these are seen as ideal communities where anonymity has a leveling effect so that rich and poor, young and old, men and women can, in the best case scenario, relate to each other without prejudice. The "Awakening Tribe," for instance, is a virtual New Age community, "a group of people who come together—in person and electronically—to study and learn, to work and play, and to be both teacher and student for each other. . . . Together we are modeling our newly emerging community—VIRTUAL COMMUNITY dedicated to developing, demonstrating, preserving and teaching the nature and dynamics of our common unity."[61] For many participants the Internet is a model for the future global community because it is democratic and erases factors like gender and race. Anthropologist Michael F. Brown observes that the channelers he studied had a key metaphor that he calls connection to "the universal All-That-Is," a concept that "finds a perfect match in the utopian language of the Internet's many poets, who celebrate its role in 'wiring human and artificial minds into one planetary soul." Observations such as this lead to the belief, shared by many in the overlapping worlds of New Age thought and computer-mediated communication, that the Internet is "the first step toward communion with universal mind."[62]

The Internet offers a multitude of sources that Neopagans and New Agers can draw on to create personalized religious identities. Like workshops, retreats, festivals, and communal living, it also provides opportunities for them to transform self-identity and to immerse themselves in a reality that is multilayered, fluid, and experimental. On the Internet, gender can be switched, age can be manipulated, and masks and costumes can be tried on in order to expand the bounds of the self and of religious community.

### At the Turn of the Millennium (1999–2000)

Like other apocalyptic religious people, some New Agers have set specific dates for the New Age, even while there remains no consensus as to when the

Age of Aquarius will begin, if it has not already. One of the most significant date-setting events was the Harmonic Convergence of the 1980s when participants believed that individuals all over the planet working together at the same time could cause global shifts in consciousness and could move the world closer to their ideal of how it should be. According to art historian Jose Arguelles, who developed the concept, "the dates August 16–17" were "the beginning of the final twenty-six year period of the Mayan calendar's 5,200-year Great Cycle, the return of Quetzalcoatl, the Mayan god of peace, and the culmination of the Aztec calendar and the close alignment of the seven planets among other things." Predicting that the convergence would mark an important planetary shift, Arguelles asked people throughout the world to gather to meditate and pray at sacred sites and powerful places like Sedona, Arizona and Mount Shasta, California to celebrate and to "create a complete field of trust by surrendering themselves to the planet and to the higher galactic intelligences which guide and monitor the planet."[63] Since 1987 Arguelles has continued to speak and organize New Age events that focus on peace and calendrics. Witch Laurie Cabot acknowledged that many people criticized the convergence for being a "doomsday watch for the world to end," but she sees it as something much more positive. For her its real purpose was "the alignment of our intentions with the evolving future of the earth and its communities of life." The convergence was successful, she claims, because it heightened "awareness about the interconnectedness of spirit and earth." As individuals become more aware of and work toward planetary change, the theory goes, that change will come about.

As the year 2000 approached, apocalyptic thinking surfaced again in New Age and Neopagan communities. At the end of the 1990s *Magical Blend*, a magazine devoted to New Age and Neopagan issues, put together a book of predictions by famous New Agers about the new millennium. Astrologer Barbara Hand Clow and others believed that we were living through "a critical leap in human evolution" as humanity approached the turn of the millennium.[64] Psychologist and popular author Jean Houston agreed that "Something profound is happening in the cosmos of the psyche" and "We live in self-created chaos to hasten our own meeting with ourselves."[65] She observed in her autobiographical book, *A Mythic Life*, that "as we approach the end of the millennium, it seems as if every shadow that ever was has been brought out to dance in the Walpurgis Night of the closing century."[66] The promise of the New Age eased the anxiety for many as the 1990s came to an end. New Age writer Marsha Sinator suggested in her essay for *Solstice Shift* that we are "evolutionary infants." Those who cultivate "the twenty-first

century mind . . . transfigure inner hurts or troubles into some beneficent vision."[67] So the fear and trepidation many people felt as the year 2000 approached could be turned into a powerful and productive force for change.
Houston, like many other New Agers, sees the current condition of humanity as a stage in an evolutionary plan. In a dialogue with the goddess Athena,
she asks what the task for humans is and the goddess responds:

> to be part of the awakening; to give to many beings—human and arche-
> typal—their impetus to evolve, to serve as planetary catalytic agents of
> this. The seeding and coding is already within human beings. The impe-
> tus often is not, or, if it is, it has gotten fogged by the demands of their
> lives and the loss of meaning. . . . As you grow the relationship to your
> archetype, the archetype dwells more and more within you. Then we can
> be bridged into your world, and you to ours. . . . It becomes a healing ex-
> change, with the archetype holding the higher "pattern" of "you" that
> can come through—not just for the healing of you but for the "wholing"
> of you and the deepening of the world.[68]

Neopagans and New Agers believe that they are part of an awakening culture that holds the best vision for a viable future on this planet. And they promote their goals with new emphases and new means that have come into
prominence since the 1960s. In this they are not alone, but they serve as prime
examples of important shifts in American religiosity.

New Age and Neopagan beliefs and practices signify a trend in American
religion at the end of the twentieth and beginning of the twenty-first centuries that resists institutionalization and gives value to personal experience.
Whether or not the Aquarian Age has arrived, religious life has been utterly
transformed since the 1960s. New Age and Neopagan gatherings are important cultural and religious sites that exemplify the migration of religious
meaning-making activities out of American temples and churches into other
spaces. Scholars of American religion have described this shift as the "disestablishment," "secularization," or increasing personalization of religion.
Mainline denominations such as the Methodist and Episcopal churches lost
numbers from the 1960s on, while independent conservative Protestant
churches grew rapidly.[69] These new independent churches emphasized the
role of the pastor or religious teacher, an individualized search for knowledge using the Bible as guide, and the importance of a personal experience of
sacred power. Sociologists of religion and other observers of the American
religious landscape point to two major trends in American religious life since

the 1960s: the decline of membership in the mainline churches—Methodist, Episcopal, Presbyterian, etc.—as independent congregations draw members away, and the personalization of religion. I would add another dimension to the theory of secularization and personalization: the rise of alternate ritual spaces in which people find religious community. The American religious landscape since the 1960s has been shaped by a battle for the future and the increasing movement of religion into other spiritually meaningful spaces, such as public memorials, Promise Keepers conventions (Christian men's gatherings), and Christian rock festivals, which contribute to the growth of nondenominational churches, as well as Neopagan festivals and New Age gatherings, music festivals, raves, the Burning Man festival (featuring art and ritual performances), holistic health fairs, and drum circles.[70] These events provide a communal experience during which individuals feel they can step outside their daily lives into another kind of reality, where personal experience is more important than codified belief.

# CHRONOLOGY

| | |
|---|---|
| 1838 | Phineas Parkhurst Quimby encounters mesmerist Charles Poyen in Belfast, Maine and begins his spiritual healing career. |
| 1848 | Spiritualism begins when the Fox sisters of Hydesville, New York report hearing mysterious rappings in their house. |
| 1875 | Helena Petrovna Blavatsky and Henry Steel Olcott form the Theosophical Society in New York City. |
| 1888 | The Hermetic Order of the Golden Dawn begins meeting in England. |
| 1893 | The World's Parliament of Religions is held in Chicago, introducing American citizens to Asian religions and cultures. |
| 1910 | Aleister Crowley joins the Ordo Templi Orientis (Oriental Templar Order or OTO), which he heads from 1922 to 1947; he incorporates many of his own teachings into its systems of initiation. The OTO continues to be an influential branch of Neopaganism. |
| 1915 | AMORC (Ancient and Mystical Order of the Rosae Crucis), an early Rosicrucian group, is founded in New York City. |
| 1931 | The Association for Research and Enlightenment (ARE) is founded to disseminate the teachings of psychic Edgar Cayce. |
| 1947 | Kenneth Arnold, a U.S. Forest Service employee sent to look for a downed plane in Washington State, reports seeing nine brightly lit, spherically shaped flying objects near Mount Rainier and sets off decades of speculation about UFOs. |
| 1949 | Gerald Gardner's *High Magic's Aid*, a fictionalized account of a witch coven, is published. |

1952     Norman Vincent Peale publishes *The Power of Positive Thinking* and ushers in the human potential movement.

1954     Gerald Gardner's *Witchcraft Today*, a pseudo-anthropological study, is published and eventually becomes one of the founding documents of contemporary Paganism.

         Aldous Huxley's *The Doors of Perception* is published and becomes popular for its account of psychedelic experiences.

1955     *The Urantia Book*, a channeled document that provides evidence for other inhabited worlds, is published.

1956     George King, an Englishman influenced by Theosophy, founds the first UFO religion, the Aetherius Society, in London.

1959     Jack Kerouac publishes *The Dharma Bums*, a fictionalized account of the lives of the Beat poets.

1961     Robert Heinlein's science fiction classic *Stranger in a Strange Land* is published.

         *Black Elk Speaks*, an account of the life of a Lakota medicine man, is reissued in paperback.

1962     Esalen Institute is founded in Big Sur, California and becomes an important New Age center offering various psychological therapies as well as bodywork and spiritual teachings.

1963     Peter Caddy, his wife Eileen, and their friend Dorothy Maclean start a garden on a barren, sandy peninsula in northeast Scotland that eventually becomes the New Age community of Findhorn.

         Timothy Leary and his family move to Millbrook, New York, one of the first communes, to further his experiments with psychedelics.

1965     The Immigration and Nationality Act is passed, ending a quota system that effectively barred Asian immigration. The influx of Asian religious teachers results in the growing popularity of meditation and other Asian religious practices as well as the spread of images of Asian deities and Asian religious ideas like karma and reincarnation.

         The U.S. paperback edition of J. R. R. Tolkien's *Lord of the Rings* is published.

1966     Robert Graves's *The White Goddess* is published and becomes an inspiration for Neopagans seeking new forms of deity.

1967     The Church of All Worlds and Feraferia, two important Neopagan groups, are founded.

1968     Timothy Leary publishes *The Politics of Ecstasy*, his treatise on psychedelic drugs and spiritual experience.

1970 *East West*, one of the most influential New Age magazines, begins publication.

1972 The first Seth book, *Seth Speaks*, is published by medium Jane Roberts.

1973 The Institute of Noetic Sciences is founded to promote the study of consciousness.

1974 Circle, a Neopagan organization, is founded to promote education, counseling, research, and spiritual healing.

1975 The Covenant of the Goddess is organized to bring together all types of practitioners of Witchcraft.

1976 *A Course in Miracles*, the text of messages channeled through medium Helen Schucman, is published.

1977 The Omega Institute for Holistic Studies is founded in Rhinebeck, New York to educate people about holistic healing and spiritual traditions from around the world.

1979 Starhawk publishes *The Spiral Dance: A Rebirth of the Ancient Religion of the Great Goddess*, which contributes to the growth and popularity of Neopaganism by making ritual techniques available to anyone.

1981 The first Starwood festival takes place, blending New Age and Neopagan interests.

1982 Theosophist and channeler David Spangler returns to the United States from Findhorn to form a New Age community in Wisconsin.

1983 Shirley MacLaine's autobiographical account of her experiences with channeling and other New Age practices, *Out on a Limb*, is published.

1985 Circle Sanctuary's Lady Liberty League is started to support Neopagans involved with struggles for religious freedom.

1987 The Harmonic Convergence, predicted by Jose Arguelles to be the beginning of a new age of consciousness, occurs.

1989 The Bay Area Pagan Assemblies (BAPA) is formed.

1993 James Redfield's *The Celestine Prophecy* is published, describing the mysterious disappearance of a Peruvian manuscript and the author's spiritual journey to find it.

1993 Neopagans take part in the World's Parliament of Religions.

   The Pagan Educational Network (PEN) is founded to educate the public about Neopaganism and to advocate for religious freedom in cases involving Neopagans.

1996          The Witches' Voice, a Neopagan news and networking site, first becomes available on the Internet.

1998          The first annual Pagan Pride Day takes place on September 19 in cities across the United States.

2000          Jose Arguelles establishes the Foundation for the Law of Time to work toward making a thirteen-month, twenty-eight-day calendar a world standard to "replace the time of war with the time of peace."

# NOTES

## 1. Ancient Mysteries in Contemporary America

1. Although "Feri" has other spellings among its practitioners, I have chosen to use this one throughout this chapter since I begin with a ritual that was labeled "Feri."

2. Chant attributed to Gabriel Carillo, teacher and elder in the Bloodrose line of the Feri tradition.

3. Chant attributed to T. Thorn Coyle, Feri teacher, from her album *Give Us a Kiss*, www.thorncoyle.com.

4. Chant attributed to Gabriel Carillo.

5. Sharon Knight, e-mail communication, 15 March 2003.

6. Dedication of merit—a Buddhist practice adapted by Neopagan priest Sam Webster. E-mail communication from Sharon Knight, 15 March 2003.

7. The name for Knight's band, "Pandemonaeon," comes from magician Peter Carroll's theory of five ages. They are the shamanic, pagan, monotheistic, rational, and finally, the Pandemonaeon, the age we are currently in. It is "characterized by a return to shamanic sorcery fueled by recent discoveries of quantum physics" www.pandemonaeon.com (23 March 2003).

8. "Victor Anderson's Feri Tradition," www.geocities.com/Athens/Rhodes/5569/faery_Trad_Intro.html (20 March 2003).

9. Penny Novack, "A Belated Voice," www.witchvox.com/passages/victoranderson.html.

10. Cholla, "Ecstasy and Transgression in the Faery Tradition," www.feritradition.org/witcheye/ecstasy.html (18 March 2003).

11. "The Basic Feri Creation Myth," www.geocities.com/Athens/Rhodes/5569/faecreation.html (20 March 2003).

## 2. Introduction to the Religious Worlds of Neopagans and New Agers

1. Diana and Gary are composites of the hundreds of Neopagans and New Agers I interviewed.

2. Both quotes are from the book jacket of *The Celestine Prophecy* (New York: Warner, 1993).

3. http://www.maui.net/~shaw/celes/celestine.html#New%20Civilization%20Network (23 January 2003).

4. Stormy from Canada on Amazon.com (21 January 2003).

5. www.circlesanctuary.org/liberty (15 February 2003).

6. www.cog.org (12 November 2002).

7. This observation was informed by discussions with Michael York, Adrian Ivakhiv, Michael Strmiska, and other members of the nature religion scholars e-mail list.

8. M. Macha NightMare, personal communication, 27 March 2003.

9. Michael Brown, *The Channeling Zone: American Spirituality in an Anxious Age* (Cambridge: Harvard University Press, 1997), 4.

10. Ibid., 2.

11. Brown, 7.

12. Starhawk, *The Spiral Dance: A Rebirth of the Ancient Religion of the Great Goddess* (New York: Harper and Row, 1979), 29.

13. Jane Roberts, *The Seth Material* (New York: Bantam, 1970), 6.

14. Ibid., 293.

15. Ibid., xiv.

16. Brown, 1.

17. The Findhorn Community, *The Findhorn Garden* (New York: Harper & Row, 1975), 54.

18. Ibid., 59.

19. Starhawk, "A Response to Charlotte Sallen," *the Pomegranate* 16 (May 2001): 2.

20. Ronald Hutton, *The Triumph of the Moon: A History of Modern Pagan Witchcraft* (Oxford and New York: Oxford University Press, 1999), 50.

21. Morning Glory Zell, "Pan," *Green Egg* 27 (104) (Spring 1994): 12–13.

22. Julia Butterfly Hill, *The Legacy of Luna* (San Francisco: HarperSanFrancisco, 2000), 9.

23. "Dialogues With Our Elders," *Earth First! Journal* 23 (2) (Jan. 2003): 72.

24. Both quotes from Ashalyn, "Shasta Vortex Adventures: Fostering Awareness through Experience," in *Mount Shasta Welcomes* (Mount Shasta, CA: Ashalyn and Kim Solga, Winter 2003), 2.

25. Shawn Eyer and David Fideler, "How Athena Came to Nashville," *Green Egg* 27 (104) (Spring 1994): 5–7.

26. Quoted in J. Gordon Melton, ed., *New Age Almanac* (Detroit: Visible Ink Press, 1991), 369.

27. *Noetic Sciences Review* 33 (Spring 1995): 37.

28. Shakti Gawain, *The Path of Transformation* (Mill Valley, CA: Nataraj Publishing, 1993), 45.

29. Marian Green, *Magic for the Aquarian Age: A Contemporary Textbook of Practical Magical Techniques* (Wellingborough: Aquarian Press, 1983), 11.

30. Starhawk, "Report from Ottawa," e-mail communication, 27 November 2001, and Barbara J. Graham, "School of the Americas Protest protected by First Amendment rights: Reclaiming Witches Network with Jesuits to Hold Ritual and Spiral Dance at Ft. Benning," e-mail communication, 28 January 2001.

## 3. Early Varieties of Alternative Spirituality in American Religious History

1. Catherine Albanese discusses "metaphysical religion" in *Nature Religion in America: From the Algonkian Indians to the New Age* (Chicago: University of Chicago Press, 1990); "alternative reality tradition" is the term Robert Ellwood invokes in *Alternative Altars: Unconventional and Eastern Spirituality in America* (Chicago: University of Chicago Press, 1979); "harmonial religion" is identified by Sydney Ahlstrom as an important American religious tradition in *A Religious History of the American People* (New Haven and London: Yale University Press, 1972); and Eugene Taylor focuses on "shadow culture" in *Shadow Culture: Psychology and Spirituality in America* (Washington, DC: Counterpoint, 1999).

2. Jon Butler, *Awash in a Sea of Faith: Christianizing the American People* (Cambridge, MA and London: Harvard University Press, 1990), 9.

3. David D. Hall, *Worlds of Wonder, Days of Judgment: Popular Religious Belief in Early New England* (New York: Knopf, 1989).

4. Boston, 1684.

5. Butler, 73.

6. Butler consulted estate inventories and discovered that in Virginia, aristocratic household libraries included many occult books, especially those by astrologers.

7. "Spiritual hothouse" is Butler's phrase; Taylor claims the period can be characterized as "a seething cauldron" and "a highly unstable atmosphere"; in *The Burned-Over District: The Social and Intellectual History of Enthusiastic Religion in Western New York, 1800–1850* (Ithaca and London: Cornell University Press, 1950), Whitney R. Cross sees the antebellum Northeast as "a storm center"; in his essay "The Making of a New Order: Millerism and the Origins of Seventh-Day Adventism" (Ronald L. Numbers and Jonathan M. Butler, eds., *The Disappointed: Millerism and Millennarianism in the Nineteenth Century* [Bloomington: Indiana University Press, 1987]), Jonathan Butler describes the era as "the antebellum American assault on limits" and "freedom's ferment"; and Ann Braude says it was marked by "religious anarchism" in her study of spiritualism, *Radical Spirits: Spiritualism and Women's Rights in Nineteenth-Century America* (Boston: Beacon, 1989).

8. Quoted in Ahlstrom, 491.

9. Paul E. Johnson and Sean Wilentz, *The Kingdom of Matthias* (Oxford and New York: Oxford University Press, 1994), 6.

10. Cross, 3.

11. Taylor, 119.

12. Butler, 242.

13. Ahlstrom, 1019.

14. Hazen, 116.

15. Taylor, 104.

16. Ahlstrom, 483.

17. From the introduction to Emanuel Swedenborg, *The Universal Human and Soul-Body Interaction*, ed. and trans. George F. Dole (New York: Paulist Press, 1984), 4.

18. W. B. Yeats, "Swedenborg, Mediums and the Desolate Places," http://www.sacred-texts.com/neu/celt/vbwi/vbw21.htm (7 May 2003).

19. Swedenborg, 25.

20. Taylor, 66.

21. Taylor, 67.

22. Taylor, 69.

23. Yeats, "Swedenborg."

24. Butler, 255

25. Braude.

26. Braude, 54.

27. Braude, 173.

28. Craig James Hazen, *The Village Enlightenment in America: Popular Religion and Science in the Nineteenth Century* (Urbana and Chicago: University of Illinois Press, 2000), 82.

29. Braude, 138.

30. Braude, 139.

31. Braude, 139.

32. Bruce F. Campbell, *Ancient Wisdom Revived: A History of the Theosophical Movement* (Berkeley: University of California Press, 1980), 20.

33. Taylor, 159.

34. Catherine L. Albanese, *America: Religions and Religion*, 3rd ed. (Belmont, CA: Wadsworth Publishing, 1999), 272.

35. Taylor, 146.

36. Albanese, *America*, 269.

37. Carl Bode, *The American Lyceum: Town Meeting of the Mind* (New York: Oxford University Press, 1956), 3.

38. Irene Briggs and Raymond F. DaBoll, *Recollections of the Lyceum and Chautauqua Circuits* (Freeport, ME: Bond Wheelwright Co., 1969), 21.

39. Stephen J. Stein, *The Shaker Experience in America: A History of the United Society of Believers* (New Haven and London: Yale University Press, 1992), 225.

40. Albanese, *America*, 240.

41. Stein, 326.

42. Taylor, 104.

43. "Elements of Phrenology: Sentiments" in "The Brontes: Texts, Sources, and Criticism," http://faculty.plattsburgh.edu/peter.friesen/default.asp?go=227 (7 May 2003).

44. Robert C. Fuller, *Alternative Medicine and American Religious Life* (Oxford and London: Oxford University Press, 1989), 81.

45. Helena P. Blavatsky, quoted in "Introductory Reincarnation Quotes from Theosophy," http://blavatsky.net/quotes/reincarnation-introductory.htm (7 May 2003).

46. Taylor, 141.

47. Stephen Prothero, *Purified by Fire: A History of Cremation in America* (Berkeley and Los Angeles: University of California Press, 2001), 26.

48. Stephen Prothero, *The White Buddhist: The Asian Odyssey of Henry Steele Olcott* (Bloomington and Indianapolis: Indiana University Press, 1996), 57.

49. Blavatsky quoted in Silvia Cranston, *HPB: The Extraordinary Life and Influence of Helena Blavatsky, Founder of the Modern Theosophical Movement* (New York: Putnam, 1993), 117.

50. Prothero, *White Buddhist*, 52.

51. Prothero, *White Buddhist*, 57–58.

52. Annie Besant (1847–1933) succeeded Blavatsky in the English Theosophical Society and William K. Judge took over the New York branch; that group split into several factions, including Rudolph Steiner's Anthroposophy, when Judge died in 1896. Kathleen Tinghley emerged as the leader of one faction and in 1897 she started a utopian community in Point Loma, California, near San Diego. When Tingley died in a car accident in the 1920s, Besant also took over leadership in the United States.

53. On Western Esotericism, see Wonter J. Hanegraaff, *New Age Religion and Western Culture: Esotericism in the Mirror of Secular Thought* (New York: SUNY, 1998).

54. See Ellic Howe, *The Magicians of the Golden Dawn: The History of a Magical Order* (London: Routledge, 1972) and Ingrid Merkel and Allen G. Debus, *Hermeticism and the Renaissance: Intellectual History and the Occult in Early Modern Europe* (Washington, DC: Folger Institute, 1988).

55. Jenkins calls the period between 1910 and 1935 "the first new age" and "the period of emergence." *Mystics and Messiahs: Cults and New Religions in American History* (Oxford and New York: Oxford University Press, 2000), 70–71.

56. Jenkins, 171.

57. Phillip Lucas, "The Association for Research and Enlightenment: Saved by the New Age," in Timothy Miller, ed., *America's Alternative Religions* (Albany: SUNY Press, 1995), 353.

58. Jenkins, 84.

59. Jenkins, 87.

60. Jenkins, 88.

## 4. The 1960s Watershed Years

1. In his preface to the 1972 edition, John G. Neihardt describes the book's previously modest reception and its burst of popularity during and after the publication of the 1961 edition. *Black Elk Speaks: Being the Life Story of a Holy Man of the Oglala Sioux As Told Through John G. Neihardt* (New York: Pocket, 1972).

2. Sydney E. Ahlstrom, *A Religious History of the American People* (New Haven: Yale University Press, 1972), 951.

3. Stephanie Coontz, *The Way We Never Were: American Families and the Nostalgia Trap* (New York: Basic, 1992), 24.

4. Ibid., 25. Coontz argues, however, that these kinds of figures are misleading, as is the popular television stereotype. In fact, many families lived in poverty, especially if they were not white, and domestic violence was not uncommon, even in the suburbs.

5. Ibid., 35.

6. Quoted in Huston Smith, *Cleansing the Doors of Perception: The Religious Significance of Entheogenic Plants and Chemicals* (New York: Putnam, 2000), viii.

7. Robert Ellwood, *The Sixties Spiritual Awakening: American Religion Moving from Modern to Postmodern* (New Brunswick: Rutgers University Press, 1994), 43.

8. Quoted in James Hudnut-Beumler, *Looking for God in the Suburbs: The Religion of the American Dream and Its Critics, 1945–1965* (New Brunswick: Rutgers University Press, 1994), 61.

9. Paul Goodman, *Growing Up Absurd* (1956; reprint, New York: Vintage, 1960), 172.

10. Ibid., 180.

11. Jack Kerouac, *The Dharma Bums* (1959; reprint, New York and London: Penguin, 1976), 70.

12. Keith Thompson, *Angels and Aliens* (New York: Fawcett Columbine, 1991), 145.

13. Catherine Albanese, *Nature Religion in America: From the Algonkian Indians to the New Age* (Chicago: University of Chicago Press, 1990), 357.

14. Martin Gardner, *Urantia: The Great Cult Mystery* (Amherst, NY: Prometheus, 1995).

15. Theodore Roszak, *The Making of a Counterculture* (Garden City, NY: Doubleday, 1969), 62.

16. Peter Clecak, *America's Quest for the Ideal Self: Dissent and Fulfillment in the 60s and 70s* (New York and Oxford: Oxford University Press, 1983).

17. Lauren Kessler, *After All These Years: Sixties Ideals in a Different World* (New York: Thunder's Mouth Press, 1990), 178–79.

18. Ahlstrom, 1080–1082.

19. This idea is discussed by Christopher Lasch in *The Culture of Narcissism: American Life in an Age of Diminishing Expectations* (New York: Norton, 1978).

20. Clecak, 22. Clecak identifies "the quest for personal fulfillment . . . . everyone had to compose his or her own story; autobiography threatened to displace his-

tory as a dominant way of making sense of things" (21, 27). "Subjectivity is supreme," as is switching religions, writes Ellwood (327–28).

21. In *Getting Saved from the Sixties: Moral Meaning in Conversion and Cultural Change* (Berkeley: University of California Press, 1982), Steven Tipton criticizes the stripping away of moral authority from major institutions and withdrawal into the refuge of private life. Robert N. Bellah documents the widespread focus on the self and "self-cultivation" in *Habits of the Heart: Individualism and Commitment in American Life* by Robert N. Bellah, Richard Madsen, William M. Sullivan, Ann Swidler, and Stephen M. Tipton (San Francisco: Harper & Row, 1985). They tell, for example, the story of a man "on his search for the self he would like to be" (60). Also see Kessler, 177.

22. Phillip E. Hammond, *Religion and Personal Autonomy: The Third Disestablishment in America* (Columbia: University of South Carolina Press, 1992), 10. Although Hammond concludes that the "third disestablishment" is "another step in the direction of secularization" (175), the New Age and Neopagan movements, which are characterized by a high level of personal autonomy, are hardly "secular," nor are widespread beliefs in astrology and ghosts.

23. Roszak, 140–41.

24. Ellwood, 9.

25. Robert Wuthnow, *After Heaven: Spirituality in America Since the 1950s* (Berkeley and Los Angeles: University of California Press, 1998), 53.

26. Roszak, xiii.

27. Roszak, 47.

28. Roszak, 147.

29. Free, *Revolution for the Hell of It* (New York: Dial, 1968), 85.

30. Quoted in Michael York, *The Emerging Network: A Sociology of the New Age and Neo-Pagan Movements* (Lanham, MD: Rowman and Littlefield, 1995), 18.

31. Julian Beck quoted in Roszak, 151–52.

32. Quoted in Kessler, 174.

33. Clecak, 93. Each focus of dissent, writes Clecak, "searched out its neglected and frequently misinterpreted past" (224). The sixties counterculture is described in detail by cultural analyst Theodore Roszak in *The Making of a Counterculture*. My analysis of American culture and American religion in the 1960s and early 1970s is also informed by Robert S. Ellwood, *The Sixties Spiritual Awakening*; Morris Dickstein, *Gates of Eden: American Culture in the Sixties* (New York: Penguin, 1977); Christopher Lasch, *The Culture of Narcissism*; Todd Gitlin, *The Sixties: Years of Hope, Days of Rage* (New York: Bantam, 1987); Steven Tipton, *Getting Saved from the Sixties*; Kessler, *After All These Years*; and William Braden, *The Age of Aquarius: Technology and the Cultural Revolution* (Chicago: Quadrangle, 1970).

34. Clecak, 145, 203.

35. Roszak, 40.

36. Ellwood, 34, 134.

37. Ellwood, 202.

38. Ahlstrom, 589. In "Ritual is My Chosen Art Form: The Creation of Ritual as Folk Art Among Contemporary Pagans" (in James R. Lewis, ed., *Magical Religions and Modern Witchcraft* [Albany: SUNY Press, 1996], 93–119), Sabina Magliocco discusses Neopagan ritual invention as "folk art," and especially the use of folkloric materials and the writings of folklorists and other academics. Magliocco points out that "like the romantic movements of nineteenth century Europe, Neopaganism makes extensive use of folkloric materials to recreate the lost ethos of the past" (95).

39. Quoted in Margot Adler, *Drawing Down the Moon: Witches, Druids, Goddess-Worshippers, and Other Pagans in America Today* (1979; reprint, Boston: Beacon, 1986), 285.

40. Ibid., 293.

41. Peter O. Whitmer, *Aquarius Revisited: Seven Who Created the Sixties Counterculture That Changed America* (New York: Macmillan, 1987), 75. For a history of Esalen, see William Truett Anderson, *The Upstart Spring: Esalen and the American Awakening* (Reading, MA: Addison-Wesley, 1983). See also www.esalen.org.

42. Timothy Miller, *The 60s Communes: Hippies and Beyond* (Syracuse: Syracuse University Press, 1999), 27.

43. Ibid., 47.

44. Ibid., 117.

45. Ibid., 119.

46. Ram Dass and Paul Gorman, *How Can I Help?: Stories and Reflections on Service* (New York: Knopf, 1990), 7.

47. Adrian Ivakhiv, *Claiming Sacred Ground: Pilgrims and Politics at Glastonbury and Sedona* (Bloomington and Indianapolis: Indiana University Press, 2001), 174.

48. (New York: Coward-McCann,, 1968), 15.

49. Ram Dass, *Be Here Now, Remember* (San Cristobel, NM: Lama Foundation, 1971).

50. Leary, *The Politics of Ecstasy* (New York: Putnam, 1968), 13.

51. Ibid., 225.

52. Timothy Miller quotes Allen Ginsberg in this regard: "life should be ecstasy. We need life styles of ecstasy and social forms appropriate to whatever ecstasy is available for whoever wants it" (113).

53. Quoted in Ellwood, 321.

54. Charles A. Reich, *The Greening of America* (New York: Bantam, 1970), 284.

55. See Clecak, 22. In *The Sixties: Years of Hope, Days of Rage*, Todd Gitlin sees the cultural context from which the sixties counterculture emerged as responsible for its contradictions (hope followed by rage being just one of these): "This generation was formed in the jaws of an extreme and wrenching tension between the assump-

tion of affluence and its opposite, a terror of loss, destruction, and failure" (12). At rock concerts and other large gatherings as well as in communes and individual lives, the 1960s counterculture expressed a similar innocence and hope equated with childhood. Writing in 1977, Morris Dickstein agreed that "the sixties were a period that believed in magic and innocence, that had a touching faith in the omni-potence of individual desire" (*Gates of Eden*, 210).

### 5. Healing and Techniques of the Self

1. Lisa Peschel, "One View on the Ethics of Healing," *Meʒlim: Practical Magick for Today* 5 (3) (1994): 15–18.

2. Janet Farrar and Stewart Farrar, *The Life and Times of a Modern Witch* (Custer, WA: Phoenix Publishing, 1988), 113–14.

3. Ibid., 114.

4. Raymond Buckland, *Buckland's Complete Book of Witchcraft* (St. Paul, MN: Llewellyn Publications, 1986), 135–36.

5. Michael Brown, *The Channeling Zone* (Cambridge: Harvard University Press, 1997), 77.

6. Fred M. Frohock, *Lives of the Psychics: The Shared Worlds of Science and Mysticism* (Chicago and London: University of Chicago Press, 2000), 26–27.

7. For case studies from her healing practice see *Proud Spirit: Lessons, Insights & Healing from the Voice of the Spirit World* (New York: Morrow, 1997).

8. Berkeley Holistic Health Center and Shepherd Bliss, ed., *The New Holistic Health Handbook: Living Well in a New Age* (Lexington, MA: Stephen Greene Press, 1985), 16.

9. Starhawk, *Truth or Dare: Encounters with Power, Authority, and Mystery* (San Francisco: Harper & Row, 1987), 200.

10. Marilyn Ferguson, *The Aquarian Conspiracy: Personal and Social Transformation in the 1980s* (Los Angeles: J. P. Tarcher, 1980), 172.

11. Annette Hinshaw, "Maps for Healing," *Meʒlim: Practical Magick for Today* 5 (3) (1994): 2.

12. Circle Sanctuary Web site, www.circlesanctuary.org/healing/spiritualhealing.htm (15 December 2002).

13. Farrar and Farrar, 116.

14. Both quotes from e-mail communication, 9 April 1995.

15. Kenneth Deigh, "Rediscovering Shamanism," *Meʒlim: Practical Magick for Today* 5 (3) (1994): 12–13.

16. Ibid.

17. Shakti Gawain, *The Path of Transformation: How Healing Ourselves Can Change the World* (Mill Valley, CA: Nataraj Publishing, 1993), 32.

18. In his study of cross-cultural views of body and illness, anthropologist Andrew Strathern describes healing rituals that aim to connect spirit and body to keep

"spirits in their place." *Body Thoughts* (Ann Arbor: University of Michigan Press, 1996), 130.

19. Jane Roberts, *The Seth Material* (New York: Bantam, 1970), 177–89.

20. Ibid., 188–89.

21. Bliss, ed., 12.

22. Laurie Cabot, *Power of the Witch: The Earth, the Moon, and the Magical Path to Enlightenment* (New York: Delta, 1989), 253.

23. Bernie S. Siegel, M.D., *Love, Medicine and Miracles: Lessons Learned About Self-Healing from a Surgeon's Experience with Exceptional Patients* (New York: Harper & Row, 1986), 5.

24. Edward C. Whitmont, M.D., *The Alchemy of Healing: Psyche and Soma* (Berkeley, CA: North Atlantic Books, 1993), 15 and 191.

25. Larry Dossey, *Reinventing Medicine: Beyond Mind-Body to a New Era of Healing* (San Francisco: HarperSanFrancisco, 1999), 3.

26. John Nelson, ed., *Solstice Shift: Magical Blend's Synergistic Guide to the Coming Age* (Charlottesville: Hampton Books, 1997), 215.

27. This case and many others in which spiritual healers are in conflict with the state are detailed in political scientist Fred M. Frohock's *Healing Powers: Alternative Medicine, Spiritual Communities, and the State* (Chicago and London: University of Chicago Press, 1992), 13–32.

28. http://www.edgarcayce.org/health/hh_index.html (20 January 2003).

29. Buckland, 193–94.

30. Robert C. Fuller, *Alternative Medicine and American Religious Life* (New York and Oxford: Oxford University Press, 1989), 113.

31. Both quotes are from ibid., 110–11.

32. Farrar and Farrar, 115.

33. Shirley MacLaine, *Dancing in the Light* (New York: Bantam, 1985), 324–25.

34. Starhawk, *The Spiral Dance: A Rebirth of the Ancient Religion of the Great Goddess* (1979; reprint, San Francisco: Harper & Row, 1989), 70.

35. Ibid., 72.

36. Graham Harvey, *Contemporary Paganism: Listening People, Speaking Earth* (New York: New York University Press, 1997), 208.

37. Margot Adler, *Drawing Down the Moon: Witches, Druids, Goddess-Worshippers and Other Pagans in America Today* (1979; reprint, Boston: Beacon, 1986), 463.

38. Brown, 55.

39. Don Handelman, "Postlude: The Interior Sociality of Self-Transformation," in *Self and Self-Transformation in the History of Religions*, ed. David Shulman and Guy Stroumsa (Oxford: Oxford University Press, 2002), 238.

40. Marian Green, *Magic for the Aquarian Age: A Contemporary Textbook of Practical Magical Techniques* (Wellingborough: Aquarian Press, 1983), 18.

41. Gawain, 39.

42. Gawain, 27.

43. My understanding of healing narratives is informed by the work of Cheryl Mattingly in *Narrative and the Cultural Construction of Illness and Healing*, ed. Cheryl Mattingly and Linda C. Garro (Berkeley: University of California Press, 2000).

44. Shuman and Stroumsa, eds., 247.

45. Nelson, 128.

**6. "All Acts of Love and Pleasure Are My Rituals": Sex, Gender, and the Sacred**

1. From Esalan (www.esalen.org) and Omega (www.eomega.org) Web sites (3 March 2003).

2. E-mail communication, 19 April 1995.

3. Margot Adler, *Drawing Down the Moon: Witches, Druids, Goddess-Worshippers, and Other Pagans in America Today* (1979; reprint, Boston: Beacon, 1986), 125.

4. Marianne Williamson, *A Return to Love: Reflections on the Principles of a Course in Miracles* (New York: HarperCollins, 1993), 250.

5. Naomi Goldenberg, *The Changing of the Gods: Feminism and the End of Traditional Religions* (Boston: Beacon, 1979), 4.

6. Ibid., 9.

7. Cynthia Eller, *Living in the Lap of the Goddess: The Feminist Spirituality Movement in America* (New York: Crossroad Publishing, 1993), 155.

8. Quoted in ibid., 150.

9. Quoted in Margot Adler, *Drawing Down the Moon: Witches, Druids, Goddess-Worshippers and Other Pagans in America Today* (1979; reprint, Boston: Beacon, 1986), 189.

10. *The Goddesses and Gods of Old Europe: Myths and Cult Images* (Berkeley: University of California Press, 1982).

11. *Earliest Civilizations of the Near East* (New York: McGraw-Hill, 1965).

12. Estes, *Women Who Run with the Wolves: Myths and Stories of the Wild Woman Archetype* (New York: Ballantine, 1992), 10 and 6.

13. Jean Shinoda Bolen, M.D., *Crossing to Avalon: A Woman's Midlife Pilgrimage* (San Francisco: HarperSanFrancisco, 1994), 81.

14. Ibid., 53.

15. Ibid., 56.

16. Ibid., 67.

17. Starhawk, *Truth or Dare: Encounters with Power, Authority, and Mystery* (San Francisco: Harper & Row, 1987), 42.

18. Ibid.

19. Ronald Hutton, *The Triumph of the Moon: A History of Modern Pagan Witchcraft* (Oxford: Oxford University Press, 1999), 341.

20. See for instance Hutton and Cynthia Eller, *The Myth of Matriarchal Prehistory: Why an Invented Past Won't Give Women a Future* (Boston: Beacon, 2000).

21. Bolen, 128–29.

22. Marion Zimmer Bradley, *The Mists of Avalon* (New York: Ballantine, 1982), 178.

23. Ibid., 181.

24. Merlin Stone, *When God Was a Woman* (New York: Dial, 1976), 144.

25. June Brindel, *Ariadne* (New York: St. Martin's, 1980), 119.

26. Ibid., 242.

27. Personal interview, 9 July 1993.

28. Starhawk, *Truth or Dare*, 296–97.

29. Ruth Rhiannon Barrett, "The Power of Ritual," in Wendy Griffin, ed., *Daughters of the Goddess: Studies of Healing, Identity and Empowerment* (Walnut Creek, CA: Altamira, 2000), 186–87.

30. Jone Salomonsen, *Enchanted Feminism: The Reclaiming Witches of San Francisco* (London and New York: Routledge, 2002), 216.

31. Michael Brown, *The Channeling Zone* (Cambridge: Harvard University Press, 1997), 104–105.

32. Starhawk, *Truth or Dare*, 296. A few months later, some of the men who had been at the feast created a rite of passage for one of their sons when he reached puberty.

33. Hutton, 37.

34. Hutton, 179.

35. Hutton, 194.

36. Hutton, 41.

37. Wendy Griffin, "The Embodied Goddess: Feminist Witchcraft and Female Divinity," *Sociology of Religion* 56 (1) (1995): 42.

38. Eller, 2.

39. Starhawk, *The Spiral Dance: A Rebirth of the Ancient Religion of the Great Goddess* (1979; reprint, San Francisco: Harper & Row, 1989), 97.

40. Judy Harrow, "Polarity: Doubting the Basics," *Enchanté: The Journal for the Urbane Pagan* 12 (1992): 12.

41. Sam Keen, *Fire in the Belly* (New York: Bantam, 1991), 100.

42. "Pan," *Green Egg* 27 (104) (Spring 1994): 13.

43. Personal interview, July 1993.

44. Personal interview, July 1992.

45. Brown, 64.

46. Starhawk, *The Spiral Dance*, 9.

47. Bolen, 257.

48. T. M. Luhrmann, *Persuasions of the Witch's Craft: Ritual Magic in Contemporary England* (Cambridge: Harvard University Press, 1989), 229.

49. Lone Wolf Circles, "Environmentalism and the Goddess," *Green Egg* 26 (102) (Autumn 1993): 28.

50. Both descriptions are from the Rites of Spring program, 1997.

51. Text from flyer available at Pantheacon 2003, San Jose, CA.

52. *Voice of the New Earth* (Feb. 2003):46.

53. Shakti Gawain, "Trusting Your Inner Power," *East West* 19 (11) (1989): 47.

54. Carl Jones, "Elixir," *Gnostica: Esoteric Knowledge for the New Age* 5 (10) (June 1978): 12.

55. Carl L. Weschcke, "Tantric Occultism," *Gnostica: Esoteric Knowledge for the New Age* 5 (10) (June 1978): 50.

56. Caroline Myss, *Anatomy of the Spirit: The Seven Stages of Power and Healing* (New York: Harmony, 1996), 144.

57. Aluna, *Green Egg* 27 (104) (Spring 1994): 19.

58. Aluna, 17.

59. Aluna, 17.

60. Janet Farrar and Stewart Farrar, *The Life and Times of a Modern Witch* (Custer, WA: Phoenix Publishing, 1987), 76.

61. Ibid., 76.

62. Adler, 110.

63. Farrar & Farrar, 78.

64. Ibid., 84.

65. Jean Marie Angelo, "Trusting Your Inner Power: Shakti Gawain," *East West* 19 (11) (1989): 46.

66. John Nelson, ed., *Solstice Shift: Magical Blend's Synergistic Guide to the Coming Age* (Charlottesville: Hampton Books, 1997), 215.

67. Jean Houston, *A Mythic Life: Learning to Live Our Greater Story* (San Francisco: HarperCollins, 1996), 233.

### 7. The Age of Aquarius

1. Catherine L. Albanese, *America: Religions and Religion*, 3rd ed. (Belmont, CA: Wadsworth, 1999), 356.

2. Margot Adler, *Drawing Down the Moon: Witches, Druids, Goddess-Worshippers and Other Pagans in America Today* (1979; reprint, Boston: Beacon, 1986), 237.

3. Albanese, 358.

4. Melinda Bollar Wagner, *Metaphysics in Midwestern America* (Columbus: Ohio State University Press, 1983), 165.

5. Marian Green, *Magic for the Aquarian Age: A Contemporary Textbook of Practical Magical Techniques* (Wellingborough: Aquarian Press, 1983), 32.

6. Marilyn Ferguson, *The Aquarian Conspiracy: Personal and Social Transformation in the 1980s* (Los Angeles: J. P. Tarcher, 1980), 19.

7. Ibid., 18–19.

8. (New York: Simon & Schuster, 1992), 29.

9. Sun Bear with Wabun Wind, *Black Dawn, Bright Day: Indian Prophecies for the Millennium That Reveal the Fate of the Earth* (New York: Simon & Schuster, 1992), 221.

10. Ibid., 223.

11. Laurie Cabot, *Power of the Witch: The Earth, the Moon, and the Magical Path to Enlightenment* (New York: Bantam Doubleday Dell, 1989), 291.

12. *Fireheart: A Journal of Magic and Spiritual Transformation* 7 (1993) (Maynard, MA: EarthSpirit Community, 1993), 73.

13. Marianne Williamson, *A Return to Love: Reflections on the Principles of a Course in Miracles* (New York: HarperCollins, 1993), 285.

14. "Who On Earth Is the Goddess?" www.caw.org/articles (7 March 2003).

15. John Nelson, ed., *Solstice Shift: Magical Blend's Synergistic Guide to the Coming Age* (Charlottesville: Hampton Books, 1997), 120.

16. Michael F. Brown, *The Channeling Zone: American Spirituality in an Anxious Age* (Cambridge: Harvard University Press, 1997), 141.

17. Nelson, 147.

18. Nelson, 133.

19. Nelson, 146.

20. Wagner, 138–39.

21. Quoted in Wagner, 161.

22. Adrian Ivakhiv, *Claiming Sacred Ground: Pilgrims and Politics at Glastonbury and Sedona* (Bloomington: Indiana University Press, 2001), 8.

23. Nelson, 174.

24. Peter Caddy, *In Perfect Timing: Memoirs of a Man for the New Millennium* (Forres, Scotland: Findhorn Press, 1996), xiv.

25. David Spangler, "The Meaning of Gaia: Is Gaia a goddess, or just a good idea?" *In Context: A Quarterly of Humane Sustainable Culture* 24 (Late Winter 1990): 44.

26. Adler, 389.

27. www.psnw.com/~galfo/gaia/vision.html (7 March 2003).

28. Harbin Web site, www.harbin.org (28 March 2003).

29. www.earthspirit.org (28 March 2003).

30. "Wild Magick Guidebook" (Needmore, IN: Elf Lore Family, 1994).

31. "Planetary Consciousness," in J. Gordon Melton, et al., *The New Age Almanac* (New York: Visible Ink Press, 1991), 425.

32. Helen Berger, *A Community of Witches: Contemporary Neo-Paganism and Witchcraft in the United States* (Columbia: University of South Carolina Press, 1999), 83.

33. Starwood XV (1995) publicity flyer.

34. Berger, 82.

35. Petherwin, "Honoring the Earth and Ourselves Through Pagan Burial Grounds," www.feri.com/frand/Wicca10.html (24 March 2003).

36. Shakti Gawain, *The Path of Transformation: How Healing Ourselves Can Change the World* (Mill Valley, CA: Nataraj Publishing, 1993), 169.

37. Albanese, 364.

38. www.starhawk.org (26 March 2003).

39. Vivianne Crowley, "Healing in Wicca," in *Daughters of the Goddess: Studies of Healing, Identity* (Walnut Creek, CA: Altamira, 2000), 161–62.

40. Cabot, 290.

41. Starhawk, "How To Conjure Justice" at http://www.starhawk.org/activism-writings/spiralswebs.html (14 January 2003).

42. Alex Wright, "New Age Message for Christians," *The Guardian*, http://www.guardian.co.uk/comment/story/0.3604.914681.00.html (15 March 2003).

43. Hanna Rosin, "Witches Stir Controversy in the Army," *Washington Post*, June 8, 1999, A1.

44. Clarence Page, "Bewitching Logic: All Religions or None Should Be Tolerated on Military Bases," *The Salt Lake Tribune* (6/17/99).

45. http://forerunner.com/champion/XOO38.html.

46. Johanna Michaelsen, *Like Lambs to the Slaughter: Your Child and the Occult* (Eugene, OR: Harvest House Press, 1989), 32.

47. Ibid., 299.

48. Ibid., 298.

49. Roger Elwood, *The Christening* (Eugene: Harvest House Press, 1989).

50. "The Doctrine of Self Intruding on Our Lives," *The Fundamentalist Journal* 7 (2) (Feb. 1988): 32–49.

51. www.circlesanctuary.org/liberty (19 March 2003).

52. Wendy Rose, "The Great Pretenders: Further Reflections on Whiteshamanism," in M. Annette Jaimes, ed., *The State of Native America* (Boston: South End Press, 1992).

53. Quoted in Sarah M. Pike, *Earthly Bodies, Magical Selves: Contemporary Pagans and the Search for Community* (Berkeley: University of California Press, 2001), 140.

54. "Meatless Pemmican: Indian Tribes, Identity, and Pan-Indianism in 20th-Century American Culture." Unpublished paper.

55. Looking Horse, "Lakota Spirituality, Lakota Sovereignty," *Colors* (Minneapolis, Jan. 1995): 14.

56. "New Agers and Native Wisdom: A Dialog on the NATCHAT list," 21 February 2003, http://www.hartford-hwp.com/archives/41/021.html (20 May 2003).

57. http://www.hanksville.org/sand/intellect/newage.html (20 May 2003).

58. My thanks to one of the anonymous reviewers of my book proposal for this apt phrase.

59. Internet communication, 21 June 1995.

60. Brown, 125.

61. www.awakeningtribe.org (14 January 2003).

62. Brown, 125.

63. Both quotes from Ivakhiv, 48.

64. Nelson, 135.

65. Nelson, 154 and 156.

66. Jean Houston, *A Mythic Life: Learning to Live Our Greater Story* (San Francisco: HarperCollins, 1996), 270.

67. Nelson, 96.

68. Houston, 319.

69. See for instance Robert Ellwood, *The 60s Spiritual Awakening* (New Brunswick: Rutgers University Press, 1994).

70. For an account of Promise Keepers see George Lundskow, *Awakening to an Uncertain Future: A Case Study of the Promise Keepers* (New York: Peter Lang, 2002); Robin Sylvan's *Traces of the Spirit: Religious Dimensions of Popular Music* (New York: New York University Press, 2002) includes discussions of raves and other musical events; Randall Balmer's film, *Mine Eyes Have Seen the Glory*, has a segment on Christian rock festivals; my essay on the religious aspects of Burning Man, "Desert Goddesses and Apocalyptic Art," appears in Katherine McCarthy and Eric Mazur, eds., *God in the Details* (New York: Routledge, 2001).

**Age of Aquarius**   A utopian future of peace and equality. A symbol for what New Agers believe will be a new kind of enlightened consciousness. Some astrologers theorized that when the sun entered the constellation of Aquarius on the day of the spring equinox, the Aquarian Age would arrive and create cosmic change. Aquarius is usually shown as a man with a water pot, pouring out a stream of water.

**ascended masters**   These beings inhabit a spirit world where they evolved separately from humans. Ascended masters can be contacted through certain ritualized techniques and are available to help humans along their spiritual paths.

**astral plane**   An invisible and spiritual level of reality.

**astrology**   An ancient system of divination based on the alignment of the stars.

**athame**   Ritual knife used by Neopagans and Wiccans. Often used in casting a circle at the beginning of a ritual.

**aura**   The subtle energy field around a person; also present in plants and animals.

**The Bear Tribe**   An organization blending New Age and American Indian beliefs, founded by Ojibwa Indian Sun Bear.

**Beltane**   May 1 or May Day, an Irish name meaning "bright fire." A day to celebrate fertility and the abundance of life.

**Blessingway/Wiccaning**   Rite of passage honoring the birth of a child that is designed to initiate the child into the community.

**ceremonial magic**   Derived from Renaissance magical traditions and often incorporating Jewish mysticism or kabbalah. Contemporary ceremonial magic rituals involve working in a circle and using visualization and meditation.

***chakras***   A Hindu term for spiritual energy centers in the body. The seven *chakras* are located along the spinal column.

**channeling**   The use of altered states of consciousness, such as meditation and trance, to contact invisible beings from other times or dimensions and to transmit messages from them through writing or speaking.

**circle**   As a noun, it means the basic Neopagan ritual form oriented to the four cardinal directions, a safe and consecrated space in which ritual work can be done. As a verb, it refers to the process of generating ritual space or conducting a ritual.

**coven**   A small group of Witches that gathers for rituals, usually guided by a priestess, priest, or both.

**CUUPS**   Covenant of Unitarian/Universalist Pagans. A Neopagan organization within the Unitarian/Universalist Church.

**crone**   Elder or wise woman.

**crystals**   Used for healing and fortune-telling, including gemstones of different colors associated with astrological signs.

**devas**   Invisible spirits, often related to plants. They may also be seen as a kind of angel.

**Druidism**   New religion based on ancient group of British Isles tree-worshippers.

**ecofeminism**   A perspective and philosophy originating in the convergence of environmentalism and feminism, based on the assumption that the exploitation of women and the degradation of nature are linked.

**fall or autumnal equinox**   September 21. A celebration of the harvest and recognition of the relationship between the earth and the sun; a day when daylight and darkness are equal.

**feminist spirituality**   A goddess-based religious movement that honors women's life experiences.

**Feri tradition**   A Neopagan tradition based on the teachings of Victor Anderson (1917–2001). It has influenced many other branches of Neopaganism, especially through the writings, rituals, and activist work of Starhawk, who was trained by Anderson.

**Findhorn**   A New Age community and retreat center in northern Scotland with elaborate gardens.

**the goddess**   Neopagan and New Age deity of whom images are drawn from archaeological finds and ancient Greek, Roman, Egyptian, and other texts.

**handfasting**   Neopagan marriage. Some are long-term commitments while others are for "a year and a day," to be renewed at a later time if the participants are willing.

**harmonial religion**   Philosophy based on the understanding that harmony exists between humans and cosmos, spirit and matter, and that they are not separate or distinct.

**Harmonic Convergence**   New Age prophet Jose Arguelles predicted that this convergence, "the beginning of the final twenty-six year period of the Mayan calendar's 5,200-year Great Cycle, the return of Quetzalcoatl, the Mayan god of peace, and the culmination of the Aztec calendar and the close alignment of the seven planets among other things," would occur in 1987 and would usher in a new era marked by a collective shift in human consciousness characterized by unity, love, and peace.

**The Hermetic Order of the Golden Dawn** An organization founded in England in the late 1880s and dedicated to ritual magic. It incorporated a wide variety of religious teachings and secret societies from around the world, including Freemasonry, astrology, and Tantric techniques.

**holistic healing** An approach to illness that involves treating the whole person, body, mind, and spirit.

**homeopathy** Developed by Samuel Hahnemann (1755–1843) in Germany; a system of medical treatment that relies on giving small doses of a remedy that would produce in a healthy person symptoms of the disease treated.

**Imbolc** February 1. Celebrates the first signs of spring and sometimes honors the Celtic goddess Brigid.

**invocation** A ritual method that involves calling to specific deities or spiritual beings and inviting them to be present in the ritual space.

**iridology** Diagnosing disease by observing the eyes. Assumes that parts of the body correspond to specific areas of the iris.

**kabbalah** Jewish mystical tradition.

***karma*** A doctrine derived from the Hindu belief that the condition to which each soul is reborn is the result of good or bad actions performed in previous lives, and that actions in this life will affect future incarnations.

***kundalini*** An energy that flows through the spine. A concept taken from Hinduism.

**Lammas/Lugnasad** August 1. A festival that marks the beginning of autumn and the first harvests.

**lyceum** A type of educational forum begun in nineteenth-century America for sharing scientific, spiritual, and cultural knowledge.

**macrobiotics** A special vegetarian diet and way of life based on ancient Asian practices and developed in the United States through the teachings of George Ohsawa and Michio Kushi.

**magick/magic** Changing one's own consciousness at will. May also include the idea of effecting change in the world outside of the self. Some Neopagans add the "k" to distinguish it from stage magic.

**meditation** A practice of developing awareness and altering the consciousness involving controlled breathing and stilling one's flow of thoughts.

**medium** A person, male or female, who transmits information from an invisible being, or who contacts the spirit world and conveys messages from a spirit guide.

**Mesmerism** A movement based on the belief that there is a universal occult energy, an invisible magnetic fluid flowing between planets and other heavenly bodies, earth, animals, plants, and humans. Mesmerists taught that spirit and matter are not separate; that humans, nature, and the divine are all connected; and that healing could be accomplished by manipulating this fluid.

**Mount Shasta**   Sacred mountain in the Cascades Range in Northern California near the Oregon border that is a New Age destination.

**naturopathy**   A major branch of the holistic health movement based on the idea that humans should live in harmony with nature and that natural healing is preferable to prescription drugs and other orthodox medical treatments.

**New Thought**   A religious movement founded in the nineteenth century that blended different religious beliefs and often included mental healing. Some New Thought healers and teachers felt they should help people harness their mental powers for the purpose of healing, while others saw the power of the mind as a way to move proactively through the world seeking financial success.

**occult**   Secret or hidden knowledge. Often transmitted through levels of initiation in secret societies.

**pantheism**   The belief that the divine or god dwells in everything, that humans, nature, and the divine are one.

**pentacle/pentagram**   A five-pointed star, sometimes misunderstood to be a satanic symbol. Its points symbolize the elements of fire, air, water, earth, and spirit.

**phrenology**   Method of diagnosing personalities based on the shape of the skull. Originally called craniognomy; developed by Franz Joseph Gall (1758–1828), a medical student in Vienna.

**polyamory**   An alternative lifestyle practiced by some New Agers and Neopagans that means "many lovers." A Neopagan organization called the Church of All Worlds spreads information about the philosophy and practice of polyamory.

**polytheism**   The belief in many gods and goddesses.

**psychic**   Someone with extraordinary powers, who can often see into the future. Psychics may offer information for a fee to clients who want predictions about the future or insight into aspects of their personal lives.

**rebirth/reincarnation**   The continuity of the soul through many lives. This belief is borrowed from Asian religions like Hinduism and Buddhism. New Agers and Neopagans believe that past lives can be accessed through meditative techniques or visualization.

**reflexology**   A form of bodywork or massage that is usually focused on the foot, which is seen as a microcosm of the body. Parts of the body correspond to specific places on the foot.

**Samhain**   October 31 or November 1. A festival to celebrate the harvest and to honor the dead. Neopagans believe that this is the time of year when the boundary is thinnest between the land of the dead and the land of the living.

**Sedona**   New Age and tourist destination in the "Red Rock region" of northern Arizona. Seen as a place of power where special energies are available for use in spiritual growth.

**shamanism**   A practice or way of life, usually thought to be based on ancient traditions, that includes some kind of out-of-body journey or trance experience.

**skyclad**   Naked; used in reference to Neopagan rituals practiced in the nude. May refer to clothing-optional Neopagan festivals.

**Spiritualism**   A movement that originated in New York State and involved spirits, often of dead loved ones, communicating through human mediums.

**spring or vernal equinox**   March 21. Celebrates the harmony of earth and sun, and the return of spring, at a point when days and nights are of equal length.

**Stonehenge**   A Neolithic stone circle in England of ancient but uncertain origin that symbolizes ancient pagan religions such as Druidism and has become a sacred site where contemporary Druids, among others, hold gatherings.

**summer solstice/Midsummer**   June 21. Celebrates the longest day of the year.

**Tantrism**   An ancient Asian practice based largely in India and Tibet that involves yoga and breathing as well as sexual-spiritual techniques.

**Theosophy**   A religious tradition blending Asian and western thought. Theosophists look to the past and to ancient cultures for truth and wisdom. They hope that through their reinvention of past cultures and revival of ancient myths and rituals they will usher in a new age of enlightenment.

**vegan**   Vegetarian who consumes no animal products.

**visualization**   Painting pictures with the mind. For instance, this might involve imagining an injured part of the body as whole and well again. It is also a technique used for spiritual growth.

**Wheel of the Year**   Neopagan calendar of festivals and holidays that marks the circular movement of the seasons beginning with Samhain through the fall equinox. The wheel is sometimes based on the ever-changing relationship of a goddess and a god as they move through the cycle of the seasons.

**Wicca**   Another name for Witchcraft. Sometimes used to distinguish it from the negative portrayal of witches in the media and in fairytales.

**Wiccan Rede**   "An it harm none, do what you will." One of the few doctrines shared by Wiccans and most Neopagans.

**yoga**   Refers to a Hindu philosophical system or to physical exercises known as hatha yoga.

**Yule/winter solstice**   December 21. Midwinter festival on the shortest day of the year to celebrate the return of the sun.

# RESOURCES FOR THE STUDY OF NEW AGE AND NEOPAGAN RELIGIONS

## Selected Bibliography

This bibliography includes scholarly and secondary texts of interest to students of New Age and Neopagan religions, but does not list all sources cited in the notes.

Adler, Margot. *Drawing Down the Moon: Witches, Druids, Goddess-Worshippers, and Other Pagans in America Today.* 1979; reprint, Boston: Beacon, 1986. National Public Radio reporter Adler's journalistic account of a wide variety of Neopagan organizations.

Ahlstrom, Sydney. *A Religious History of the American People.* New Haven and London: Yale University Press, 1972. A classic history of the diverse streams of American religiosity through the 1960s.

Albanese, Catherine L. *America: Religions and Religion,* 3rd ed. Belmont, CA: Wadsworth Publishing, 1999. Overview of American religions that also explains how metaphysical religion fits into the larger history.

Albanese, Catherine L. *Nature Religion in America: From the Algonkian Indians to the New Age.* Chicago: University of Chicago Press, 1990. Traces the development of religions that emphasize the importance of nature, with considerable attention paid to the New Age and Neopagan movements.

Bellah, Robert N., Richard Madsen, William M. Sullivan, Ann Swidler, and Stephen M. Tipton. *Habits of the Heart: Individualism and Commitment in American Life.* San Francisco: Harper & Row, 1985. Classic sociological study based on interviews that argues for the kind of personalization of religion common among Neopagans and New Agers.

Berger, Helen. *A Community of Witches: Contemporary Neo-Paganism and Witchcraft in the United States.* Columbia: University of South Carolina Press, 1999. Sociological study of the Earthspirit community in Massachusetts.

Berger, Helen, Evan A. Leach, and Leigh S. Shaffer. *Voices from the Pagan Census: A National Survey of Witches and Neo-Pagans in the United States*. Columbia: University of South Carolina Press, 2003.

Braude, Ann. *Radical Spirits: Spiritualism and Women's Rights in Nineteenth-Century America*. Boston: Beacon, 1989. Historical study of nineteenth-century spiritualism.

Brown, Michael. *The Channeling Zone: American Spirituality in an Anxious Age*. Cambridge: Harvard University Press, 1997. Anthropological study of channeling in contemporary America, including first-person accounts of channeling sessions.

Campbell, Bruce F. *Ancient Wisdom Revived: A History of the Theosophical Movement*. Berkeley: University of California Press, 1980. Places the Theosophical movement in its historical context and explores the roles and impact of Henry Olcott and Helena Blavatsky.

Cranston, Silvia. *HPB: The Extraordinary Life and Influence of Helena Blavatsky, Founder of the Modern Theosophical Movement*. New York: Putnam, 1993. An exhaustive biography of Blavatsky, including analysis of her works and her impact on Theosophy and related movements.

Eller, Cynthia. *Living in the Lap of the Goddess: The Feminist Spirituality Movement in America*. New York: Crossroad Publishing, 1993. Critical and scholarly study of feminist spirituality with descriptions of ritual events and analysis of beliefs.

Ellwood, Robert. *The Sixties Spiritual Awakening: American Religion Moving from Modern to Postmodern*. New Brunswick: Rutgers University Press, 1994. Scholarly study of the variety of religious expressions during the 1960s and analysis of religious aspects of the 1960s counterculture.

Ferguson, Marilyn. *The Aquarian Conspiracy: Personal and Social Transformation in the 1980s*. Los Angeles: J. P. Tarcher, 1980. Discusses the many developments in science, religion, and medicine that seem connected in their focus on a new or Aquarian Age.

Frohock, Fred M. *Lives of the Psychics: The Shared Worlds of Science and Mysticism*. Chicago and London: University of Chicago Press, 2000. Profiles of many psychics, stories of their healing techniques, and analysis of their scientific and religious views.

Fuller, Robert C. *Alternative Medicine and American Religious Life*. Oxford and London: Oxford University Press, 1989. Survey of nineteenth- and twentieth-century alternative religious and healing practices including crystal healing and chiropractic and osteopathic techniques.

Gardner, Martin. *Urantia: The Great Cult Mystery*. Amherst, NY: Prometheus Books, 1995. Skeptical and critical view of the origins of the Urantia book and its account of the teachings of extraterrestrials.

Griffin, Wendy, ed. *Daughters of the Goddess: Studies of Healing, Identity and Empowerment.* Walnut Creek, CA: Altamira Press, 2000. Essays by both scholars and participants in a variety of Neopagan and feminist spiritual practices.

Harvey, Graham. *Contemporary Paganism: Listening People, Speaking Earth.* New York: New York University Press, 1997. Overview of Neopagan beliefs and practices, with a focus on Neopaganism in Great Britain.

Hazen, Craig James. *The Village Enlightenment in America: Popular Religion and Science in the Nineteenth Century.* Urbana and Chicago: University of Illinois Press, 2000. Examines nineteenth-century alternative medicine and healing, including Mesmerism and Spiritualism.

Hutton, Ronald. *The Triumph of the Moon: A History of Modern Pagan Witchcraft.* Oxford and New York: Oxford University Press, 1999. Exhaustive history of the origins, leading figures, beliefs, and practices of Neopaganism from 1800 to the late 1990s.

Ivakhiv, Adrian. *Claiming Sacred Ground: Pilgrims and Politics at Glastonbury and Sedona.* Bloomington and Indianapolis: Indiana University Press, 2001. Describes New Age and Neopagan beliefs and practices concerning sacred sites.

Jenkins, Henry. *Mystics and Messiahs: Cults and New Religions in American History.* Oxford and New York: Oxford University Press, 2000. Looks at the history of and controversies about new religious movements.

Luhrmann, T. M. *Persuasions of the Witch's Craft: Ritual Magic in Contemporary England.* Cambridge: Harvard University Press, 1989. A psychological anthropologist reports on her experiences as a participant-observer, with an emphasis on psychological explanations for magical beliefs.

Magliocco, Sabina. *Neo-Pagan Sacred Art and Altars: Making Things Whole.* Jackson: University Press of Mississippi, 2001. Describes the role of the arts in Neopagan ritual life and includes photographs of a wide range of Neopagan altars and artwork.

Melton, J. Gordon, ed. *New Age Almanac.* Detroit: Visible Ink Press, 1991. Encyclopedic overview of New Age figures, organizations, and events with brief but numerous entries.

Pike, Sarah M. *Magical Selves, Earthly Bodies: Contemporary Pagans and the Search for Community.* Berkeley: University of California Press, 2001. An ethnography of Neopagan rituals and festivals, including discussion of conflicts between Neopagans and other religious cultures.

Prothero, Stephen. *The White Buddhist: The Asian Odyssey of Henry Steele Olcott.* Bloomington and Indianapolis: Indiana University Press, 1996. Biographical account of Olcott's role in the Theosophical Society and his travels and activist work in India.

Roszak, Theodore. *The Making of a Counterculture.* Garden City, NY: Doubleday, 1969. An observer's critical analysis of the 1960s counterculture.

Salomonsen, Jone. *Enchanted Feminism: The Reclaiming Witches of San Francisco.* London and New York: Routledge, 2002. Focuses on the theology and ritual of one important Neopagan organization.

Sutcliffe, Steven J. *Children of the New Age: A History of Spiritual Practices.* London and New York: Routledge, 2003. Historical look at the emergence of the New Age movement in Great Britain and contemporary practice, with special attention to the Findhorn community.

Wagner, Melinda Bollar. *Metaphysics in Midwestern America.* Columbus: Ohio State University Press, 1983. An anthropological study of an alternative religion in the Midwest, including accounts of meditation, spiritual healing, and psychic readings.

York, Michael. *The Emerging Network: A Sociology of the New Age and Neo-Pagan Movements.* London: Rowan and Littlefield, 1995. Examines similarities and differences between these two movements, with an emphasis on theology and belief.

## Journals and Newsletters

*Body & Soul.* Articles on bodywork, holistic healing, and various New Age spiritual practices. http://www.bodyandsoulmag.com

*Circle Magazine.* Published by Circle Sanctuary. Includes poems, photos, articles, announcements, and networking information. P.O. Box 219, Mt. Horeb, WI 53572.

*In Context: A Quarterly of Humane Sustainable Culture.* Publishes articles on New Age spirituality and environmental issues. http://www.context.org

*Magical Blend Magazine.* Focuses on mostly New Age and some Neopagan topics. http://www.magicalblend.com

*The Noetic Sciences Review.* Covers spiritual issues and the scientific study of human consciousness. http://www.noetic.org/ions/new.html

*Nova Religio.* Scholarly journal covering many kinds of new religious movements, including Neopagan and New Age religions. http://www.ucpress.edu/journals/nr

*The Pomegranate: The Journal of Pagan Studies.* http://www.equinoxpub.com

*Reclaiming Newsletter.* Publication of Bay area Neopagan organization that conducts public rituals and offers educational opportunities. P.O. Box 14404, San Francisco, CA 94114.

*SageWoman.* Journal for women of all ages. P.O. Box 641, Point Arena, CA 95468.

## Web Sites

*Access New Age—All Things Esoteric and Spiritual.* Esoteric Web links and astrological information. http://www.AccessNewAge.com

*Alternative Health News.* http://www.altmedicine.com

*The American Society for Psychical Research.* http://www.aspr.com

*Ananda Marga.* Sponsors centers that teach meditation, yoga, and other spiritual practices. http://www.anandamarga.org

*Ancient Ways.* Berkeley, California book and supply store for Neopagans. Sponsors two large Neopagan gatherings: Pantheacon and Ancient Ways Festival. http://www.ancientways.com

*ArnDraiocht Fein: A Druid Fellowship.* Druid rituals, information on gatherings, and articles about contemporary Druid worship. http://www.adf.org

*The Association for Consciousness Exploration.* Sponsors of Starwood and other New Age and Neopagan events. http://www.rosencomet.com/index.html

*Avatar Search: Search Engine of the Occult Internet.* http://www.AvatarSearch.com

*The Awakening Tribe.* http://www.awakeningtribe.org

*Bay Area Pagan Assemblies.* Lists open circles and drumming circles in the San Francisco Bay area. http://www.bapa.net/

*The Celestine Prophecy Home Page.* http://www.maui.net/~shaw/celes/old_celestine.html

*The Church of All Worlds.* Articles on CAW and various aspects of Neopaganism; lists of events. http://www.caw.org

*Circle Sanctuary.* Networking information and educational articles on Neopaganism. http://www.circlesanctuary.org

*Circle's Lady Liberty League.* Religious freedom news and information. www.circlesanctuary.org/liberty

*Committee for the Scientific Investigation of Claims of the Paranormal.* Publisher of the *Skeptical Inquirer.* http://csicop.org

*Covenant of the Goddess.* http://www.cog.org

*Covenant of Unitarian Universalist Pagans.* http://www.cuups.org/content/intro.html

*Earth Religions Legal Assistance Network.* http://www.conjure.com/ERAL/eral.html

*The Earthspirit Community.* Memorials, information on Neopagan gatherings, and networking. http://www.earthspirit.org

*Edgar Cayce's Association for Research and Enlightenment (ARE).* An organization established to spread the teachings of psychic Edgar Cayce. Includes listings of conferences and classes, books, and educational articles. http://www.are-cayce.com

*Esalen Institute.* http://www.esalen.org

*The Findhorn Foundation and Retreat Center.* http://www.findhorn.org

*Full Circle Events.* Sponsors events in the San Jose, California area and publishes a newsletter. http://www.FullCircleEvents.com

*Guide to Intentional Communities.* http://www.ic.org

*Gurdjieff International Review.* http://www.gurdjieff.org

*Harbin Hot Springs and Heart Consciousness Church.* http://www.harbin.org/harbin. htm?13,13

*The Institute of Noetic Sciences.* http://www.noetic.org/ions/new.html

*The Lama Foundation.* An intentional community and educational center influenced by many spiritual teachers, especially Ram Dass. http://lamafoundation.org

*The Lucis Trust.* Information and books on Alice Bailey and the Arcane School based on her teachings. http://www.lucistrust.org

*The Omega Institute.* http://www.eomega.org

*Pagan Educational Network.* Articles and information on environmental issues, alternative technologies, and educational resources. http://www.PaganEdNet. org

*The Pagan Federation.* A worldwide networking organization. http://www. paganfed.demon.co.uk

*Reclaiming.* San Francisco Bay area Neopagan organization that conducts public rituals and offers educational opportunities. http//www.reclaiming.org

*Seth Network International.* A meeting place for readers of the Seth material, channeled through medium Jane Roberts. http://209.81.10.123/

*Serpentine Music Productions.* Online Neopagan music catalog. http://www. serpentinemusic.com

*Spiritual Connections Online Bookstore.* http://www.spiritualconnectionsgroup.com /book.php?ISBN = 04465186X

*Starhawk's official site.* Articles on many aspects of Neopaganism and reports from Starhawk's political actions. http://www.starhawk.org

*Starwood Festival.* Neopagan festival in western New York. http://www. rosencomet.com/starwood

*Sun Bear's Unofficial Home Page.* Information about Sun Bear's teachings and the Bear Tribe, the organization he founded to blend New Age and American Indian beliefs. http://www.liteweb.org/wildfire/

*The Witches' Voice.* A news clearinghouse and networking site with a bulletin board and educational articles about Witchcraft and other forms of Neopaganism. http://www.witchvox.com

*Z. Budapest.* Z. Budapest's site includes an online Dianic University for the study of women's mysteries. http://www.zbudapest.com

# INDEX

Personalization, 21; and divinity, 26;
and future transformation, 171–72;
and healing, 31; 1960s, 73–75, 182–
83nn20–22; and religious practices,
30–31; and stereotypes, 22. *See also*
Eclecticism
Phrenology, 53, 55
*Piercing the Darkness* (Peretti), 162–63
Pilgrimages, 34, 35, 121
Piscean Age, 143, 146
Planchette, 52
Planetary healing, 23
*Planetary Herbology: An Integration of
Western Herbs Into the Traditional
Chinese and Ayurvedic Systems*
(Tierra), 93
*The Politics of Ecstasy* (Leary), 75, 85,
174
Polyamory, 137, 141
Positive thinking, 23, 70
*The Power of Positive Thinking*
(Peale), 70, 174
*The Power of the Witch* (Cabot), 160
Poyen, Charles, 47, 173
Prabhupada, A. C. Bhaktivedanta, 83
Pranic healing, 105
Pre-Christian nature religions, 19, 27,
124–25
Pregnancy, 121–22
Price, Richard, 80
Prophet, Elizabeth Clare, 165
Psychedelic drug culture, 83–85;
chronology, 73, 174; and commu-
nity, 81; Huxley on, 69–70, 84; and
sensuality, 86–87
Psychic healing, 16, 24–25, 47. *See also*
Healing
Psychic powers, 23, 84, 93
Puritanism, 45

Quimby, Phineas Parkhurst, 46–47, 53,
61, 173

Rainbow Ray focus group, 82
Rajneesh, Bhagwan Shree, 83
Ram Dass, Baba (Richard Alpert), 73,
82, 83–84, 85, 88
Ramtha, 16, 24, 28
Rand, Ayn, 79
Rape, healing from, 108–9, 131
Rapping, 52
Ravenwolf, Silver, 17–18
Raye, Marina, 112–13, 150
Reclaiming Coven, 130
*Recovering the Soul* (Dossey), 102
Redfield, James, 16–17, 175
Reflexology, 55
Reform. *See* Social activism
Regardie, Israel, 59–60
Reich, Charles, 86–87
Reiki, 22, 104
Reincarnation, 15; and early twentieth-
century religious movements, 63,
64; and 1960s, 83; and nineteenth-
century religious movements, 57,
60
*Reinventing Medicine: Beyond Mind-
Body to a New Era of Healing*
(Dossey), 102
Religious freedom/persecution, 18,
164, 168, 175
*Religious History of the American
People* (Ahlstrom), 48
Religious practices, 30–31. *See also*
Ritual
Religious specialists, 14, 23, 81, 165
Renaissance occult tradition. *See* West-
ern Esotericism
Retreats/sanctuaries, 32, 80,
153–54. *See also* Community;
Gatherings
"Revolutionary Letter #7" (DiPrima),
77–78
*Revolution for the Hell of It* (Hoffman),
75–76

# COOPERATIVE LEARNING & EDUCATIONAL MEDIA

## & EDUCATIONAL MEDIA

### COLLABORATING WITH TECHNOLOGY AND EACH OTHER

# COOPERATIVE LEARNING & EDUCATIONAL MEDIA

## COLLABORATING WITH TECHNOLOGY AND EACH OTHER

:::

**DENNIS ADAMS**
University of Minnesota, Duluth

**HELEN CARLSON**
University of Minnesota, Duluth

**MARY HAMM**
San Francisco State University

:::

**EDUCATIONAL TECHNOLOGY PUBLICATIONS**
**ENGLEWOOD CLIFFS, NEW JERSEY 07632**

Library of Congress Cataloging-in-Publication Data

Adams, Dennis M.
   Cooperative learning & educational media: collaborating with
technology and each other/Dennis Adams, Helen Carlson, Mary Hamm.
      p.   cm.
   Includes bibliographical references.
   ISBN 0-87778-219-9
   1. Team learning approach in education. 2. Group work in
education. 3. Educational technology. I. Carlson, Helen.
II. Hamm, Mary. III. Title. IV. Title: Cooperative learning and
educational media.
LB1032.A32       1990                                        89-28709
371.3'95 -- dc20                                               CIP

Printed in the United States of America.

Library of Congress Catalog Card Number:
89-28709.

International Standard Book Number:
0-87778-219-9.

*First Printing: January, 1990.*

# ACKNOWLEDGEMENTS

We would like to acknowledge the contributions of Greta Gaard in Chapter Three. Special thanks are also extended to the Interactive Videodisc Group, College of Education and Human Service Professions, University of Minnesota, Duluth: Larry Bright, Eugene Grossman, Mark Nierengarten, Iver Bogan, Harry Watts, Terrie Shannon, and Dennis Falk.

# PREFACE

Why is American industry gasping for breath as it fights for its high-tech life? A recent MIT study identified three major stumbling blocks for American industry and technology. The first was the decline in worker productivity as the result of inadequate educational preparation. The second was relatively low levels of on-the-job training by American corporations. And the third was our national inability to cooperate.

Collaborative interaction is recognized as vital to international relations, national politics, communities, family relationships, and the workplace. It is also a means for improving communication and creating the kind of school/work culture in which mutual assistance flourishes. In an effort to stay competitive American industry has turned to the "work team" method of grouping workers and managers. In general, this on-the-job method of grouping has been found to be a flexible and effective way to creatively motivate personnel. A similar process is gaining ground in American schools. Cooperative small group learning is coming to be viewed as an important supplement to whole class instruction and having individuals work alone.

Like educational technology, ideas about group learning have gone through a number of incarnations. The quality of the schools and the competitive ethos of traditional instruction are now the subject of national concern. Failing schools, dwindling academic achievement, low self esteem and alienated students are causing fear of change to evaporate. American education is reexamining models of teaching, learning and school structure.

Educators are focusing their efforts to improve education on programs, like cooperative learning, that have been proven effective by evaluation data.

The benefits of cooperative learning, implemented through a joint teacher-administrator approach, are widely viewed as having the potential to make a significant contribution to restoring the quality and utility of our schools. It is important that such an opportunity should not be lost through fear, misunderstanding, or lack of reliable research information.

As classroom organizational approaches move toward new group work procedures, machines increasingly facilitate our communication with information and with each other. An explosion of new ideas is taking place in technological applications. Technology has seeped into just about every sector of American culture. It has become the environment in which an increasing amount of thinking and communicating is taking place. The jobs of the future will require workers who can deal with rapidly changing technology and work cooperatively in a group situation.

While group learning and democratic education are not new concepts, today's cooperative team learning takes on new dimensions. Teachers are viewed as principal agents for initiating change and creating high quality learning environments for students and their technological associates. In classrooms structured to accommodate cooperative learning groups, responsibility replaces individual competition as pupils strive to reach learning goals. As students explore together to accomplish a group task the accomplishment of one student helps all the others. Conversely, the discouragement of individuals is met with group concern. Interaction, positive group interdependence, collaboration and individual accountability are important parts of the framework for collaborative models.

This book sets out to fuse cooperative learning strategies with a wide range of communication technologies: computers, television, interactive videodiscs and hypermedia. It is intended for a broad range of readers — from the novices to those highly skilled in developing the new media. We examine issues, present practical ideas and explore the controversy surrounding the role of collaboration in both low and high tech learning environments. Cooperative models and methods are explained in a way that can amplify learning with technology as simple as pencils and as complex as computer-controlled hypermedia. The intent is to draw the reader into thinking about the changes possible today — and the future of classroom organization and effective teaching.

Americans must now live by the product of technological tools and the collective thinking abilities of the students our schools graduate. To focus on learning and intellectual achievement, rather than control, requires both new instructional arrangements and better use of technology in the curriculum. Yet schools have been slow to adapt to either the information age or the need for teamwork in the workplace. It is one thing to demand first-rate program evaluations before something new is adopted. It's quite another to obstruct change that is demonstrably beneficial.

The theme of electronic media and collaboration runs throughout this book. Yet it is recognized that there is no substitute for individual accountability. Similarly, new media must be tempered with the old. In a technologically and literacy intensive future neither the written word nor printed word can be ignored. Textbooks may be monotonously similar, but there is no substitute for the way *print* can convey metaphor, or connect to a rich literary tradition.

When "a picture is worth a thousand words," that picture usually appears within a context of printed words. Regardless of how accessible non-print information becomes, there will be no substitute for a well written sentence. New media does, however, allow us to build on visual concepts on a scale undreamed of in the past. Schools are also starting to recognize that there are certain kinds of information—like understanding the human circulatory system — that are transmitted most effectively when there is a visual component.

Librarians, among the most vigilant caretakers of traditional literacies, recognize that new electronic media have assumed a pivotal role in reading, writing and communication. These "information specialists" realize that we are on the verge of a new alliance between old and new literacies. Microcomputers, software, compact discs, interactive videodiscs, audio tape "books," camcorders, and video cassettes (a real circulation booster) are becoming part of their collections.

One cause for concern is the widening gap between the traditional print media and the more popular electronic varieties. A recent Gallop poll found that only a small percentage of American children frequently read for pleasure. Reading was ranked last among activities in which children reported engaging. TV viewing was ranked first in popularity and time commitment. Everyone agreed that reading was important. But only girls, with well educated parents, were reported to be avid readers. And after fifth grade there was a significant drop in reading interest reported in all groups.

Education relates importantly to the whole range of communications media and to the roles of collaboration, imagination and experience in fostering personal growth. Over a billion people around the globe watch at least five hours of television a day. Tens of millions use computers daily on the job. Whether looking into a cathode ray tube at home or at work, viewers have often been placed in a kind of psychological solitary confinement. This book suggests ways to break out.

The nature of work and learning are being transformed as advanced information technologies, including computers and their associates, spread across the social and economic landscape. Competitive, isolated, paper/pencil tasks have been replaced by technologically intensive work environments that require higher levels of thinking and collaboration. What's going on represents nothing less than cultural change on an industry wide basis. As new opportunities unfold the function of literacy and the nature of work will be transfigured. Our living standard and power in the years ahead will depend upon our national ability to learn new skills, cooperate and use high technology.

The video screen is evolving into a learning tool infused with potential from developments in microcomputers, artificial intelligence, simulation, interactive video, hypermedia, and telecommunications. When combinations of "old" and "new" media are combined with the skills of collaboration, critical thinking and group problem solving the result can foster student self esteem and academic achievement (Carlson & Falk, 1986). If education and its media associates are approached in a spirit of collaboration, a new synergy will develop between communications technology and its users.

One of the major questions we sought to explore was how cooperative learning and technological tools can support and amplify literacy and each other. Another concern was how current educational practices are informed by ideas, concepts and practical methods for improving learning  with the whole range of information technologies. A variety of cooperative learning techniques, suited to varying learning styles, are outlined in a way that will help teachers move beyond chalk, talk, and solitary activities. In addition, we have provided practical methods to go along with ideas, issues and trends in collaborative learning and emerging technologies.

The book is intended for teachers, parents, media specialists, administrators and others curious about the newly converging concepts of cooperative learning and educational technology. It provides those responsible for educational experiences with collaboration strategies and procedures for applying technology in the classroom. We believe that by building a dynamic and literate learning environment, with a team approach, students will also be able to transfer cooperative models to the world of work and the need for self-generated life-long learning.

## Reference

Carlson H. & Falk, D. (1986). *Learner Analysis for Interactive Videodisc Instructional Design: Understanding Groups Videodisc Series.*   Duluth, MN: Center for the Advancement of Learning Technologies Interactive Videodisc Research Group, Occasional Paper 87-2.

# CONTENTS

# COOPERATIVE LEARNING & EDUCATIONAL MEDIA
## COLLABORATING WITH TECHNOLOGY AND EACH OTHER

# 1

## COOPERATIVE LEARNING
## Building a Team Spirit in the Classroom

American education is working with an increasingly diverse group of pupils. Changing demographics mean a changing cultural balance in the workplace by the 21st century. Only two out of five new workers will be white males. Today students who are linguistically and culturally "different" make up at least half of school populations in many states. The reality of schooling today is at odds with how the general public remembers their own school days. Chewing gum and running in the hallway are no longer the most serious problems.

In order to serve as many disadvantaged students as possible, teachers and the curricula must not be remote from culture and interests of students being served. Inner city youth, for example, frequently share such common traits as alienation, low self esteem, poor health care, and nutrition-related deficiencies (Carnegie Foundation for the Advancement of Teaching, 1988). Many children escape from the negative consequences of poor academic performance by devaluing academic skills and seeking satisfaction outside of school. Some students need a special kind of support. But the schools, starved of funds and personnel, can do little about it.

Financially strapped urban and rural schools are struggling. Without increased funding, excellence usually occurs at the expense of equity. Schools that are doing well get the rewards; those that aren't become worse off than ever. The educational reform movement has left the basic needs of many students unmet. The American dream is more like a nightmare for many youth as they miss out on educational advantages from early childhood education to job training. Concerns have also been raised about the inequality of educational possibilities as minority youngsters who stay in school are put on the lowest expectation track. A subtle message of low self worth comes through. And history has shown that pouring contempt on people may very well make some of them contemptible.

As far as classroom organization is concerned, we do have some proven techniques that can stretch the possibilities for equity. We know that young people need more personal attention in school. Studies have shown advantaged as well as disadvantaged students significantly benefit from collaborative learning techniques (Sharan & Shachar, 1988). Even the most outstanding students can reach higher levels of achievement when tutoring others. Pupils with less information can drive and motivate the students with more. Self worth for all students is enhanced through the collaborative process. Academically talented students are not just providing a service, by teaching others they themselves actually come to understand the material better (Kraft, 1985).

In the late twentieth century socialization seems to be more difficult for young adults of all social classes. Faced with the possibility of downward social mobility, more and more of them are unable to build productive careers or raise families. The "me generation" is finding that serving themselves at the expense of others is a hollow ideal. Even the more self centered have reached the limit on the number of homeless they are willing to step over to get to the limo. In the final analysis it's how one uses freedom for the good of everyone that counts. What can be done to help persons of all ages, but particularly the young, gain prosocial skills in a multicultural society? Can cooperation and collaboration skills underlying prosocial behavior be learned? Can new, emerging technologies contribute effectively to this learning?

## Cooperative Learning and Tomorrow's School

New technological work requirements are changing the educational equation at an ever accelerating rate. The factory model, with its top down organization, has been replaced in the world outside of school by new concerns about collective responsibility (Levine & Trachtman, 1988). This leaves today's students ill served by the silent and frequently isolated teaching techniques formed in the days of factory assembly lines. There is general agreement that we need to move schools into the information age.

Long held educational models of teacher talk, textbook memorization, tracking, and moving pupils from box to box (with a bell) are poor examples for future workers and professionals. Even those students who "adjust" are finding that the skills learned no longer count for much when they leave school. In the new workplace power is frequently shared, collaboration encouraged, and higher levels of thinking required.

Cooperative learning is one of the most useful organizational ideas recently advanced for changing the educational process, engaging the minds of students, and connecting schooling to the world of work. While collaboration in the classroom is not new, it has only recently gained serious attention from educational researchers. Even the mass media seems interested. A 1989 issue of *The New York Times,* for example, referred to cooperative learning as "the coming wave in American education."

The basic concept revolves around teacher organized active small group learning environments. Students cluster together, discuss topics and learn to take charge of their own learning. Team spirit, rather than individual rivalry, is stressed as students learn to work together in mixed ability groups. Students work together to accomplish a learning goal and their team is held responsible for each group member's learning. The students' objective is not only to complete a task, but to learn something as a team. The success of one student aids others.

Recent research suggests cooperative groups produce more and better ideas than students working alone. Cooperative discussion has proven that it can increase retention and improve the problem solving ability of all students. Discussion aids learning as peers encourage each other. Not surprisingly, one of the clearest findings is that cooperative learning improves social relations among students (Slavin, 1989).

Blueprints for collaborative knowledge building include strategies for connecting thinking to collaborative groups. Students learn how to jointly  search out information on questions generated by individuals or the group. They learn techniques for analyzing, interpreting, negotiating and communicating their information as a team. Instead of the traditional emphasis on competitive individual performance students are encouraged to pool their talents to help each other learn, and come up with group products.

Within cooperative learning groups the student's role

also changes. The role of collaborative researcher replaces the traditional notion of student as a passive knowledge recipient. Learning starts with curiosity, moves toward students' interpretation of the subject's meaning in their lives, and is then connected to other areas of knowledge. Children learn by "talking out," assimilating ideas through group interaction, and assuming a higher level of responsibility for what they set out to learn.

### Teaching as an Act of Social Collaboration

The more options students have the more learning takes on an element of ambiguity similar to the world of work in the late twentieth century. This requires shared curriculum development and decision-making by knowledgeable professionals (teachers) working in an environment that allows time for creative planning, risk-taking, action research, and thoughtful evaluation. Educators need to move from the certainty of textbooks and teacher's manuals. This requires teachers who have a deep understanding of their subject matter and a thorough knowledge of the characteristics of effective instruction. Keeping up-to-date in either area isn't easy.

Updating teaching methodology works best with the mutual support of colleagues. A team approach to renewal can help teachers overcome isolation while building the professional networks so useful to life-long learning. When it comes to inner city schools and a sustained multicultural curriculum, new teachers have been shown to do better if they receive mentoring from knowledgeable and experienced teachers who know how to reach urban students. The technological possibilities for doing this are also being explored. For example, there is a federally funded computer network at Harvard University that links beginning teachers by microcomputer to veteran teachers, professors, and each other.

To develop comfort with the fluid character of today's knowledge the old model of teaching *as telling* must be replaced with one that might be described as teaching as choreography or teaching as coaching. Getting students excited about a subject and linking it to meaning is an act of pedagogical leadership. When teachers take responsibility for how schools are managed and students take on more responsibility a synergy of teaching and learning develops. Instead of rivalry in the teacher's room, or in class, a team spirit can emerge. This provides group support as individuals internalize ladders of knowledge and wrest personal meaning from what's being studied.

New models for teaching and learning cannot be put in place without going beyond considering social opportunities and overall school structure. Support for new learning strategies and the need for institutional changes are interwoven. Without a high level of political, social, and economic support it is difficult to talk about empowering teachers or improving the texture and richness of learning. Fortunately it's not all gloom and doom. We seem to be moving towards a societal consensus, supported by the public and leaders in just about every field, that neglecting our educational institutions will prevent the human retooling necessary for serving the needs of the 1990s and beyond.

# Cooperative Learning:
# Changing Attitudes and Values

Cooperative learning can help us with social values and subject matter accomplishment. Numerous studies of cooperative learning have shown significant student gains on measures of academic achievement, measures of social relationships, self esteem, and cross-cultural relationships (Slavin,1989; Sharan & Shachar, 1988). These well documented benefits are causing educators to reexamine their assumptions about institutional organization and learning environments.

The ways we choose to spend our teaching/learning time convey implicit messages to students about what is valued and important. Traditionally most class time was spent listening to the teacher or working on isolated paper and pencil tasks. If such large amounts of time are devoted to the learning of isolated facts the underlying assumption conveyed is that education means a tedious mastering of a narrow range of skills, emphasizing product. Important educational matters are much broader. Like cooperative learning, they represent more of an attitude toward the world than a set of subskills.

## Balancing Competition and Cooperation

Competition, anxiety, a product orientation, and not feeling part of a learning group have been identified as problems that inhibit children's development. Schools have traditionally been competitive institutions. Competition increases as students move up through the system. The messages sent through this model are that quick, "right" answers are valued. As a result children learn to depend on the "faster" students to provide answers and on the teacher for validating their thinking. Focusing on completing assignments quickly, children rarely stop to question the reasonableness of their response or the meaning behind it. Such pedagogical techniques not only inhibit students' self reliance but do little to produce literacy.

Research also points to the fact that levels of anxiety significantly inhibit achievement (Bulmahn, Young, 1982). When a competitive structure is bonded to an abstract style of presentation, anxiety is usually the major product. In such a stressful environment many students withdraw into themselves as they seek out the psychological equivalent of desert islands — unreal, but there. Cooperative learning attempts to deal with these concerns by maximizing interaction and changing what is valued in the learning process. The result can be classrooms where learning is both more possible and more productive.

When working in collaborative groups students have a better chance to explore ideas, justify their views and synthesize knowledge within a supportive environment. Instead of quiet isolated "workers" reluctant to share answers, shielding their papers from other students' eyes, students are encouraged to share ideas, collaborate together and pool their knowledge to solve or resolve problems. Learning is a cooperative rather than a competitive endeavor. This need to teach young people to think and work in groups is expressed repeatedly in the literature. We now have widely respected evidence that cooperative groups lead to growth in higher order thinking (Hertz-Lazarowitz et *al.*,1980; Sharan & Shachar, 1988). Unfortunately classroom practice often falls into the dark hole between knowledge and practice.

In response to these issues professional associations are calling for an emphasis on group learning that relies on reasoning skills more than rote. In a recent statement, the American Association for the Advancement of Science called for a common core of collaborative learning that stresses thinking skills and problem solving over memorization of details. One of the key features of cooperative learning that they refer to is the need for students to pool their critical thinking — giving and receiving help. This is supported by the literature that goes on to suggest that such interaction correlates with higher levels of critical thinking and risk taking (Webb, 1982).

In developing collaborative learning structures it's necessary to create a learning environment in which it is safe to make mistakes and learn from those mistakes. This type of classroom structure maximizes social interaction and focuses on learning that is as exciting as it is pleasurable. Such an organizational model does not require adapting one's thinking to the person "in charge," but encourages the sharing of knowledge in a way that contributes to a shared understanding.

## The Specifics of Cooperative Learning

It usually takes more than one or two tries with cooperative learning to get cooperative groups going. Students, like teachers, must be eased into the process through a consistent routine. The more someone works in small groups the easier it becomes. When high achievers from traditional classrooms have to work in a group they often have initial problems because they are accustomed to being rewarded for easy to come by answers that require little thinking. It may take some time and teacher assistance for them to become comfortable working cooperatively.

### Shared Leadership and Group Task Behaviors

Collaborative structures for human interaction involve shared leadership. This means that many roles must be performed by group members. Each member of a group takes responsibility for making sure that group members work toward a goal — while maintaining a good feeling about the group. This doesn't mean using the "team spirit" to suppress dissent or intimidate individuals.

These can all be called task and maintenance functions. They involve specific task behaviors:

1. *Clarifying or elaborating* — interpreting or building on another's information.

2. *Information or opinion giving* — sharing information relevant to the group.

3. *Information or opinion seeking* — requesting information relevant to the group.

4. *Summarizing* — pulling together information already shared.

5. *Managing* — establishing a process which helps the group achieve its goal.

Organizing an agenda or plan of action for the group is an essential part of shared leadership. Students need to learn how to give and receive information so as to continue progress on a group task. Summarizing and clarifying that information is also an important group strategy. Sometimes it is necessary to test the consensus of a group — how many members agree that a particular direction is advisable or that a particular conclusion is accurate.

## Maintenance Behaviors

In addition to these task behaviors, a group member also needs to display empathy for other group members and their feelings. At times it is crucial to reflect on the process of the group and the feelings group members express. This assures that each member of the group has an opportunity to express opinions and ideas. When group interactions become tense, a release of that tension is needed; perhaps a funny joke will ease members' frustrations. Creating harmony may result when one group member acknowledges that another group member is upset.

A brief outline of maintenance behaviors includes:

1. *Compromising* — "giving in" when necessary to other group members.

2. *Empathizing and encouraging* — showing understanding and helping others feel a part of the group.

3. *Gatekeeping* — giving everyone a chance to speak in the group.

4. *Releasing tension* — harmonizing interactions in the group.

5. *Sharing group feelings and processes* —
   helping the group to examine how it is feeling
   and operating.

It is useful for teams to evaluate the effectiveness of each group meeting as soon as it is over. This provides feedback and insights into the group process. As the team learns to focus its energy on the learning task, it also learns to focus on itself to help its members grow and develop. Compromising, encouraging, sharing and productive tension release are learned behaviors and as such need time, coaching, and commitment. When task and maintenance behaviors are in balance, group members can work collaboratively to achieve important goals.

## Individualistic, Competitive, and Cooperative Goal Structures

The goal structure of a group also has a significant bearing on the group's ability to interact effectively. Three different goal structures have been identified: individualistic, competitive, and cooperative. In individualistic goal structures, the person works alone, moving at his or her own pace to achieve a particular end product or process. When competitive goal structures exist, one person achieves a goal at the expense of another. If, for example, a normal curve is used for grading purposes, only a certain number of pupils can attain an "A." Given this competitive ethos, if some pupils achieve high grades, certain others must receive low grades.

A cooperative goal structure allows all members to mesh their individual goals with a group goal through a process called positive interdependence. This means that each person's individual objective is met at the same time that the group meets its goal. Coupled with the idea of positive interdependence is the concept of individual accountability. Each group member is responsible for a particular task and accountable for her own knowledge or his own area of contribution to the group (Johnson, 1974; Slavin, 1988).

**Peaceful Conflict Resolution and Problem Solving**
Another key task in cooperation and collaboration is an ability to resolve conflicts in a peaceful manner. When conflict escalates, group members take unyielding stances and refuse to consider other points of view. Groups members who can use negotiating and problem solving are skillful in deescalating conflict.

Problem solving is a useful group strategy to assist in conflict resolution. This systematic five step process of constructively addressing conflicts includes:
1. Defining the problem and its causes.
2. Generating alternative solutions to the problem.
3. Examining advantages and disadvantages to each alternative.
4. Deciding upon and implementing the most desirable solution.
5. Evaluating whether the solutions solve the problem.

Group members must define exactly what the problem is. On occasion, this can be difficult, but it is worth the effort. Once the problem is defined, group members can then suggest alternative solutions for the problem and explore the consequences of each of those alternatives. The group members then make a decision to try an alternative and to review the results within a stipulated period of time (Filley, 1975; Stanford, 1976).

Problem solving resolves conflict and allows group members to continue with their work. Children as young as four and five years of age are able to use this problem solving approach as they resolve conflicts over such things as the possession of materials ( Spivack, Platt, & Shure, 1976). Educators and parents have also found problem solving approaches to be helpful in dealing with classroom and family conflict (Dinkmeyer & McKay, 1976; Gordon, 1976; Gordon & Burch, 1974).

Negotiating is also a learning part of problem resolution. It involves mutual discussion and arrangement of the terms of an agreement. The process of learning to "read" another's behavior for clues as to a problem solution is crucial in being able to guess what will appeal to another person and how to make a deal in which each participant's preferences or needs are considered (Katz, 1982; Rubin and Everett, 1982).

Complementing the task and maintenance functions are such communication skills as active listening. This means both attending to and responding to group and individual efforts. Active listening allows all group members to be fully in tune with each other. Acknowledging the content, feelings, or meaning of what another person is communicating lends itself to goodwill and understanding. Gatekeeping (group monitoring) assures that all members of the group participate and are secure in the knowledge that they are contributing to the group (Carkhuff, 1985; Eagen, 1986).

# Models of Cooperative Learning

Programs can vary in terms of both task structures and reward contingencies. Four different cooperative learning methods have been extensively developed and researched. The Teams-Games-Tournaments (TGT) and the Student Teams and Achievement Divisions (STAD) are two general methods adaptable to most subject matter and grade levels. Team Assisted Instruction (TAI) and Cooperative Integrated Reading and Composition (CIRC) are designed for specific curricula and grade levels. All methods incorporate concepts of individual accountability, team rewards and equal opportunities for success, but approaches differ.

In the STAD and TGT approaches new material is first presented by the teacher to the whole class. Following this initial presentation, pupils are organized into mixed ability learning teams. Students work within their teams to insure that all members have mastered the lesson objectives. In the Student Teams Achievement Division approach students take individual quizzes on the material, whereas in the Teams-Games-Tournaments method group members are asked questions orally in tournaments with other teams. This team competition involves three tournament tables where students of similar abilities from different teams accumulate points for their team. In both cases, scores are kept for both individuals and teams or groups.

Other cooperative methods include the Jigsaw approach, where a different portion of a learning task is completed by each group member. This entails mutual cooperation. For example, pupils within one group might be required to read a certain text, with each group member assigned a particular potion of that text. Each pupil becomes an expert for that certain section, although all pupils must pass a test on the entire passage. Often, the "experts" from different groups meet to discuss material before returning to their home groups to present and discuss their assigned material. Positive effects on both achievement, particularly for minority children, and cross ethnic friendships have resulted (Sharon,1980; Ziegler, 1981).

The research on the effects of cooperative learning also suggest:

* Positive effects on academic achievement measures:
  - improved performance on vocabulary tests
  - higher achievement scores on tests mathematics computation and problem solving

* Improvement on interpersonal measures:
  - mutual concern
  - friendships between pupils of different races and ability levels

* Improved attitudes:
  - toward school
  - students' perceptions of peer support for their own performances, and self esteem

(Madden & Slavin, 1983; Stallings & Stipek,1986).

## Use of Cooperative Goal Structures

A variation on the task specialization model for cooperative learning involves each group member completing a different type of task. For example, students may present a play as a culminating activity for a unit of study. Each group member has a different task, from building set scenery, to creating script, to acting, and each is accountable for this task. The group evaluation rests on the quality of the play. The use of these types of cooperative goal structures with pupils has resulted in high interpersonal interaction, effective communication, and powerful peer facilitation of each other's learning. This results in high levels of trust, divergent thinking and risk-taking (Johnson, & Johnson, 1974).

Cooperative goal structures used in other varieties of learning tasks, ranging from learning to play golf, to solving mazes, were also more effective than competitive or individualistic goal structures (Johnson, Maruyama, Johnson, Nelson, & Skon, 1981). In general, it is important to include both group goals and individual accountability to increase achievement in classroom learning tasks. The provision of both group goals and individual accountability increases student achievement (Newmann & Thompson, 1987; Slavin, 1988).

## Mainstreaming:
### A Collaborative Model for Pupils and Teachers

One dual-focused collaboration model placed pupils with learning disabilities into regular classrooms and used teams of regular and special educators to serve all students in those classrooms. The pupils worked in heterogeneous cooperative groups in reading/language arts and mathematics. Regular classroom teacher team members structured the physical environment and developed the broad educational goals and curricula, while special educator team members adapted methods and materials to meet the needs of both learning disabled and low achieving pupils.

In this mainstreaming model of cooperative learning pupils with learning disabilities were served with special instruction removed from the regular classroom. They were compared with pupils with learning disabilities and low ability in cooperative models. The latter students had significantly higher academic achievement in reading comprehension and math computation. Learning disabled pupils also felt more satisfied and perceived their work as less difficult. Teachers who worked with other professionals on this collaborative model were positive about the support system which developed and referred to it as a "burnout prevention model" (Carlson, Ellison, & Dietrich, 1988).

Each of these areas: shared leadership, cooperative goal structures including individual accountability, peaceful conflict resolution, and excellent communication skills are essential for effective collaboration and cooperation. These key components contribute to a model of cooperation and collaboration which can be used for the development of instructional designs as well as models for the use of older, newer, and emerging technologies.

One of the strongest findings from the research is that students benefit socially as well as academically from cooperative learning. The outcomes are overwhelmingly positive for improving relationships between students of different backgrounds and academic levels (at all grade and subject levels). The widespread use and effectiveness of these learning models contributes to their attractiveness to teachers (Good & Brophy, 1989). The process of collaboration also seems to add to the enjoyment of learning and improving the educational experiences of many students.

# Cooperative Learning Environments

## The Role of the Teacher
## in the Cooperative Classroom

Once the curriculum of the past is viewed from a safe distance (like Dick and Jane in the old reading textbooks), it can be seen as a quaint anachronism. But while your professional life is squeezed into its narrow confines, the charm escapes you. Traditional goal structures tended to be teacher centered with teachers controlling learning by imparting knowledge, maintaining control, and validating thinking. Teachers have traditionally controlled the learning that goes on by knowing the end product of the learning experiences—as well as the sequence of activities and procedures needed to achieve the learning goal.

Successful implementation of cooperative learning requires deep conceptual understanding of the process by teachers *and* students. Small-group cooperative learning involves significant changes in the role of the classroom teacher. In the cooperative learning classroom the teacher is faced with the difficult task of encouraging students to become responsible for their own learning. One of the goals is to have students rely more heavily upon their classmates for assistance in doing a task and evaluating an answer. Only after they have checked with everyone in the group can they ask the teacher for help.

When the classroom organization is built on cooperative learning, teachers specify the instructional objectives, provide the appropriate materials, and arrange the classroom to maximize social interaction. Additionally it's the teacher's job to set the task, explain the cooperative goal structure, observe the student interactions, and help students solve problems.  Teachers must also pay attention to the learning process, social relationships within the groups, and evaluation of the group products.

In a collaborative setting the teacher helps children gain confidence in their own ability and the group's ability to work through problems and consequently rely less on the teacher as the sole knowledge source.  Students are motivated more by the social contact with their peers and by their sense of achievement as they succeed in challenging tasks through the group effort rather than through strict, step by step, teacher direction.

Students in cooperative learning settings frequently raise questions and ideas which often go well beyond any teacher's guide. To keep up-to-date teachers must also continue being  learners and become comfortable with saying "I don't know" or "let's find out" as students push them in new learning directions unimagined and unplanned.

A conceptual reexamination of classroom grouping structures is needed to form collaborative learning groups.  This involves substantive change more than superficial refinements.  Cooperative classroom environments will not materialize overnight, without effort. Teachers need to understand and actively seek to create them.  Once teachers reconstruct their classrooms for group work, many will find that their best instincts were correct and that they could have promoted better learning all along.

### The Student's Role Is Changing

A shift in student attitudes must also occur if a collaborative learning environment is to succeed.  Getting over years of learned helplessness will take time.  The school experience has taught students that the teacher is there to validate their thinking and direct learning. Upon entering school students have been constantly compared with one another for grades and recognition. For many teachers direction on the smallest detail becomes the order of the day. Students learn that it's easy to predict their success based on their past performance. Getting over these dated modeling structures takes time.

It is important that students understand that simply "telling an answer" or "doing someone's work" is not helping a classmate learn. Helping involves explaining with an example or learning to ask the right question to help a classmate grasp the concept. These understandings need to be actively and clearly explained, demonstrated, and developed by the teacher. Students need supportive relationships between the subjects they study and either their peers or knowledgeable adults. By connecting with others, cooperative learning is more of a "culture" or set of values that pervade the classroom than it is a technique.

Attitudes also change as students learn to work cooperatively instead of taking individual ownership of ideas. Students share rather than compete for recognition; evaluating the learning outcomes rather than hurrying to finish the task. Small groups can write collective stories, edit each others writing, solve mathematics problems, correct homework, prepare for tests, investigate science questions, examine artifacts, work on a computer simulation, brainstorm an invention, create a sculpture, or arrange a new rap music tune. Working together students synthesize what they have learned, collaboratively present information, coauthor a written summary or communicate a concept through the subtlety of art.

## Benefits for Students

A major benefit of cooperative learning structures is that students — many of whom feel isolated — are provided with group support. The small group provides safe opportunities for trial and error as well as a safe environment for asking questions or expressing opinions. More students get chances to respond, raise ideas or ask questions. As each student brings unique strengths and experiences to the group and contributes to the group process, respect for individual differences is enhanced.

The group also acts as a motivator. Risk-taking becomes easier as ideas are pushed beyond what an individual would attempt or suggest. The quality and quantity of thinking also increase as more ideas are added, surpassing what the individual could do alone. Group interaction enhances idea development and students have many opportunities to be teachers as well as learners (Kraft, 1985).

Small cooperative group structures extend children's resources as they pool strategies and share information. More withdrawn students can easily become more active. And students who often have a hard time sticking to a task receive group assistance so they can learn to monitor their time better and become a productive member of the group. The unity of the group has been found to extend beyond the classroom, to the playground and social situations (Adams & Hamm, 1989).

## Teaching Advantages

Dividing the class into groups means the teacher has six or eight groups (instead of 25 to 35 individuals) to make good contact with each day. Sometimes when children are placed in pairs there are even more groups. No matter what the group size, each of the 25 to 35 individuals can act as aides in the classroom. Students monitor each other while creating a spirit of cooperation and helpfulness. Students are also better listeners within a cooperative structure. Students must agree to collectively ask for help so they ask better questions and are more eager for teacher input.

Cooperative learning helps teachers spend less time being policemen as students learn they are capable of validating their own values and ideas. Teachers are freer to move about, work with small groups and interact in a more personal manner with students. Cooperative group learning can also be arranged so there is less paperwork for the teacher. Six, eight, or even a dozen coauthored papers is less than 24 or 32. In this structure teachers have time to continue to be learners themselves, opening channels they may never have imagined.

## Organizing the Classroom

Cooperative learning will not take place with students sitting in rows facing the teacher. Desks must be pushed together in small groups or replaced with small tables to facilitate group interaction. Resource and hands-on materials must be made readily accessible. Collaboration will not occur in a classroom which requires students to raise their hands to talk or not move out of their desks. Responsible behavior needs to be developed and encouraged. This means removing authoritarian approaches to discipline and raising our expectations of students — trusting them to be responsible for their own learning and behavior.

Other changes involve the noise level in the room. Sharing and working together even in controlled environments will be louder than an environment where students work silently from textbooks. Teachers need to learn to evaluate whether noise is constructive. We need to get over the traditional factory model of schooling where communication has to be justified.

Evaluating cooperative learning necessitates a variety of procedures. Some learning outcomes will undoubtedly continue to be measured by such instruments as standardized tests, quizzes, and written exams. Cooperative learning demands more subjective measures — like work samples and student portfolios. Students and teachers need to be more involved in evaluating learning products and the learning climate.

## Structuring Cooperation Between Learners

Various heterogeneous group structures are quite different from the usual "ability grouping" that forms the traditional tracking system. In the cooperative organizational structure students are usually more able to set a personal learning agenda, distinguish hypotheses from verified information, and recognize reasoning based on misconceptions. Collaboration invites students to be active players in classroom activities. Topical projects, writing assignments or journal reaction papers are examples of activities that require group planning, negotiating and collaborative distribution of work.

One way to bring group activities to closure is by forming a panel or roundtable. As groups do try to reach consensus they can create an analysis grid whereby comparisons and contrasts can be made as well as students' speculations about outcomes. Within the tension of discussing different points of view, learning takes place.

### Aids to Collaborative Learning

*   Collaboration works best when students are given real problems to solve.

*   A collaborative environment grows slowly nurtured by teachers who consider everyone a resource.

*   Learning to think as a team that "sinks or swims" together can help many students learn more.

*   A collaborative environment works best if it allows risks and mistakes.

*   Collaborative learning allows practice in solving problems.

*   Individuals learn best when they are held individually responsible for group subtasks.

*   The less academically talented develop better learning attitudes when they work with "successful" students.

*   Roles often change; student as tutor or teacher—and teacher as learner.

## Changes in the Learning Environment

Cooperative learning takes time and work to develop. Teachers and administrators must make a conscious effort to collaboratively build educational structures that have high standards and democratically serve the diversity of students in our schools today. Researchers who are concerned with the inequality of learning possibilities fostered by traditional classroom organization suggest that we should reduce the general preoccupation with competition and ability grouping (Jussim, 1986). Cooperative learning would also appear to have a natural role to play in overcoming the suppression of human aspirations that have played such a central role in competitive tracking models.

The traditional system of school and classroom organization is no longer enough. It will take more than tinkering to get the job done. Model schools can help, but major change will require educational vision and greater societal commitments than we have seen to date. It's a question of priorities. The public tends to put its wallet where its values are. And even when values change, it takes time for victimized institutions — like schools — to catch up.

Teachers need to be actively involved in learning new strategies and goal structures. And they need support while implementing new skills. Change takes resources, time, and systematic staff development. It also takes practice for the vital energy inherent in new skills to become part of a teacher's repertoire. Inservice workshops can help provide assistance as teachers try activities and share experiences. But, in the final analysis, they need to give and receive feedback from colleagues within a supportive environment of collaboration.

Changes in the organization of learning require an environment where it is safe to make mistakes and where it is safe to learn from those mistakes. Social interaction, creativity, inventiveness, discovery and critical thinking are crucial ingredients that must be applied to the collaborative learning process. Cooperative learning, like any other proven method, is only as good as the ability of its practitioners to model the behavior. For the teacher the best way to deal with team spirit in the classroom is to join in. The question is, how long will it take for successful examples to spread?

## References

Adams, D. & Hamm, M. (1989). *Media and Literacy.* Springfield, Illinois: Charles Thomas Publisher.

Bulmahn, B. & Young, D. (1982). On the transmission of mathematics anxiety. *Arithmetic Teacher,* 30: 155-56.

Carkhuff, R. (1985). *The Art of Helping: Trainer's Guide.* Amherst, Massachusetts: Human Resource Development Press.

Carlson, H., Ellison, D., & Dietrich, J. (1988). *Servicing Low Achieving Pupils and Pupils with Learning Disabilities: A Comparison of Two Approaches.* Duluth, Minnesota:University of Minnesota, Duluth and the Duluth Public Schools. (ERIC Document Reproduction Service No. ED 283 341.)

DeVries, D. & Slavin, R. (1978). Teams-games-tournaments: Review of ten classroom experiments. *Journal of Research and Development in Education,* 12, 28-38.

Dinkmeyer, D. & McKay, G. D. (1976). *Systematic Training for Effective Parenting.* Circle Pines, Minnesota: American Guidance Service.

Eagen, G. (1986). *The Skilled Helper: A Systematic Approach to Effective Helping.* Belmont, California: Wadsworth.

Filley, A. C. (1975). *Interpersonal Conflict Resolution.* Glenview, Illinois: Scott Foresman.

Good, T. L. & Brophy, J. (1989). Teaching the lesson. In R. Slavin (Ed.) *School and Classroom Organization.* Hillsdale, NJ: Lawrence Erlbaum Assoc.

Gordon, T. (1976). *P. E. T. Parent Effectiveness Training: The Tested New Way to Raise Responsible Children.* New York: New American Library.

Gordon, T. & Burch, N. (1974). *T. E. T. Teacher Effectiveness Training.* New York: David McKay Company.

Haines, D. B. & McKeachie, W. J. (1967). Cooperation versus competitive discussion methods. *Journal of Educational Psychology,* 58, 386-90.

Hertz-Lazarowitz, R., Sharan, S. & Steinberg, R. (1980). Classroom learning styles of elementary school children. *Journal of Educational Psychology,* 72, 99-106.

Johnson, D. W. & Johnson, R. T. (1974). *Learning Together and Alone: Cooperation, Competition, and Individualization.* Englewood Cliffs, NJ: Prentice-Hall.

Johnson, D. W., Maruyama, G., Johnson, R., Nelson, D., & Skon, L. (1981). Effects of cooperative, competitive, and individualistic goal structures on achievement: A meta analysis. *Psychological Bulletin,* 89, 47-62.

Jussim, L.(1986). Self-fulfilling prophecies: A theoretical and integrative review. *Psychological Review,* 93, 429-445.

Katz, L. (1982). Professional judgment in preschool teaching. In J. Sword and A. Das (Eds.) *Proceedings of the Second Annual Conference on Early Childhood Education.* Duluth, Minnesota: Advisory Council of the Early Child Care and Development Programs of the University of Minnesota, Duluth, 21-31.

Kraft, R. G. (1985). Group inquiry turns passive students active. *College Teaching,* 33, (4): 149-54.

Levine, M. & Trachtman, R. (Eds.) (1988). *American Business and the Public School: Case Studies of Corporate Involvement in Public Education.* New York: Teachers College Press.

Madden, N. & Slavin, R. (1983). Effects of cooperative learning on the social acceptance of mainstreamed academically handicapped students. *Journal of Special Education,* 17, 171-182.

Newmann, F. M. & Thompson, J. (1987). *Effects of cooperative learning on achievement in secondary schools: A summary of research.* Madison, Wisconsin: University of Wisconsin, National Center on Effective Secondary Schools.

Rubin, K. H. & Everett, B. (1982). Social perspective-taking in young children. In S. G. Moore & C. R. Cooper (Eds.), *The Young Child: Reviews of Research,* (vol. 3). National Association for the Education of Young Children.

Sharan, S. (1980). Cooperative learning in small groups: Recent methods and effects on achievement, attitudes and ethnic relations. *Review of Educational Research,* 50, 241-271.

Sharan, S. & Shachar, H. (1988). *Language and Learning in the Cooperative Classroom.* New York: Springer-Verlag.

Slavin, R. (1983). *Cooperative Learning.* New York: Longman.

Slavin, R. (1988). Cooperative learning and student achievement. *Educational Leadership,* 54, 31-33.

Slavin, R.E. (1989). *School and Classroom Organization.* Hillsdale, NJ: Erlbaum.

Spivack, G., Platt, J. & Shure, M. (1976). *The Problem Solving Approach to Adjustment.* San Francisco: Jossey-Bass.

Stallings, J. & Stipek, D. (1986). Research on early childhood and elementary school teaching programs. In M. Wittrock (Ed.), *Handbook of Research on Teaching and Learning.* New York: Macmillan.

Stanford, B. (Ed.) (1976). *Peacemaking: A Guide to Conflict Resolution for Individuals, Groups, and Nations.* New York: Bantam.

Webb, N.M. (1982). Student interaction and learning in small groups. *Review of Educational Research,* 52, 421-445.

Ziegler, S. (1981). The effectiveness of cooperative learning teams for increasing cross-ethnic friendship. Additional evidence. *Human Organization,* 40, 264 -268.

# 2

## TELEVISION
## Interpreting Changing Media Messages

The introduction of television, like any other major medium, has resulted in a shift in the mental posture of its users. For many people the video screen has been used as a partial substitute for human relationships. It's hard to build a sense of community in the age of TV. Television can, however, cut two ways. From C-Span to cable access TV to teleconferencing, new possibilities are being developed for using video to facilitate the building of a sense of community. If viewers are taught how to become confident users, consumers, and producers in this medium, then it can serve as a connecting link between people.

Television has proven that it has the power to create certain kinds of audience consciousness and affect major world events. It has also caused major changes in social behavior, lifestyles, thinking patterns, and our interpretation of the news. TV has the unique ability to focus on broad social and political issues and bring them closer to the visceral level of personal experience. In addition, media attention has helped mobilize communities around issues.

In the last decade research on the effect of television has begun to throw some light on how new communications media affect cognitive and affective development. The perception of television reality, it seems, is a mediating factor in forming personal behavior, relationships, and social attitudes across age groups (Greenfield, 1984). Children need to learn early on, in both a theoretical and hands-on fashion, how a medium, like television, works. Learning about this area involves understanding the role that media technology plays in shaping thinking habits, social behavior, and political ideas. Whether it's in the family or in the schools, gaining some understanding of media messages requires learning in groups (Hodge & Tripp, 1986).

There is general agreement that children's reality is being shaped by electronic illusions. From toy advertisements reinforcing sexual stereotypes to Channel One's commercially sponsored news programs for high school students, television sends messages of how to look, which roles to emulate and what to think. There is even a video game revival with Atari and Nintendo putting full-sized games like "Li'l Miss Makeup" and "G.I. Joe" into pocket size units. Whatever the size of the screen, the video message remains the same — girls apply makeup, boys fight. In the language of TV, husbands "help" wives with domestic chores, suggesting that little change in sex roles has taken place on the home front. It is little wonder that researchers have found heavy TV viewers (as young as three years old) have more stereotyped views of sex roles and minorities than light viewers (Greenfield, 1984). Since changing the programming is so difficult, we had better work on changing the viewers. Television offers an ideal source for developing critical thinking and cooperative learning skills with students.

Instructional television (ITV) is now being reassessed after more than a decade in limbo. Educators are finding that simply watching ITV, or an educational film, without any pre- or post-viewing activities doesn't make much sense. The old TV style of simply covering information at length didn't really teach. With better programming and better teaching methods teachers are again looking to new instructional TV programs for connecting to learning (Baker & O'Neil, 1987). Use of short instructional videos, for example, has proven effective in motivating students and exploring relationships in cooperative groups.

Like it or not, television plays a major role in our lives and will continue to be a part of our future. Tomorrow's students will need to be able to decipher and communicate intelligently within the vast media culture that fills nearly every corner of their lives. This chapter examines television's role in learning and suggests collaborative strategies for helping students assess video messages. Both of these processes must be taught so that students can disentangle the web of images and consumer messages. The question is, how might this powerful medium be used to assist human learning, thinking, and group communication?

## Television's Role in Perceptual Learning

Psychologists have long known that learning and thinking are linked to visual representations. Television adds power to the imagery. It has been found that many children come to rely on their televised concepts, even if they run contrary to verbal explanations or personal experience (Dorr, 1986). Older children can often extract meaning from the conventions of video production —zooms, pans, tilts, fade outs and flashbacks. But distinguishing fact from fiction or extracting realistic meaning from what is viewed is more difficult. Using strategies of group problem solving with attention to critical viewing can help teach about this visual subject matter and group communication itself.

Sometimes the very texture of the programming and the subtlety of video insights can have a corrosive effect. Children often construct meaning for television content without even thinking about it. They attend to stimuli, and form meaning based on their experience. How well television content is understood varies according to similarities between viewers and content, viewers' needs and interests, and the age of the viewer. For example, toy ads that adults dismiss as simply "cute" may have more profound effects on children.

Research on TV viewing suggests that it is not vocabulary limitations alone which impede children from grasping some adult content. Younger children lack fundamental integrative capacities to "chunk" (group) certain kinds of information into meaningful groups which are obvious to older children. Piaget, a leader in developmental learning, showed how certain notions of time and space are beyond children's grasp before particular age-related developmental levels are reached. Young children who have not developed strategies for tuning out irrelevancies may be particularly vulnerable to the current tendency to mix news with entertainment ("infotainment"), tabloid TV, "short shows" and other unwanted adult content. Families are central to sorting things out.

The greater the experiential background, the better chance children have to organize content into meaningful chunks. The ability to make subtle judgments about video imagery is a developmental outcome that proceeds from stage to stage with an accumulation of viewing experience. Thus different age groups reveal varying levels of comprehension when they view TV programs. Eight-year-olds, for example, retain a relatively small proportion of central actions, events or settings of typical programs. Even when they retain explicit content younger children fail to infer interscene connections. Improvement in comprehension occurs with maturity. But substantial understanding of the medium requires training. Collaboration can add power to the process.

There is general agreement that students learn best if they take an active role in their own learning. Cooperative strategies which engage students in examining, comparing, clarifying and evaluating enhance individual experiences. Relying upon a host of cognitive inputs, individuals select and interpret the raw data of experience to produce a personal understanding of reality. It's what you think when you look at TV, not only what's in the imagery. Ultimately it is up to each person to determine what he or she pays attention to and what he or she ignores.

What's understood while viewing depends on the interplay of images and social conditions. Each person uses the available physical stimuli, human psychological apparatus and information processing schemes taught by his culture to interact with and make sense of the world. In this respect reacting to TV and its content is no different from any other experience and influences in life. Video has the same range of good and bad potentials. Music videos, for example, have been charged with everything from inciting "sexual promiscuity" to "powerful inspiration." The truth, depending on the video clip, probably lies some place in between. It is important to study these various corners of popular culture because they demonstrate a vital element of what's going on in a changing society. In this sense, television is as valid a source of information as what is learned on the street or in school. It is just as possible to internalize ideas from electronic visual imagery as it is from conversation, print, or personal experience.

Contrary to popular belief television is not automatically a passive or mindless entertainment (marketing) device. Whether it's positive or negative in its programming, television can be a stable object of thought for children on which they exercise their growing mental capacities. Recent research shows that children must do active work to watch TV, make sense of its contents and utilize its message (Anderson, Bryant,1983). Children often exhibit evaluative activities, including judging and assigning worth, assessing what is admired, and deciding what positive and negative impressions should be assigned to the content. In this sense children are active participants in determining television's meaning.

Due to an emphasis on show business values, fictional treatment and magical effects, television is likely to distort awareness of reality. Research shows heavy television viewers have a vision of the world which is more like what they watch than it is like the real world. Data reviewed from the U.S. Department of Health and Human Services also suggests that children more heavily oriented toward TV viewing are likely to be less imaginative. And children already predisposed to imaginative activities are less attracted to the TV medium.

In spite of the negatives, heavy viewing does not automatically result in stunted personal growth, poor academic achievement, or an inability to work in groups. Several Japanese studies have found that students who viewed a great deal of TV got better grades than those who didn't. Television, it seems, is too diffused and contradictory in content to push things in a particular direction on its own. As such, the medium depends on popularity and reflects its users, as much as it does the group doing the programming.

## Developing Thinking Tools
## for Assessing Television Messages

Today's television consumers need to be knowledgeable about the medium and able to effectively communicate and critically interpret its message and meaning. Collaborative learning objectives for television literacy include students being able to:

1. *Understand the grammar and syntax of television* as expressed in different program forms.

2. *Analyze the pervasive appeals of television advertising*.

3. *Compare* similar presentations or those with similar purposes *in different media*.

4.    *Identify values* in language, characterization, conflict resolution, and sound/visual images.

5.    *Identify elements in fragmented presentations* associated with the concepts of plot,story-line,theme, characterizations, motivation, program formats, and production values.

6.    Utilize strategies for the *management* of duration *of viewing* and program choices.

7.    *Describe the technical processes of television*, including those dealing with electronics and production.
(Anderson & Bryant, 1983)

## Collaborative Learning, Television and Parents

While psychologists, media specialists, educators and others examine the effect of television on youngsters, several national groups are attempting to create a more media literate society. A related concern is that adults must be familiar with media messages if they are to assist children. Otherwise TV becomes an equal opportunity oppressor.

Research shows that students' social, cultural, educational, and family context influence what messages they take from the medium, how they use television, and how "literate" they are as viewers. Parents, in collaboration with teachers and peers, can significantly affect what information children gather from television. They can also exhibit an informed response and point out misleading TV messages. The schools, family, and the media itself can help children learn how to process video information.

The viewing habits of families play a large role in determining how children approach the medium. The length of time parents spend watching television, the kinds of programs viewed, and the reactions of parents and siblings toward programming messages all have a large influence on the child. Influencing *what* children view may be done with: rules about what may or may not be watched, interactions with children during viewing, and the modeling of certain content choices.

Parents can provide a sense of connectedness by collaborating with the child as viewing selections are made. By explaining content, and discussing how the program content relates to the child's world, adults can go a long way in helping children extract meaningful connections. They should take care, however, not to build curiosity for undesirable programs ("forbidden viewing"). When this is done children will frequently react by moving *towards* the undesirable programming. Parental interest and support are key elements in assisting students as they learn to work with others to interpret how media messages are shaped by advertisers, editors, and others who own or work in the "consciousness" industry.

Whether co-viewing or not, the viewing choices of adults in a child's life (parents, teachers, etc.) set an example for children. If parents are heavy watchers of public television or news programming then children are more likely to respond favorably to this content. Influencing the settings in which children watch TV is also a factor. Turning the TV set off during meals, for example, sets a family priority. Families can also seek a more open and equal approach to choosing television shows — interacting before, during and after the program.

Parents can also organize formal or informal activities outside the house that provide alternatives to TV viewing.  And since some TV viewing will happen anyway, it is important to connect with the media literacy learning going on at school.  Helping children become more intelligent video consumers is a shared responsibility.

## The Role of the Video Screen

Television is a convenient nemesis for those inclined to worry about the decline of educational and social standards.  The video screen is often accused of robbing children of their play, shortening attention spans, and  getting in the way of clear thinking.  Critics also blame television for the decline in literacy and point to its jumble of fleeting images as responsible for problems ranging from students being in poor physical condition to the decline in higher level thinking skills.   Television is also blamed for a decline in a common core of cultural knowledge and civic skills.  There is evidence to support some of these claims.  A recent Roper poll, for example showed that only about one American in ten could name the Chief Justice  of the Supreme Court, but the majority knew the name of the judge on TV's "People Court."  Is there any hope that a virus of wisdom is breeding behind — or in front of — the visual wallpaper?  Changing the programming is most difficult, but even the most severe critics hold out the promise that the family and the school can positively alter the meanings arrived at by watching television.

Print is not the sole path to wisdom.  Television is a

potentially positive force to be reckoned with in any educational future. New areas can be opened to public view from the U.S. Senate to the democracy movement in China. It takes effort to cut through the visual clutter, but it is possible for children to become active, powerful, and intelligent decoders of television. Programs can be rich in educational meaning and civic value. And it they aren't, they can be picked apart by cooperative group analysis.

**Commercial Television and Perception**

Television, from its inception, has been a great marketing tool. The dominant visual format of commercial TV has little tolerance for intelligent argument, guesswork, questioning or explanation. The imagery merchants, it seems, often can't distinguish between what they have a right to do and *what's right to do.* On television substance and logic are often replaced by image, gesture and the values of merchandising and show business. Commercial children's programming often flounders under an excess of sheer cuteness.

Grounds for critical scrutiny can be found in the nature of the video medium itself. The way images are used often leaves little to the imagination or intellect — sometimes sound cues even tell us which emotion or mood is appropriate. In spite of its limitations, television provides access into millions of minds and has the latent ability to extend literate thought. For example, more people have seen the BBC television production of Shakespeare than have viewed five hundred years of stage plays.

Today electronically produced visual imagery is being called upon to play a more fundamental role in thinking, learning, and how we experience products of the mind. High definition TV — and its film quality pictures — is in the process of giving the imagery even greater power over the viewer's senses. Is there any credence to the canard that, even at today's level, too much viewing can unbalance young, impressionable minds?

Studies of how children retain certain kinds of material (presented by various media) show that children tend to comprehend more of what they see on television than what they read or hear on the radio (or audiotape) — and they remember it longer. Children are more attracted to action (and sound effects) than dialogue, but once that action is viewed, it tends to be remembered. When children are fed a constant diet of television programming they tend to internalize the attitudes and values and identify with the powerful characters (Anderson & Bryant 1983).

Can TV can serve as an instrument that will help implement educational visions? The power for visual learning afforded by this electronic image manipulator should not be underestimated. Whatever the programming, critics agree that television has a certain harsh power that is very compelling for large numbers of people. It's just as likely to become a source of illumination as it is to be a colossal time waster. And if too many people waste time with it, we have a strong reason for serious study.

Television may promote different mental skills than those developed by reading and writing, but these skills are not necessarily inferior. TV's wide accessibility has the potential for making learning available for groups of children who do not perform well in traditional classroom situations. Connecting TV with collaborative learning strategies provides a vehicle for reaching these students.

Rather than viewing in isolation and withdrawing into the medium, the emphasis is on sharing, discussing and evaluating.

The Public Broadcasting System has been helping by providing free programming for years. Cable TV also seems interested in helping schools. Turner Broadcasting's Cable News Network, for example, offers school districts a curriculum guide to go along with their Sunday-night "Week In Review" program. The project is produced jointly with the National School Boards Association. The Discovery Channel, the Arts & Entertainment Network, and C-Span are putting on more  commercial-free documentaries for schools. A nationally syndicated TV news service, *Children's Express,* is proof that given the right resources, children can even produce good programming. Sadly, many schools are reluctant to tap this resource. When schools ignore good instructional video the result is most severe for those who don't do well with the print medium.

### Reaching Children with Television

A two class system becomes ever likely from day to day. Unless we begin to act now, all of us are going to pay an increasingly high price. Breaking the cycle of "disadvantage" demands the use of every weapon in the educational arsenal. Helping children cooperatively develop a larger framework of connectedness and a sense of commitment to learning will enlarge their lives. But closing technological windows would  also hinder the efforts to retool American schools.

Many disadvantaged children live a dual life in the classroom and the streets. They have less experience with books and with school-like situations. In contrast their backgrounds may provide an advantage in learning from television because of greater exposure and more acceptance of the medium at home. Television's perceived relation to the "real world" makes it a useful partner in a comprehensive sustained effort to reach the millions of children and young adults who are on the brink.

There are some good educational TV programs that capitalize on the developmental realities of how children can learn and process information in groups. Studies of children's programs found that the visually dramatic techniques of television were more successful in teaching early reading skills than traditional methods (Anderson & Bryant, 1983). This research also suggests that video media is more closely matched to the mental processes of beginning readers than print. Easier may not be better, but TV holds attention longer and can act as a powerful agent of socialization.

Quality educational programming has proven that it can encourage groups of children to discover their creativity — while giving them the tools to visually restructure subject matter concepts. Thoughtful strategies for using the video medium for progress have been developed by Children's Television Workshop. Many of their programs are aimed at helping children who are experiencing difficulty in learning to read. Early programs like "Sesame Street" and "The Electric Company" improved a wide variety of beginning reading skills. Research on the subject is clear; television can teach specific reading skills if children haven't already learned the skill. The mathematics and science programs "3-2-1 Contact," "Newton's Apple" and "Square One TV" have also proven effective in reaching their target audience. "Square One," for example, not only deals with mathematics, but parodies the video medium itself.

One of the missing elements in educational broadcasting is expanded teacher, community, and youth participation in shaping richer learning possibilities. Transforming TV from a passive to an active medium is essential in tapping its full teaching potential. Learning requires active social involvement and personal mental effort. Several educational series, like "Voyage of the Mimi," fill the bill. This program gets children actively involved by sending the child's school (or parents) closely related computer programs, print materials, and even a videotape of the program if the broadcast is missed. In this mode the print, video and computer mediums stand alone, yet dovetail together to teach the same concept. This kind of innovative programming redefines the boundaries of three media by simply using technology that most schools have in place.

**Learning About the Real World**

Just as there are some exemplary TV programs for children, there is also a dark side. The average child does not spend much time watching educational programming. This is partly due to its scarcity — with some quality programs, like "The Electric Company" losing their funding. Others have been crowded out by "deregulated" commercial TV. The result is that young people are most likely to spend long hours watching lowest common denominator programs and commercials.

On Saturday mornings younger children get half hour cartoons of the likes of "Rambo," "GI Joe," "He-Man," and "Masters of the Universe," which feature animated toys. The only relief in this genre are the saccharine sentimentality of "My Little Pony" and "Pound Puppies."

Many of these programs are usually nothing more than extended commercials for the toy companies—some of whom give a share of the toy sale profits to broadcasters.

Children below the age of seven are particularly susceptible to the commercial influence of television. They are often unable to distinguish the ads from the rest of the program. This is particularly true when the whole series is based on a toy product. Children remember commercial messages. They can recite the slogans, sing the jingles, recognize the brand names and influence their parents to buy advertised products. From Cabbage Patch dolls, to breakfast cereal, to designer clothes, children have become a major market for TV advertising. Without the help and collaboration of adults and peers they become easy prey. You can get some indication of the quality of children's commercial programming by asking the following questions: *Can you tell it has a writer? Does it have a point to make? Is it fun to look at?* and *Is there something that an adult can take from it?*

TV has an extraordinary mass effect and the ability to create public opinion. As a mass medium it touches so many people that it has a tremendous potential for stimulating thinking. Like the sea, it is full of possibilities that may be hard to see, but hold out immense possibility for harvest and use. Particularly if its nuances are understood, television can go beyond stereotypes to teaching about other cultures. The U.S./U.S.S.R. audience participation "Space Bridge Program" serves as one example. Discerning TV programs can result in the questioning of predigested assumptions about what other societies should be. Doors can be opened to a world beyond the home, community, and national boundaries. The fact that television sometimes distorts that world view and "children already spend too much time watching TV" are arguments for making sure that children can think about it critically.

For the parts of the world that won't fit onto a TV screen, concrete direct experiences in the actual environment are the best teachers. There seems to be at least some truth in the notion that *we remember about 10% of what we hear, 40% of what we see, and 70% of what we hear, see, and do something with.* But sometimes the real experience isn't available... practice is needed first... or the subject is too distant in time and space.

Electronic media can help students go beyond seeing and hearing to provide opportunities for group experience. It is possible to learn about the real world from electronic imagery, computer simulation, or simply thought. What's found on the street is not necessarily the best teacher; concrete experience does not hold the only key to reality. In art and science the human construction of reality is to some degree an invention. In a theatrical play, for example, reality is frequently a clever illusion. In spite of its flaws, television can add to a child's perceptual universe.

## Developing Critical Viewing Skills
## Through Visual Literacy

Media literacy involves an understanding of all media formats — not just what we see, but what we read and hear. Visual Literacy has been defined as the ability to comprehend and create visuals in a variety of moving and non moving media in order to communicate effectively. This involves components of writing, reading, comprehension, critical evaluation, and production. There is a cumulating body of research that shows the importance of images in learning and its transfer to real world situations.

The power of visual images and the need to understand them is not new. From cave drawings to medieval cathedrals to children's book illustrations, pictures have played a major role in human communication. Illustrations, photographs, charts and graphs increase children's learning of meaningful written and verbal material. It has been found that teaching with images can help students focus on lessons, retain information, and improve psychomotor skills. The same research has also shown that children who view illustrations can recall 40% more of a story than students who just listen (Olson, 1984). It seems that illustrations and internal representation can improve retention and comprehension.

Effective use of imagery adds interest and enhances student involvement with the material they are working with. Projected images such as slides, transparencies, political cartoons in the newspaper, or illustrations in a book, can promote visual thinking and recall. Children can also comprehend more and creatively solve problems through internal imaging. This includes techniques such as "close your eyes and imagine," or a guided fantasy tour (Bagley & Hess, 1984).

The effective utilization of images can help students understand the content of classroom material and remember that information for both the short and long term. The question is, how many teachers are exposed to training that provides them with the skills needed for teaching visual literacy?

As schools become more and more distant from their students' non-school world, television has become the universal curriculum. Becoming a critical consumer of that medium requires some understanding of how that relatively new visual medium uses pictures to tell stories. Understanding television imagery means understanding the form and content of mass media messages. It implies an understanding of how to place those messages in a context and understanding how the various social, political, and industrial forces shape the message. It also relates to issues of media induced social conformity and economic alienation. Critical viewing skills go hand in hand with the ability to examine, evaluate, and interpret television messages. This skill reaches across subjects to ask questions about the visuals surrounding us today, as well as the more complicated imagery promised for tomorrow.

## Collaborative Activities for Constructive Viewing

A good organizational structure for connecting critical viewing and cooperative learning is to schedule classroom time to provide for a variety of learning modes:

* 1/5 for teacher talk and discussion
* 1/5 for students to work in pairs
* 1/5 of the class for students to work in small groups
* 1/5 of the time for whole class instruction and sharing
* 1/5 of class time for individuals to work alone

### 1. Help Students Critically View
### What They Watch

Students must be guided in decoding and looking critically at what they view. Students can identify individual elements and classify them into various categories, then relate the whole to their own experiences, drawing inferences and creating new conceptualizations from what they have learned. Working in pairs or small groups, have students examine the plot and story line of a taped segment from a favorite program. Identify the message of the program. What symbols, camera techniques, motion sequences, setting, lighting, etc. does the program use to make its message? Some time may need to be spent with the class in identifying these. What does the director do to arouse audience emotion and participation in the story? What metaphors and symbols are used?

### 2. Compare Print and Video Messages

Have students follow a current event on the evening news (taped segment on a VCR) and compare it to the same event written in a major newspaper. A question for discussion may be: How do the major newspapers influence what appears on a national network's news program? Encourage comparisons between both media. What are the strengths and weaknesses of each? What are the reasons behind the different presentations of a similar event? Having students answer these questions in small groups can help a passive medium, like television, become more experiential.

### 3.Spice Up a Presentation or Discussion with Short Video Segments

Using a VCR, make frequent use of 3 to 5 minute video segments to illustrate different points. This is often better than showing long videotapes or a film on a video cassette. For example, teachers can show a five minute segment from a video cassette movie to illustrate how one scene uses foreshadowing or music to set up the next scene. In "Ghandi," for example, danger is foreshadowed when the white minister first appears in a South African scene. In the next scene we see an encounter with white toughs.

### 4. Analyze the Daily Use of Media

After compiling a list of favorite TV programs, or music videos, assign student teams to analyze the reasons for their popularity; examine the messages these programs send to their audience. Do the same for favorite books, magazines, newspapers, films, songs, and computer programs. Look for similarities and differences between the media.

### 5. Examine Advertising Messages

Advertisements provide a wealth of examples for illustrating media messages. Move students progressively from advertisements in print to television commercials, allowing them to locate features (such as packaging, color and images) that influence consumers and often distort reality. Analyze and discuss commercials in children's TV programs: How many minutes of TV ads appear in an hour? How have toy manufacturers exploited the medium?

What is the broadcasters' role?    What should be done about it?

### 6. Act Out Your Own Ad

Creative drama, mime, and movement can stretch observation skills and ease the tensions of individuals working in unison in front of other groups.  In this activity students work together to create and act out a short one or two minute ad.  The product or topic can be chosen by the teacher or left to the students' ingenuity.  No props are necessary, little or no memorization is required, plenty of group action is involved with nobody left out.

### 7.Create a Scrapbook of Media Clippings

Have student groups construct a scrapbook of newspaper and magazine clippings on television and its associates.  Paraphrase, draw a picture, or map out a personal interpretation of the articles.  Share these with other student teams.

### 8. Create New Images from the Old

Have student groups take rather mundane photographs and multiply the image, or combine it with others, in a way that makes them  interesting. Through the act of observing and discussing in the group it is possible to build a common body of experiences, humor, feeling and originality. And through collaborative efforts students can expand on ideas and make the group process come alive.

## 9. Use Debate as a Stepping Stone for Critical Thought

Debating is a communications model that can serve as a lively facilitator for concept building. Taking a current and relevant topic, and formally debating it, can serve as an important speech/language extension. For example, the class can discuss how mass media can support political tyranny, public conformity or the technological enslavement of society. The discussion can serve as a blend of social studies, science, and humanities study. You can also build the process of writing, or video-taping from the brainstorming stage to the final production.

## 10. Evaluate Television Programs

Visual and television literacy includes the ability to evaluate the quality of a program as a basis for selective viewing. Discussing the various types of programs with children and developing criteria for evaluating them is a way to develop awareness. Here is an example of a group program evaluation:

## Television Evaluation Form

Name of Evaluators_____

Name of TV Program_____

Viewing Date_____Time_____

**Short answer**   *Add details on the back.*

1.  Where did the program take place? _____
2.  Describe the opening scene. _____
3.  How was the mood affected by the use of music, color, and space?_____
4.  How did this program use visual space?_____
5.  Briefly   describe   the   story   line   (plot).
6.  Were you able to predict the outcome? Explain.
    _____
7.  Which character in the program would you become friends with?_____Why?
8.  What would you change in the program's sequence of events? _____
9.  Was the photography effective?_____Explain.
10. Describe any close-up or zoom-in shots.  What was their message?_____
11. Was the dialogue believable? _____ Give an example._____
12. On a scale from one to ten (ten highest) how would your group rate this program? _____ Explain your rating._____
13. What did you learn from this program? _____
14. On the back of this sheet contrast (map) the differences between this and another favorite TV program.
15. Explain any similarities between this program and stories that you've read about similar events.
16. Suggest a sequel to this program.
17. Other comments about the program.

## 11. Evaluate a Newscast

Critically evaluating the quality of a news program is a way to get at important issues and learn how newscasts go about revising and editing their stories. Some questions to explore might include:

1. Are all the major news stories reported? (You may need to look at major newspapers for some of this information.)
2. Is adequate background information supplied?
3. Is the visual and spoken content presented objectively?
4. Are significant stories treated differently from those more trivial?
5. How has the news program taken on some of the entertainment values of popular sitcoms?
6. Is the information reported the same as that on other channels?
7. What happens if they do a quality program and people don't respond by watching?

## 12. Guided Imagery

The technique of guided imagery can increase listening comprehension of a video segment by getting the student involved and thinking about it before viewing. (This technique was developed for students learning a second language.) The teacher has to preview the video and lead students on a mental tour (before viewing), stopping to have students fill in the blanks. Students close their eyes while the teacher tells the story, pausing for several 30 to 60 second intervals (during the pause the student mentally makes up what is happening). Once students become adept at guided imagery, teachers can set the situation (or show the first part of the video segment) and allow students to make up the middle and end. Encourage the students to explain why they feel the story will turn out a particular way. When the predicting and discussion are finished, show the video, and see how the predictions compare to the actual story. By having the students form a mental picture, predicting the outcome, and then discussing the prediction, you are getting the students more involved in listening than by simply having them watch the video and taking notes.

### 13. Write Letters to TV Stations
(They are required to respond.) Newspapers often get opinion letters, but they are rare indeed at a television station. For each letter received a station manager figures that as many as 10,000 people may have a similar opinion. So one discriminating video consumer can speak with quite a voice while getting practice with traditional media skills (writing). Remember some decision makers at TV stations are older white males. If they have to decide between a story on golf or adolescent relationships, golf will win out every time. In all of these activities the validity of each student's point of view must be supported. This will help them, in turn, to support the legitimacy of their peer's view.

### 14. Listening in Pictures: Mapping
Before viewing, give a brief synopsis of the video segment. For an example we used the movie *Julie*

*of the Wolves,* by Jean Craighead George (French conversation). This is the story of a young Eskimo girl, Miyax (sometimes known as Julie), who runs away from a bad situation and is lost in the Arctic wilderness without food or compass. She connects with a pack of wolves and is accepted. She survives many months and in doing so learns about her own strength and becomes reacquainted with her Eskimo past. After viewing students construct a visual, or a map or outline by using questions to prompt thinking:
 -What is the probable theme of the
  story?
 -What skills would you need to survive
  in the Arctic?
 -What hazards might you face in the
  wilderness?
 -How might a person befriend a pack of
  wolves?
Summarizing:
After viewing a selected portion of the video or reading the book, several maps might be developed for various aspects of the story.

### 15.Questions for Critical Viewing
* How are images used to communicate?
* How did the creator of the visual image
  expect the viewer to actively engage
  the image?
* How does your social background affect how you
  receive (or construct) the message?
* Visuals are authored in much the way print
  communication is authored. How does the

author of the image manipulate the viewer
through such things as point of view, size,
distortion or lighting?
* What mood was created by the imagery?
* When you close your eyes and think about
the visual experience what pictures do you
see? What sounds do you hear? Does it
remind you of anything?

## Student Video Productions and Becoming Intelligent Consumers of Television

In the last few years camcorders have become a part
of everyday life in America. These small home-video
cameras can give students at many grade levels some
power over video by helping them understand the production process. As local and national networks begin to use
some brief shots of fast breaking news events some experts are calling camcorders a democratizing technology.
Giving students a prime tool of mass communication is
much like giving them a computer that can do desktop
publishing. By doing their own video productions students
can go a long way towards answering the question of how
TV programs are made. Students will discover, among
other things, that television programming is made by people working with technology. They will also find that a
video segment or program is not just a collection of elements, but a series of esthetic judgments that are made
to suggest a system of relationships between the parts.
Like a written essay, a video production tries to tell a
story in a way that captures interest.

Even younger students can use the new lightweight

VHS or 8mm camcorders. If the teacher isn't familiar with the equipment, it's helpful to assign two interested students with camcorders at home to become familiar enough with them to teach a few basic techniques to others. Students can form investigative groups and identify areas that will require special expertise. Once this is done crew assignments are chosen by pairs and decisions are made about how to combine their work into a single product.

Before anything is recorded, have the group *think*, *plan*, and *visualize* what they will shoot. Writing an outline helps students figure how long they will spend on each scene. (Winging it simply doesn't work.) Groups can put together coherent themes for scenes developed by individuals or partnerships. A good starting point is to simply ask students to write a short scene about some situation that makes them laugh, cry, or get angry. Scenes that are well thought through are much easier to film.

Next, students can figure out how to get what they have written onto a storyboard. A storyboard is a visual sketch of precisely what will take place. It might be thought of as a cartoon-like scene sequence depicting what will be shot. Students can sketch out their productions on paper and place them in a loose leaf notebook for reference. Pages can be revised and decisions made about how to move the concepts (advanced students might do a script) into video and sound. (Remember that it takes time to learn to function as a group.)

## Simple Camera Techniques

To begin with students can examine quality TV programs, films, photographs and paintings to understand how visual artists heighten the intensity of an image with light. A tour of a local museum would probably be more useful than a TV studio. Efforts must be made to help students understand some of the philosophy behind frame composition.

*Holding the camera steady* is one of the most difficult things for beginners. It is important to use a tripod, and learn how to brace the camera to get a steady shot — lean against a tree, fence, on someone's shoulder, anything to prevent the camera from jumping around.

Figuring zones of coverage and how cameras and people should move is another common difficulty for students new to video production. You usually move the video camera up or down, right or left, but not both in the same shot. It is important that students realize the camera not be moved without a reason. The video will look jerky if the camera is allowed to bounce around. Learning how to figure zones of coverage and how both cameras and people will move is also important.

Natural or artificial *lighting* can be a powerful tool for controlling  mood and understanding. As students learn how to control how light falls on a subject they shorten the distance between ideas and the video screen. Have students experiment with several light sources to see differences. It's a good idea to show several professional productions and identify lighting sources, changes, and how these techniques convey messages. The ability of light and shadow to shape objects affects the composition of the frame.

Teach students how to pan, tilt and zoom. A panoramic or *pan* shot is a horizontal move of the camera. A tilt shot goes up or down. Students can practice tilting up, pausing, changing camera angle, and tilting down. To *zoom* start with a long shot (to establish where the action is taking place) and then zoom in. Beginning students may have a tendency to do too many zooms without good reason. More advanced students can try to cover the zoom with movement of the subject or the camera.

There are other production techniques which students need to develop an awareness of and spend time experimenting with. Some of these include learning how to:

1. *stop and start action*
2. *bridge sharp changes between scenes*
3. *allow visual action to carry the scene*
4. *use sound as a motivator*
5. *pace the production* (On a video tape information can usually get through to people at a faster pace than we think.)

Conceptually students can be encouraged to:

1. *treat one concept at a time*
2. *introduce their topic immediately*
3. *break subjects into clearly defined sections*
4. *plan how to involve the viewer*

Assign each student a specific responsibility as part of the crew, hold them responsible for their area, and make sure they get full credit (on the video) for what they do. With all of these techniques it is important that the camera isn't moved without a reason. Remember the very amateurishness of student productions can be refreshing. Enthusiasm and heart can communicate to people. With just a few of the basics, students' experimentation and common sense will take them further than some mechanical processes.

Children seem more comfortable than adults in adopting new uses of video. As television production and editing technology evolves we will have cheaper and easier to use equipment. This will give students additional freedom and opportunity to create special effects and aesthetically pleasing visuals. Learning the conventions of electronic imagery can also help students look for creative meaning while becoming more intelligent video consumers.

Using music video, for example, can help students work together to collectively accept, reject, and critically sort out how television offers students a place to stand in relation to other individuals or groups. Other short video segments can be used to teach specific production skills such as editing, story-lines, computer graphics, lighting, visual imagery, symbolism, camera angles and photographic styles. Intensive scrutinizing of carefully chosen video samples — ads, or whatever — can also help students identify the function of sound in other video productions.

Whatever the topic, when the final production is put together the group compares the beginning with the ending. How does the ending bring closure on the narrative, unity of plot, and specific devices of motivation? When two shots are joined the group discusses whether the shots are graphically continuous and what rhythmic relations have been created.

## Ideas for Student Video Production

### 1. Create Original Music Videos
Have students create their own music videos based on a favorite song.

## 2. Design a Poetry Video
Assign students to write, record and shoot a poetry video based on their own original writing.

## 3. View and Produce Scenes from Different Perspectives
To understand how music adds texture to a film or video story, view a scene — like the airplane segment from *Out of Africa* — with the sound off. Then view it a second time with the sound on. Using camcorders, encourage students to use closeup shots and panning, tilting and zooming techniques. Then have them add music to the track.

## 4. Create a Short Video Segment
Have students design a video segment from a movie video. Students build their own story or TV ad from selected video segments and add their own soundtrack taking selected parts from the dialogue.

## 5. Jigsaw Editing
Give students 10 or 12 short segments of video and have them arrange each clip under the following headings: Setting: Characters: Motivation: Time: Plot: Cause & Effect: Based on their classifications, have them design a coherent film.

## 6. Practice Video Techniques
Create a TV advertisement using video techniques such as flashbacks, cuts, and dissolves. Have students demonstrate how these techniques convey messages to consumers.

### 7. Photography Guessing Game

Encourage students to take part in the adventure of acquiring and viewing just about anything in the environment. Start by encouraging students to view objects from a different perspective. Zoom in on an object, hold, tape, and have students guess what it is from the close-up. Then have students shoot their own close-ups for discussion.

### 8. Shooting a Single Scene

Using a single scene, see how many different ways you can view that scene. Discuss the effects of camera angle, panning, and zooming techniques.

### 9. Using a Video Camera for Storytelling

After critically viewing popular programming, such as music videos, students can construct their own set of electronic images to go with the music. Indeed, the very act of using a video camera for storytelling can become a personal tool, seeing through the electronic void—helping to open doors to visual and technological literacy.

### 10. Video Time Line

Videotape a short but telling scene from a common theme in the life of the group. Have the students imagine where their life fits on the continuum. Describe visually the major elements of the past and what will happen in the future. Use a computer graphics program to print out a long time line.

### 11. Two Minute "Bites"
Have students work together as a crew with one responsible for sound, one for lighting, one for camera work and one for direction. Tape a community event. Boil it down to a two minute segment. (Discuss what similar evening news boil-down techniques do to a story.)

### 12. Disseminating Your Production
If several student groups are doing a similar short project, hook up two VCRs and record one tape with all the material on it. Take that tape to the cable company and have them show it on the public access channel. (All cable companies are required to provide free public access — and most of them are more than willing to play a VHS video cassette.) As with writing in the language arts, it is important that students share their work with a real audience — sometimes it's the class and other times it's the whole community.

### 13. Helpful Resources
There are some simple computer programs, for grades six and up, that can easily add captions, credits and animated sequences to any video production. Using an Apple II series computer students can add information screens directly to the videotape (VCR Companion, Broderbund,17 Paul Drive, San Rafael, CA, $60). An advanced "Desk Top Video" project is being piloted in twenty schools chosen by the National School Boards Associations' *Institute for the Transfer of Technology to Education.* Using Commodore hardware (Amiga

2000) this computer/video project ranges from video yearbooks to student-produced news reports shown on local cable access channels.

The practical video production suggestions in this chapter are designed for different skill and experience levels (excluding broadcasting professionals). Whether it's elementary school children with camcorders, or crews of older students with Super-VHS or Hi8 video cameras, cooperative groups aren't just conveniences. They are absolutely necessary for video production. The whole crew concept is built around collaboration and individual accountability.

In the process of shaping and "writing" with camcorders students gain some feeling of control over our dominant communications medium. In addition student television productions form a natural work-group base for learning about cooperative skills. Such group investigations have been shown to have a positive influence on motivation, social relations in class and academic achievement (Sharan, 1984).

## Converging Media Technology

Many educational TV programs are now more visually striking than in years past. New television technology allows cameras to view things previously seen only with devices like electron microscopes, or radio telescopes. Adding computer memory to the video screen can push beyond "real" images to a computer graphics simulation. The digitization of one picture allows the computer to zoom in or provide three dimensional imagery of the elements from any angle. Computer graphics can take over from there. Students can "see" what it's like to be in the middle of an atom or looking at the galaxy—where no camera has gone before (or science for that matter). The supremacy of physical proximity is no longer quite as omnipotent.

Whether it's computer generated or imagery produced with a video camera, youngsters can get as close to understanding with electronic devices as they can in books or through discussion. This is especially true if electronic imagery can be coupled with concrete activities. Actual chemical experiments can be viewed at the micro level with new video cameras, graphically simulated by computer, and done by students with real chemicals.

We are getting to the point where image and reality can amplify each other. A characteristic of any effective media is its ability to change how we use our senses to process thought and perceive reality. Like traditional reading and writing, it is not a simple matter of decoding symbols, but the construction of meaning. The video image is more vivid than print — and it certainly speaks well to a new generation. In fact, the ease with which the electronic image involves all of our senses is unparalleled in the history of communications.

The video display terminal has many ways of helping us get closer to hidden realities. As computers give us interactive control over video images distinctions between television, computing, speech, images, writing and reading are becoming less severe. Various technological hybrids are creating new media realities that integrate the unique characteristics of each medium.

It is important to discuss the social, moral and political significance of technology itself. Technology isn't neutral. Our experience with video or computers amplifies a particular set of cultural assumptions that form the language of our thinking. As we search for what we can do with machines it is important to help students understand that any technology they use reinforces certain aspects of culture. Any search for meaning must incorporate traditional communication skills with electronic imagery. Both can serve as collaborators. Linking new literacies to concrete curriculum-wide improvements can even enhance older literacy traditions.

Using electronic windows (even if they are made of refracted glass) can allow students access to images on their own terms. The power to recreate reality — through any medium — is built on all sources of mental development. Making the best use of media is a constant juggling act that requires a respect for the inherent values of all modes of communication. There is little question that intelligently opening up of broader literary vistas necessitates an ecological balance between modes of communication. They each carry meaning to the alerted eye.

If educators refuse to deal with a major piece of today's communications puzzle then their professional future will be shaped by a vision they do not share. Teachers, curriculum specialists, parents, media technicians, scientists and humanists all share a common cause: exploring pedagogical possibilities and rejecting any model that cheapens thought or human dignity. Like Emerson's dictum on the one true use of books *"they are for nothing but to inspire."*

## References

Adams, D. & Hamm, M.(1987). *Electronic Learning: Issues and Teaching Ideas for Educational Computing, Television, and Visual Literacy.* Springfield, IL: Thomas.

Anderson, D. & Bryant, J. (1983). *Watching TV: Understanding TV Research on Children's Comprehension.* New York: Academic Press.

Bagley, M. & Hess, K. (1984). *Imagery in the Classroom.* Monroe, NY: Trillium Press, Inc.

Baker, E. L. & O'Neil, H. F. (1987). Assessing instructional outcomes. In R. M. Gagne (Ed.) *Instructional Technology: Foundations.* Hillsdale, NJ: Erlbaum

Bronowski, J. (1978).*The Origins of Knowledge and Information.* New Haven: Yale University Press.

Bry, A. (1978). *Visualization: Directing the Movies of Your Mind.* New York: Barnes & Noble Books.

Bullough, R. V.(1987). *Multi-Image Media.* Englewood Cliffs: Educational Technology Publications.

Campbell, J. (1982). *Grammatical Man: Information, Entropy, Language and Life.* New York: Simon & Schuster.

Carlisle, R.(1987). *Video at Work in American Schools.* Bloomington, IN: AIT, Agency for Instructional Technology.

Doerken, M.(1983). *Classroom Combat: Teaching and Television*. Englewood Cliffs, NJ:  Educational Technology Publications.

Dorr, A.(1986). *Television and Children*. London: Sage Publications.

Fleming, M. & Hutton, D. (Ed.) (1983). *Mental Imagery and Learning*. Englewood Cliffs, NJ : Educational Technology Publications.

Frye, N. (1988). *On Education*. Ann Arbor: University of Michigan Press.

Gibson, J. (1979). *The Ecological Approach to Visual Perception*.  Boston: Houghton Mifflin.

Greenfield, P. (1984). *Mind and Media*. Cambridge: Harvard University Press.

Hodge, B. & Tripp, D. (1986). *Children and Television*. Stanford, CA: Stanford University Press.

Mathis, G. (1986). *How to Produce Your Own Videoconference*. White Plains, NY: Knowledge Industry Publications.

Olson, D. R.(1984). *Media and Symbols: The Forms of Expression, Communication, and Education*. Chicago: The University of Chicago Press.

Reiser, R. & Gagne, R. (1983). *Selecting Media for Instruction*. Englewood Cliffs, NJ: Educational Technology Publications.

The Report of the National Task Force on Educational Technology. (1984). *Using Technology to Change the Direction of American Education*. U.S. Government Printing Office.

Sharan, S. (1984). *Cooperative Learning in the Classroom: Research in Desegregated Schools*. Hillsdale, NJ: Erlbaum.

Salomon, G. (1981). *Interaction of Media, Cognition and Learning*. San Francisco: Jossey-Bass Publishers.

Slater, R. (1988). *This Is CBS: A Chronicle of 60 Years*. Englewood Cliffs, NJ: Prentice-Hall.

Verna, T. (1987). *Live TV*. Stoneham, MA: Focal Press.

# 3

## COMPUTERS AS COOPERATIVE TOOLS

In the eighties we witnessed the beginning of widespread computer use in the schools. Two early goals were the study of computing itself (programming, computer literacy, etc.) and the integration of the technology into educational practice. As computer literacy and programming diminished in importance, computer applications and courseware became more important than ever. Increasingly, rich software and more advanced hardware are reaching a stage where they can transform student ability, power, and achievement.

In the early days, computers were often harnessed to repeat the educational mistakes of the past: electronic workbooks and drill, drill, drill. Some critics felt that computers would help schools become impersonal warehouses of rote learning. With each child hard at work in an isolated cubicle some programs reinforced poor pedagogy in yet another idiom. The attitudes of the teaching community changed during the 80s as the general level of computer familiarity become more pervasive. By the end of the decade software and courseware were in place that made use of the unique characteristics of computers; simulation, modeling, desktop publishing, data bases, and so on. The risks paid off.

The indications are that the 1990s will witness new relationships between technological tools, learners, teachers, the curriculum, and classroom organization. A recent study funded by the Carnegie Corporation suggested that children need to collaborate with each other and that individual learners had to have a close learning relationship with at least one teacher. In the same vein, teachers needed mentors and colleagues that can be depended on. When it comes to educational computing, teachers of different grade levels and subjects have a great deal to teach each other about how computers can be used effectively. In collaboration with each other, teachers can be armed with the right computer assisted tools of the trade — emphasizing thinking, writing, and doing.

Surveys of teachers indicate that they view computers as a potential ally in the teaching-learning process. Yet many still report reluctance in using them. There were a number of problems mentioned. The most frequent was lack of time to learn about the equipment (hardware) and programs (software). Teachers say that they just haven't gotten the training needed to integrate the technology into their classroom routine. Another problem is their computers are often kept in labs where teachers have little access. Teachers also mention a shortage of quality software resources; this even makes curriculum integration difficult for those that are familiar with educational computing (U.S. Congress Office of Technology Assessment, 1988).

By 1984, about 350,000 computers were in schools across the United States. Today, that number has risen to nearly 3,000,000 and we are still wrestling with how they can best aid teaching. The majority of elementary schools have five or more computers, and half of the secondary schools have fifteen or more. Apple continues to lead the field, winning the K-12 market with ease. Tandy and IBM, with their MS-DOS machines, have carved out market niches, like business education and integrated learning systems. IBM may edge in a little more. But projections suggest that market share will remain about the same as school related hardware and software double in quantity by 1993.

America is changing. Schools must not only reflect that change but lead us into the 21st century. Teacher training is the key to having the schools use computers successfully. Teachers must learn to integrate technological applications into the curriculum in a manner that makes learning more interactive. Computers were a hot topic in the 80s but it will be the mid-90s before the schools can be brought up to speed.

Teachers need help from the academic research community in deciding how computers can best be used. Opportunities for a deeper understanding must not be missed. Some basic questions must be answered before teachers can decide on the most effective emphasis. For example: should computers be used to enrich existing instruction or to gain access to new audiences through a different delivery system? Whatever the answers, teachers are adopting a less resistant approach to technology and  students are increasingly learning via VCR tapes, computers, and interactive videodiscs.

## Computers in the Classroom

By the mid-80s we started to see educational software which used the unique characteristics of the computer medium to enhance the learning environments. Language arts and English teachers began to realize that spelling and style checkers give students new tools for interacting with their writing. In the natural and social sciences, simulations have provided students with safe nuclear experiments and surrogate experiences from history. Information can be embedded in visual narratives to create context that gives meaning to dry facts. Applications in biology, chemistry, engineering, ergonomics, physics, psychology and physiology allow teachers to create simulations which conform to the normal laws of the universe.

Research shows that students benefit when they are given control over system parameters so they can explore their effects. For example, the computer can let pairs of students discuss and visually compare (in real time) how high a dropped ball would bounce on Neptune or Mars. In a similar cooperative vein students can explore an art museum — calling up text to explain the conditions under which the artist created the painting that they are viewing.

Computers have been found to increase socialization among students. The curriculum materials that are most effective and most popular are those that provide for social interaction. Student can collaborate by working in pairs on even the more traditional program. And capitalizing on computer-controlled interactive activities can reach small groups of children through many senses.

## The Teacher's Role

There were only 30,000 microcomputers in the schools in 1980. The "computer revolution" didn't work out quite as dramatically as many predicted in the early

1980s. In spite of the problems, anyone who has used computers in the classroom will tell you that they are not just another fad, they are here to stay.

The successful use of computers means involving students and educators in the learning process in new ways. As with any medium, the vitality of computer use depends on talented teachers. Professional knowledge about children, learning, curricula and classroom organization goes hand-in-hand with the competencies needed to apply courseware sensibly. Helped along with informed adult energy, computers can do more than facilitate the exchange of ideas and improve writing skills. They can help sharpen a student's power to think critically and develop independent judgments.

Even the most successful use of computers in the classroom will not solve our serious social and educational problems. But failing to use the medium will leave the schools less able to cope with these difficulties. Becoming competent and confident users of this technology is important if the schools are to meet the demands of a changing society. It is equally important to understand the social, economic, political and educational contexts of the technology that shapes our lives. As these "smart machines" enter into grand alliances with other technology, they will become  common adjuncts to the human teacher and peer group. Future computers and their technological associates will alter the learning environment to the point where old methods of classroom organization will disappear.

In the world outside of school, computers are seen as real tools for real people. A similar view would be appropriate for schools. Teachers may have to make some changes in how they teach, but computers can never serve as electronic teacher replacements. There is no substitute for educational leaders who exhibit an informed exuberance.

Computers are not teaching machines to dispense isolated learning, but instruments to meet integrated curricular goals. Computer programs can facilitate thought while serving as a unique and useful supplement to traditional media. There is general agreement — in practice and in the literature — that working on computers in cooperative pairs is usually better for beginners than working alone (Costanzo, 1989). Sharing with peers, in a supportive small group, is just as important in learning with computers as it is with any other medium.

Computers are only a part of a much broader technological revolution. In the early days instructional television programs and computer software were passive. This is changing. Just as newsprogramming and videodiscs have enlivened video, the best new computer programs make computing interactive. Peer sharing and coaching can add more active elements to a computer program that is not all that engaging. In opening up avenues of communication educators must decide which technology is best for which students and which set of objectives fit the technology. By the time students get to high school they should be able to develop genuine group goals and use computers to access information, process words, create images and solve problems.

**Computer Using Educators Should Be Able to:**

1.   Generally understand the social and economic impact of computers.

2.  Knowledgeably discuss how computers work and how they are used outside of school.

3.  Evaluate and use software in different educational settings.

4.  Identify sources for computer education materials in relevant subject  areas.

5.  Relate learning theory and principles of child development to the creation of a computer learning environment.

6.  Discuss major issues in computer education.

7.  Apply their knowledge of curriculum development to develop supplemental materials for use with computer software.

8.  Operate and use at least one brand of microcomputer.

9.  Describe the purposes and major features of applications software — using word processing, problem solving and simulation programs.

10. Interpret the research findings, theory and literature in the field.

11. Plan, implement, and evaluate computer related activities.

The current climate of educational reform has created an opportunity for teachers to become leaders of the effort to create schools that are better places to teach and learn in a spirit of cooperation. As they are called upon to become more sophisticated managers of students' learning, teachers increasingly use computers to help students think through their decisions, allowing them to see the potential consequences of different actions.

Using computers, like using any other media, should be directed at achieving some instructional purpose. This goes beyond having a few computer programs in a learning center at the back of the room where a student goes when everything else is done. Computers can be used to teach traditional content and open doors to knowledge in ways that other media can't.

Competency needs vary according to the discipline being taught, the curriculum, and the grade level. Most teachers would not think of assigning a chapter from the history or science book without some kind of lead in and some follow up activity. The same thing is true for learning on computers. Students should not be left to fend for themselves when the computer enters the process. Like any good learning material, computer software needs to be enhanced and extended by an enthusiastic instructor.

## Selecting and Evaluating Software

No media, person, idea, book, musical composition or work of art should be kept beyond the reach of rational criticism. Some guidelines for critiquing software might include a checklist such as this:

## SOFTWARE CHECKLIST

1. What skill is the program trying to teach? And is this a skill that fits into my curricular objectives?

2. Does the computer courseware create high levels of engagement for students?

3. What examples does the program use to teach these skills?

4. What kinds of teaching techniques are used?

5. What prerequisite skills do students need to use this piece of software?

6. Where does this piece of software fit into the learning sequence for this topic?

7. What directions need to be given to students before using the software?

8. What activities would serve as a follow up to this software program?

9. How will students' performance be evaluated?

10. What other materials would enhance the skills developed by this program?
    No matter how careful the selection process the most important question is: *Do you like it?*

### Student Software Critiques

Students can also evaluate computer software by sifting through some of the software evaluations in magazines.  They can even send for a few samples or check a program out of the curriculum library.  Children and young adults can learn a great deal by doing their computer program reviews along book report lines.  One of the first tenets of book review criticism is to critique what is taken for granted.  Another is that a critic must have at least a little affection for the media being critiqued.

Assuming they know the basics of how to turn the computer on and load a program, students can quickly check to see if the flow of a program makes sense.  If they have time, they can help each other try out the software as they think a successful or unsuccessful student might.  What happens when mistakes are made?  Is it more fun to fail than to succeed?

There are time consuming evaluation issues surrounding the multitude of software programs to be dealt with.  Simulation, Logo microworlds, word processing, interactive literature, spreadsheets, database managers, expert (AI) systems or getting the computer in contact with the outside world (telecommunications) through a modem/software combination all increase the potential for influencing impressionable minds.  That is too large a universe for the teacher to figure out alone.  Other teachers who use computers are an excellent source of help with what works in the classroom.  Students can also take some of the responsibility.  This task is more reasonable and the analysis process itself is an excellent learning vehicle.

The most interesting way to approach the software evaluation process is  similar to a book, movie or television program review. Like book or film critics, similar points tend to run through different small group evaluations — even though the process is very subjective. It's important to consider whether or not a particular piece of software is motivating and easy to integrate into their instructional program. But the bottom line is: *Do the students like it?* Without question, teachers and students are the ones who experience the consequences of making good or bad choices in software selection. And they are the ones who most quickly learn the consequences of poor choices.

## Criteria for Software Evaluation

The same criteria that are applied to other instructional materials can be applied to evaluating educational computing courseware. The following list is an example:

1. Does the software meet the age and attention span demands of your students?

2. Does the program hold the student's interest?

3. Does the program develop, supplement or enhance curricular skills?

4. Does the program require adult supervision or instruction?

5. Children need to actively control what the program does. To what extent does the program allow this?

6. Can the courseware be modified to meet individual

learning needs?

7. Can it be adjusted to the learning styles of the user?

8. Does the program have animated graphics which enliven the lesson?

9. Does it meet instructional objectives and is it educationally sound?

10. Does the program involve higher level thinking and problem solving?

### Activity for Evaluating Software
### Student Evaluation Form

Name of student evaluators _____
Name of software program_____
Publisher_____Subject_____
1. How long did the program take?_____minutes
2. Did you need to ask for help when using this program?
3. What skills do you think this program tried to teach?__
_____
*Please circle the word that best answers the question.*
4. Was the program fun to use?   yes      no      somewhat
5. Were the directions clear?      yes    no      somewhat
6. Was the program easy to use?  yes    no      somewhat
7. Were the graphics good?  yes    no      somewhat
8. Did the program get you involved?  yes    no  somewhat
9. Were you able to make choices in the program?
10. What mistakes did you make?_____

11. What happed when you made a mistake? _____
12. What was the most interesting part of the program?
13. What did you like least? _____
14. What's a good tip to give a friend who's getting started
    with this program? _____

*Extended activities:*
   * Make up a quiz about the program and give the
     questions to other students in the class who have
     used the program.
   * Create your own soundtrack for part of the program.
   * Make up a student guide for the program. Use your
     own directions and illustrations.
   * Interview other students who have used the program
     and write down their responses.
   * Write a review of the program for a magazine.

## Cooperative Activities for Enhancing Computer Assisted Learning

### 1. Integration with Other Materials
After having students use a program like *Oregon
Trail* (MECC), assign students to read the his-
toric book by the same title. Encourage comparisons between the events in both sets of materials. Have students use the simulation program
again and offer insights into the hardships they
encounter based on their reading. If you have the
documentation (instructions) that goes along
with the program, then you have another whole
set of activities.

## 2. Use One Piece of Software as a Follow-up to Another

There are many programs which supplement, enhance or augment others. Select those you feel lend themselves to sequential or integrated learning lessons. For example, after students have written a story using a word processing program like *Bank Street Writer*, have them use a painting program or Koala pad to illustrate their writing.

## 3. Drill and Practice Software Tournament

This activity is designed to be used with drill and practice software which reinforces concepts taught, but not mastered by students. (Practice on multiplication facts, spelling words, etc., falls into this category.) If students are unfamiliar with the software program, demonstrate the program they will be using. Allow time to answer questions, provide practice demonstrations, etc. Once students are familiar with the program:

1. Divide the class into learning teams to practice desired concepts. Structure the teams so that students of varying ability levels are on all teams. Instruct students to practice with their team using the drill and practice software program. Allow time for each team to polish their skills, and master the concepts.

2. When students feel their teams are ready, split up the teams into two to three person tournament tables composed of members of different teams. It's a good idea to select tournament

teams whose members are of similar ability levels (for example, students who have performed well on this skill would be grouped together on one tournament table, and students who were having more difficulty would be grouped together on another).

3. Using the same piece of software, team representatives try to win points for their team. Each student from a tournament table might play 3 or 4 rounds of a drill and practice activity and keep a record of right and wrong answers for each member of the tournament table.

4. After the tournament, the people at each table with the highest scores (greatest number of correct answers) receive 6 points to take back to their team. Those with the second highest scores receive 4 points, those with the least highest number receive 2 points. Winning teams are determined by total team scores.

### 4. Robot Treasure Hunt
This activity is designed to help students build a conceptual understanding of programming. Divide students into groups of two or three. Their assignment is to hide a treasure of their choice, then develop step by step directions (a program) of how to get to the hidden treasure. When the student teams have finished writing their treasure programs, have them exchange programs with another team. They then become the "robots" and follow the program directions to

the hidden treasure. Have students make a written note of "bugs" in the program as they attempt
to find the treasure.    Programs and treasures
are returned to the original team along with suggestions for "debugging."

## Collaborative Writing with Computers

The increased popularity of collaborative writing in
high school and college composition courses is similar to
the way writing is done in the workplace (Anderson,
1985). Writing teachers try to prepare students for writing on-the-job by creating assignments which most
closely simulate the kinds of writing they will be expected to perform in their professions.

Writing in collaborative groups has other justifica-
tions as well.   Through such groups, or literacy circles,
students learn strategies for negotiation and conflict
resolution.   The isolation of the individual writer is re-
lieved by working with a writing group which shares a
common task. Motivation is easier to sustain when sudent
writers feel responsible not only to a teacher but to each
other.  Most important, collaborative writing groups offer
students a real audience — which is built in to every step
of the writing process (Bruffee, 1983).  Students give and
receive immediate feedback with each other, and as the
group becomes more familiar with each member's
strengths and idiosyncrasies, a method for effective collaboration can evolve.

### A Practical Classroom Example
Over the last few years major changes have been

made in writing courses, gearing them more towards preparing students for the workplace, further academic work, and life-long learning. The example here is from Greta Gaard's Macintosh lab connected via Appleshare to a computer network (Gaard, 1989). This Appleshare network allows collaborative writing groups to communicate without the imposition of scheduling restraints: for example, one member of a collaborative writing group can create a document in the morning of one day, store that document in the conferencing file on the Appleshare network, and her group members can access a copy of her document whenever their schedules permit. The collaborative writing courseware program includes tutorials for writing proposals, memos, short reports, instructions, and long reports.

In this pilot program students use the MacWrite and MicrosoftWord programs. They also made use of the MacDraw, MacPaint, and CricketGraph programs. At the outset of the collaborative writing task, classes were given a list of possible strategies for collaboration (Ede & Lunsford, 1986). The team strategy was the most popular among groups with two or four members, while groups with three members chose a variety of configurations that somehow emphasized the particular strengths or leadership of one member.

## Sample Strategies That Work
*Team emphasis*
    A. Team plans and outlines. Each member drafts a
       part. Team compiles parts and revises the whole.
    B. Team plans and outlines. One member writes
       entire draft. Team revises.
    C. Team plans and writes draft. Half of the team

revise the draft without consulting the other team members.

*One member emphasis*
D. One member plans and writes draft. Team revises.
E. One member plans and writes draft. This draft is submitted to other members who revise the draft without consulting the writer of the first draft.

*Assignment emphasis*
F. One member assigns writing tasks. Each member carries out individual tasks. One member compiles the parts and revises the whole.
G. One member dictates. Another person transcribes and revises.

An individual writer's satisfaction with the collaborative writing task was found influenced by seven factors:

| | |
|---|---|
| *Control* | —the degree of control the writer has over the text |
| *Credit* | —the way credit is given |
| *Response* | —the ability to respond to others who may modify the text |
| *Procedure* | —an agreed-upon procedure for solving disputes among coauthors |
| *Flexibility* | —the amount of flexibility tolerated in using preestablished formats |
| *Constraints* | —the number and kind of constraints (deadlines,length and style requirements) imposed on the writers |
| *Status* | —the status of the project within the organization |

In this computer-collaboration project the reports of conflict decreased as time went on. In the final collaboration report, most writers were pleased with the outcome of their work. Comments from the group of four are representative of many other groups:

> In the beginning of this assignment, we did not work together particularly well as a group, primarily because none of us was willing to give in to another's suggestions. By the time the project was near completion, we were much more open to each other's ideas, comments and suggestions. Despite certain conflicts, we seemed to pull through the ordeal with a good paper and a sense of what it takes to collaborate on a report with everyone's reputation at stake (i.e., grades).

> During the last four days, we became an effective and efficient team.

> ...we worked well together when the 'heat was turned on'.

Over and over, groups reported being pleasantly surprised at the diversity and complementarity of skills among the group members:

> The group really evolved as a team. Our members' respective skills complemented each other and each person fulfilled a necessary function for the group.

> Working as a group was great for combining the various skills each of us possessed, and finding the connections we had to get the job done faster and easier than it would have been if we would have done it alone.

> The talents each of us utilized in this paper were different, and I think this enhanced the final product.

> I think collaborative writing can work very well, if group members work well together as ours did.

Certainly, difference could have been viewed as a drawback, but from the start difference was stressed as an asset and students were encouraged to talk about each writer's idiosyncrasies so that these could be utilized in their collaborative strategy. Apparently, the tactic succeeded; several groups said they would work together again.

Student writers will tend to view their group activity as more important if it is given adequate time in class (Allen, *et al.*, 1988). Though many elementary schools are working towards preparing students for computer use, at this stage many high school and college teachers are still introducing first-time users to computers. By providing instructional and peer support for students learning to use computers, writing programs perform a valuable function in preparing students for the writing and group work skills so necessary on the job.

## Collaboration Choices

Pairs of students tended to choose a team approach, while groups of three tended to choose some form of a one-member emphasis. Once the strengths, weaknesses, and idiosyncrasies of the group members were revealed, groups who chose to adjust their collaboration strategies were more likely to accomplish set tasks, and to be more satisfied with their group process as well as with their writing products. Members of the group which did not adjust to its own strengths and idiosyncrasies found themselves learning more about interpersonal dynamics than about writing, clearly because that topic continued to dominate their group meetings.

## Conflict

Most conflict episodes occurred in the planning stages of the project, a time when the most important decisions were made together by people who were, for the most part, unfamiliar with each other's work habits. As students became acquainted, the number of conflict episodes dropped. Instead of producing a period of high conflict, the final week of the project created an atmosphere of pressure which encouraged group members to unite behind a common goal.

## Satisfaction

Individual writers' satisfaction with their group product was intricately related to their group's flexibility in terms of their chosen collaborative strategy. For example, as it always happens, some students had to fall behind in their group responsibilities for personal reasons, and found their groups willing to readjust task allocations so that the work would still be fairly divided at the outcome. Those students were very vocal about their satisfaction with their groups. Moreover, students began to complement other group members on their willingness to work.

### Decisions for Future Teaching

Although all teachers using the Macintosh lab distributed step-by-step instructions for using the computers and the Appleshare network, students continued to report computer-related problems, whether in the software use itself, or in accessing the network, or a particularly violent computer infection. Knowing a little bit about computers beforehand was a definite plus. While not every beginner experienced problems, learning computers and collaborative writing simultaneously was too difficult for some students. And finally to the question "do collaborative writing groups really work?" Yes, but *only as well as the people in them* (Gaard, 1989).

## Creativity and Skill Training

Basic skills, the creative process, and computing need each other. Spontaneity and the creative imagination are elements of achievement that are central to the development of human thinking and freedom. There is no creative thinking or freedom in a solitary vacuum. A person with a creative style of thinking needs to be stimulated by others. Creative abilities, like connecting disparate concepts or giving novel ideas a chance, require a mix of traits and abilities. And, when teaching thinking is the question, it is always time to begin. Computer-based learning technologies can embody powerful ideas which can be shared across subject areas. Language makes us human and literacy makes us civilized, but it's technology that makes us powerful.

## The Interaction Between Creative Thinking and Basic Skills

The intellectual tools developed in one area can foster originality in another. Skills can combine with creative factors to generate learning across a wide range of subjects. Skill without imagination is stifled, while imagination without skill aborts the image. Although basic and imaginative skills may seem antithetical, one without the other is limiting. In reading, you need a few basic subskills to get started — but without the higher level context of good literature and imaginative thinking it leads nowhere. The reverse situation is equally dismal—a great imagination can destroy its potential without at least some skills being in place.

No matter how creative a concept, there is an implicit connection to subskills. For either basic skills or creativity to be developed requires that each area support the other. It is fine to challenge the framework of narrowness often associated with basic skills, for without connections to higher levels of thinking they lead nowhere. The two areas have a curiously symbiotic relationship. A major difficulty which most teachers encounter is getting students to depart from the skills framework in a disciplined and informed fashion. Computer-based technology can be an informed associate in this process.

Creativity is more than originality. There is a strong connection between creativity (including originality and novelty) and basic academic skills. The notion of having to choose between the two is one of the worst mistakes we could make, for the two feed on each other. From middle school on, students are often tracked. The youngsters at the top get an emphasis on creativity. For those on the bottom, the emphasis is on basic skills and discipline. Cooperative learning allows the two groups to be mixed. This way students on the bottom are not cheated out of a good education.

There is little question that educational computing has a role to play in helping students develop an unconditional positive regard for one another. Computing would seem to be a natural for bridging the gap between the old view of "the basics," imaginative thinking skills, and breaking through the artificial limits of school imposed isolation.

## The Computer as an Expressive Medium and Skill Builder

Computers are not good or bad, they are powerful. Like words, paint, or clay the computer can also be used as an expressive medium. Skills and imagination belong together. In mathematics, for example, the act of creating requires a prerequisite skill base of mathematical structure and pattern. Poetry also relies on the writer's mastery of language, form and meter. The computer is a medium of human expression which can be used as an extension of these skills and creativity. Imagination and the basics, poetry and mathematics can emerge from the technology together.

The flexibility of computers allows the imagination to select and combine elements on various levels. Mathematical patterns found in nature, like fractiles, can be generated so that visual models are easily manipulated on the computer for creative problem solving. Thus, the computer allows students to learn problem solving and basic skills in a more dynamic manner.

Like composers who create by sitting at the piano and making things up, the computer also permits creative play. This aspect of computers deserves at least equal time with basic skill building. Children using a Logo program, for example, can manipulate complex geometric concepts in math while creating their own visual compositions with musical accompaniment. The editing process allows them to add, delete and "arrange" to their satisfaction.

Computer generated visual models — whether basic skills or flights of fancy — can be manipulated with flexibility and creativity. The opportunity is created for moving across media using computer graphics, numbers, words or music. Children create their own microworlds, imagine, *and* build skills which can be freely explored. The computer provides a language of thinking and a means of expression where permission is granted to be oneself.

The traditional notion of educators is that if fluency, flexibility, and originality were systematically taught, true creativity would follow. Unfortunately, it isn't that simple. To begin with, teachers have to teach it. Secondly, fluency doesn't count for much if all the ideas generated are simply trivial. And if flexibility clouds issues or discourages group decision making it can impede learning. Even originality might be simply a social accommodation, rather than either intuitive boundary-pushing or barrier breaking. We need to question some of our most basic assumptions about fostering basic skill.

Unfortunately, the most common school practice encourages children to be plodders who see the rules as con-

duits for action, rather than as collaborative spring-
boards for changing realities.  Taking risks, dealing with
failure, the desire to be surprised, and enjoying ambiguity
are all essential elements in creative behavior.  All are
difficult for teachers to model and for many students to
accept.  After all, simply accepting the directions from
someone in authority is always easier.

In the real world we learn more about creativity from
our failures, accidents, and the personal restructuring of
our reality in the face of uncertainty.  Gaining the help of
a supportive group reduces the fear of failure.  This fear
prevents some students from even trying creative activities.  The computer can rekindle interest by allowing the
students to take risks and make mistakes without a loss
of self esteem.

As a dynamic communication instrument the computer can act as a generator for collaboration, creativity,
and skill-building.  Students, even if they are great dis-
tances apart, can use the computer and a modem to jointly
create new ideas and look at basic skills in a new way.
Computers can also give visual dimension to metaphors
and help students go beyond the literal in understanding
what they are reading and writing about.  What better way
is there to ensure that the basics are taught in depth, than
to include the basic intellectual tools and symbol systems
— reinforced through exploratory computer-based instruction?

## The Future of Human-Machine Interaction

The 1990s will bring increasingly powerful multi-media computers into the educational system. Even today it's possible to connect to a videodisc and CD ROM player. The synthesis of visual, auditory and manual cues goes along with the new emphasis on empowering students and teachers. Technological tools can help creativity and inventiveness permeate all aspects of a child's learning. This process requires fresh metaphors and fresh pedagogical ideas to manage the computerization that is transforming our educational environment.

As tomorrow's schools struggle with social change, new technology, a rapidly expanding knowledge base and a multicultural school population, there is an ever increasing need to help students understand basic skills *and* develop higher order thinking abilities. As we all work to manage our own learning — both present and future — the ability to creatively think and solve problems cooperatively will become more important than ever. Working creatively with conflicts means viewing them as possibilities for the cooperative improvement of education.

As schools move through the 1990s computers will be viewed as just one part of the technology equation. The school microcomputers of the early 80s were the electronic learning equivalent of the worksheet. Computers are now multimedia devices capable of full motion video, voice recognition, interactive graphics and touch sensitive screens. With the right software and peripheral devices, PCs can now turn a disk of data into a book in a few minutes, making high quality personalized publishing a reality. And Steve Jobs wants nothing less than "the *world* in a backpack." His NeXT computer already has a large *island* or two on CD-ROM. The world will prove more difficult. Technology and educational development decisions made today will be with us at the beginning of the new millennium. Experts predict that in the 21st century we will have self improving thinking machines that seem more like living things (Moravec, 1988).

## Adapting Software for Collaboration: A Dozen Favorites

*Audubon Wildlife Adventures*
*Grizzly Bears*
Computer Advanced Ideas

*Bank Street Writer III*
Scholastic

*The Children's Writing*
*& Publishing Center*
Learning Company

*Decision, Decisions*
*& Geoworld*
Tom Snyder

*Geometric Supposer*
Sunburst

*Muppet Slate*
Sunburst

*Oregon Trail*
MECC

*Science Toolkit*
*Module 1, 2*
Broderbund

*Solve It*
Sunburst

*Talking Text Writer*
Scholastic

*Where in the World Is*
*Carmen Sandiego?*
Broderbund

*Word Bench*
Addison-Wesley

## Directory of Publishers

Addison-Wesley Publishing
Jacob Way
Reading, MA 0186

Computer Advanced Ideas
2902 San Pablo Ave.
Berkeley, CA 94702

Broderbund
17 Paul Drive
San Rafael, CA 94903

Learning Company
6493 Kaiser Drive
Fremont, CA 94555

MECC
3490 Lexington Ave. N.
St. Paul, MN 55126

Scholastic Inc.
2931 E. McCarty St.
Jefferson City, MO
65102

Sunburst Communications
39 Washington Ave.
Pleasantville, NY 10570

Tom Snyder Productions
90 Sherman St.
Cambridge, MA 02140

## References

Adams, D. & Hamm, M. (1987). *Electronic Learning.* Springfield, IL: Charles Thomas Publishing.

Adams, D. & Hamm, M. (1986). *Educational Computing: Issues, Trends and a Practical Guide.* Springfield IL: Charles Thomas Publishing.

Allen, N., Atkinson, D., Morgan, M., Moore, T. & Snow, C. (1988). What experienced collaborators say about collaborative writing. *Journal of Business and Technical Communication,* 1, 70-90.

Anderson, P.V.(1985). What Survey Research Tells Us About Writing at Work. In L. Odell and D. Goswami (Eds.) *Writing in Nonacademic Settings.* New York: The Guilford Press.

Bruffee, K. A. (1983). Writing and Reading as Collaborative or Social Acts. In J.N. Hays, J.R. Ramsey, & R.D. Foulke (Eds.). *The Writer's Mind: Writing as a Mode of Thinking.* (pp. 159-169). Urbana, IL: NCTE.

Costanzo, W.(1989). *The Electronic Text: Learning to Write, Read, and Reason with Computers.* Englewood Cliffs, NJ: Educational Technology Publications.

Ede, L. & Lunsford, A. (1986). Why Write...Together: A Research Update. *Rhetoric Review,* 5(1), 71-81.

Erikson, T.(1986). *Off and Running: The Computer Off-line Activities Book.* Berkeley, CA: EQUALS.

Felici, J. & Nace, T.(1987). *Desktop Publishing Skills.* Reading, MA: Addison-Wesley.

Franklin, S. (1987). *Making the Literature, Writing, Word Processing Connection: The Best of the Writing Notebook 1983-1987.* Mendocino, CA: The Writing Notebook.

Gaard, G. (1989). Collaborative Theory and Collaborative Practice in the Electronic Classroom. University of Minnesota. Paper presented at 1989 NCTE Conference.

Gardner, H. (1982). *Art, Mind and Brain: A Cognitive Approach to Creativity.* New York: Basic Books.

Gardner, H. (1985). *The Mind's New Science.* New York: Basic Books.

Goldenberg, E. P. & Wallace, F. (1987). *Exploring Language with Logo.* Cambridge: MIT Press.

Hofstadter, D. (1985). *Metamagical Themes: Questing for the Essence of Mind and Pattern.* New York: Basic Books.

Kagan, J. & Lamb, S. (1987). *The Emergence of Morality in Young Children.* Chicago: University of Chicago Press.

Moravec, H. (1988). *Mind Children: The Future of Robot and Human Intelligence.* Cambridge, MA: Harvard University Press.

Pagnoni, M. (1987). *Computers and Small Fries.* Garden City, NY: Avery.

Pea, R. & Sheingold, K. (1987). *Mirrors of Minds: Patterns of Experience in Educational Computing.* Norwood, NJ: Ablex.

Perkins, D. N., Lochhead, J. & Bishop, J.(1987). *Transfer and Teaching Thinking.* Hillsdale, NJ: Lawrence Erlbaum Associates.

Rheingold, H. (1985). *Tools for Thought: The People and Ideas Behind the Next Computer Revolution.* New York: Simon & Schuster.

Roberts, N. *et al.* (1988). *Integrating Computers Into the Elementary and Middle School.* Old Tappan, NJ: Prentice-Hall.

Schulman, E. & Page, R. (1987). *Spreadsheets for Beginners.* New York: Franklin Watts.

Solomon, Cynthia (1986). *Computer Environments for Children: A Reflection on Theories of Learning and Education.* Cambridge: MIT Press.

Stark, J. & Metz, L. (1988). *Improving Teaching and Learning Through Research.* San Francisco: Jossey-Bass.

Swigger, K. M. & Swigger, B. K. (1984). Social patterns and computer use among preschool children. *AEDS Journal,* 17(3).

Thomas, R. (1988). *ClassWorks: Appleworks for the Classroom.* Eugene:ICCE.

U. S. Congress Office of Technology Assessment. (1988). *Power On! New Tools for Teaching and Learning.* Washington, DC: U. S. Government Printing Office.

Webb, N.M.(1985). Cognitive requirements of learning computer programming in group and individual settings, *AEDS Journal,* 18(3).

Williams, K. (1988). *Technologies of Control: The New Interactive Media for the Home.* Madison: University of Wisconsin Press.

# 4

## COOPERATIVE MODELS AND
## INTERACTIVE VIDEODISC TECHNOLOGY

Each use of new media and technology promises more effective, efficient and satisfying learning. Sometimes it is, sometimes it isn't. And sometimes it's like a steamroller going over the landscape, if you aren't part of it you're part of the parking lot. How various types of technology affect the complex learning process leads to a consideration of various issues. The presentation of symbol systems, the means employed to learn content, how students interact with peers, and the interaction of technology and learners are all part of the picture.

Interactive videodisc technology links videodiscs to a controlling computer. This allows the user to access memory or still images in a manner that combines print and graphics. One of the most frequently heard comments about this technology is how it changes the student from a passive observer to an active participant. Learners actively work together to quickly access all types of information in a way that makes sense to them. As part of this process it's important for the teacher to know how to structure a cooperative learning environment that builds on technology to respond to human variability.

Using interactive videodisc technology allows all types of symbol systems to be accessed by teams of learners in an elaborate and adaptive manner. When symbol systems are presented, they differ in notationality, with verbal systems being more semantic and pictorial systems being more visual. Video presentations tend to highlight the action properties of a narrative, while print versions emphasize informational characteristics.

It is not clear exactly how learners internalize these different presentations. What is clear is that students experience more than they understand and that it is experience that most influences behavior. Movement from the real experiences of the learner to pictorial representations and finally to verbal schemas has been proposed as a model for learning. Theorists speculate further that all symbols (pictorial or verbal) become part of the learner's conceptual framework and are decontextualized (Bruner, 1964; Kosselyn, 1981; Salomon, 1979; Adams & Hamm, 1987).

The means employed to learn content may affect the learner and attitudes about learning. Learners differ in the way they employ symbols to represent, store, and manipulate information. It seems reasonable that an instructional presentation which is closely matched to the learner's communicational symbol system is easier for the learner to recode and comprehend. Interactive technology can be used to compensate for learner deficits as well, such as when the zoom feature is used to increase learner cue-attending skills (Salomon, 1974, 1979).

Learners are not always accurate selectors of their own instructional technology. High ability students, in traditional educational settings, may select directive, structured technology because it is perceived as a certain route to successful test performance. If this happens educators will not be able to capitalize on the fact that many high ability students profit from undergoing the fatigue of judging for themselves. On the other hand, low ability students may need guidance in selecting unstructured technological offerings which might also prove to be inadequate (Clark, 1982).

In thinking about the new interactive technologies, three general questions thus arise: How does the presentation relate to internalization of concepts on the part of the learner? How does the means employed to learn affect groups of learners? How do specific learner characteristics and technological attributes interrelate?

**Technology Which Is Responsive to the Learner**

Interactive videodisc systems are controlled by the student and provide immediate feedback in response to their instructions. The user can address a variety of video, audio, and graphics data simply by touching a screen or clicking a mouse. Laser videodiscs store 54,000 still frames on the single side of a 12-inch silver colored disc. There is room for about thirty minutes of moving images and two thirty minute audio tracks on one side of the disc. The ability to rapidly access frames randomly leads to interactivity between user and technology (Seal-Warner, 1988).

Hardware capabilities have been rated according to a three point scale. Level I interactive video gives the least amount of interactivity. The program is largely linear — although the picture stops can be encoded on the disc. It usually allows the learner to control the movement through the provision of random access, remote control, freeze framing, forward and reverse movement, slow motion, scanning, and step framing.

Level II videodisc media represents an intermediate level of interactivity. The control program is recorded on the disc and it works very well when the content is unchanging. The videodisc players have their own microprocessor with a memory size from 1 to 5K. This level has all of the features of Level I as well as the ability to branch and monitor learners' performance.

Level III connects an external computer to the videodisc player. It's ideal for changing content and presents the highest level of interactivity. It builds on the strength of television and computers as instructional devices. A single videodisc program can be used with several computer programs. The two audio tracks can be accessed by different audiences and can provide simple or advanced levels of commentary. Different languages can also be used on the two tracks. Text and graphics generated by the computer can either be superimposed over the video material or shown independently (Bayard-White, 1986).

Tape-based interactive systems have some of the same features, but are not as popular as videodisc systems. They have the advantage of being recordable and the disadvantage of wait time, as the tape player winds and rewinds to the appropriate location. Several systems include cue-toned, frame-coded tape which can be used in conjunction with computers and a range of tape players. They can also be used with a range of computers and authoring systems (Wright, 1988).

**Potential Advantages of Interactive Technologies**
Interactive technologies can provide instructional variations to meet differing learning styles, ability or

knowledge levels, and personal preferences. For example, learners could choose to become familiar with the vocabulary of Spanish speaking Americans through auditory means, through visual means, or through a combination of the two. Further, they can access more difficult conversations in Spanish if, through a pretest, they demonstrate basic competence in vocabulary and grammar.

After taking a learning styles survey to determine instructional preferences, users could select to learn basic concepts about group interaction either inductively or deductively. In the inductive track, learners would have a chance to see many examples illustrating a concept, to develop personal descriptions of those examples, to receive feedback from a person skilled in facilitating group interaction, and to compare their ideas with those of the expert mentor on the videodisc. In the deductive track, the learner would first receive the definition of a concept and a brief explanation. This would be followed by video examples illustrating the particular concept (Carlson & Falk, 1986; Videodisc Research Group, 1986).

**Effectiveness of Interactive Technologies**

The focus of evaluation for new, interactive technologies has often centered on the acquisition of specific skills through training rather than on broader conceptual frameworks. Generally learners have benefited from instruction using interactive videodisc technology. They have received higher achievement scores and experienced greater satisfaction than learners using traditional instructional methods. The instruction has also proven to be cost effective (Abrams, 1986; Browning, 1986; Pieper, 1985; Thorkildsen, *et al.*, 1983).

Criticisms have arisen when researchers fail to identify learner characteristics, media characteristics, conceptual frameworks, or the qualities of the dependent variables. The research suggests that technology isn't very effective when the learner is viewed as a passive recipient of instruction who does not interact with the instruction being presented (Salomon & Clark, 1977; Sheingold, Kane, & Endreweit, 1983). To be effective, students (in pairs or small groups) must be able to work their own way through the material.

Do learners who use interactive technologies become more involved and active in their own education? There is support for an affirmative answer. As learners create a personal path through a disc program, they gain feelings of competence as well as specific knowledge. The more interactive and collaborative video instruction becomes, the greater the learning (Seal-Warner, 1988). For example, a student who has the opportunity to use videodiscs to explore a city by "driving" through its streets comes to know a "learning" environment rather than a teaching situation.

Combining text with moving and still imagery has resulted in a powerful learning medium. A practical example can be found in a videodisc developed by Apple Computer Inc., that allows groups of learners to place any word in the Constitution in context. This program also lets them create additional contexts based on personal preferences and needs. A good example deals with Civil Rights. This issue can be explored through a series of dramatizations, ranging from the Dred Scott decision to Martin Luther King's "I Have a Dream" speech.

Another locally developed example used a Macintosh HyperCard program, a CD-ROM drive, and a videodisc player to go back in history. In this program students could view television news, newspaper reports, and the opinions of historians. The material was all from the summer of 1969: the Vietnam War, student protests, the moon landing, President Nixon, the beginning of an opening to China, and the Kennedy accident at Chappaquiddick. Students explore the relationship between historical elements, and the historians' views about how time changes the relative importance of different events. After going through this material students hold small group discussions about how these events made a difference in national direction.

## Collaborative Learning and Interactive Technologies

The basic components of cooperative learning have been identified, as have the key characteristics of interactive technologies. What happens when cooperative learning and interactive technologies merge is now beginning to be explored. A recent study found that learners who worked with a partner in a collaborative manner and used videodisc technology achieved higher scores in both content knowledge and observation skill tests than learners who worked alone with technology or those who worked with a partner using traditional reading materials. They also completed instruction in an efficient manner and with a relatively high degree of satisfaction (Carlson & Falk, 1987). The same research suggests that collaborative learning with real and media projected partners is highly engaging.

# Incorporating Cooperative Models Into the Interactive Media Process

Some serious interactive media design choices are now in the process of being made. One of the most important is how to increase student motivation by incorporating group goals into the communications process. Another decision, with important implications for the future, is how to make the technology personalized and intimate enough to function as a surrogate group member.

As a new communications infrastructure is being shaped, some "ecologists" of media are arguing for human-machine diversity, connectedness, and cooperative association. They suggest that when cooperative models are incorporated into the design of interactive technologies, it is important to consider the types of mediating processes which might be used, the types of peer interaction which might occur, and the cognitive processes which could be utilized (Bossert, 1988). Each of these processes has implications for how interactive media can be used cooperatively.

## Mediating Processes

The controversy which occurs when opinions in a group differ can foster new social perspectives and problem solving. Oral rehearsal and summarization of information takes place as comprehension develops. Cognitive conflict can result in positive peer interaction, friendship and acceptance (Johnson & Johnson, 1985). Mediating processes parallel the basic concepts of shared leadership and peaceful conflict resolution outlined earlier. For example, group processing which allows reflection on task and maintenance behaviors tends to improve both academic learning and social cohesion (Brandt, 1987; Yager, *et al.,*1986).

### Peer Interaction

The types of peer interaction which promote learning include the opening of intellectual doors through exploration rather than quick answers. This helps the learners discover correct procedures or underlying frameworks for information (Webb, 1985). A good interactive program should not allow the student to abdicate their right to explore and think.

Social interactions among peers also shape learning. If the prior achievement of some pupils works to depress the lower achieving pupils, then both social and academic learning may suffer (Bossert, 1988). Pupils can improve their own learning by coaching their peers. It is also important to inform students about who they can assist and who they can receive assistance from (Cohen, 1986). Differentiated tasks which provide for interdependence among students are helpful in creating mutual high regard and an equality of participation among group members.

### Cognitive Processes

Specific cognitive processes have been identified as helpful in increasing achievement. These include relating new information to what was learned previously, paraphrasing or reviewing information, and checking information with others.

The degree of ambiguity in a learning task is a factor in how pupils focus their attention. Of the four tasks of a typical classroom — memory, procedural, opinion, and comprehension — students have the most trouble with comprehension. Pupils may avoid comprehension tasks by refocusing them into memory, procedural, or opinion tasks. In cooperative learning experiences, clear sequences of activities increase pupil satisfaction and facilitate comprehension.

Clear specification of the goals and objectives for learning is a necessary prerequisite for the productive collaborative use of interactive technologies. The use of students as "teachers," who give explanations, often results in more learning than having the teacher give convergent answers to a question. Creation of separate, yet interdependent tasks, along with heterogeneous grouping, may be necessary to avoid role confusion and high-status pupil domination of group interaction. Broad multidimensional learning environments that have a great deal of student interaction may be more congruent with the many possibilities inherent in both cooperative learning models and interactive technologies.

## Formats for Cooperative Use of Interactive Technologies

Collaborative models can be beneficial when interactive technologies are used in learning. Of the many formats available, five are particularly useful in promoting a convergence of cooperative learning and interactive technologies:

1. *Interruptible Design to Teach Facts* — useful when specific knowledge and information needs to be learned and practiced.

2. *Simulation with Decision Making* — allows debate and cognitive conflict related to complexity of group interaction and the process of making decisions.

3. *Problem Solving Based on Data Gathered* — combines individual exploration of assigned data available on a videodisc with group summaries of this data; this, in turn, is related to various solutions to a designated problem.

4. *Critiquing Human Interactions* — encourages individual critiques of problematic situations presented on videodisc or frame-coded videotape and the sharing of these critiques with a small cooperative group.

5. *Recording Behavioral Data* — allows pairs of learners to create sensitive coding formats for the documentation of specific behaviors.

These five formats range from those which promote the acquisition of specific information to those which deal with broad issues of problem solving. All incorporate mediating processes such as constructive controversy, rehearsal of information, positive peer interaction or cognitive operations such as explanation and consensus testing. All promote shared leadership with a balance of task and maintenance functions, effective communication, and peaceful conflict resolution.

**Interruptible Programs Which Teach Facts**
This format is valuable when the purpose of instruc-

tion is to have students learn and apply information in a specific way. In this procedure a video scenario is presented and the students interact with the situation. The instructional videodisc program then stops and the learner is instructed to meet with another student to complete practice exercises. This type of exercise requires the learners to periodically stop, discuss the rules, and apply them to specific case study forms. The learners must arrive at agreement prior to the final submission of the project to the larger group or the teacher. If the group work is satisfactory, each learner demonstrates competence with a final test that holds the individual accountable.

Alternating "teacher" and "student" roles during the formal completion exercise gives the student the benefit of giving and receiving assistance. Requiring learners to give explanations for their answers is also beneficial. Reminding the learners to use relevant task behaviors —information giving, receiving, summarizing, clarifying, and consensus testing—leads to a further elaboration of ideas. Appropriate maintenance behaviors, such as creating empathy, can also promote an atmosphere of collegiality.

Instructors could consider the following questions as they use interruptible videodisc designs with learners:

1. Has the specific information to be learned
   been communicated in a clear, concise manner?

2. Do the  video and audio examples engage
   and motivate the learner?

3. Are the directions about the processes clear
enough for the learners to maximize knowledge
acquisition in a cooperative manner?
  - Have the use of peer explanation and oral
    rehearsal been suggested?
  - Have clarification and empathic response been
    recommended?
  - Do the learners know how to periodically
    reflect on what is proving effective for them?
  - Was the suggestion made that learners
    periodically alternate "teaching" and "learning"
    roles?

4. Has individual accountability been coupled
with positive group interdependence?

By considering each of these questions, an instructor
can enhance the learning that occurs in the collaborative
use of interactive technology.

Interruptible design applications engage learners in a
variety of ways. For example, to learn a particular math
concept students can be presented with information on
videodisc or videotape. This information may very well
involve using accompanying sets of manipulative materials. During a pause in the instructional program, pupils
meet to solve problems related to the math concepts presented on disc. They review the content and discuss solutions to the problems. Students agree on solutions to the
problems and then explain those solutions to the larger
group or to the teacher. This facilitates content learning
and social skill development (Carlson & Falk, 1987).

The interruptible format using interactive technology
alternates a personalized program of instruction (via

Level III videodisc) with a practice period using cooperative interaction. In addition, such a model can also be employed by an instructor using an already produced videodisc or tape. Simulated groups where learners participate with surrogate group members is yet another way to structure collaboration.

### Simulations Which Involve Decision Making

Simulations, available through interactive technologies, can also serve as powerful vehicles for cooperative learning. Rather than a convergent approach, they demonstrate the complexity of human interaction and allow divergent responses to be discussed and debated. This process allows for cognitive controversy which can deepen the students' understanding of basic concepts while encouraging higher order analysis, synthesis, and evaluation.

When using this format, instructors may consider the following questions:

Have the cooperative processes to be used (in creating divergent responses to the simulation) been specified?

Has the use of cognitive controversy been reviewed?

Do students understand the importance of gatekeeping and when arriving at a group consensus?

Have the steps in peaceful conflict resolution been reviewed?

Have group members been asked to periodically reflect on what is effective for them?

Do students know about the importance of backing up ideas with information and reliable data?

## Problem Solving Based on Data Gathered

In discs related to problem solving learners are asked to assume a role and assist in finding a solution to their problem. Exploration can be made possible through a Level III interactive videodisc program. This would allow the student access to such resources as a directory of community services which describe community resources and opportunities for contacting educational and human service workers in a mythical community.

When a group of learners uses this type of interactive program cooperatively, they may want to begin by defining the problem presented on the disc in a precise manner. As part of developing alternative solutions to a group generated question, pairs of learners can divide up the community resource database for exploration. The group members then meet back at an appointed time to present data summaries and to further develop alternative solutions.

In using this collaborative model, learners first debate the problem and then use consensus testing to assure that each group member agrees on the problem definition. Group members volunteer to explore specific portions of the data recorded on the videodisc. Each member is accountable to the rest of the group for a specific part of the data. Group members then meet to provide their individual reports and to summarize and clarify the types of community resources available. Group discussion leads to further exploration of alternatives based on data provided.

This model, which starts and ends with group discussion, uses the interactive technology as part of differentiated tasks. Each group member is held accountable for a different part of the whole assignment. When each part is contributed, it allows the total group to continue in an interdependent manner.

As an instructor using this model, it is important to ask the following questions:

1. Have the learners been informed of the steps used in the problem-solving approach?

2. Have the key factors involved in shared leadership, effective communication, and successful collaboration been reviewed?

3. Do the students understand the importance of individual task completion in an interdependent model of interaction?

This format can be used in a variety of ways with students at different grade levels. For example, children could define a problem or problems related to the pollution of the environment. They then could use a videodisc which has a variety of data recorded on it (photographs, newspaper highlights, governmental statistics related to environmental issues). Each child then would be responsible for recording data either by topic (acid rain, air pollution, garbage disposal, greenhouse effect) and by type of data (newspapers, photographs, reports). The interactive technology allows sorting in a variety of ways for different purposes. Making individual reports back to the whole group generates further discussion related to various alternative solutions to environmental problems.

In this format, learners first meet to collectively

define a problem. The next step is using interactive technology as a data source for further discussion and problem solving. Closure occurs when the small groups get back together to discuss their findings. This model successfully combines interactive technologies and cooperative learning models.

**Critiquing of Situational Scenarios**

In a disc related to understanding cultural diversity (Videodisc Research Group, 1987), groups of learners begin by viewing a series of interactions between American educators and refugee children from Southeast Asia. In these scenarios, various interactions happen. For example, the school principal rushes through an explanation of the all the forms which must be completed as part of the registration process — thoroughly confusing the family. Another problem occurs when the classroom teacher takes the children into a puzzling cafeteria and speaks in a patronizing manner about the fun the children will have there.

Working in groups, learners carefully observe the interactions in the scenarios, replaying as necessary. Each learner then writes an independent critique which is then shared with the group. The group members then develop a group report, analyzing the various scenarios. The group analysis is compared with the comments of a refugee sponsor which are recorded on the videodisc. The idea is to get learners working with the disc to confront their preconceptions, take off their cultural blinders and examine values that have been taken for granted.

In observing situations such as these, students may observe different behaviors. By completing an individual report prior to sharing opinions, each learner has the opportunity to summarize her personal opinion.  Discussing different opinions creates an opportunity for multicultural understanding.  The next step is to create a group summary clarification.  Comparing and contrasting the composite views of the group with that of the expert refugee sponsor allows the higher order thinking skills of analysis and evaluation to be used.

Instructors using this type of interactive technology to  foster collaboration need to address several questions:

1.  Have the students been prepared for carefully observing the interactions of the people involved— noting both verbal and non-verbal behavior?

2. Have behaviors which promote academic learning in groups — cognitive controversy, explanation, and discussion — been reviewed?

3. Have the learners reviewed effective group interactions related to task and maintenance behaviors, communication skills, and peaceful conflict resolution?

4. Have questions been developed which will facilitate the application of the key concepts needing to be learned?

This model can be applied in many circumstances. For example, pupils could observe other classes at the same grade level from different regions whose interactions  have been recorded on videodisc.  They could begin by writing down their individual reactions to perceived cultural differences and similarities.  These could then be compared in a small group. Interactive technology allows for such things as replays and pauses to enable rechecking of observations. Through writing a group report of the observations, explanations would be deepened and understanding strengthened.

This model allows maximum benefit from both the interactive technology and the collaborative models of learning. Individual accountability is also present when learners write personal critiques of the interactions. Positive interdependence occurs through the writing of the group report. In addition, observational skills are developed and the higher order thinking skills of analysis, synthesis, and evaluation are used.

### Recording of Behavioral Data

In a disc related to understanding effective communication skills (Videodisc Research Group, 1989), learners have an opportunity to record, in minute detail, each communication behavior they see in videodisc scenarios. Working first in pairs with an instructional program, they record behaviors for each video segment. Debate about both what is recorded and the method of recording sharpens the depth of observations.

Students are then asked to produce and  critique a videotape of their own communication interactions as they discuss a topic assigned by the teacher. The learners may retape themselves until they feel satisfied with their demonstration of effective communication. This format has a number of advantages which combine the salient features of both interactive technology and cooperative learning models. By taking advantage of user services within the computer program, learners can replay segments in two ways — with audio track audible and with audio track inaudible. This allows observation of both verbal and non-verbal behavior. Discussion and debate about the content and methodology of observational recording allows controversy to be used in a manner that strengthens understanding.

In using a format which promotes collaboration in behavioral data recording, the following questions need to be addressed by an instructor:

1. Does the interactive technology program have abundant material to observe?

2. Have alternative methods for effective group interaction and the recording of behavioral data been reviewed?

3. Do students know about the learning benefits of peer teaching?

4. Have the basic concepts related to shared leadership, effective communication, and peaceful conflict resolution been reviewed?

5. Have the criteria to be used in the evaluation of the learner produced videotape been clearly stated?

This format can be used in many ways with learners at many grade levels. For example, recording observations of a particular species of animal portrayed on a videodisc could allow high school biology students to further their understanding of animal life. The scientific method becomes more meaningful as students debate the specifics of their observations.

The combination of collaboration and interactive technology can be effective in the arts as well. Comparisons between one painting and another can happen easily as learners work together to record observations. Positive interdependence is created as the learners develop a joint report of their observations. Individual accountability can be realized if the learners are required to analyze new data and submit individual reports.

This model involves working in pairs or small groups, discussing and debating information, and arriving at consensus. It illustrates an effective way to combine collaboration and interactive technology. Interruptible programs which teach facts, simulated decision making, and higher level thinking are a good use of interactive technology. When this is coupled with cooperative groups the interactive avenues of electronic communication can be traveled at a much higher speed.

## Group Configurations Which Promote Collaboration and Cooperation

In addition to considering design formats which offer the potential for success in using interactive technologies cooperatively, there are different group configurations which also influence the learning environment. Two group configurations will be considered here — learning in pairs and learning in small groups. Following a description of the configuration, a summary of data gathered from learners using these two formats will be given.

### A Comparative Study: Learning in Pairs or Alone while Using Interactive Technologies

To learn about effective group interactions in elementary classrooms, teacher candidates were randomly assigned to different instructional groups. Some students used the Level III videodisc instructional program alone while others worked collaboratively in pairs. Students were videotaped as they completed the instruction and were stopped three times to reflect on the process. They described their academic learning and the thinking skills which they used. Students also reflected on their attitudes about the instruction and completed individual written tests of main concepts presented.

When reporting on the thinking skills used, students who worked alone differed from those who worked in pairs. For example, students who worked in pairs stated that they reviewed directions together and clarified meanings. This made the task easier to complete. These students also reported that they discussed and analyzed material presented on the videodisc prior to entering a response into the computer. Controversy arose at times. However, it appeared to lead to more thorough understanding of the content presented. Students working in pairs also indicated that they appreciated the empathic support of their fellow students.

Students who worked alone stated that they found the scenarios to be engaging and engrossing due to the color and graphics. They also found the self-pacing of the program and the ability to review and repeat sequences to be beneficial. Rather than the analysis and synthesis reported by students working in pairs, students who worked alone emphasized learning definitions and applying these to examples on the videodisc. Many students commented about the isolation of working with the equipment and stated that they desired more human contact.

Students were given content, observation, and satisfaction surveys at the conclusion of the instruction. The content test measured knowledge of basic concepts taught through the disc program. The observation skills test included student recording and analysis of the behaviors of the members of an elementary cooperative group which they had not previously seen. The satisfaction survey included a Likert rating scale for a series of statements related to both the instructional design and the technical aspects of the program.

In general, an analysis of variance revealed that students who worked in pairs to learn the material in a deductive manner received significantly higher scores in the content and observation skill tests. However, there were no significant differences in overall satisfaction between students working alone or in pairs (Carlson, 1989).

### Learning in Small Groups Using Interactive Technologies

To use the disc related to understanding groups, a peer teaching/small group model was compared with individual/consultation use of a Level III videodisc program (Videodisc Research Group, 1986). In the small group model, student peer teachers used the Macintosh HyperCard and Voyager Stacks to develop a program with selected segments of interaction from those recorded on the videodisc. These peer teachers then developed discussion outlines to facilitate small group cooperative learning experiences while using the interactive technology.

During the group experience, students were asked by their peer teacher to observe behaviors and record their individual observational data on specially created forms. Group members then discussed and debated their data before receiving "expert" feedback from the videodisc program.

In the individual use model, students had access to a self-paced computer program highlighting the same video sequences and observational data recording sheets as those used in the small group. Students were free to consult peers as they worked through the program. They also had access to the same "expert" feedback from the videodisc program as that available in the small group. A peer lab assistant was available for consultation related to both the content and process of learning.

Content and observation tests — as well as satisfaction surveys — were used to report student reactions to the types of instruction. Again, students who engaged in the small group peer teaching model scored significantly higher in content and observation skill tests than students working alone (Carlson, 1989).

Students expressed satisfaction with the discussion and the support offered by fellow students as well as the peer teachers. They commented about the individual attention of the peer teachers who animated the discussions. This was in marked contrast to learners using the individual/consultation approach. They continued to feel isolated with the technology which seemed to lack human empathy. The availability of consultation did not prove effective in increasing satisfaction.

These results corroborate the key issues described at the beginning of this section. By allowing debate and constructive controversy, the peer teachers facilitated explanations of ideas rather than convergent "right" answers. Through checking with others, group members engaged in the paraphrasing and clarifying of information. A balance between task and maintenance functions was encouraged by the facilitators and group members. The presence of such cooperative learning techniques mean higher levels of academic achievement when students are using interactive videodisc courseware (Carlson, 1989).

The personal responses of the peer teachers to individual learners and the small group as a whole was another positive aspect of this model. The ability to "read" non-verbal expressions of frustration or confusion allows clarification to occur. In addition, a peer teacher trained in effective communication and peaceful conflict resolution enhances the cooperation and collaboration within a small group (Webb, 1985).

Peer teachers can select examples from a wealth of material on a disc and use these examples to facilitate learning in cooperative groups. When peer teachers are rotated each member of the group has an opportunity to serve as both teacher and learner. This enhances the status and learning of each group member. This small group peer teacher configuration has much to offer as new programs and technology put educators in a position to design their own interactive programs.

Working in pairs to learn content and observation skills is more effective than working alone with the technology. Being part of a small group with a peer teacher who promotes cooperative learning is more effective and satisfying than working in a consultative manner with the technology. The use of such strategies as debate, discussion, personalized response, rehearsal, paraphrasing combined with a balance of task and maintenance behaviors, effective communication, and peaceful conflict resolution appears to promote high academic achievement. The addition of a peer teacher appears to enhance the satisfaction of the learners as well.

The two configurations — learning in pairs and learning in small groups with peer teachers — have proven beneficial to students. Combining the best of videodisc scenarios with the best of interactive programs is in itself positive. But when these are then used with cooperative learning models, there is potential for even higher levels of academic and social skill development.

Both type of format and type of group configuration need to be considered carefully by instructors planning to combine cooperative models with interactive technologies. When the kinds of task/technology variables, group/pupil variables, and process/outcome variables for instruction are carefully listed, a selection of both format and group configuration can be made with greater confidence.

## Students Collaborating with Instructional Designers in Videodisc Production

Students at the elementary and secondary level can participate as data gatherers in the development of interactive technologies. As part of this process small cooperative groups can provide a forum for choosing, analyzing, summarizing, and submitting information. This kind of curriculum building process involves individual responsibility with positive interdependence. The common goal is to build an exceptional interactive program.

### An Example: Pupils Collecting Data Sources for a Major Project

In the London Public Records Office is the most extraordinary record of of a country that has ever been written. Called the *Domesday Book,* it was drawn up over 900 years ago, in the year 1086, at the request of William the Conqueror. It has 888 pages with column after column of facts about eleventh century England, including 13,400 place names and the names of the 2 million people who lived in England at that time. It is an administrative document presenting a pattern of living social relations in terms of the land and labor of the entire country. The reader comes to know the daily life of Chaucer-like characters from the hill farms of Devon to the herring fishmen of Yarmouth, from the lead miners of Derbyshire Peak to the burgesses of Norwich and Chester. This remarkable technical record brings the world of the eleventh century to the reader of today, making contact with the local courts, the torrential rain, the cold, the famine, and ruined fruit crops. Basic elements of English life are revealed in the pages of this record, a remarkable technological achievement for its time.

On the nine hundredth anniversary of the Domesday recordings, England again decided to record its life, but with new dimensions. Students across England were asked to become involved in the collection of data related to their lives and that of their neighbors. Elementary and secondary pupils replicated the Domesday Project. Pupils around the country located interesting local legends, took pictures of sites important to them, and wrote stories about their daily lives. Literally thousands of bits of data were collected.

The new videodisc technologies were viewed as the

ideal vehicle for the organization of this type of data. The design team, working collaboratively with students, created an instructional design. They developed nested map menus, and used computer-controlled pictures that allowed users to view the country from space and zoom in on general pictures of the countryside, city pictures and neighborhoods. If the user pressed Birmingham on the map of England, for example, they would see first an aerial photograph of the city and receive some general information. When a city map appeared, they would see photographs and receive information about a particular neighborhood. If users would go on to select a neighborhood map, they then could access specific streets, view scenes, and even enter public structures.

All the basic building blocks for this new *Domesday* videodisc were gathered by elementary and secondary students. Creation of such a product, in collaboration with a videodisc design team, was important to many segments of society. It was particularly useful in helping students understand the relationship between street, neighborhood, city, county, and country. For older pupils and adults, the design team added reprints of major newspaper articles and texts of major government and scientific reports. The user could even see photographs of newspaper articles reporting current events in the city at the time the disc was made.

For urban students, an important feature of the Domesday disc was the opportunity to take surrogate walks around a farm, a country house, and village streets. Likewise, rural students could explore city marketing and cultural centers. Pupils made plans outlining the direction of their simulated travel. This, in turn, led to an understanding of simple maps. The software used allowed up to five lines of text to be added to each picture. This way the students used the disc to create their own databases, displaying maps and photographs complete with captions (Homer, 1989).

### A Suggested Model for the Future

A basic model where pupils serve as data gatherers for a design team creating instructional programs for interactive technologies has many possibilities for the future. Pupils could replicate portions of the Domesday project through collecting data about their own neighborhoods and cities. Pupils in different states or countries could combine materials for cross-cultural learning.

The design team could then take student samples and combine the video and audio materials with computer data bases for instructional programs facilitating hypothesis generation on the part of pupils. These hypotheses could then be tested with data stored on disc in a manner that helps students gain selection and higher order thinking skills.

## Pupils as Design Team

Another model for the development of new interactive technologies is using the pupils themselves as major players in the design process.

### An Example: Pupils Developing Community Related Interactive Resources in Appalachia

During his first year of teaching English in a high school in the Appalachian Mountains of northeast Georgia, Eliot Wigginton helped his students found a quarterly magazine they named *Foxfire.* The contents of the magazine were drawn from the indigenous Appalachian culture. With tape recorders and cameras, students developed reports based on the culture of the region. These included compositions related to blacksmithing, planting by the signs of the Zodiac, building log cabins, cooking in a fireplace, tanning hides, and making banjos. Other articles were philosophical reminiscences of the lives of the region's inhabitants.

The *Foxfire* Press publishes such works of regional interest. One of their recent books was *Aunt Arie: A Foxfire Portrait,* which formed the basis of the Broadway play, "Foxfire." Foxfire also has a video program that was developed in a student-designed studio. Programs broadcast on cable television included conversations with people who have been involved in Rabun County government for long periods of time, demonstrations of log cabin building, education in local schools and environmental studies of the local area that introduced the interdependence of species. By listening to Foxfire music in collaborative groups, students also learn to sing and play traditional musical instruments.

Through these and other efforts connected with Foxfire, students learn the basic skills of writing, photography and editing, and become engaged in a personal confrontation with their own heritage (Foxfire, 1985). The next logical step is just being taken. It involves using interactive video to paint some of these traditions with more vivid colors.

## A Suggested Model for the Future

With the interactive technologies now available, it is possible to follow a student-created design team model such as that implemented through Foxfire. Pupils in any community can use new camcorders, along with the more familiar audio recorders and cameras, to compile a record of their own environment. Rather than relegating the material to print media, pupils can now make their own interactive videotape.

Simple flow charts, created by elementary or secondary students, can illustrate how the collected community materials might be organized. As storyboards are created to illustrate the interrelationship of audio, video, and computer inputs, pupils gain abilities to present information in new and interesting ways. Students in other parts of the country can examine and record their heritage, much as the Foxfire student teams have done.

## Teachers Working with Design Team

Teachers, like students, can learn from participating in the design process. To ensure the connection between cooperative learning, interactive technology, and the curriculum the design team needs teacher representation. Their involvement not only assists teachers in a life-long professional renewal process, but ensures that the final product is used. Without involving the instructors who will use the disc, it would be like dressing up with no place to go — a wonderful interactive videodisc collecting dust on a shelf.

### An Example: Using Interactive Media
### to Develop Instruction for Beginning Teachers

The staff development faculty of a local school district wanted to use collaborative techniques and interactive technologies to assist beginning teachers as they struggled with effective classroom management strategies. The first step was to review the various concepts of classroom management. Next they selected the strategy of "using interpersonal problem solving" for emphasis.

In the first meeting with the videodisc design team, the staff development director described the objectives, content and strategies used in solving classroom management problems. They also explained different uses of the strategies with younger and older learners — and the anticipated effects.

The media design team members shared the basics of interactive videodisc instruction: the touch screen, mouse, user control, and simulations. Next the new teachers practiced various reactions to such classroom situations and explored the consequences of different actions using the already developed interactive videodisc, *Missing the Obvious.* This disc was quite useful because experienced teachers helped develop it and performed in some of the classroom scenes (The IVIS Project, 1989).

With the advent of programs like HyperCard new possibilities exist for the teacher development of interactive curriculum materials. Techniques related to modification of methods and materials for pupils with special needs, and strategies related to the whole language approaches for the teaching of reading all lend themselves to teacher designed interactive technologies. Working as an interdisciplinary team, teachers can help each other learn design skills which will allow them to create effective instructional programs across a variety of subject areas.

## An Example: Teachers Collaborate in the Creation of a Disc about Medieval Times

One of the least understood periods of history is that of medieval times. By bringing together middle and high school faculty from various social sciences (economics, sociology, history, geography, political science) and the fine arts (literature, art, music), this medieval disc incorporated a variety of subjects. The intent was to help teachers make connections between subjects in a way that illustrated the totality of knowledge.

For example, a series of slides showing works of art from medieval times are more powerful when combined with sequences of music and excerpts from literature. When social scientists add excerpts from primary source materials and video simulations, perspectives on family and community life in various medieval villages come alive. Various sorting options permitted learners to organize data by topic or date — allowing the final product to reflect elements that the learner decided were the most important.

Through creating objectives, content chunks, flowcharts, and storyboards, teachers gained design skills useful in planning further programs. To accomplish these design tasks, the administrative structure of the school had to support interdependent collaboration through organizational structures that allowed design team members from different subject matter areas to work together (Bright, Carlson, Grossman, & Shannon, 1985). Collaboration with instructional technology and teachers in other disciplines does take time. If teachers are to be involved on a weekly basis then they need to be supported by administrators with released time.

## A Model for the Future

Teachers can work as members of professional inter-active media design teams or design less complex programs with small groups of colleagues. With a little instruction they can use new HyperCard type programs to specially tailor commercially available material. The instructional design skills which teachers gain from working on the structure of interactive media can contribute to improved general planning skills for other phases of instruction (Carlson, 1989). Thus, the process could be used as a faculty development effort to improve teaching. An additional benefit is that interactive media endeavors that involve teachers, in the early stages, will more closely match the needs of practitioners.

The possibilities for involvement of either pupils or teachers in the interactive media design process is a potential that is just beginning to be tapped. The media itself is growing in a number of directions and taking on descriptive names like "hypermedia," "hypertext," "fluid media," and "multimedia." The labels are evolving, but they all describe the connection of different media across a whole range of applications and markets. Evidence is now emerging that coupling these emerging technologies with cooperative learning models has much to offer students and teachers.

Developing a set of clear cut quantitative rules for analyzing rapidly evolving interactive media will have trouble accounting for the interest generated in users. The power of the medium to summon the full range of human communication outpaces any effort to evaluate all of its outcomes. Therefore it is important to preserve options.

For new media to be fully successful requires new cooperative attitudes, different instructional assumptions, innovative design skills, and a willingness to change. At a recent poetry reading Elizabeth Bishop expressed this need for such connectedness when facing new worlds:

> *The year's doors open like those of language to the unknown. Last night you told me we shall have to think up signs, sketch a landscape, fabricate a plan on the double page of day and paper. Tomorrow, we shall have to invent once more the reality of this world.*

## References

Abrams, A. (1986). *Effectiveness of Interactive Video in Teaching Basic Photography Skills*. Las Vegas, Nevada: Association for Educational Communications and Technology. (ERIC Document Reproduction Service No. ED 267 754.)

Adams, D. & Hamm, M. (1987). *Electronic Learning*. Springfield, IL: Charles Thomas.

Bayard-White, C. (1986). *An Introduction to Interactive Video*. London, England: Council for Educational Technology for the National Interactive Video Centre.

Bossert, S. (1988). Cooperative activities in the classroom. In *Review of Research in Education.* Washington, D.C.: American Educational Research Association, 15, 238-250.

Bossert, S., Barnett, B., & Filby, N. (1984). Grouping and instructional organization. In P. Peterson, L. C. Wilkinson, & M. Hallinan (Eds.), *The Social Context of Instruction: Group Organization and Group Processes.* New York: Academic Press.

Brandt, R. (1987). On cooperation in schools: A conversation with David Johnson and Roger Johnson. *Educational Leadership,* 45, 14-19.

Bright, L., Carlson, H., Grossman, E. & Shannon, T. (1985). Technology in Preparing Teachers for an Information Age. Paper presented at the thirty-second world assembly of the International Council on Education for Teaching. Vancouver, British Columbia.

Browning, P. (1986). Interactive video in the special classroom: A pilot study. *Computing Teacher,* 13 , 36-38.

Bruner, J. S. (1964). The course of cognitive growth. *American Psychologist,* 19, 1-15.

Carkhuff, R. (1985). *The Art of Helping: Trainer's Guide.* Amherst, Massachusetts: Human Resource Development Press.

Carlson, H. (1989). Effectiveness of interactive videodisc instructional programs in elementary teacher education (Submitted for publication).

Carlson, H., Ellison, D., & Dietrich, J. (1988). *Servicing Low Achieving Pupils and Pupils with Learning Disabilities: A Comparison of Two Approaches.* Duluth, Minnesota:University of Minnesota, Duluth and the Duluth Public Schools. (ERIC Document Reproduction Service No. ED 283 341.)

Carlson, H. & Falk, D. (1986). *Learner Analysis for Interactive Videodisc Instructional Design: Understanding Groups Videodisc Series.* Duluth, Minnesota: Center for the Advancement of Learning Technologies Interactive Videodisc Research Group, Occasional Paper 86-1.

Carlson, H. & Falk, D. (1987). *Instructor Manual for Understanding Groups in Education and Human Services.* Duluth, Minnesota: Center for the Advancement of Learning Technologies Interactive Videodisc Research Group, Occasional Paper 87-2.

Carlson, H. & Falk, D. (1987). *Student Handbook for Understanding Groups in Education and Human Services.* Duluth, Minnesota: Center for the Advancement of Learning Technologies Interactive Videodisc Research Group, Occasional Paper 87-1.

Carlson, H. & Nierengarten, M. (in press). Subject matter experts: A key to designing interactive videodiscs. *Educational Technology.*

Clark, R. E. (1982). Antagonism between achievement and

enjoyment in ATI studies. *Educational Psychologist,* 17, 92-101.

Cohen, E. (1986). Talking and working together: Status, interaction and learning. In P. Peterson, L. C. Wilkinson, & M. Hallinan (Eds.) *The Social Context of Instruction: Group Organization and Group Processes.* New York: Academic Press.

*Foxfire* (1985). Fabun Gap, Georgia: Foxfire Fund.

Homer, A. (1989). Let your fingers do the walking. *Interactive Video in Education Update,* 2:1, 3.

*The IVIS Project* (1989). London, England: National Interactive Video Centre.

Johnson, D. & Johnson, R. (1985). Classroom conflict: Controversy versus debate in learning groups. *American Educational Research Journal,* 22, 237-256.

Kosselyn, S. M. (1981). The medium and the message in mental imagery. *Psychological Review,* 88, 46-66.

Pieper, W. J. (1985). *Interactive Graphics Simulator: Design, Development and Effectiveness Cost Evaluation.* (Report No. AFHRL-TR-84-38.) Denver, Colorado: Essex Corporation. (ERIC Document Reproduction Service No. ED 253 211.)

Salomon, G. (1979). *Interaction of Media, Cognition, and Learning.* San Francisco, California: Jossey-Bass.

Salomon, G. (1974). Internalization of filmic schematic

operations with learners' aptitudes. *Journal of Educational Psychology,* 66, 499-511.

Salomon, G. & Clark, R. E. (1977). Reexamining the methodology of media and technology in education. *Review of Educational Research,* 47 (1), 9-12.

Seal-Warner, C. (1988, Spring). Interactive videosystems: Their promise and educational potential. *Teacher's College Record,* 89(3), 373-383.

Sheingold, K., Kane, J. H., & Endreweit, M. E. (1983). Microcomputer use in schools: Developing a research agenda. *Harvard Educational Review,* 58 (4), 412-432.

Sustik, J. M. (1981). An interactive videodisc project in art history. *Performance and Instruction,* 20 (9), 10-13.

Thorkildsen, R., Allard, K. & Reid, B. (1983). The interactive videodisc for special education project: Providing CAI for the mentally retarded. *The Computing Teacher,* 10 (8), 73-76.

Videodisc Research Group (1986). *Understanding Groups.* Minneapolis, Minnesota: University Media Resources Center.

Videodisc Research Group (1987). *Understanding Cultural Diversity: A Case Study from Southeast Asia.* Minneapolis, Minnesota: University Media Resources Center.

Videodisc Research Group (1988). *Problem Solving in*

*Education and Human Service Professions.* Minneapolis, Minnesota: University Media Resources Center.

Videodisc Research Group (1989). *Developing Effective Communication Skills.* Minneapolis, Minnesota: University Media Resources Center.

Webb, N. (1985). Student Interaction and Learning in Small Groups: A Research Summary. In R. Slavin, S. Sharan, S. Kagan, R. Hertz-Lazarowitz, C. Webb & R. Schmuck (Eds.), *Learning to Cooperate, Cooperating to Learn.* New York: Plenum Press.

Wright, T. (1988, September/October). Interactive video tape systems: A round-up of current products and applications. *Interactive Update,* 1(7), 25-7.

Yager, S., Johnson, R., Johnson, D. & Snider, B. (1986). The impact of group processing on the achievement in cooperative learning groups. *The Journal of Social Psychology,* 126, 389-397.

# 5

## EDUCATIONAL RENEWAL
## Avenues of Communication
## and Collaboration

Hypermedia and cooperative learning can help our ailing educational structures improve and prepare for the 21st century.  But, as Einstein said, *"God is in the details."*

Some educational fundamentalists view learning as an individual act where tight control and better test scores are the keys to success.  Is simply doing more of what we are doing now a little like the proverbial rearrangement of chairs on the Titanic?  Many of those involved with education agree that it is.  There is also general agreement that it will take new approaches to keep the ship afloat.

## Collective Responsibility
## and New Learning Tools

Corporate success in the late twentieth century is coming to be equated with a change in the old "general staff" mentality — seeking out ways to give workers a sense of collective responsibility.  Unions, in turn, are voting for cooperation and solving problems informally, rather than through grievance procedures. Like European and Japanese competitors, American companies are shedding top-down management styles for participatory decision-making and work teams. As our international competition has realized early on, this also requires a constant updating of the workforce. Many of the most successful on-the-job training models combine learning to work in groups and skill training through interactive media — helping workers learn and make connections between concepts in their own way.

Economists tell us that about half of any nation's increase in productivity comes from the knowledge and skill growth of its population. Corporate America is coming to agree. They realize that at the end of World War II our workforce was at the top, in terms of educational levels, and now it's struggling to catch up. A recent report by the American Society for Training and Development calls for increased support for the public schools and for more on-the-job training. It goes on to support the idea that the quality of any workforce depends on the educational level of its population.

Enlightened companies combine on-site learning centers with varying levels of collective responsibility. They have also found that productivity improves when people consider themselves part of the decision-making process, have a chance to make changes, and are encouraged to improve the system. And it's not just management. The United Automobile Workers Union, for example, has opted for what they call a "jointness" team concept that gives workers more participation in decision-making. This approach also gives workers the chance to rotate jobs and learn new skills.

It is now generally agreed that the possession of a flourishing educational and technological base is fundamental to national culture and productivity. The concern is real. From economists to legislators we hear the clarion call for meaningful education change. Beyond generalities, however, there are few suggestions as to what should be changed — or how. School programs may get some attention, but changing the technological vehicles of instruction — or the overall school or classroom structure — takes a great deal of sustained energy and commitment.

Change comes more slowly to educational institutions than it does to industry. Schools still do not provide for cooperative teacher planning or for cooperative practices to take place in the classroom. Worse yet, some school districts have not even picked up on the notion that treating people with dignity — and enhancing their feeling of self worth—can lead to greater productivity.

The initial phase of this country's decade long effort at changing schools revealed a complicated pattern of unmotivated learners, substandard teacher training, dull curriculum materials, outdated technology, and little relationship to the workplace. The mass media is, on occasion, even more critical, suggesting that national prosperity is fading in a wash of individual incompetence and outdated learning tools. The result of many of these early efforts at school reform were competency tests and teacher-proof materials — reinforcing chalk, talk, textbooks and the bureaucratic structure of school organization.

The second wave of school reform is more promising. It includes the encouragement of new instructional delivery systems and giving teachers a collaborative voice in professional decision making. But as H.G. Wells noted in a similar context, *this is the beginning of a beginning.* We are now entering a fulcrum period for schools — with visually-intensive technology, a shared knowledge base, and cooperative organizational structures sharing center stage.

As boundaries between media dissolve, we see a fusing of information technologies into "hypermedia." The process is leading to new learning tools which incorporate computer control, sounds, and moving images. Of course, predicting the future of technology and schooling is a little like foreseeing a 747 while watching the Wright brothers.

Many see hypermedia and cooperative learning as on the cutting edge of the educational future. Pessimists view one as a trendy toy and the other as hurting rugged individualism. Here we argue that when powerful technological tools are coupled with proven collaborative structures the learning process can be transformed.

### Developing Partnerships

Encouraging higher levels of collective responsibility — and peer support for academic achievement — represents the essence of cooperative learning. Schools have traditionally viewed collaboration as cheating. It isn't. The research strongly supports collaboration and the instructional use of team goals — with students sharing materials, encouraging each other and really caring how well others in the group are doing. The elements of goal, task, and reward interdependence are quite different than physical proximity or having the fast students help the slow ones when they are finished. Developing a high level of interpersonal and small group skills means going beyond individual assignments at the same table. It means cooperation on a grand scale, with students reaching personal goals by helping everyone else in the group reach *their* goal. Under these conditions groups seek outcomes beneficial to all.

Educators can't help but notice that when exemplary companies couple interactive learning tools with collaborative organizational structures the result is greater productivity. When the appropriate instructional design methodology connects to interactive technology — and a shared vision — researchers have found positive changes in individual attitude and enhanced organizational effectiveness. This would seem to be enough to make both the grouping and the technological possibilities worthy of serious consideration in our efforts to improve the national educational infrastructure.

As we enter the last decade of the twentieth century work is becoming ever more technically complex, ambiguous and group oriented. There is a glut of rapidly evolving information to be managed at all levels, and companies do not have the luxury of time when it comes to training. The educational sector needs to be in sync with this new interdependent reality as it leads the way in providing some kind of intellectual connection between the past, present, and future.

Developing a team spirit is just as important in the classroom as it is in any organizational setting. But it takes more than simply getting people to work together in groups and structuring a set of relationships to accomplish team goals. The level of productivity depends on the development of interpersonal skills, positive interdependence, technical competencies, technological enhancement, and the potential for life-long learning.

Interactive media can amplify the pooling of resources and ideas, allowing students to reach further than they would dare on their own. In the process hypermedia can help the teacher by being a non-human information provider, allowing the teacher to concentrate on being a facilitator, mentor, and coach. When individual accountability is coupled with hypermedia technology, effective instructional methods, and cooperative learning, the quality of intellectual life in the classroom is bound to change for the better.

### Letting Go of Mindsets

Certain organizational structures and teaching tools may break new ground, but the idea that they are without antecedents is an illusion. Learning to cooperate and cooperating to learn occupies a treasured place in the history of American schooling — from colonial times to the one room country schoolhouse. High levels of interpersonal competition is a relatively new phenomenon. Hypermedia also has its antecedents. Scholars have long had a slow version of hypertext — using a card catalog and educated hunches to sort through nonsequential information, synthesize diverse points of knowledge and discuss implications.

Hardware-intensive training programs have a more recent but not wholly successful track record in the military and in industry. Some of the early machine-based training experiences were said to replace Valium and Novocaine as the numbing drug of choice. Neither the technology nor the programming was there to provide motivating materials. Since the expectations were so high, the first computer drill and practice (CAI) programs were even more disappointing. They had two solitary cycles:

*tell & ask* and *ask & tell*. Worse yet, they either pitted person against person, or individual against machine.

New technology programming and interpersonal interaction changes the scene. Instead of competitively learning alone some of the most recent interactive media take a team approach — from training tank crews to airline pilots. All of this is more than the technological equivalent of moving from an icebox to a refrigerator. Hypermedia is adding a new algorithm to the training equation.

## A Never-ending Cycle of Learning

Today technology and the knowledge needed in school and on the job are changing at an ever accelerating rate. Historians tell us that today's newspaper contains more information than a person in the sixteenth century would have to deal with in a lifetime. Academic concepts, tools, equipment, and products that are new and novel today may be obsolete in five years. Some of the products that will be in daily use in ten years have yet to be invented. With this incredible growth comes a never-ending need to train and retrain everybody. Formal schooling is never complete, at best it's a solid introduction that can be built on. Graduation is now simply the completion of one more stage of preparation for future learning.

As we move towards a technologically-intensive society, schools, government and industry are faced with an accelerating requirement for continual skill improvement. Human teachers and trainers simply can't handle the volume of learning that's required. How can we best retool our human assets? Successful public sector agencies and private companies are relying more and more on interactive media courses to teach higher level skills and shared responsibility to workers. The equipment being tested ranges from Brown University's multi million dollar "Intermedia" project to Apple Computer's Macintosh/HyperCard, a low budget alternative.

Hypermedia is helping dissolve the boundaries between information technologies. This fusion of computers, television, and other technologies has shown that it can:

* Provide a high level of clarity and transference.

* Prepare personnel to leave the course ready to perform the job task.

* Minimize the risk to operators and complex equipment.

* Allow for the teaching of more information in less time.

* Help personnel see across job classifications to the big picture without being enslaved by someone else's time and method of presentation.

## Interactive Media and Reconceptualizing Education

*The information age is a condition of technological change, group oriented decision making, and constant uncertainty, At the very time the world is in a state of permanent **white water** the schools are providing **calm-water** skills.*
                                        - Patricia McLagan

From the popular press to the most serious journals the realization has finally sunk in that the key to our competitiveness as a nation — and our soul as a country — is the education of our people. Lessons that incorporate collaborative learning principles and interaction with the most advanced technological vehicles of instruction may seem out of place amidst the chalk dust. Neither the co-operation nor the technology is that far beyond the educational horizon, and both closely model the workplace of the future.

If young people are going to be adequately prepared for the world of tomorrow then the schools must move beyond the precedents and procedures of a fading industrial society. Besides group cooperation and human judgment new information age structures require a continuous process of learning that makes use of available technological vehicles. Education, government, labor, and industrial organizations must now work together to coordinate life-long learning structures.

Developing a collaboration is a creative process of deciding how to apply influence, when to introduce a new idea, and balancing criticism with empathy. When teachers get the idea that it's possible to be major players in the educational renewal process, change — in that most reluctant of partners (schools) — will take place.

The evidence strongly suggests that combining cooperative learning and interactive information technologies can be effective in rapidly achieving training outcomes across institutional barriers. Together they can provide a much needed framework in the drive to develop a "seamless partnership" between new organizational models, the schools, the workplace, technology and the future.

Americans have usually done well when confronted by

situations in which technology rapidly remakes global realities. Using hypermedia to electronically walk from one medium to another fits right in. Like books, there are good and bad models. If the animation, graphics, sound, moving images, printed text, and instructional design are of high quality, "learners" of any age can browse through all kinds of information and interact with it in a way that builds on  higher order thinking skills. New ways of mixing print and imagery also allow students to discover new connections to knowledge.  Bringing multimedia elements together through thought-like linkages between imagery and text is as much a new state of mind as it is a new technological application.

## Cooperative Learning and Educational Access

As far as schooling is concerned, the cooperative learning movement has a growing set of research tested approaches for making group learning more productive. And, with tracking being declared discriminatory by organizations as diverse as the Rand Corporation and the N.E.A., there are few alternatives on the horizon. Currently there is a high level of general interest in improving the public schools and at least making a dent in the growing underclass. While the educational establishment may have cold feet, the American public's are blistering hot.

Separating "fast" and "slow" learners dates back to the 1830s. As educators mint the cliches they sweat to achieve some — and avoid others. Do tracking systems allow teachers to "tailor studies to students' varying abilities" or do "children do better when they are in classes with children who do better?" The Educational Testing Service suggests the latter. E.T.S. also notes that the majority of minority students are placed in lower tracks —

without their agreement. This hardening of the categories starts as early as when students are placed in reading groups on the basis of some subjective definition of "ability" — the "bluebirds," "blackbirds," and the "gorillas." By the time they get to junior high school their label might as well be carved in stone.

It has taken some time, but solid information pointing to the defects of tracking is no longer eluding us. There is a growing consensus that tracking is a subtle form of racial discrimination that has long been misused. As the evidence accumulates more and more educators are coming to believe that there is something wrong with putting children in classes that are, at best, remedial. It gives them a message that they can't make it. And whatever talent that child may have had is lost. Researchers suggest that low-track children need high-track children as role models (Maeroff, 1988).

Overcoming these obstacles to knowledge building will take more than apocalyptic angst. In *Faust*, Goethe makes the observation that deliberate design, changes in social attitudes, and *pure luck* are connected in the educational and technological products of the human mind. Social commitment and chance have a larger role to play in educational reform than is generally recognized.

In our search for the school of tomorrow it is important to consider teacher training, school organization, curriculum design, technological possibilities, a student's socioeconomic status and the limitations of deliberate design. There is an educational and political energy in the air that could result in significant change. From newly tested approaches like cooperative learning in the classroom to technological empowerment with hypermedia, fresh ideas are in the air.

The transformations of the late twentieth century are having an accelerating effect on education. We are at a major divide in our accelerating technological, social, economic, and educational history. From converging technologies to new organizational approaches, ideas are developing that can energize the curriculum. But will today's invigorating gales last long enough to allow the many small beginnings of educational change to grow and spread?

## The Knowledge Building
## Potential of Technology

Educational systems do not exist in some kind of pristine isolation. To educate children in the late twentieth century requires going beyond what has traditionally been considered to be the domain of educators. Broader technological and social influences are bound to have an effect on learning. Hypermedia and cooperative learning are two bright possibilities. In other institutions they have proven capable of promoting thoughtfulness and group investigation. Using the best of both could create a powerful synergy that is more meaningful than any of the elements taken alone.

Major literacy goals have to be more than listing the common ideas that all literate persons should share — *a la* E. D. Hirsch and *Cultural Literacy*. This means making connections between subjects and developing a critical mind to search for knowledge throughout life. We are in the process of shifting what it means to be literate from a memory base of knowledge acquisition to knowing how to find and use channels of information. Knowing how to learn is more important than the facts accumulated.

Interactive technologies are no longer in the deep dark dungeons of computer companies and the major research universities. New technological tools can provide us with random access to information through multiple senses. Along with team efforts they can help put immediacy, color, and bite into learning. If you have an Apple Macintosh you have probably used *HyperCard* or *Supercard* or *Course of Action*. If you have an IBM you may have used *Guide* or *KnowledgePro*. All five are hypertext products that have already gained favor with computer users. Many of us are even connecting videodisc players and CD-ROM units to our PCs and using prerecorded optical discs. The next step will probably be adding erasable CDs to this mix.

Today's school equipment has dozens of pieces of computer software that claim to incorporate some hypermedia features. New classroom organizational methods — along with advancing methods for mixing media — will make connections between points of knowledge in a fundamentally different way.

## Children Helping Children

### Guidelines for Structuring Groups
### Using Hypermedia Resources

Our society is in the process of shifting its focus away from a memory-based system of individual evaluation to evaluating work groups on their ability to find and connect information. Classroom practice suggests that one good way to structure collaborative investigations with technology is when:

1. Groups of about six students identify subtopics for two students to jointly explore (in a manner that adds to the overall group goal).

2. Pairs of students make and carry out plans for gathering and exchanging information.

3. After analyzing the information that is found—as a partnership and a small group—decisions can be made about how the information can be combined into a single whole group product. (It is important for everyone to note how much *individual students* learn from the cooperative experience.)

4. The group decides how to present it to the whole class—demonstrations, exhibitions, experiments, creative dramatics, readers theater, or any other method that might actively involve the whole class.

5. Students evaluate themselves, their group, and the rest of the class.

Our preliminary research suggests that when this type of collaborative investigation is combined with *HyperCard* constructed hypertext there is a positive effect on reading comprehension, motivation, research skills, and the quality of group work produced. Adding the videodisc dimension seems to pull in a wider range of learning styles. Collaboratively using hypermedia may also put students ahead in hard to measure intangibles such as social skills — relative to those receiving whole class instruction. But we did not find a significant difference (as compared to pupils receiving one-on-one tutoring) on the standardized achievement tests administered to individuals (Adams and Hamm, 1989).

Hypermedia can help connect disciplines and free students from someone else's preferred mode of presentation. This means that the expert or "writer" is no longer the ultimate authority on *how* the information is presented. The learner can still choose to follow the author's path through the information, it's just no longer the only route. The individual or small group decision making inherent in the hypermedia process can incite the imagination of students by helping learners make critical and creative associations. This is not an insignificant accomplishment, for associations between ideas — and the fluidity of such associations — has long been viewed as central to the creative process.

If the best of technology and scholarship could be brought together to define and teach, it just might be possible to boost our educational *and* societal future. Learning how to learn and learning to work with others, particularly others who share similar concerns, is a key to discovering multiple solutions to new knowledge. Americans have always loved team sports, now we have to learn how to carry this concept into the classroom, the boardroom, and the workplace. Technology can add power and help us turn up the volume.

## Interactive Media, Collaboration
## and Knowledge Grids

For those interested in education and communication, understanding new media networking technology is important. Satellite technology, computer networks, and hypermedia are already changing the way we communicate and learn. The convergence of video, computers, networking and publishing technology will open a whole new range of information options and presentation formats. Technologically advancing media will transform the human ability to learn, express and communicate. In the future it will be crucial as students use the technology to explore key concepts, solve problems and grasp a new world of ideas.

We are living in a time when human communication is swinging from the end of one era to the beginning of another. Even the local delicatessen has a FAX machine for taking orders. Almost unnoticed nearly a million Americans use either *CompuServe*, *The Source*, or *Dow Jones* computer networks. Educational researchers are starting to use more specialized networks like *TechNet* (AECT), *SpecialNet,* and *DeafNet.*

When many telecommunications networks began, in the early 1980s, print (on the video display terminal) was the primary medium. Now, all of the major participants in the computer and telecommunication industry are in the process of reframing how we view information by including graphics and moving video. Schools are just beginning to recognize the possibilities that stem from cross linking information from distant sources. It is time to identify the resources and supports that can help classroom teachers use networking  effectively.

As computer accessed databases become more visually intensive they quietly start to change the way individuals access world knowledge — *and* the way the world has access to them. The dark side of this access is that government agencies, credit bureaus, and the press have become adept at covertly tapping these vast networks to gather, examine, and cross-reference vast amounts of personal information about individuals. As we move towards a new communications technology there is a need to reexamine the balance between the public good and personal privacy. The basic questions of how to fuse basic democratic rights with a wide range of rapidly advancing technologies has yet to be asked—let alone answered.

Today's networks have problems that go beyond snooping. We need more sources of information, more moving visuals, and networking programs that are easy for an amateur to just pick up and use. Copyrights were designed to help get ideas around by supporting creative efforts. If interpreted too strictly the "good stuff" might not get on the grid. It's very important to get the best information on future networks — otherwise we will have great roads with little of consequence to travel around on them. And without quality information, interactive technology will be underutilized.

Teaching students how to use new communications technology is becoming more and more like teaching them to *think* — with a combination of conscious control and intuition. Learners need to take from — and add to — the knowledgebase that's out there. Hypermedia, simulation, artificial intelligence and telecommunications are core technologies that will influence learning, our lives, and our deepest assumptions. In the process learning will become more like doing personally interesting research with teammates, than like traditional learning where knowledge is poured into an isolated recipient. If the constraints are loosened on technology's potential impact, future collaborators will range from humans across the state to machines on  other planets.

## Personalized Learning of the Future

For many educators acquiring the knowledge needed to teach will require a subtle, but important, shift in beliefs.  To make information "hyper," for example, requires software that can help the user spontaneously gather and view pieces of visual, print, or sound information in an associative fashion. This means less teacher control over a process that is more active, relatively noisy, and quite different from learning through a linear flow of print.  As new media technologies incorporate knowledge about thinking, learning, and problem solving into their approach these communications devices will vastly  increase in power.

Rather than forcing our thoughts to move around as a preplanned program does, multimedia devices of the future will allow learners to move around concepts in a manner that best fits in with their thinking pattern.  Such information can be transmitted and received anywhere—allowing users to get outside themselves and join others to explore unknown intellectual landscapes.  Hypermedia telecommunications programs will allow users to team up, create a window on  their computer screen and selectively hop down a variety of distant database alleys.

Within a few years we will have computer-controlled programs that gather information much as a good research assistant would—cutting through the clutter to give you what you need. Like good science and good art, hypermedia can make connections between things that might not seem related— accelerating, amplifying, and personalizing the knowledge acquisition process. Future programs will be able to decide, when they come across something unexpected, whether or not it should be passed along to the human user. Artificially intelligent interactive media will attend to learning style preferences and comb databases and the network television to assemble a net of images and words that reflect a viewer's needs. In the near future these computer-controlled devices can be told what kind of information to look for, what kind to ignore, and what mix of visual/print information to bring back to the viewer.

As connectivity software and media hardware merge and become more refined the stage will be set for powerful ingredients of future learning; artificially intelligent peers and tutors from around the world. Better links to databases will make many libraries, information utilities, databases and television broadcasts available in seconds. This kind of travel on knowledge grids requires students to act more like *researchers* than traditional *learners.*

New interactive media and knowledge grids will give students fresh, fast, free-associative images that are as much like an action painting that you can feel as they are like printed text that you can intellectually comprehend. A multiplicity of visually linked representations can provide a dynamic for learning that goes beyond what is possible with static media such as books and blackboards. Increasingly hypermedia devices can fashion subject matter in a unique manner. For example, interactive media simulations can retrieve stored images of notable scientists (doing experiments), and artists (explaining various creations). When simulation is added to this technological soup, students can enter an electronic environment, experiment with a pioneer researcher, develop a structure for asking the right questions, and graphically see the consequences of their decision making. The goal of these programs is not only to convey the way in which these human artists or scientists think and work, but let students electronically collaborate with these experts. The result can be a total immersion in the creative situation under study.

Like other important technological applications, electronically accessed networks of knowledge will take time to *fully* develop. It will be a long time before it will be safe to assume that most of the information we need is even in the database. All of it may never be there. The changes brought by the automobile, for example, took some forty or fifty years to unfold. Technological development time is now more compressed, but it still takes time. As these knowledge grids develop it will be possible to visually transport the best teacher and learning activities from one site to hundreds (simultaneously). As cooperative learning fuses with new learning networks students will be challenged to think and collaboratively explore with thoughtfulness and imagination. By the 21st century electronic knowledge grids will connect the individual to the world.

### Expanding Educational Resources

We are heading toward individualized learning-research technology that provides access to the world of ideas based on our terms. Cooperative learning groups can help. Groups can provide support and give assistance.

Students may want ready made answers, but in the final analysis, individuals must be held accountable for providing enough of their own energy to cut through *the fatigue of finding things out for themselves.*

Access to distant teachers, peers, library resources, and video databases will change the way that groups are formed and the way that information is accessed and transmitted. It will also change traditional definitions of what it means to be a "literate" person. Computer-controlled networks hold immense potential for a real revolution in learning through electronic collaboration and easy access to the latest information. The ideal of keeping our knowledge up-to-date is coming within our grasp as technology gives us access to the most recent information, learning strategies and machine associates.

We are now in the process of putting together the technological elements needed to give us interactive access to a personalized set of learning experiences. New media are being created that will transform human learning, expression, and communication. We must spend at least as much time developing a modern philosophy of teaching and learning. Understanding the characteristics of effective instruction is an essential piece of future literacy puzzles. We can also give teachers and students intellectual and technological tools to search the range of choices and select new solutions.

Much of the important information in the world is already is the process of being stored electronically. The challenge is to make sure that all of this information can be democratically accessed *in* the right place *at* the right time. While learning to use what's available today, we need to start building the infrastructure and the traffic control patterns for the personalized knowledge highways of the future. Education and technology can serve as a "traffic cop," helping us avoid the electronic equivalent of junk mail. Avoiding these informational traffic jams is a high priority because inundating people with facts diminishes knowledge. Education and technology can help us quickly sort through what we need to know, assist in preventing mental gridlock, and show us the limitations of knowledge.

Integration of basic skills, habits of the mind, wisdom, and cooperative traits of character will be affected —one way or another—by the communications technology already on the horizon. Like de Tocqueville, we might just as well be optimistic and believe *that at certain intervals great reforms arise, and new ideas, supported by social forces and new technologies, suddenly change the face of the world for the better.*

## References

Adams, D. & Hamm, M. (1987). *Electronic Learning.* Springfield, IL: Charles Thomas  Publisher.

Adams, D. & Hamm, M. (1989). *Media  and Literacy.* Springfield, IL: Charles Thomas Publisher.

Collins, B. (1988). *Computers, Curriculum, and Whole Class Instruction: Issues and Ideas.* Belmont, CA: Wadsworth Publishing.

Gibson, W. (1987). *Count Zero.* New York: Ace Publishing.

Hall, G. & Hord, S. (1987). *Change in Schools: Facilitating the Process.* Albany, NY: State University of New York Press.

Hall, N.(1987). *The Emergence of Literacy.* Portsmouth, NH: Heinemann.

Hills, D. (1985). *The Connection Machine.* Cambridge: MIT Press.

Hogan, J.(1987). *Minds, Machines and Evolution.* New York: Bantam/Spectra.

Kobayashi, K.(1986). *Computers and Communications.* Cambridge: MIT Press.

Lawler, R.(1985). *Computer Experience and Cognitive Development: A Child's Learning in a Computer Culture.* Chichester, England: Horwood.

Maeroff, G. (1988). Withered hopes, stillborn dreams: The dismal panorama of urban schools. *Phi Delta Kappan,* May 1988, 633-8.

Stecher, B. (1987). *Effective Strategies for Computer In-service Training.* Pasadena: Educational Testing Service.

Useem, E. (1986). *Low Tech Education in a High Tech World.* New York: The Free Press.

Van Enckevort, G. (Ed.) (1986). *Distance, Higher Education and the Adult Learner.* Heerlen, The Netherlands: Open Universiteit.

## Online Networks for Educators

*CompuServe,* P.O. Box 20212, Columbus, OH 43220.

*Dialog Classroom Instruction Program,* Administration, 1901 No. Moore Street, Suite 500, Arlington, VA 22209.

*Einstein Consumer Service,* Educational Broadcasting Corporation, Learning Link, 356 W. 58th St., New York, NY 10019.

*Electronic Networking Association* (ENA), 2744 Washington Street, Allentown, PA 18104.

*FrEdMail* (Free Education Mail), 4201 Allen School Road, Bonita, CA 92002.

*Interactive Communication Simulations* (ICS), University of Michigan, School of Education, Ann Arbor, MI 48109.

*Iris,* MECC, 3490 Lexington Avenue North, St. Paul, MN 55126.

*National Geographic Kids Network,* National Geographic, Washington, D.C. 20036.

*The Online Journal of Distance Communication,* University of Alaska, 11120 Glacier Highway, Juneau, AL 99801.

*Pals Across the World,* 4974 SW Galen, Lake Oswego, OR 97035.

*The Source,* 1616 Anderson Rd., McLean, VA  22101.

*W/Pug*, Box 144, Malverne, NY 11565.

# APPENDIX

## Cooperative Learning Activities
## with Traditional Audio-Visual Resources

The central focus of this book is on cooperative learning and the relative newcomers to educational technology — television, computers, interactive videodiscs, hypermedia and telecommunications. But for many of today's classroom instructional media needs, more traditional audio-visual resources still have a role to play. Film projectors, filmstrips, still cameras, audio tape, record players, and overhead projectors *can* help in the creation of a cooperative learning environment. Here we have outlined a selection of collaborative methods involving this generation of technological aids.

### Film

The skills students need for viewing films are similar to those needed for viewing television or reading a book. Of course each medium has different attributes. But they all require adaptation and collaborative reinforcement of the skills learned to insure growth toward sophisticated use. Using film in the classroom is more than simply turning on the projector. Teachers need methods to connect this medium to the curriculum.

*Before viewing* activities can: focus attention, provide motivation, expand subject knowledge, increase comprehension, and facilitate cooperative learning strategies. The possibilities include:

* Making predictions based on the title or the first few minutes of the film.

* The introduction of new vocabulary and the small group development of a prediction outline or map.

* A group discussion of major concepts and visual clues.

There are a number of ways that the teacher can increase student learning *during film viewing:*

* Students can be encouraged to use self monitoring techniques learned in cooperative groups.

* Place the projector on still mode and use the picture for predicting ahead or for discussion.

* A short film can be shown twice. The viewing assignments can be different for the second viewing. For example, the sound can be turned off and students can take turns doing the narration.

* Stop the film at a certain point and use a VCR to show a contrast or comparison. This way different ideas, happenings, cultures, or theatrical interpretations can be examined. For example, two very different treatments of the same scene from a Shakespearian play could be compared.

* Stop the projector or VCR and ask some higher level questions like "How would you feel if..."

*After viewing* activities can help students make the connection between new knowledge, personal experience and previously learned concepts. After viewing students can work in cooperative groups:

* Each individual can share at least one new idea learned.

* Students reach a group consensus on the main ideas.

* Groups construct a summary outline or story map.

* Teams come up with either an oral or written group answer to *who, what, where, when, how, and so what.*

The teacher would not use all of these techniques at the same time, but a mixture based on learning objectives and student interest.

**Photographic Media**

Filmstrips, slides, photographic prints and photo-copied images can assist in teaching content, aesthetic sensitivity, and psychomotor skills (Eastman Kodak, 1979). Whether they are being used in large or small groups, filmstrip and slide projectors are easy to stop for questions and answers. The teacher or group member running the projector can adjust the pace to accommodate individual interest and need.

Small cooperative learning groups can use pictures to arrange visual sequences or as a springboard for exploration and discovery. Curriculum units can use pictures to engage children in study across a wide range of subjects. In the *Reading Pictures* kit, for example, children working together learn how pictures from award winning children's books were created and why  they  are suited for the story being illustrated.  This way elementary school students learn how printed text and images work together to produce meaning.  Critical thinking, visual literacy, reading, writing, oral language and collaborative learning skills stem from such a "whole language" unit.

Photography can be studied as a subject itself or it can serve as a vehicle for teaching the usual subjects in the curriculum.  When teaching subject matter this medium can serve as a primary information source or an instructional aid.  Photographs can also assist in introducing or following up a unit.

*A Cooperative Group Photography Activity*

We tested a collaborative photo technique that was borrowed from David Hockney, the artist.  He refers to this collage technique as a "joiner" and  describes how even five pictures of part of someone standing still will, when placed together, cause the eye to linger five times as long as a single picture.

*Procedure:*

Divide the students into pairs and  have them take turns photographing each other doing something— descending a staircase, for example.  The pictures are taken in rapid succession and taken in for development.  The students are also asked to bring in photocopies of pictures from home; a few magazine pictures and words can also be added.  The next step, after the pictures are developed, is for each small group to come up with a collage by gluing slightly overlapping images onto a large piece of colored tag board. The goal of this activity is to help build critical thinking and visual literacy skills — as students work together to compare, categorize and evaluate. The finished product can then be displayed on bulletin boards around the school.

### Using Photographic Media to Explain a Field Trip

Working in pairs, on a field trip, students can use one camera and photograph what they see as important. A small cooperative group can then pool their photos to develop a presentation plan for slides—or a mural type display center of still photographs and captions.

### Audio Media

Audio tape, records, and CDs are the main storage devices for audio media. This medium includes music, sound effects, books on tape, and newscasts of historical events. As students teach others they can choose from a wide range of enrichment topics and pick out short segments as discussion points. If noise is a problem, various headphone arrangements can be set up.

Audio programs that are supplemented with printed material can help some students and hold the attention of others for longer periods of time. Many young people even do traditional classroom assignments better with music going in the background. As cooperative models enter the classroom, students can bring in short segments that they have recorded to share with other students. The very limitations of audio can help in the development of listening skills. Like any media, the selection of audio tools should be based on their potential for enhancing the learning environment.

*A Collaborative Guided Imagery*
*Activity with Audio Media*

This type of activity can help develop listening and imagination  skills. Teachers report that it can also serve as a writing starter — and even increase comprehension when the story is part of the reading curriculum.

*Procedure:*

Turn the lights off and have students sit quietly with their eyes closed... read or tell a story with sound effects or music in the background.  Pause for thirty seconds every so often to let students mentally fill in the blanks. For example:  "You are walking along a tropical beach... feel the sun on your face, the wind in your hair and the sand under your feet. You see a large  box floating next to the shore... wade in to it, open it up... what do you see? (*Pause*  for 30 seconds.)  Now drag the box up onto the beach and open it up again... take whatever is in it out and do something with it. (*Pause* for a minute or two.)  Turn the lights on and have the students open their eyes and share what they have found with a partner. Each pair decides how something might be done with both sets of objects seen in the box.  They then report their scenario to their group or the whole class.

## Collaboration with Overhead Projectors

Overhead projectors are used more for lecture type presentations than they are for cooperative learning. Still, there are some collaborative activities that can make use of their capacity for enlarging small objects. Jointly made black and white sketches or cartoons can be permanently "burned" onto transparencies by using the Thermofax machine found in most schools.  If this isn't possible, felt pens can be used to draw or trace illustrations for pairs of students to briefly present to a small group or to the whole class.

*Group Communication Activity*
*Using the Overhead Projector*

Overhead projectors can help in other cooperative learning activities. A good example here is a technique developed to build vocabulary, self concept, and communication skills.

*Procedure:*

Students work in pairs. A large piece of paper is taped on the wall or chalkboard and students take turns standing next to it as the overhead projects their shadow. They take turns tracing each others head silhouette onto the paper. Silhouettes are cut out and taped or glued onto a large piece of construction paper. Using magazines, students cut out words or sentences describing each individual and tape them onto their silhouette. Words that describe both partners are placed in between the cutouts. The completed chart is then presented to the small group or to the whole class.

The success of any media or grouping technique depends largely on how it is used to promote teaching and learning. This means that the teacher, with peer encouragement, must determine how, when, where and under what conditions a medium or technique is to be used. No matter which generation of instructional media chosen, it is hoped that teachers and administrators will acknowledge the need for collaborative professional support in integrating technology and cooperative learning techniques into the classroom routine.

## References

Adams, D., Crandall, A., Eckhoff, B., Woods-Elliott, C. (1980). *Sparks for Learning.* Watertown, MA: ESN Press.

Arnheim, R. (1969). *Visual Thinking.* Berkeley, CA: University of California Press.

Bagley, M. T. & Hess, K. (1987). *Imagery in the Classroom.* Monroe, NY: Trillium Press.

*Beginning Creative Photography for Graphic Communications.* Rochester, NY: Eastman Kodak Company, 1979.

Cox, C. (1982). Children's preferences for film form and technique. *Language Arts,* 59(3), 231-238.

Cullinan, B. (Ed.) (1987). *Children's Literature in the Reading Program.* Newark, DE: International Reading Association.

National Council of Teachers of English (1989). *Focus on Collaboration.* Urbana, IL: NCTE.

Sinnott, J. (1989). *Everyday Problem Solving.* New York: Praeger.

Stewig, J. W. M. (1989). *Reading Pictures: Exploring Illustrations with Children.* New Berlin, WI: Jenson Publications.

# Index